Making Home(s) in Displacement
Critical Reflections on a Spatial Practice

Making Home(s) in Displacement

Critical Reflections on a Spatial Practice

Edited by
Luce Beeckmans, Alessandra Gola, Ashika Singh,
and Hilde Heynen

Leuven University Press

The publication of this work was supported by the Research Foundation-Flanders (FWO) Project 1215920N and the KU Leuven Fund for Fair Open Access.

Published in 2022 by Leuven University Press / Presses Universitaires de Louvain / Universitaire Pers Leuven. Minderbroedersstraat 4, B-3000 Leuven (Belgium).

Selection and editorial matter © Luce Beeckmans, Alessandra Gola, Ashika Singh, Hilde Heynen, 2022
Individual chapters © The respective authors, 2022

This book is published under a Creative Commons Attribution Non-Commercial Non-Derivative 4.0 International Licence.

The license allows you to share, copy, distribute, and transmit the work for personal and non-commercial use providing author and publisher attribution is clearly stated.
Attribution should include the following information: Luce Beeckmans, Alessandra Gola, Ashika Singh, Hilde Heynen (eds). *Making Home(s) in Displacement: Critical Reflections on a Spatial Practice*. Leuven: Leuven University Press, 2022. (CC BY-NC-ND 4.0)
Further details about Creative Commons licenses are available at http://creativecommons.org/licenses/

ISBN 978 94 6270 293 6 (Paperback)
ISBN 978 94 6166 408 2 (ePDF)
ISBN 978 94 6166 409 9 (ePUB)
https://doi.org/10.11116/9789461664082
D/2022/1869/2
NUR: 648

Layout: Crius Group
Cover design: Daniel Benneworth-Gray
Cover illustrations:
Front: Mohamad Hafez: *Unpacked*, 2020, © Mohamad Hafez, www.mohamadhafez.com;
Back: Wafa Hourani: *Qalandia 2067*, 2008 © Wafa Hourani. https://www.wafahourani.com/qalandia-2067

Table of Contents

PREFACE   9

INTRODUCTION   11
Rethinking the Intersection of Home and Displacement from a Spatial Perspective
Luce Beeckmans, Ashika Singh & Alessandra Gola

PART 1 – **CAMP**

CHAPTER 1   45
To Shelter in Place for a Time Beyond
Anooradha Iyer Siddiqi & Somayeh Chitchian

CHAPTER 2   61
Towards Dwelling in Spaces of Inhospitality
A Phenomenological Exploration of Home in Nahr Al-Barid
Ashika Singh

CHAPTER 3   83
Who/What Is Doing What?
Dwelling and Homing Practices in Syrian Refugee Camps –
The Kurdistan Region of Iraq
Layla Zibar, Nurhan Abujidi & Bruno de Meulder

CHAPTER 4   117
In the Name of Belonging
Developing Sheikh Radwan for the Refugees in Gaza City, 1967-1982
Fatina Abreek-Zubiedat

PART 2 – **SHELTER**

CHAPTER 5   139
At Home in the Centre?
Spatial Appropriation and Horizons of Homemaking in Reception Facilities for Asylum Seekers
Paolo Boccagni

CHAPTER 6   155
Bare Shelter
The Layered Spatial Politics of Inhabiting Displacement
Irit Katz

CHAPTER 7   173
Refugee Shelters done Differently
Humanist Architecture of Socialist Yugoslavia
Aleksandar Staničić

CHAPTER 8   197
Years in the Waiting Room
A feminist Ethnography of the Invisible Institutional Living Spaces of Forced Displacement
Maretha Dreyer

PART 3 – **HOUSE**

CHAPTER 9   221
Gendering Displacement
Women Refugees and the Geographies of Dwelling in India
Romola Sanyal

CHAPTER 10   239
Homing Displacements
Socio-Spatial Identities in Contemporary Urban Palestine
Alessandra Gola

CHAPTER 11
Mediating between Formality and Informality
Refugee Housing as City-Making Activity in Refugee Crisis Athens
Aikaterini Antonopoulou

265

CHAPTER 12
Making Home in Borgo Mezzanone
Dignity and Mafias in South Italy
Anna Di Giusto

285

PART 4 – HOUSE

CHAPTER 13
News from the Living Room
Historiography and Immigrant Agency in Urban Housing in Berlin
Esra Akcan

305

CHAPTER 14
The Nubian House
Displacement, Dispossession, and Resilience
Menna Agha

327

CHAPTER 15
Trans-national Homes
From Nairobi to Cape Town
Huda Tayob

347

CHAPTER 16
Static Displacement, Adaptive Domesticity
The Three Temporary Geographies of Firing Zone 918, Palestine
Wafa Butmeh

367

CODA
About the Displacement of Home
Hilde Heynen

395

ABOUT THE AUTHORS

417

© Henk Wildschut, Gardens in Calais Camp (picture series), 2017.

Preface

This edited collection of papers was born out of a doctoral workshop and conference held in Brussels, Belgium, in March 2019 and entitled, *Displacement & Domesticity since 1945: Refugees, Migrants and Expats Making Homes*. This was a themed conference sponsored by the European Architectural History Network (EAHN), The Royal Flemish Academy of Belgium (KVAB) and KU Leuven's Faculty of Architecture. Many people, including the editors of this book and many of its contributors, were involved in the organisation of both the workshop and conference. Special thanks go to the organising committee – Alessandra Gola, Anamica Singh, Ashika Singh and Hilde Heynen – for overseeing the conference from beginning to end.

At the time, the goal of the organising committee was ambitious but simple: to bring together scholars, activists and architects involved in the (re-)thinking of what it means to imagine, design and create 'homes' in contexts of human displacement. The notion of home itself was placed in relation to domesticity, not with the intention to interiorise or to privatise the concept, but in order to draw attention to spatio-material effects and processes of home-making, which differ from more traditional and idealised associations of comfort and security. Although the origins of this project are rooted in architectural circles, the intellectual agenda was from the start set up as interdisciplinary. Therefore, the conference opened its call to and welcomed papers from the fields of architectural history, theory and practice, ethnography and sociology of space, human and cultural geography, migration studies, as well as post-colonial studies and decolonial criticism, and philosophy. Hence, the conference's goal was to bring together scholars who shared *a spatialised and interdisciplinary approach to the intersection of displacement and making of home(s)*. This objective remains very much the focus of this edited volume.

The origins of this edited volume are more than circumstantial. The theme resonates not only with a number of conferences and workshops that emerged around the same time, but also with fraught and ongoing political situations both now and in the past. Among the former, those with a focus on migration, architecture and space include: 'Urban Arrival Infrastructures' (Cosmopolis Centre for Urban Research, VUB, 2015); 'Inside Out – Outside In: Shifting Architectures of Refugee (In) Habitation' (Max Planck Institute, 2019); 'Infrastructures of Care: Spaces of Refuge and Displacement' (The Bartlett, UCL, 2019); and 'Moving, Living, Investing, and Surviving: Housing and Migrations in Uncertain Times' (IMISCOE, 2020).

Many of these intellectual activities arose in response to the so-called European refugee 'crisis' of 2015 and, indeed, there is much to be said and is being said about the *poverty* of the response from European States and institutions. Yet, with this edited volume, architects and scholars from various interdisciplinary fields have also endeavoured to draw from and account for broader geographies of displacement and home-making: from institutionalised accommodation in Europe to households and urban spaces in locations such as Palestine, Lebanon and South Africa. All go to show that human displacement and emplacement have long and significant histories, each with its particular trajectories. Therefore, there is still much to explore and to analyse, especially in order to foster more positive and open attitudes and practices in relation to the movements and settlements of people. This edited volume seeks to take a few more steps in that direction.

It should be further noted that the writing and the editing of this volume unfolded during the Covid-19 pandemic. This global event, which has not left untouched the lives of virtually everyone on the planet, has brought renewed attention and even a new understanding with regard to the relationship between making home(s) and displacement. Displacement can represent both the integration of people's lives into a globalised framework of movement and social relations, and the disruption of everyday lives when this framework begins to fracture. The latter is not due to the flow of global mobility per se, but can be due to new regimes of state control and practice as well as the minor and major adjustments that we must make in and to our lives when the health of the general public is at stake. All of us have in multiple ways had to adapt to these changing circumstances that have already had deep and probably long-lasting political, social, economic and cultural ramifications. It is without doubt, however, that people living in conditions of uncertain accommodation, poverty, occupation and systems of containment (e.g. prisons, detention centres, refugee camps, etc.), are put under ever greater strain in order to survive and, within this, to maintain a sense of human dignity. And yet, what we believe and hope is that this global experience, however variously it has manifested itself, will open the chapters of this edited volume up to a deeper understanding of human lives and homes in displacement.

INTRODUCTION

Rethinking the Intersection of Home and Displacement from a Spatial Perspective

Luce Beeckmans, Ashika Singh & Alessandra Gola

Making home is arguably one of the most universal and, at the same time, social, cultural, and place-specific processes that characterise human life. The latent tension therein between the universal and the particular, or between the general and the contextual, becomes all the more evident when home is made under conditions of displacement, whether this be forced, chosen or the result of changing climates, landscapes, global geopolitical and economic conditions or population demographics. An exploration of this tension – between the 'making of home(s)', on the one hand, and 'displacement', on the other – is, however, largely lacking, and this is all too often due to the ways in which these two concepts are juxtaposed and even upheld as contradictory positions. Yet, while it is important to underscore the disparities operative in practices of making home(s) and displacement, we find ourselves at a point, living in a highly globalising world – of which short- and long-term transnational migration is inherently part – where a mere juxtaposition of both concepts cannot remain unreviewed or unchallenged. In fact, not unpacking and unsettling what continues, particularly in policy, to be seen as a contradiction would do an injustice to the lived experiences, multiple subjectivities and activities of many people in the world across space and time. As the chapters of this book will show, migrants' and refugees' homemaking is restricted neither to a place, nor indeed to one home in particular, but should rather be conceptualised as a transnational practice.

Therefore, with great anticipation we watch an ever-growing field of scholarship that systematically scrutinises how people who are 'on the move' and displaced create, reproduce and re-enact home in various circumstances (e.g. Dossa & Golubovic, 2019; Brun & Fabos, 2015; Boccagni & Brighenti, 2015; Levin, 2016; Motasim & Heynen, 2011). Scholars often point to the double meaning of home that emerges as both "a bounded place" and "a meaningful and emotionalized kind of relationship with place" (Boccagni, 2017, p. 5). This edited volume intends to build upon this growing scholarship in both an empirical and a theoretical capacity. It endeavours in particular – inspired by the literature within the fields of urban planning and architecture on this topic (e.g. Lozanovska, 2019; Akcan, 2018; Cairns, 2004) – to explicate a critical reflection on making home or homes in displacement as a *spatial practice*. Thereby, as this introduction will explain, it seeks through the methodological primacy of architecture, space and spatial agency to shed important and necessary light on the complexity of what is materially and socially operative at the intersection of making home(s) and displacement.

Rethinking narratives beyond the opposition of making home(s) and displacement

The material cultures and lived experiences that emerge from the intersection of home and displacement can rarely be separated from their complex cultural, social, economic and political contexts (Fiddian-Qasmiyeh, 2020; Pasquetti & Sonyal, 2020). For this reason, investigations into the making of home(s) in displacement have often demanded an interdisciplinary approach including, but by no means limited to, sociology, ethnography, architectural and urban theory, geography, philosophy, feminist and critical theory, and the political sciences. In this interdisciplinary scholarship, homemaking practices are often viewed as political (cf. Gola, 2021a; Singh, 2020; Ramadan, 2013; Duyvendak, 2011; Isoke, 2011; Malkki, 1992); the result of socio-cultural and psychological processes of socialisation (Foucault, 1977; Lawrence-Zúñiga & Low, 2003); and related to acculturation, alienation and hybridisation (Feldman, 2006; Ahmed, 1999; Bhabha, 2004; Berger, Berger & Kellner, 1973). Because of this methodological (and, at times, epistemological) diversity, it is important to expand at first more deeply on the two key concepts of this book, namely 'making home' and 'displacement'. While we do not intend conceptually to delimit what these terms mean or how they are used, we do seek to ascertain some kind of common ground from which discussions in this book and beyond can better flourish.

Home is perhaps the more ambiguous and controversial of these two terms. Although home may for many typically invoke ideas of stability and comfort, there seems to be no basic definition, nor any systematic way of defining home or the homeplace that would appeal to or appease everyone (cf. Mallett, 2004; Somerville, 1989; Saunders & Williams, 1988). Home has been defined as a socio-spatial unit, a psycho-spatial condition and something of a "warehouse" of emotions and sentimental attachments (Easthope, 2004). It is variously described as conflated with or related to housing and family (Rykwert, 1991; Rybczynski, 1986); to the development of self and community (Massey, 1994); as well as to gender identities and relations (Baydar & Heynen, 2005; Madigan et al., 1990); and to migration (Ahmed et al., 2003; Rapport & Dawson, 1998). Many authors also reflect on the importance of dwelling or, as it were, the ontology of being-at-home (Young, 2005; Heidegger, 1971), not to mention on the 'ideal' home (Shove, 1999). In all these interpretations there remains, nonetheless, the view that "privileging one, or certain, places against all the others [is] one of the few constants of the human condition' (Heller, 1995, pp. 1-2). Depending on the homemaker then, home might refer to various or multiple places and sentiments. And yet, what seems a rather core element to home's development is the spatial and material processes involved in *making* home.

There is a multitude of reasons to be critical of a focus on homemaking and the homeplace. Anti-capitalist, feminist and post-colonialist theory alike have criticised home as a space and practice of gendered and racial violence, asymmetrical power relations, privatisation and commodification, and colonial socialisation and oppression (e.g. Arnold, 2004; Honig, 1994; Sibley, 1995; Said, 2000). In the past century alone the modern architectural movement has further propagated traditional European gender norms throughout the globe by reifying the vision of women as the ideal care-takers of 'their' mass-produced and standardised kitchens (Hayden, 1981; Colomina, 2007). However, the focus on 'making home' in our book highlights, and does not seek to dispel, a number of tensions, problematic assumptions and roadblocks that are ever operative in the process. It realises that there is always a gap between the real and the desired side of home, posing challenges to everyday practices, norms and ideals. Home – *not* as some space of belonging rendered 'pure' by some idea of fixed and impermeable boundaries – is still something fundamental to the way we interact with the world and other people (cf. hooks, 1991). In making home(s), power relations, identities and memories, the associations of beauty and the sublime are transposed onto a space or, indeed, onto a number of spaces or moveable places, endeavouring to uphold a sense of security, freedom and control, and scope for creativity and regeneration. The making of home(s) in this sense cannot be limited to the appropriation and transformation of domestic spaces; it is also entangled with establishing access to legal and political representation as well as to community, rural- or urban-based, and citizenship (cf. Akcan, 2018; Low, 2016; Yuval-Davis, 2011; Dadusc, Grazioli & Martínez, 2019).

Nowhere are these tensions and problematics of making home(s), and the means by which people strive to resolve or overcome them, more visible than in situations of displacement. Displacement is very generally understood as the movement of people away from home, nominally, from their country of origin; and it is most typically depicted in the form of forced displacement and in cases of underprivileged migration. Although many chapters in this book focus on recent migrations, forced and otherwise, a more conceptual reflection on displacement which integrates a historical and global perspective can be illuminating. Indeed, displacement in the most basic of senses can be described as a situation "where a new or alien element is introduced into a more or less stable context" (Heynen, 1998, p. 2). Displacement can therefore occur prior to any physical movement away from a place as landscapes and demographics transform in response to modern and post-modern industrialisation (King, 2014), colonialism (Crinson, 1996), immigration and emigration (Dossa & Golubovic, 2019; Tayob, 2019; Lopez, 2015), occupation and war (Weizman, 2007; Graham, 2004). In this regard, human displacement is perhaps as old as the existence of *homo sapiens*, and yet displaced people are still treated to a large degree with caution, suspicion and even outright hostility. Seemingly regardless of the ubiquity of the pehenomenon, that homes may be made in displacement appears extremely difficult to accept for many politicians and policy-makers, as well as for some scholars.

As editors of this book, we believe that there is an ever-growing need to break away from such reactionary perspectives as they risk not only overtly romanticising the homeplace (especially as a rooted and immobile state of affairs and things), but also demonising displacement. Displacement is thus viewed through a rather reductive lens. But, ultimately, the material cultures and lived experiences derived from living in displacement cannot be comprehended in only the two notions of being-at-home and being-without-it; there is always something in between, and sometimes home is even mobile (Meier & Frank, 2016). By placing emphasis on displaced people as *actors* and as *active* in the process of making home(s) we propose to problematise, challenge and further enlarge this lens. We thus advocate reflecting on making home(s) in displacement as an immanent complex *practice*, which heavily depends on the socio-cultural, political and economic background of the homemaker(s), and in which a multitude of other socio-cultural, temporal, economic, political and spatial actors and factors are at work.

Making homes in displacement as a *spatial* practice and as spatial agency

Making home(s) in displacement is also a *spatial* practice, one which intrinsically relates to the shaping of the built environment. With this edited volume we aim to rethink the intersection of home and displacement from a spatial, material and thus architectural perspective, as this still remains underexplored in existing literature. In Western thought, as argued by Stephen Cairns (2004), architecture and migrancy are often brought together as counterparts within a more general binary relationship which "privilege[s] such principles as settlement, stability and permanence over those of movement, flux and fluidity" (p. 1). And yet, Cairns adds the point that, however "closely identified migrants were with nomadic styles of mobility, their aspirations were oriented towards stability and settlement" (ibid.). Alternatively, this edited volume seeks instead to nuance, rethink and ultimately undermine this (Eurocentric) binary relationship between architecture and migrancy, and between home and displacement altogether.

In this respect, we propose that, if thought through more critically and from a long-term historical and broad global perspective, there is nothing intrinsically permanent about architecture as there is nothing intrinsically fluid about migration in spatial terms. Built environments and human settlements are and have always been in motion and in transition, and migrants have always been as much engaged in processes of deterritorialisation (or displacement) as of reterritorialisation (or emplacement). One of the most important aspects of this latter process of reterritorialisation is the making of homes, which can also occur in transit. Here we use the plural of 'home' to point to the materiality of the process, which can range from a modest spatial occupation and appropriation of an existing place or building to a radical (re-)construction of it, and which differs from the singular of 'home' as pointing to an emotional relationship with a place, as in Boccagni notion of "homing". We therefore align with Mirjana Lozanovska's (2015) pioneering book in which she asserts that "buildings and places associated with migration tell us about central questions of belonging, culture, community and home" (p. i). Since this material, physical and architectural lens on (forced) migration still remains insufficiently mobilised, that is, as a key to unlock knowledge and add new insights to the scholarship present within the social sciences, our edited volume aims to explore this assertion further. Although the social sciences have to some degree already encountered a 'spatial turn' during the last few decades, their focus still is predominantly on 'social space' rather than on 'spatial space'.

By articulating the homemaking experiences of migrants and refugees as spatial practices, we aim to bring to the fore their 'spatial agency' (Awan et al., 2011) as fundamental in the fabrication of the built environment. This objective resonates with recent feminist architectural histories of migration, for instance, by Anooradha Iyer Siddiqi (2018), that aim to destabilise and decentre certain historiographical presumptions, for example, by attributing architectural authorship to non-experts, such as migrants who "may have lacked signature, but not significance" (online; see also Siddiqi & Lee, 2020). Therefore, we aim to confront the presumption of powerlessness and inertia attached to the labels of 'migrants' and 'refugees', categories with which many people subsumed under them would not identify (often precisely for this reason). The challenge in this approach is to avoid romanticising – and even fetishising – the spatial agency of those who have been historically, socially and politically marginalised, for it is clear that displaced persons must often operate in very precarious circumstances. Instead, the intention of this book is to acknowledge the significance (and, indeed, signatures) of migrants' and refugees' contributions to the built environment and to the production of everyday (material) life.

Hence, this edited volume seeks to underscore how these practices produce new and alternative meanings within the pre-existing codification applied to everyday living environments. Rather than considering displacement a condition of homelessness that is associated merely with loss and passivity, we argue that displacement is a spatial practice through which displaced populations contribute to processes of territorialisation, homemaking on different spatial scales, and urbanisation. As a consequence, rather than passive beneficiaries of humanitarian aid or 'bare lives' in states of exception, refugees and migrants are largely portrayed here as active urban agents and (infrastructural) change-makers. Their spatial agency is then not considered as a naturally positive element, but problematised and unravelled in the different contributions of this edited volume.

Simultaneously, this approach delves into the manifold spatial relations that surround migrants' and refugees' daily life, highlighting their connection with apparently remote socio-spatial contexts through, for instance, the (transnational) exchange of place-making and homemaking practices via their involvement in complex networks of people, places and references that bond the local and the global (Beeckmans, 2021b; Tayob, in this volume). Moreover, while Cairns (2014) might perceive a distinction between "architecture-by-migrants", "architecture-for-migrants" and "architects-as-migrants" (p. 23), we believe (and the chapters in this book underscore this point) that the overlaps and tensions between these categories render their categorical separation somewhat artificial. For instance, even within institutionalised "architecture for-migrants", which might be designed by architects who live and work as migrants, an "architecture-by-migrants" also occurs. Additionally, if we consider "migrants-as-architects" (and thereby also not prioritising Eurocentric institutional understandings of architectural practices), it becomes ever more apparent that making homes in displacement takes place against a background of power relations, hierarchal inequalities and opportunities in which the spatial agency of (forced) migrants is always in a dialectic with several forms of spatial governmentalities (Legg, 2007).

For a deeper analysis of migrants' spatial and architectural agency in the process of homemaking it is particularly interesting to look at Lozanovska's recent book on *Migrant Housing* (2020), in which she elaborates on Tadao Ando's (1991) idea that the process of inhabitation involves 'battles' with the house. Whereas Ando's notion of 'battling' relates to how clients often do not feel at home in architect-designed houses, Lozanovska uses the concept to explain how embodied dwelling habits (or *habitus*) that migrants bring with them often do not 'fit' with local housing forms in immigrant cities (see also Boano & Astolfo, 2020). In the subsequent physical 'battling' between migrants and houses, Lozanovska not only considers the agency of the migrant but, by referring to the psychoanalyst theories of Slavoj Zizek (2006), she also conceptualises the house as an active agent that draws the migrant into action, which is in line with Bruno Latour's concept of *actant* (1999). In this edited volume we also aim to break with the conventional reading of the house (or built environment, more generally) as a passive agent in the homemaking process, and instead seek to foreground the multi-layered interaction between the builder-migrant and the migrant-housing. In this case, rather than forming a radically distinct form of architecture, making homes in displacement constitutes a recalibration of existing vernacular forms by adding to it material practices coming from elsewhere, resulting in what we could call a "transnational housing vernacular" (Beeckmans, 2021a).

In this sense we aspire to break with a certain tendency in architectural history to exclude from its annals the practices and architectural makings of 'non-experts' in the fabrication of the built environment as they are not seen as authorities within a tradition (cf. Siddiqi, 2018; Dalal et al., 2018). This book challenges this position insofar as it seeks to bring to the fore the spatial decisions, strategies and practices of those whose impact certainly resonates globally on what is often called the 'age of migration' (Castles & Miller, 1993). Ultimately, our effort to challenge and broaden the canon of architectural histories and theories concerns establishing a legitimate position within architectural scholarship for all those place-makers and homemakers that have hitherto been marginalised by it. Equally, by including contributions that unpack this topic in a variety of geopolitical and historical contexts, written by a diversity of authors, we aim to liberate the bibliography in current architectural scholarship and challenge the continuous (re-)production of Eurocentric academic knowledge in this field. Therefore, this book endeavours to expand the scope of architectural scholarship to embrace the emerging thinking on the intersection of displacement and home, while at the same time significantly contributing to it by adding a spatial focus.

The global politics of making home(s) in displacement

We propose that by *spatialising* the process of making home(s) in displacement, it becomes ever more salient that this spatial practice is also a deeply political one. The spatialisation of the existing epistemologies and methodologies pertaining to making homes in displacement serves to illuminate how these spatial practices are laden with presumptions and multiple ambiguities, which include but are not limited to the effects of modern capitalist privatisation, repressive gender roles as well as nationalist and (neo-)colonialist politics. Further to instigate critical reflection on the global politics of the spatial practice of making homes in displacement, we shall outline below some topics and themes – of which some are age-old and others more recent – that appear central to any discussion about the intersections of making home(s) and displacement in the context of a globalised world.

By expanding on home as a dynamic and multi-scalar entity, we endeavour to point to the relational nature of its socialisation and materialisation. This point opposes a much more common understanding of home as a fixed (usually, domestic) place that connotes and values above all else stasis, nostalgia, enclosure and security and which is very often placed in opposition to what is deemed 'other' or external to the demarcations of a particular homeplace or homeland (Massey, 1994, pp. 167-168). In this regard, this edited volume's project entails looking at home through its interrelations with other places and 'elsewheres', and embracing how the notion and sentiment can be embedded in a place or in a constellations of places that are in continuous contestation (ibid., p. 169). In this view, home emerges as a terrain where power regimes of different natures simultaneously take place, and where power is exercised and renegotiated at different spatial scales. That is to say, each home mediates "flows of power within and beyond the household" (Pilkey, Scicluna, & Gorman-Murray, 2015, p. 129), thereby intertwining the domestic sphere with the public (be it rural or urban) and, ultimately, with the global. Home, or the absence of it, both in its unicity and multiplicity, reflects the (ever-changing) interplay between intimate, familial, private and broader social, economic and political spheres of influence. This is particularly the case for homes made in displacement, which often find themselves under several regimes of power at the same time on various spatial scales.

Amongst the power relations at work in the concept of home are our understandings of gender and the value of reproductive labour (Baydar & Heynen, 2005; Rendell et al., 1999; Young, 2005). As a result, processes of homemaking are heavily influenced by gender cultures of time and place (Beebeejaun,

2017). Emphasised in the literature are often those cultures that uphold a strict binary between two genders (nominally, male and female) and endorse a patriarchal system which upholds gendered understandings of space that measure expectations of spatial agency against specified physical and metaphorical territorialities (Massey, 1994, p. 70; see also McDowell, 1993; Weisman, 1992). Migration from one place to another inevitably unsettles home as a social and spatial entity. Moreover, it has the potential to reset the social capital associated with individuals and households. Experiences of displacement may also challenge existing patriarchal systems by affecting domestic regimes and disrupting prevailing divisions of reproductive labour (Massey, 1994, p. 167; see also Amadiume, 2017). While the fear of losing one's sense of cultural identity to a displaced situation or context can propel people to tighten gender schemes in everyday practices and domestic spaces, which can emerge as the desire to control women's activities and bodies (e.g. France's ban on the niqab, burqa and burkini), alternatively, the disruption of everydayness and domesticity in displacement also represents the chance to reflect critically on gender roles and their spatial expressions in public and domestic life, generating new patterns of gender-related practices (cf. Gola, 2021a; Benchelabi, 1998; Daley, 1991).

In most cases, gender constructs, insofar as they are conceived as per the mundane realities of displaced homemaking, often drive distinctive expectations, imaginaries and attitudes towards the private and public lives of members of a household, especially women. Women, with regard to their home life, can end up in varied ways expressing resourcefulness and resilience as well as frustration and longing, combined with a sense of both belonging and loss (cf. Salih, 2017; Ahmed, 1999). As we have painfully witnessed only recently during the Covid-19 pandemic, in times of 'crisis' women remain expected to uphold and ensure the smooth operation of reproductive and care work, even under rising vulnerable (spatial) conditions and increased levels of domestic violence (UN Women, 2020). Moreover, although often providing essential care work both in their domestic and professional lives, the tasks related to which can certainly overlap in space and time, women are not granted ownership over the spaces in which this care occurs, putting them in precarious and dependent positions of powerlessness. As neoliberal capitalist systems repeatedly limit possibilities of organising care work more collectively, the transition towards a more stable home setting does not always accompany the empowerment of women (Power & Mee, 2020; Federici, 2018).

Parallel to this, a new collective sensitivity regarding the manifold implications of home and displacement has arguably been fostered (albeit in a very short timespan) as a result of the global health crisis. The spread of Covid-19 has changed and advanced global understandings of the material dimensions of homemaking. Indeed, anti-Covid measures, such as lockdowns (or stay-at-home orders), social distancing and curfews, shed light on and magnify existing socio-spatial inequalities and conditions of precariousness related to the material aspects of everyday life. The pandemic has not only thoroughly reshaped domestic regimes and homemaking practices, a fact which can be seen in the pressures exacted on our abilities to secure physical and mental well-being (Usher et al., 2020; Beeckmans, 2021b), but it has also recalibrated the relationship between private and public realms. Limited access to public space, and its essential micro or semi-public facilities, have forced us to address issues of exclusion and segregation, and critically re-draw "the right to the city" (Harvey, 2003). That said, although we may brave the same storm, we are not all in the same boat. People living in conditions of uncertain accommodation, poverty, occupation and systems of containment (e.g. prisons, detention centres, refugee camps, etc.), and with commitments to caring for others, are put under ever greater strain to survive and to maintain a sense of human dignity in those spaces (Beeckmans & Oosterlynck, 2021).

With access to housing and to public spaces being a matter of governance, spatial governmentality, social control and political-ethical principles (Szczepanikova, 2012), homemaking in displacement inevitably gives rise to new forms and patterns of (spatial) exclusion and inclusion, inequalities as well as geographies of power (Massey, 1994, p. 160). Indeed, the struggle to find the bearings of one's (new) home is often conceived as a struggle for empowerment, one that is regularly affected and countered by institutions, legislation, policies and planning. By framing home in terms of these power relations (gender and health, then, being but two multi-layered and deeply entrenched aspects), we outline the premise that the construction of any 'homey' environment is a political issue. Importantly, what follows is the acknowledgement of the unsettling of individual and intimate relationships that are associated with or systemically embedded in the difficult and precarious housing and homemaking pathways of refugees and migrants (Beeckmans & Geldof, 2021), and the contextual dissolution of 'Home' – as a social, cultural or even national ideal – during this process (Ahmed, 1999, p. 330). The subsequent dis-location of identity (Dixon & Durrheim, 2000) corresponds in turn to the creation of complex, multiple and, at times, contradictory senses of belonging, the result of socio-spatial-temporal cross-referencing within broader transnational fields (cf. Beeckmans, 2019; Hall, 2013; Heynen & Loeckx, 1998; Morley, 2001; Schulz & Hammer, 2003).

That said, it could also equally be argued that, by making homes in displacement, migrants exert a form of "infrastructural citizenship" (Lemanski, 2019). By appropriating and adapting infrastructures, such as existing housing or institutional shelters, (urban) citizenship is also negotiated, claimed and pursued (Dadusc, Grazioli & Martínez, 2019). In that view, housing as a particular type of urban infrastructure is not only the context but also the substance of citizenship struggles (Holston, 2008). Or, as Amin (2014) notes, "the liveliness of infrastructure involves more than its character as the object of community struggle" (p. 138; see also Lepofsky & Fraser, 2003). Yet, as making home(s) in displacement often happens within the context of contested and blurred territories and activities, it does not automatically translate into citizenship, and in many cases it simply does not even have political aspirations, but is rather part of migrants' and refugees' everyday existence and survival.

Core to our approach to highlighting the political in the spatial is the intention to decentralise and decolonise current definitions of home and displacement, and therefore achieve a broader and more pluralistic view on the matter. By this we mean acknowledging the ways in which world history unfolds through the fine grain of common gestures, relations, objects and places, which, however much their importance is noted, remain to a large extent absent from archives, official accounts of place-making and architectural history in particular. We therefore find of irreducible value the question of this discrepancy and the interrogation of what place the material expressions of the everyday have in lieu of 'grand' historical narratives. A strong focus is therefore placed on a variety of micro-historical accounts of 'homing' in displacement; this includes emphasis on instances and questions of ephemerality, everydayness, cultural and domestic reproduction, and the invocation of subjective experiences from across the globe (Gola, 2021b). In this way we contend with how "great history" is produced and what (spatial) agency displaced people are given in this process (Eckert & Jones, 2002). In doing so, we aim to expand the historical narration beyond hegemonic meta-narratives (Siddiqi, 2020) and add to a broader project of decolonising knowledge production in academia and beyond (cf. Sheppard et al., 2013; Chakrabarty, 2000; Robinson, 2002).

Interdisciplinarity as a method of doing research on making home(s) in displacement

Even though the aim of this edited volume is to shed light on making home(s) in displacement as a spatial practice, the politicised nature of making home(s) in displacement does not allow us simply to rely on the autonomy of one discipline, such as architecture or urban design, over another. Instead, we see the socio-material entanglement of 'home' and 'displacement' as an invitation to work towards a project of knowledge integration which conceptually and methodologically requires an interdisciplinary approach. This edited volume is the result of a desire to contribute to *conceptual cross-fertilisations* between architectural theory and the spatial (planning) sciences, on the one hand, and social and political theories and sciences, on the other.

This is facilitated by the fact that the discipline of architecture is intrinsically interdisciplinary: architects are unable to work in a void, but rather they need to process different strands of social, political, technical and cultural information through their designs, as do architectural scholars through their writings and theoretical and archival discoveries. In addition, the classical epistemological frameworks of architectural histories and theories often fall short of investigating and interpreting the spatial decisions, strategies and practices of those making homes in displacement. Therefore, producing knowledge on this topic is inevitably an exercise in broadening and simultaneously provincialising 'the canon' by adding new and often silent (and sometimes silenced) voices from hitherto invisible geographies (Singh et al., 2020). As such, this edited volume endeavours in its totality, by deeply embracing an interdisciplinary approach to the topic, to establish alternative epistemological frameworks for (future) research in architectural theory and history at the intersection of home and displacement, and more generally on the nexus of architecture and (forced) migration. Simultaneously, we seek to enlighten other disciplines with renewed concepts from our disciplinary backgrounds. The ultimate goal would be to overcome disciplinary divides such that theoretical frameworks from different disciplinary 'silos' could be merged better and ideas no longer get lost in translation (*Teaching Tool*, 2019).[1]

In addition to fostering conceptual innovation, this edited volume also seeks to contribute to methodological innovation by providing new heuristic frameworks for (future) research on making home(s) in displacement as a spatial practice. In order to do so, we believe that it is crucial to mobilise interdisciplinarity as a research method. The implication of this is a mixing of quantitative, qualitative and more experimental and speculative research methods that stem from different disciplines. By integrating research methods, a better understanding of a research problem can potentially be gained than when studied by distinct approaches. A 'mixed method' approach to making home(s) in displacement therefore opens up the breadth and depth of understanding and corroboration, while offsetting the weaknesses inherent in using each method alone. Within this volume many authors mix methods of research in innovative and interesting ways, offering altogether a heterogeneous repertoire of research approaches. Remarkably, many of them confessed to having struggled in doing so. They lack, on the one hand, the analytical tools and interdisciplinary background to manoeuvre confidently between different research methods. On the other hand, methodological challenges arise when one is conducting research

– like that on making homes in displacement – in a context where conventional archives or other primary sources are limited, inaccessible or in need of (re-)construction. Moreover, strategies and ethical guidelines that explore alternative primary sources, such as oral sources, are often not part of the pedagogical training of hegemonic disciplines. What also became apparent were the ways in which many authors were compelled to mix methods almost spontaneously, which prompted reflection on the methodological experimentation used only later in the research process.

Therefore, if provided with the time and distance to think through these ongoing experiments, thereby to reflect on both the methodological gains and risks they offer, we can in this edited volume already begin to distinguish between some innovative mixed methods applied to the research on making home(s) in displacement as a spatial practice:

ARCHITECTURAL ETHNOGRAPHY: As several contributions relied on participatory observations and interviews with displaced people making homes in new localities, they actually engaged in a method that has only recently been called "spatial" (Low, 2017) or "architectural ethnography" (Kalpakci, Kaijima, & Stalder, 2020; Iseki, 2018). In such an approach ethnographic methods and methods for spatial analysis are combined and result in what Lopez (2011) has described as "building ethnographies", which is to say a "fine-grained ethnographic research of the envisioning, construction, and use of building projects" (p. 1). Such 'building ethnographies', or even 'building histories', are developed mainly using the qualitative life history interviewing method, which is a form of data collection where people are asked to document their lives (and sometimes the lives of others) over a period of time. Analogously and literally, interviewees are requested to sketch in their own manner, whether this be through words or drawings, using their own personal time lines and log books, their material homemaking processes. This practice is closely aligned to the theory of 'mental mapping' (e.g. Lynch, 1960).

DEEP MAPPING AND VISUALISATION: Many contributors to our edited volume also started to visualise the ethnographic data in mappings, such as handmade drawings or through the use of new technologies for spatial data analysis. By moving beyond mere illustration, they mobilise 'the visual' as an interpretative instrument of analysis. This has the potential to provide new insights about making homes that would previously have been untapped were these authors to maintain a conventional textual analysis of their ethnographic fieldwork. In a next step, some began to add supplementary source material to their mappings, resulting in what are called 'deep mappings' (Bodenhamer et al., 2015; Brook & Dunn,

2011; Roberts, 2016) or multi-media mappings, in which historical and fieldwork data (e.g. drawings, photographs, legislative documents, archival records, etc.) are juxtaposed, blended and geo-referenced as well as enriched by other sources, such as newspaper articles or interviews. As is the case in *Diasporic Agencies: Mapping the City Otherwise* by Nishat Awan (2016), these mappings can also include reflections on "the multiple belongings of diasporic citizens, half-here and half-there", and as such are deployed to overcome "a crisis in the standard modes of architectural representation that tend to homogenise and flatten experience" (see also Hall et al., 2017). Deep mapping and visualisation are thus also used to provide insight into the multi-layeredness and multi-scalarity of making home(s) in displacement as a spatial practice.

SPATIALISATION: By engaging with a project of spatial and architectural ethnography and by developing deep mappings, and hence by maximising their spatial skills, the authors in this edited volume instantiate an attempt to spatialise the existing knowledge bases and methodologies. Spatialisation is based on the recognition that space is a common concept and field of investigation amongst many disciplines involved in the rethinking of the intersection of home and displacement, thereby providing stable, yet unexplored, ground for inter- and transdisciplinary knowledge production. This epistemological process of spatialising does not intend to neutralise (i.e. to render without positive or negative value) the operative concepts of displacement and home. In fact, the goal of spatialisation is arguably quite the opposite: namely, to make the many presumptions and multiple ambiguities with which displacement and home are laden visible and understandable. Spatialisation helps to avoid reinforcing binary relationships, for example, between empowered and disempowered, legitimate and unauthorised, allowing them instead to be viewed as embracing multiplicity and diversity. In this way space is generated for the unknown and the unknowable, which are important factors in the consideration of domesticity and displacement. Hence, in the context of our edited volume, spatialisation is not only an interdisciplinary method, but also a *political* one. As we see it, it is a method that embarks upon decolonising and provincialising canonical knowledge, thereby enabling concepts, images and writings to overcome pre-established and institutionalised binary (power) relations pervasive in social discourse, but which are also prevalent in academic research.

Spatialisation, in this sense, is core to most of, if not all, the approaches outlined in this book, especially given that it touches upon deep ethical concerns related to doing research about making homes with people who have been displaced. For instance, through visualisation, a new vocabulary for talking about homemaking in displaced situations can be developed without the need for linguistic translations (which can be difficult when speaking of rather intimate feelings and matters, or in local languages or dialects not shared by everyone involved in the research process). Certainly, this is not always the case for textual analysis, which in academia is predominantly Anglophone. Deep mappings can furthermore contain original (oral) source material that not only provides a deeper insight into one's relationship with home and displacement, but also acknowledges the importance of local and non-hegemonic scholarship, such that the authorship of 'interviewees', 'participators' and local 'research assistants' can be respected. Spatialisation, therefore, incorporates an attempt to develop knowledge that is not or, at the very least, is less oppressive than some traditional methods. Finally, spatialisation, in its intention to showcase the interaction between physical space and people, as well as the variety of actors and factors involved in this process, opens up the potential to provide a dynamic platform that could foster encounters and discussions between scholars and practitioners alike from a multitude of disciplinary, interdisciplinary and transdisciplinary backgrounds. It therefore has the opportunity to open up new collaborations and establish a (seemingly more) generous research environment for those working on the intersections of home and displacement (cf. *Teaching Tool*, 2019).

Towards more *affective* writing on making home(s) in displacement

Much academic and scientific scholarship continues explicitly or implicitly to perpetuate the presumption that one needs an 'objective' distance to observe and analyse events and experiences critically, and thereby attain 'knowledge' (as some representation of 'the truth'). Alternatively, we, as the editors of this book, contend that personal trajectories and ontological experiences constitute a different sort of operative knowledge. By engaging with lived experience as an asset to knowledge, we are better able to define our respective standpoints and highlight their plurality, while remaining sensitive to that which drives our individual and unique ways of conducting research and producing knowledge. Upon the recognition that ontology and epistemology are the results of an individual lifelong learning process (Pitard, 2017), we seek to valorise the positionality of our contributors. Therefore, in the pursuit of different, non-oppressive approaches to knowledge, one that is more consistently informed by the affections and complexity of human lived experience, it would be pertinent to dedicate some space for a critical and, more importantly, personal reflection on our *positionality* as editors and authors of this book.

As editors, we are a team of four women from various socio-cultural backgrounds, age groups and personal as well as professional trajectories. We, along with most of the authors who have contributed to the making of this book, deal day-to-day with conditions of homemaking and displacement in our respective lives, albeit some in more severe circumstances than others. Certainly, editing a book on the (spatial) experience of making homes in displacement during the Covid-19 pandemic has been challenging, but not without its heart-warming moments. In positioning ourselves as the moderators of this discussion, we recognise that our epistemological and ontological formations are influenced by multiple histories grounded in centuries of women being designated as homemakers. Like many others across the globe, alongside our professional careers, each of us participates in a society where neoliberal mechanisms of social reproduction consistently tie women (and, especially, women of colour) to the household and the bulk of unpaid work that pertains to such spaces (Mitchell, Marston, & Katz, 2004; Hopkins, 2015). Our public and intellectual activities, conversely, unfold in spaces often envisaged and dominated by (white) men (Kern, 2019; Weisman, 1992). This perspective, which includes but is not limited to our sensitivity to issues of housework, class, racialisation, gender and private and public dynamics, undoubtedly influences the tone of discussions found in this book.

Some of us live our thinking and critiques through the everyday work-life balance between family and professional tasks which can occur either in the same space or at great distance from each other. We are mothers, grandmothers, daughters and sisters; in the process of starting new jobs and projects while finalising old ones; trying to attain citizenship, family reunification or a permit to stay in our respective places of residence, some of which are occupied by foreign military powers. English is for the majority of us not our native tongue, and yet we must engage in or with it nearly daily. Many of the contributors to this volume are themselves living in displacement, sometimes having personally experienced – or continue to experience – the effects of European (neo-)colonialism, international and civil wars, internal displacements, refugeehood, statelessness and short- or long-term resettlement in foreign contexts.

At the same time, we acknowledge that we experience and discuss displacement and the making of home(s) from relatively privileged situations. Aspects of our individual profiles (including access to education and financial support, and proximity to Western institutions) enable us to engage with the issue in practical and theoretical terms, enjoying access to 'global' perspectives, while being free to enter the debate voluntarily and, therefore, with greater firmness to do so on our terms. With regard to modern demographics on migration, our identities and backgrounds would probably position us in the category of 'expats' (Gatti, 2009). Remarkably, this puts us in a advantageous position in comparison with the majority of displaced people, who deal with much less fortunate circumstances by reason of their country of birth, political conditions, race, gender, education, age and wealth. It is our aspiration that in compiling this edited volume we could provide space for the perspectives of scholars coming from more diverse contexts and cultural backgrounds. Moreover, by deliberately choosing an 'open access' publisher, we hope that this rich compilation of texts will reach a broader public than is often the case in academia.

We are not alone in either this desire or venture. Bucking the trend in architectural studies and theory, Lozanovska (2020) refers to her own book as a "migrant daughter's study" (p. 23), thereby taking the step which would allow her to elaborate on the many ethical and political questions related to the writing and research of migrant, gendered and generational subjectivities. In Lozanovska's book, this positionality as an author-subject not only results in a deeper and richer understanding of the migrant architecture in question, as it is the fruit of over thirty years of longitudinal research, but also gives way to a highly personal account of post-war migrant housing. Lozanovska describes herself as a woman for whom "(t)he house that Alberti canonises is not her house" (ibid., p. 24). She is therefore able to contribute to the project of decentralising and provincialising Eurocentric architectural historiographies and theories by adding missing histories and voices to it. In line with this, we aim with our edited volume to contribute to a decolonisation of the debate on (forced) migration, thereby breaking down distant and elitist positions (Toyosaki, 2018). We seek instead more inclusive and pluralistic perspectives that value proximity to the subject matter. We endeavour to create a more "collaborative journey" between the narrator and the reader (Pitard, 2017), which ultimately works towards a project of *affective,* instead of merely effective, scholarly writing.

Consistent commitment to a more inclusive and plural narrative in the production of knowledge, we confront making home(s) and displacement through an intersectional, feminist perspective that builds upon and engages with recent and longstanding discussions and debates on near and far space, multicultural and hybrid societies and everyday practices (e.g. hooks, 1999; Colomina, 1992; Low, 2000; Massey, 1994; McLeod, 1996; Hall, 2012; Hall, 2015; Frisch, 2015; Beebeejaun, 2017; Doan & Higgins, 2011; Shaw, 2011). This approach, we believe, best illuminates the relational aspect of making home(s) in displacement, centring attention on multiple differences and the experience of underrepresentation in power minorities, counterposing a more personal and human narrative to the disembodied register inherited by the predominantly men-driven scholarly debate from the 'enlightened' sciences (McDowell, 1993). The inclination towards a more plural production of knowledge is reflected in the composition of the editorial team and that of the authors of the book, who together produce multidisciplinary and *interdisciplinary* knowledge that shares a common interest for spatial issues and what people do in the everyday, along with their broader socio-spatial, political and historical implications.

The rationale of the book: Making Home(s) in Displacement

Making home(s) is one of the most universal and, at the same time, (culturally) specific processes, the latent tensions of which become all the more manifest when made under the conditions of displacement. Making use of certain epistemological tools from architecture and urban planning, sociology, anthropology, ethnography, material cultures, environmental psychology and human geography, to name but a few, this interdisciplinary scholarship highlights the homemaking practices of migrants and refugees as complex and highly-charged socio-cultural and psychological processes of socialisation (Dossa & Golubović, 2019), acculturation and alienation (cf. Kissoon, 2015; Nine, 2018), hybridisation (cf. Akcan, 2018; Lozanovska, 2015; Sanyal, 2014) and, ultimately, *spatialisation*. A contemporary history of migration, forced or otherwise, further concerns post-colonial and decolonial notions of belonging, citizenship, and (transcultural) appropriations. And yet, at the heart of this project lies the argument that making home(s) in displacement is a *spatial practice*, one which intrinsically relates to the shaping of a person's built environment.

Bringing together a variety of case studies from diverse geopolitical contexts and historical trajectories, this edited volume aims to nuance, rethink and, in most cases, to undermine what appears to be a contradiction between home and displacement. The chapters thereby provide an understanding of the material processes and products of homemaking in displacement at different spatial scales. In this edited volume we expound the centrality of spatial practices and spatialisations in displaced homemaking through an emphasis on four spatial sites: (1) Camp, (2) Shelter, (3) City, and (4) House. These four categories not only are physical, material spaces that recur in the different chapters of this book but rather should be interpreted as conceptual categories that, when taken together, provide a novel conceptual framework for revisiting the nexus of home and displacement from a spatial perspective.

Although these four conceptual categories represent different physical spatialities and morphologies, which have particular geo-political constellations, narratives and literatures connected to them, they occur in a wide diversity of geographical areas and throughout history. However, while providing a conceptual framework allowing for a novel spatial analysis, with this book's structure we equally intend to steer critical reflections on the multiple dimensions of such spatial categorisations beyond the clichés typically attributed them and, eventually, to challenge the categories themselves with the support of actual cases. In line with authors such as Potvin (2013), who pleaded for "humanitarian enclaves to become cities, and for cities to become true asylums" (p. 15), our structuring of this book along these four conceptual categories is meant to trigger such provocative statements. Moreover, the conceptual focus on space and spatiality in this categorisation is also a way of not falling into the trap of categorising people as 'migrants' or 'refugees' (solely), but rather of outlining the variety of actors involved in the making of such spaces. In doing this, the narrative of this volume emphasises the deep entanglement of space with history, theory, politics and the everyday spatial practices of individuals and communities. Each of the book's parts consists of a collection of four chapters.

The first half of this book introduces the 'Camp' and the 'Shelter', which are comparable infrastructures and spaces in their emergence as responses to emergencies or 'crisis' situations, yet on different spatial scales. They are both generally conceived as highly institutionalised spaces, developed and deployed by a myriad of stakeholders including state governments, architects and humanitarian organisations that deal with (forced) migration. Typically, these spaces harbour displaced persons through top-down power dynamics, which can provoke tense and deeply socially and psychologically damaging, situations (cf. van der Horst, 2004; Darling, 2011; Campesi, 2015; Brun et al., 2017; Tazzioli & Garelli, 2018). These spaces have a tendency to constrain the potential for inhabitants (who can themselves be variously categorised as 'irregular migrants', 'asylum seekers', 'internally displaced persons' or 'refugees') to negotiate their spaces, and thereby to fulfil activities and tasks that make home(s). At the same time, histories, various kinds of news and personal stories are slowly emerging from these spaces which paint pictures of resilience, resistance and endurance, all of which question the institutionalisation of these spatial typologies, create new spatialities and materialities to accommodate and *home*, even if for short periods of time, inhabitants from a multitude of backgrounds (e.g. Sanyal, 2011; Sigona, 2015; Depraetere & Oosterlynck, 2017; Katz, Minca, & Martin, 2018; Siddiqi & Osman, 2017).

CAMP: Anooradha Iyer Siddiqi and Somayeh Chitchian (Chapter 1) open our first part with a reflection on the passing and suspension of time in the ephemerality of camp spaces across Ethiopia, Bangladesh and Kenya. This chapter takes the invocative form of an analysis of a serial exhibition of images posted on Instagram during the global pandemic of 2020 and endeavours to understand how dreams of a life beyond encampment become materialised (or not) in camp spaces, thereby generating a series of paradoxical living situations while producing knowledge of them. The debate around local developments and "the dwelling of potentiality" (Povinelli, 2012) in camps further unfolds in a more theoretical interpretation of home and lived experience by Ashika Singh (Chapter 2), who takes the German tradition of the phenomenology of dwelling as her starting point, and upon which she builds, to discuss how people built transnational homes in the Palestinian refugee camp of Nahr Al-Barid, Lebanon. A post-colonial approach to lived experience, displacement and home is key here, a point that is subsequently built upon in the ethnographic observations of homemaking processes in camps in the Kurdistani Region of Iraq (KR-I) by Layla Zibar, Nurhan Abujidi and Bruno De Meulder (Chapter 3). Zibar, Abujidi and De Meulder offer a critical narrative, through selective images and interviews, of the "spatial agency" of the Kurdish inhabitants through their material appropriations of the camp space to invoke multiple and multiscalar experiences of belonging. Fatina Abreek-Zubiedat (Chapter 4) concludes this section with a critical analysis of the role modernisation and state housing policies play in unsettling the development of camps as socio-spatial units of resistance to colonial powers in the Gaza Strip, Palestine. Using extensive archival research, Abreek-Zubiedat provides a compelling critique of "professional knowledge" and of how such agendas can clash with, if not silence, the voices of actual inhabitants.

SHELTER: Here we explore the realities of reception centres and makeshift shantytowns as have been seen in Europe across space and time. To begin, Paolo Boccagni (Chapter 5) draws extensively from sociological methodologies and research to reflect on the relationship between institutional accommodation and the adaptive processes of asylum seekers who live in these spaces for short periods of time. Boccagni underscores the importance of "beautification" as part and parcel of the 'homing' process, which entails spatial agency but is not without its contradictions in an environment that systematically suppresses efforts to gain political recognition and the ability to navigate through the public sphere. Subsequently, Irit Katz (Chapter 6) elaborates precisely on this point by engaging with the writings of Hannah Arendt. By engaging with political philosophy and architectural ethnography, Katz underscores how the inhabitation of what she calls "bare shelter" takes on political meaning in situations of abandonment, such as the EU's response to the 2015 refugee 'crisis'. With an eye to the recent European response to forced migration, Aleksandar Staničić (Chapter 7) takes us on a historical journey through archival research and analysis of a reception centre designed by the architect, Mihajlo Mitrović, in the Socialist state of Yugoslavia. In doing so, he provokes questions about the historical and diplomatic role of architecture and the architect. In the last chapter of this section, Maretha Dreyer (Chapter 8) explores the advantages of a self-ethnographic and feminist approach to the everyday lives of people living in Direct Provision (asylum) centre in Dublin, Ireland. Her depiction of life as it is lived in such centres is self-aware and critical, explaining with intimate detail the inequalities of our perceptions and shelter responses to racialised migration.

By 'City' and 'House', in the second half of this book, we refer to those urban sites in which (forcibly) displaced persons endeavour to build homes, very often on their own initiative and often in severe and precarious conditions. Although these are by no means 'flexible' or 'welcoming' spaces, a fact which is made apparent via building regulations, policing and housing/squat clearances (Perera, 2019; Shildrick, 2018), the spatial and material components that make up cities and urban housing are often not as institutionalised, nor as organised under systems of surveillance and restricted movement, as camps and shelters. Yet, after leaving the asylum centre, being recognised or not as a refugee, or even without having pursued the status of asylum seeker, most newcomers 'land' in cities because of the availability of rich "arrival infrastructures" (Meeus et al. 2018, 2020; d'Auria, Daher, & Rohde, 2018) or "arrival neighbourhoods", often vulnerable to gentrification, in which more established migrants groups play an essential role because they provide networks of kinship and information necessary to access (often substandard) housing on the over-saturated, urban housing markets (cf. Schillebeeckx et al., 2019; Saunders, 2016; Wessendorf, 2018; Çağlar & Glick Schiller, 2018; Beeckmans, 2020; Pemberton & Phillimore, 2018). However, while we understand cities as the place of settlement preferred by many for making a home (Glick, Schiller, & Çağlar, 2011; Hall, 2015), this city-making mostly occurs in connection to cities elsewhere (Hou, 2013; Beeckmans, 2022). Moreover, as we interpret the homemaking process of migrants and refugees in cities, it is important not simply to transpose the traditional Western split between the public and the private spheres, but rather to envisage how they bleed into and *feed* each other, and therefore form overlapping and revivifying domains (Staeheli et al., 2009; Vasudevan, 2017). In this sense, making home(s) in the city is not strictly bound to any particular threshold or territory. Instead, homemaking processes connect domesticity to urban spaces as they form part of a broader process of the practice of "homing the city" (Low, 2016).

City: A feminist ethnographic approach is pursued and elaborated on in Romola Sanyal's (Chapter 9) investigation into women's experiences of (re)making their family homes in cities as compared to camps in the aftermath of the

Partition of India (1947). Sanyal explores and seeks to overcome the limits of archiving women's voices, seeing women instead as legitimate authors of their histories and of the homes they have made in the face of multiple, intersectional hardships. Following this, Alessandra Gola (Chapter 10) delves into questions of home and citizenship through a socio-spatial exploration of the adaptation of everyday urban spaces in migrant contexts. Her 'microstories' compare and contrast sites and people's lives in the Al-Amari refugee camp and the suburban sprawl of Ramallah, Palestine. Aikaterini Antonopoulou (Chapter 11) also explores questions of home, citizenship and city-making in the context of Athens, Greece, by comparing two vastly different responses, one formal (Alexandras Avenue refugee housing) and the other informal (City Plaza), to accommodating forced migrants in two different periods of history, prior to WWII and now. Finally, the question of urban informality and city-making is picked up by Anna di Giusto (Chapter 12), who embarks on a material ethnography of the rural slum, Borgo Mezzanone, in Italy. Di Giusto explores how people live and build in the context of laws and policies that systematically persecute and marginalise 'irregular' migrants seeking asylum.

House: The last part of this book discusses the house as part of the homemaking process. It opens with Esra Akcan (Chapter 13), who provides some insight into her recent work on Kreuzberg's urban renewal via the study of a housing complex. Akcan challenges whom we perceive as architects and what we perceive as architectural history, and makes space for the testimonies and experiences of those who actually live in these spaces. The register of architectural design as something which constantly changes in time and acquires new forms and meanings with residents is further made manifest in Menna Agha's (Chapter 14) auto-ethnographic reflection on the Nubian house. Significant here are the experiences of Nubian women in Egypt of the increasing constraints placed on their role in community life. The need to adapt domestic spaces and activities to ensure survival and dignity comes to the fore in Wafa Butmeh's (Chapter 15) exploration of the shifting temporal conditions of homemaking under heavy Israeli military control of Masafer Yatta, Palestine. In the last chapter, Huda Tayob (Chapter 16) provides unique insight via deep mapping into the socio-material effects of migrant transnational networks by investigating the narratives of home that surround Somali Malls in South Africa. Even though a form of temporary, privately-arranged accommodation, the spaces of Malls are embedded with sentiments of refuge and belonging as well as homemaking and unmaking.

The book concludes with a contribution by Hilde Heynen which, as a final reflection, further contextualises the various case studies within the epistemological framework proposed in this introduction, additionally elaborating on some key themes of the book such as the temporal, geo-political and gendered dimension of making homes in displacement. As such it provides not an end, even though it concludes the book, but rather a 'stop off' in what is a much more expansive, probably never-ending journey to explore historical and global readings on the matter of making home(s) in displacement.

Notes

1. Apart from the Teaching Tool, which was created during a workshop conducted the day before the 2019 *Displacement & Domesticity* conference, the cross-disciplinary reading list, recently produced by the HOMInG Network (Giudici, 2019) and Huda Tayob and Suzanne Hall's 'Race, Space and Architecture: Towards an open access curriculum' (2019), provides good examples of a step towards disciplinary and conceptual cross-fertilisation.

References

Ahmed, S. (1999). Home and away: Narratives of migration and estrangement. *International Journal of Cultural Studies*, 2(3), 329–347.

Ahmed, Sara. (2000). *Strange Encounters: Embodied Others in Post-coloniality*. London: Routledge.

Ahmed, Sara, Castañeda, Claudia, Fortier, Anne-Marie, and Sheller, Mimi. (2003). *Uprootings / Regroundings: Questions of Home and Migration*. Oxford: Berg.

Amadiume, I. (2017). Family and Culture in Africa. In: P. Essed, D.T. Goldberg & A. Kobayashi (eds.), *A Companion to Gender Studies* (pp. 355-369). London: Blackwell Publishing.

Amin, A. (2014). Lively Infrastructure. *Theory Culture & Society*, 31(7-8), 137-161.

Akcan, Esra. (2018). *Open Architecture: Migration, Citizenship, and the Urban Renewal of Berlin-Kreuzberg by IBA-1984/87*. Basel: Birkhäuser.

Ando, Tadao. (1991). *Tadao Ando: Beyond Horizons in Architecture*, edited by H.S. Bee, New York, Museum of Modern Art.

Arnold, Kathleen R. (2004). *Homelessness, Citizenship, and Identity: The Uncanniness of Late Modernity*. Albany: State University of New York.

Awan, N. (2016). *Diasporic Agencies: Mapping the City Otherwise*. Farnham: Ashgate.

Awan, N., Schneider, T. & Till, J. (2011). *Spatial Agency: Other Ways of Doing Architecture*. Routledge.

Beeckmans, Luce. (2021a). Diasporic place-making and multi-referential architecture in Europe: exploring the new vernacular of Afro-Christian churches. *Society of Architectural Historians Conference (SAH), paper presentation in Session 'Diasporic Architectural Histories' (Mirjana Lozanovska and Anoma Pieris)*. Montreal, Canada.

Beeckmans, Luce. (2021b) The politics of emotions of doing research on unprivileged housing and home-making while being locked down at home with my three little children. *DiGeSt: Journal of Diversity and Gender Studies, 8* (1), 7-9. https://doi.org/10.21825/digest.v8i1.18836

Beeckmans, Luce. (2022, forthcoming) Mobile Urbanism from below: the transnational exchange of place-making practices across the African diaspora. African churches as scale-makers and place-makers in European mid-sized cities.

Beeckmans, Luce. (2019). Migrants, Mobile Worlding and City-Making. *African Diaspora, 11*(1–2), 87–100. https://doi.org/10.1163/18725465-01101007

Beeckmans, Luce. (2020). A plea for greater diversity in urban redevelopment. *Flanders Architectural Review N°14. When Attitudes Take Form*. Antwerp: Flemish Architecture Institute.

Beeckmans, Luce and Geldof, Dirk. (2021, forthcoming). Reconsidering the interrupted housing pathways of refugees in Flanders (Belgium) from a 'home-making' perspective. *Housing Studies*.

Beeckmans, Luce and Oosterlynck, Stijn. (2021). Lessons from the lockdown: foregrounding non-privileged perspectives into the (post-)covid city debate. In: *Global Reflections on Covid-19 and Urban Inequalities*. Eds. Doucet, Brian, van Melik, Rianne and Filion, Pierre. Policy Press.

Bachelard, Gaston. (1994, orig. 1969). *The Poetics of Space: The Classic Look at How We Experience Intimate Places*. Boston: Beacon.

Bhabha, H. K. (2004). *The Location of Culture*. 2nd Edition (orig. pub. 1994). London and New York: Routledge.

Baydar, Gülsüm, and Heynen, Hilde. (2005). *Negotiating Domesticity: Spatial Productions of Gender in Modern Architecture*. London: Routledge.

Beebeejaun, Y. (2017). Gender, urban space, and the right to everyday life. *Journal of Urban Affairs, 39*(3), 323–334. https://doi.org/10.1080/07352166.2016.1255526

Benchelabi, H. (1998). Cultural Displacement in Brussels with Maghrebi Women. *Journal of Architectural Education, 52*(1), 3–10. https://doi.org/10.1111/j.1531-314X.1998.tb00250.x

Berger, P. L., Berger, B., & Kellner, H. (1973). *The Homeless Mind: Modernization and Consciousness*. New York: Random House.

Boano, C. & Astolfo, G. (2020). Inhabitation as more-than-dwelling. Notes for a renewed grammar, *International Journal of Housing Policy*, 20 (4), 555-577.

Boccagni, Paolo, and Brighenti, Andrea. (2017). Immigrants and Home in the Making: Thresholds of Domesticity, Commonality and Publicness. *Journal of Housing and the Built Environment* 32(1): 1-11.

Boccagni, P. (2016*). Migration and the search for home: Mapping domestic space in migrants' everyday lives.* Springer.

Bodenhamer DJ, Corrigan J, and Harris TM (Eds). (2015). *Deep Maps and Spatial Narratives.* Bloomington: Indiana University Press.

Brook, R. & Dunn, N. (2011). *Urban Maps Instruments of Narrative and Interpretation in the City.* Farnham: Ashgate.

Brun, C. et al. (2017). Displaced citizens and abject living: The categorical discomfort with subjects out of place. *Norsk Geografisk Tidsskrift-Norwegian Journal of Geography, 71*(4): 220-232.

Brun, Cathrine, and Fábos, Anita. (2015). Making Homes in Limbo? A Conceptual Framework. *Refuge* 31(1): 5-17.

Butler, Judith and Athanasiou, Athena. (2013). *Dispossession: the performative in the political.* Polity Press: Cambridge.

Cairns, Stephen. (2004). *Drifting: Architecture and Migrancy.* London: Routledge.

Çağlar, Ayşe and Glick Schiller, Nina. (2018). *Migrants and City-Making: Dispossession, Displacement, and Urban Regeneration.* Durham: Duke University Press.

Campesi G. (2015). Humanitarian Confinement. An Ethnography of Reception Centres for Asylum Seekers at Europe's Southern Border. *International Journal of Migration and Border Studies, 1*(4): 398-418.

Chakrabarty, D. (2000). *Provincializing Europe: Postcolonial thought and historical difference.* Princeton, N.J: Princeton University Press.

Castles, S., & Miller, M. J. (1993). *The age of migration: international population movements in the modern world.* New York: World.

Colomina, B. (Ed.). (1992). *Sexuality & Space.* New York: Princeton Architectural press.

Colomina, B. (2007). *Domesticity at War.* Cambridge, Mass.: MIT Press.

Crinson, M. (1996). *Empire Building: Orientalism and Victorian Architecture.* New York and London: Routledge.

Dadusc, D., Grazioli M., & Martínez, M. A. (2019). Introduction: citizenship as inhabitance? Migrant housing squats versus institutional accommodation. *Citizenship Studies,* 23(6), 521-539.

Dalal, A., Darweesh, A., Misselwitz, P., & Steigemann, A. (2018). Planning the Ideal Refugee Camp? A Critical Interrogation of Recent Planning Innovations in Jordan and Germany. *Urban Planning,* 3(4), 64-78.

Daley, P. (1991). Gender, Displacement and Social Reproduction: Settling Burundi Refugees in Western Tanzania. *Journal of Refugee Studies,* 4(3), 248–266.

Darling, J. (2011). Domopolitics, governmentality and the regulation of asylum accommodation. *Political Geography, 30*(5): 263-271.

d'Auria V., Daher R. & Rohde K. (2018). From integration to solidarity: Insights from civil society organisations in three European cities. *Urban Planning*, 3(4): 79-90.

Darke, J. (1994). Women and the Meaning of Home. In: R. Gilroy & R. Woods (eds.). *Housing Women*. London: Routledge.

Depraetere, A., & Oosterlynck, S. (2017). 'I finally found my place': a political ethnography of the Maximiliaan refugee camp in Brussels. *Citizenship Studies*, 21(6): 693-709.

Dixon, J., & Durrheim, K. (2000). Displacing place-identity: A discursive approach to locating self and other. *British Journal of Social Psychology*, 39(1), 27–44. https://doi.org/10.1348/014466600164318

Doan, P. L., & Higgins, H. (2011). The demise of queer space? Resurgent gentrification and the assimilation of LGBT neighborhoods. *Journal of Planning Education and Research, 31*: 6–25.

Dovey, Kim. (1985). Homes and Homelessness. in Altman, I. and Werner, C. (Eds). *Home envi-ronment*. New York: Plenum Press.

Dossa, P., & Golubovic, J. (2019). Reimagining home in the wake of displacement. *Studies in Social Justice*, 13(1): 171-86.

Duyvendak, J. W. (2011). *The Politics of Home: Belonging and Nostalgia in Western Europe and the United States*. London: Palgrave Macmillan.

Easthope, Hazel. (2004). A Place called Home. *Housing, Theory and Society* 21(3): 128-138.

Eckert, A., & Jones, A. (2002). Historical writing about everyday life. *Journal of African Cultural Studies*, 15(1), 5–16. https://doi.org/10.1080/13696810220146100

Feldman, I. (2006). Home as Refrain: Remembering and Living Displacement in Gaza. *History and Memory, 18*(2), 10-47.

Federici, Silvia. (2018). *Re-enchanting the World: Feminism and the Politics of the Commons*. Oakland: PM Press.

Fiddian-Qasmiyeh, E. (ed.) 2020. *Refuge in a Moving World. Tracing refugee and migrant journeys across disciplines*. London: UCL Press.

Foucault, Michel. (1977). *Discipline and Punish: The Birth of the Prison*. Translated by Alan Sheridan. New York: Pantheon.

Frisch, M. (2015). Finding transformative planning practice in the spaces of intersectionality. In P. L. Doan (Ed.), *Planning and LGBTQ communities: The need for inclusive queer spaces* New York, NY: Routledge, pp. 129–146.

Gatti, E. (2009). Defining the Expat: The case of high-skilled migrants in Brussels. *Brussels Studies*. https://doi.org/10.4000/brussels.681

Glick Schiller, N., & Cağlar, A. (2011). Locality and globality: Building a comparative analytical framework in migration and urban studies. *Locating migration. Rescaling cities and migrants*, 60-81.

Gola, A. (2021a). The Making of National Identity in the Guests' Room: the Palestinian Duyuf. *Journal of Palestine Studies*.

Gola, A. (2021b). The Material Culture of the Palestinian Duyuf. In D. Schneiderman, *Appropriated Interiors*. New York: Routledge.

Graham, Stephen. (ed.). (2004). *Cities, War, and Terrorism: Towards an Urban Geopolitics*. London: Blackwell Publishing.

Giudici, Daniela (2019). Homemaking and forced migration: A bibliography. *HOMInG-HOASI Working paper*, 5. HOASI: University of Trento.

Hall, S., King, J., & Finlay, R. (2017). Migrant infrastructure: Transaction economies in Birmingham and Leicester, UK. *Urban Studies*, 54(6), 1311–1327.

Hall, S. M. (2013). The politics of belonging. *Identities*, 20(1), 46–53. https://doi.org/10.1080/1070289X.2012.752371

Hall, S. M. (2015). Migrant Urbanisms: Ordinary Cities and Everyday Resistance. *Sociology*, 49(5), 853–869.

Hayden, Dolores. (1981). *The Grand Domestic Revolution: A History of Feminist Designs for American Houses, Neighbourhoods, and Cities*. Cambridge, MA: MIT Press.

Harvey, D. (2003). The Right to the City. *International Journal of Urban and Regional Research*, 27(4), 939/941. doi: https://doi.org/10.1111/j.0309-1317.2003.00492.x

Heller, Agnes. (1995). 'Where are we at home?' *Thesis Eleven* 41: 41(1):1-18. doi:10.1177/072551369504100102

Heidegger, Martin. (1971). 'Building, Dwelling, Thinking'. In: M. Heidegger & A. Hofstadter (trans.), *Poetry, Language, Thought*. New York: Harper & Row.

Heynen, Hilde. (1998). Patterns of Displacement. *Journal of Architectural Education* 52(1): 2-2.

Heynen, H., & Loeckx, A. (1998). Scenes of Ambivalence: Concluding Remarks on Architectural Patterns of Displacement. *Journal of Architectural Education*, 52(2), 100–108. https://doi.org/10.1111/j.1531-314X.1998.tb00261.x

Holston, J. (2008). *Insurgent Citizenship*. Princeton, NJ: Princeton University Press.

Honig, Bonnie. (1994). Difference, Dilemmas, and the Politics of Home. *Social Research*, 61(3): 563-597.

hooks, Bell. (1991). *Yearning: Race, Gender and Cultural Politics*. London: Turnaround.

Hou, J. (2013). *Transcultural cities: border-crossing and placemaking*. New York: Routledge.

Hyndman, J. (2000). *Managing Displacement: Refugees and the Politics of Humanitarianism*. Minneapolis, MN: University of Minnesota Press.

Iseki, Kaijima Stalder. 2018. *Architectural Ethnography – Japanese Pavilion Venice Biennale 2018*. Tokyo: Toto.

Isoke, Z. (2011). The Politics of Homemaking: Black Feminist Transformations of a Cityscape. *Transforming Anthropology*, 19(2): 117-130.

Jacobson, Kirsten. (2009). A developed nature: A phenomenological account of the experience of home. *Continental Philosophy Review* 42(3): 355-373.

Katz, I., Minca C. and Martin, D. (eds.) (2018) *Camps Revisited*. London: Rowman & Littlefield.

Katz, Irit. (2017). Between Bare Life and Everyday Life: Spatializing Europe's Migrant Camps. *Architecture_MPS: Web*.

Katz, I. (2017). Pre-fabricated or Freely fabricated? *Forced Migration Review, 54* (Shelter in Displacement).

Kalpakci, Andreas, Momoyo Kaijima and Laurent Stalder. 2020. Architectural Ethnographies. *ARCH+ Features, 98*.

Kern, L. (2019). *Feminist City*. London: Verso.

King, Anthony D. (2004). *Spaces of Global Cultures: Architecture, Urbanism, Identity*. New York: Routledge.

Kissoon P. 2015. *Intersections of displacement: Refugees' experience of home and homelessness*, Newcastle upon Tyne: Cambridge Scholars.

Lawrence-Zúñiga, D., & Low, S. (2003). *Anthropology of Space and Place: Locating Culture*. London: Wiley-Blackwell.

Lemanski, C. (2019) *Citizenship and infrastructure: practices and identities of citizens and the state*. London: Routledge.

Legg, Stephen. 2007. *Spaces of Colonialism*. Malden: Blackwell Publishing.

Lepofsky, J., & Fraser, J. C. (2003). Building Community Citizens: Claiming the Right to Place-making in the City. *Urban Studies*, 40(1), 127–142.

Levin, Iris. (2016). *Migration, Settlement, and the Concepts of House and Home*. London: Routledge.

Long, Katy. (2013). *The Point of No Return: Refugees, Rights, and Repatriation*. Oxford: Oxford University Press.

Lopez, Sarah Lynn. (2015). *The Remittance Landscape: Spaces of Migration in Rural Mexico and Urban USA*. Chicago: University of Chicago Press.

Lopez, Sarah Lynn. (2011). *The Remittance Landscape: Space, Architecture, and Society in Emigrant Mexico*. UC Berkeley: PhD Dissertation.

Lopez, Sarah Lynn. (2010). The Remittance House. *Buildings and Landscapes*, 17(2), 33-52.

Low, S. (2017). *Spatializing culture: the ethnography of space and place*. London: Routledge.

Low, S. (2016). Homing the City: An afterthought. *Home Cultures*, 13(2), 215–220. https://doi.org/10.1080/17406315.2016.1195097

Lozanovska, Mirjana. (2020). *Migrant Housing: Architecture, Dwelling, Migration*. London: Routledge.

Lozanovska, M. (ed.) (2015). *Ethno-architecture and the politics of migration*. London and New York, NY: Routledge.

Lynch, Kevin. (1960). *The Image of the City*. Cambridge: MIT Press.

McDowell, L. (1993). Space, place and gender relations: Part II. Identity, difference, feminist geometries and geographies. *Progress in Human Geography*, 17(3), 305–318. https://doi.org/10.1177/030913259301700301

Madigan, R., Munro, M. & Smith, S. J. (1990). Gender and the meaning of the home. *International Journal of Urban and Regional Research 14*: 625-647.

Mallett, S. (2004). Understanding Home: A Critical Review of the Literature. *The Sociological Review 52*(1): 62–89

Malkki, Liisa. (1992). National Geographic. *Cultural Anthropology, 7*(1), 24-44.

Massey, Doreen. (1994). *Space, Place, and Gender*. Minneapolis: University of Minnesota Press.

McDowell, L. (1993). Space, place and gender relations: Part II. Identity, difference, feminist geometries and geographies. *Progress in Human Geography, 17*(3), 305–318. https://doi.org/10.1177/030913259301700301

Meeus, Bruno; Beeckmans, Luce; Van Heur, Bas and Karel, Arnaut. (2020). Broadening the urban planning repertoire with an 'arrival infrastructures' perspective. *Urban Planning, 5*(3), online.

Meeus, Bruno, Arnaut, Karel and Van Heur, Bas (Eds.). (2019). *Arrival Infrastructures: Migration and Urban Social Mobilities*. London: Palgrave Macmillan.

Meier, Lars and Frank, Sybille. (2016). Dwelling in mobile times: places, practices and contestations. *Cultural Studies, 30*(3), 362-375.

Merrifield, A. (2014). *The new urban question. London*. London: Pluto Press.

Minca C. (2015). Counter-camps and other spatialities, *Political Geography, 49*: 90-92.

Mitchell, K., Marston, S., & Katz, C. (Eds.). (2004). *Life's work: Geographies of social reproduction*. Malden: Blackwell.

Morley, D. (2001). Belongings: Place, space and identity in a mediated world. *European Journal of Cultural Studies, 4*(4), 425–448. https://doi.org/10.1177/136754940100400404

Motasim, Hanaa, and Heynen, Hilde. (2011). At Home with Displacement? Material Culture as a Site of Resistance. Home Cultures 8(1): 43-70.

Nine, C. (2018). The Wrong of Displacement: The Home as Extended Mind. *Journal of Political Philosophy*, 240–257.

Pasquetti, S. & Sanyal, R. (eds.) 2020. *Displacement. Global conversations on refuge*. Manchester: Manchester University Press.

Pemberton, S., & Phillimore, J. (2018). Migrant place-making in super-diverse neighbourhoods: Moving beyond ethno-national approaches. *Urban Studies, 55*(4), 733–750.

Perera, J. (2019). *The London Clearances: Race, Housing and Policing*. Institute of Race Relations, Background Paper. no. 12. Link: https://irr.org.uk/app/uploads/2019/02/The-London-Clearances-Race-Housing-and-Policing.pdf.

Pieris, Anoma. (ed.) (2019). *Architecture on the Borderline: Boundary Politics and Built Space*. London: Routledge.

Pilkey, B., Scicluna, R., & Gorman-Murray, G. (2015). Alternative Domesticities. A cross-disciplinary approach to home and sexuality. *Home Cultures, 12*(2), 127–138. doi:10.1080/17406315.2015.1046294

Pitard, J. (2017). A Journey to the Centre of Self: Positioning the Researcher in Autoethnography. *Forum Qualitative Sozialforschung / Forum: Qualitative Social Research, 18*(3). http://dx.doi.org/10.17169/fqs-18.3.2764

Potvin, L. (2013). Humanitarian urbanism under a neoliberal regime', Paper presented at the International RC21 Conference 2013, Berlin, 1-17. Retrieved from: http://www.rc21.org/conferences/berlin2013/RC21-Berlin-Papers/24-1-Potvin-Marianne

Povinelli, E. A. (2012). The Will to Be Otherwise/The Effort of Endurance. *The South Atlantic Quarterly, 111*(3), 453-475.

Power, E. R. & Mee, K. M. (2020). Housing: an infrastructure of care, *Housing Studies,* 35(3), 484-505.

Ramadan, Adam. (2013). Spatialising the refugee camp. *Transactions of the Institute of British Geographers, 38*(1): 65-77.

Rapport, Nelson, and Dawson, A. (1998). *Migrants of Identity: Perceptions of Home in a World of Movement.* Oxford: Berg.

Robinson, Jennifer (2005). *Ordinary cities: between modernity and development. Questioning Cities.* New York: Routledge.

Roberts, L. (2016). Deep Mapping and Spatial Anthropology. *Humanities* 5(5).

Roy, A. & Ong, A. (2011) *Worlding cities: Asian experiments and the art of being global.* Chichester, West Sussex; Malden, MA: Wiley-Blackwell.

Rybczynski, W. (1986). *Home: A Short History of an Idea.* New York: Penguin Books.

Rykwert, J. (1991). 'The Idea of a Home: A Kind of Space'. *Social Research* 58(1): 51–62.

Said, Edward. (2000). *Reflections on Exile and other essays.* Cambridge, MA: Harvard University Press.

Salih, R. (2017). Bodies That Walk, Bodies That Talk, Bodies That Love: Palestinian Women Refugees, Affectivity, and the Politics of the Ordinary. *Antipode,* 49: 742– 760.

Sanyal, R. (2014). Urbanizing refugee spaces. *International Journal of Urban and Regional Research, 38*(2), 558-572.

Sanyal R. (2011). Squatting in camps: Building and insurgency in spaces of refuge, *Urban Studies,* 48(5): 877-890.

Saunders, P. & Williams, P. (1988). The constitution of the home: Towards a research agenda. *Housing Studies* 3(2), 81-93.

Saunders, Doug. (2016). Arriving on the Edge: Migrant Districts and the Architecture of Inclusion. In: *Making Heimat. Germany, Arrival Country,* edited by P. C. Schmal, O. Elser and A. Scheuermann. Ostfildern: Hatje Cantz Verlag Gmbh & Co, pp. 22-39.

Schillebeeckx, Elise, Oosterlynck, Stijn and De Decker Pascal. (2019). Migration and the Resourceful Neighborhood: Exploring Localized Resources in Urban Zones of Transition. In: *Arrival Infrastructures: Migration and Urban Social Mobilities,* edited by B. Meeus, K. Arnaut and B. Van Heur. London: Palgrave Macmillan.

Schulz, H., & Hammer, J. (2003). *The Palestinian Diaspora: Formation of Identities and Politics of the Homeland.* London: Routledge.

Shaw, Wendy S. (2011). *Cities of Whiteness.* London: John Wiley & Sons.

Shildrick, T. (2018). Lessons from Grenfell: Poverty Propaganda, Stigma and Class Power. *The Sociological Review,* 66(4), 783–798.

Sheppard, E., Leitner, H., and Maringanti, A., 2013. *Provincializing global urbanism: a manifesto*. Urban Geography, 34, pp. 893–900

Shove, E. (1999). 'Constructing Home: A Crossroads of Choices'. In: Cieraad, I. (ed.), *At Home: An Anthropology of Domestic Space*, Syracuse: Syracuse University Press.

Sibley, D. (1995). *Geographies of Exclusion: Society and Difference in the West*. London: Routledge.

Sigona, Nando. (2015). Campzenship: reimagining the camp as a social and political space. *Citizenship Studies*, 19(1): 1-15.

Siddiqi, A. I. (2020). Ephemerality. *Comparative Studies of South Asia, Africa and the Middle East*, 40(1), 24–34. https://doi.org/10.1215/1089201X-8186005

Siddiqi A.I. (2018). Writing With: Togethering, Difference, and Feminist Architectural Histories of Migration. In D. Barber, E. Rega (eds.) *Structural Instabilities*, e-flux Architecture. https://www.e-flux.com/architecture/structural-instability/208707/writing-with/

Siddiqi, A.I. and Osman, A. (2017). Traversals: In and Out of Dadaab. *Perspecta 50* (Urban Divides): 173-191.

Singh, Ashika L. (2020). Arendt in the Refugee Camp: The political agency of worldbuilding. *Political Geography*, 77.

Singh, Ashika L., Gola, Alessandra, Beeckmans, Luce, and Heynen, Hilde. (2020). Displacement & Domesticity Since 1945: Refugees, Migrants and Expats Making Homes, Following the EAHN's Sixt Thematic Conference (Brussels, 27-28 March 2019). *Architectural Histories*.

Slingenberg L., Bonneau,L. (2017). (In)formal Migrant Settlements and Right to Respect for a Home. *European Journal of Migration and Law*, 19(4): 335-369.

Somerville, P. (1989). 'Home Sweet Home: A Critical Comment on Saunders and Williams'. *Housing Studies* 4(2): 113–118.

Staeheli, L., D. Mitchell, and C. Nagel. (2009). Making Publics: Immigrants, Regimes of Publicity, and Entry to 'the Public'. *Environment and Planning D: Society and Space*, 27: 633–648.

Szczepanikova, D. A. (2012). Between Control and Assistance: The Problem of European Accommodation Centres for Asylum Seekers. *International Migration*, 51 (4).

Tayob, Huda and Hall, Suzanne. (2019). Race, space and architecture: towards and open-access curriculum. *Online paper*. London: London School of Economics and Political Science, Department of Sociology.

Tayob, Huda. (2019). Architecture-by-migrants: the porous infrastructures of Bellville. *Anthropology Southern Africa*, 42(1), 46-58.

Tazzioli, M.; Garelli, G. (2018). Containment beyond detention: The hotspot system and disrupted migration movements across Europe. *Environment and Planning D: Society and Space*, 0 (0): 1-19.

Teeple Hopkins, C. (2015). Introduction: Feminist geographies of social reproduction and race. *Women's Studies International Forum, 48*, 135–140. https://doi.org/10.1016/j.wsif.2014.06.002

Toyosaki, S. (2018). Toward De/Postcolonial Autoethnography: Critical Relationality With the Academic Second Persona. *Cultural Studies ↔ Critical Methodologies, 18*(1), 32–42. https://doi.org/10.1177/1532708617735133

Usher, K., Bhullar, N., Durkin, J., Gyamfi, N., & Jackson, D. (2020). Family violence and COVID-19: Increased vulnerability and reduced options for support. *International Journal of Mental Health Nursing, 29*, 549–552 doi:. doi:doi: 10.1111/inm.12735

UN Women. (2020). Whose Time to Care? Unpaid care and domestic work during Covid-19. Brief: Women Count. Resourced from https://data.unwomen.org/publications/whose-time-care-unpaid-care-and-domestic-work-during-covid-19.

Van der Horst H. (2004). Living in a reception centre: the search for home in an institutional setting. *Housing, Theory and Society, 21*: 36-46.

Vasudevan, A. (2017). Squatting the city: on developing alternatives to mainstream forms of urban regeneration. *The Architectural Review. Special issue 'Home', 1443.*

Weizman, Eyal. (2007). *Hollow Land: Israel's Architecture of Occupation*. London: Verso Books.

Weisman, L. K. (1992). *Discrimination by Design. A Feminist Critique of the Man-Made Environment*. Urbana: University of Illinois Press. Retrieved from 1.1

Wessendorf, Susanne. (2018). Pathways of Settlement among Pioneer Migrants in Super-Diverse London. *Journal of Ethnic and Migration Studies, 44*(2):270-86. doi: 10.1080/1369183X.2017.1341719,

Young, I. M. (2005). House and Home: Feminist variations on a theme. In S. Hardy & C. Wiedmer (eds.), *Motherhood and Space* (pp. 115-147). New York: Palgrave Macmillan.

Yuval-Davis, N. (2011). *The Politics of Belonging: Intersectional Contestations*. London: Sage Publications.

Zizek, Slavoj. (2016). *The Parallax View*, Cambridge, MA: MIT Press.

PART 1
CAMP

CHAPTER 1

To Shelter in Place for a Time Beyond

Anooradha Iyer Siddiqi & Somayeh Chitchian
Barnard College, U.S.A. | Harvard University, U.S.A.

The 'camp'

Architectures of displacement, if thematised or studied at all, are associated with the institutionalised spaces of shelter. They are primarily centred on the binarism of the formal, institutional, humanitarian and overall 'authored' understandings of shelter in relation to the 'informal', makeshift and self-made modalities thereof (Siddiqi, 2017; Siddiqi, 2023; Seethaler-Wari et al., 2021; Beeckmans et al., forthcoming 2021; Siddiqi, 2018; Katz et al., 2018; Oxford RSC, 2017; Hailey, 2009). The so-called camp is asked materially to constitute and bridge this binarism: in effect, to produce the alibi for the abstraction of modernity's ideals of sheltering the displaced. It is, in the end, an alibi for its own abstraction: the constant state of emergency. The ideal of sheltering is projected in the plan, which is first drawn and soon afterwards built in emergency. The architecture of the camp realises the hasty drawings, frozen in time, made by an emergency planner or a logistics expert, standing by, participating at the edges of an act of containment. Authorship of shelter outside this humanitarian frame is doomed to a perpetual state of so-called informality, exile, fleetingness, labelled as an outside condition. This 'informality' is based on looks alone. Architecture in this condition is aesthetically bordered (Pieris, 2019), othered and read materially as something else, *made informal* into an outside condition of existence despite its inherent formality.

Displacement, however, has a long history. It has different manifestations, in both spatial and temporal terms, including in the longue durée, for instance, as the camp has evolved from a sheltering infrastructure into a city, as well as a more recent past in which being unhoused has been equated with being homeless. Within armed conflicts, uneven economic and spatial development, military occupations, class struggles, ethno-racial and religious 'otherings', global land and water grabs, gentrification and apartheids, changing institutional terrains of governance (from the local to the supranational) have resulted in people's migrations and (im)mobilities, that is, various forms of displacement.

Despite these varied modalities and multiple subject positions produced by displacement, the main subject inhabiting displacement in both popular discourse and scholarly work is 'the refugee' or, more broadly, 'the migrant': the prime embodiment of the contemporary subject of displacement and dispossession. This subject of the modern state is reduced to a signifier of homelessness. Whether having crossed a political border or not, she is bordered into a refugee or displaced status. Border after border, everlasting borders; bordered to be sheltered; bordered to be encamped; in sum, bordered to be contained. This at once allies her with the radical homelessness some have diagnosed in the broadly modern condition (Morrison, 1997, 2012), but yet demands that she be consigned to the position of an aspirant to that modernity or an exile outside it (Mamdani, 1996), floating in a perpetual state of displaceability.

If materiality is evacuated in the plan of the camp, such an eviction seems to parallel the The draining of this melancholy subject's agency, integrity and will is paralleled in the plan of the camp, a symbol of eviction, and the object lesson of this modern-day displaceability. Why the camp? Where is the camp space? Where does it start and where does it end? If the camp becomes the locus of thought, are we to speak of the camp instead of *through* the camp? Are we to speak of the refugee instead of someone *among* the inhabitants of refuge? How do we demarcate the camp from the non-camp? How does the subject inhabit the spectrum in between? How does this bordering of both space and subject help or hinder understandings and conceptualisations of displacement and refuge? Are displacement and home even the two ends of the spectrum of inhabitation, or do they collide, fold into a concurrent and simultaneous state of displacement *and* home making (that is, *homing* while displaced and *displaced* while at home)?

Perhaps we have reached the limits of our spatial language. Our existing vocabulary is evading us, leaving us unequipped to understand. For a moment, let us think beyond 'shelter', especially beyond shelter as a function that has somehow come to be understood as independent of lives.

Inhabiting, otherwise

The spatio-temporal frame encompassing inhabitation beyond shelter complicates the totalising image of the camp as *the space* of refuge or the figure of the refugee as *the subject* of displacement. A critique of *where* and *with whom* we are looking must be simultaneously accompanied by questions of time, duration and distance—the *when* and the *while*—causing an epistemic shift of the *site*, the *time* and the *subject* of knowledge production. This is a contingent process of spatial authorship and (re)production, a yet-to-come design of the unlicensed architect, a yet-to-be-written spatial story of its yet invisible author (Siddiqi, 2018). It is *an otherwise*, constantly to be written and rewritten, arranged, de-arranged and re-arranged in an entangled web of connections. It is not to be fetishised through 'crisis' discourses of 'exceptionality'. Rather, the parameters for its emergence and design are already present, even if omitted by the gaze of the state or the discipline of architecture.

"To build is to build into existence the possibility of *an otherwise*", writes Elizabeth Povinelli (2014; emphasis added), with the aim of understanding "the dwelling of potentiality", the ability "to think and see otherwise" (Povinelli, 2012), the possibility for an alternative "stitching" together of space, a differing spatial arrangement, which "installs its own possible derangements and rearrangements", thus "creating new enclosures" while "allowing new worlds to emerge" (Povinelli, 2011). This *making* lies beyond its association with the design and the materiality of the built environment, and rather serves as a domain, zone or plane of arrangements (Povinelli, 2014; Povinelli, 2017) through which new time-space configurations are constantly formed, encountered, altered and negotiated. It is the potentiality to "*figure* space – ... create worlds ..." (Povinelli, 2011). Material evidence of times gone by and the potentiality of that to come is figured and configured by time in space, time itself figured through layers and layers of space, erased only to be remembered anew, remembered only to be erased once more. It is an understanding of *timespace* that connects displacement to emplacement, deconstruction to construction, uprooting to sheltering, abandonment to enclosure, as interdependent modalities of operation in constant negotiation with each other, in a complex and variegated temporal and spatial continuum.

This pushing of time into space fundamentally characterises life in emergency, providing the irreducible conceptual unit that denotes a camp as such. As Angela Naimou describes, "what promises in name to be a single, practical, urgent, and temporary need for refuge is almost never experienced or conceptualized this way: instead, contemporary refugee timespaces involve a complex of spatial and temporal scales as they collide, converge, interrupt, or overlap with each other" (Naimou, 2018). This cross-temporality and cross-spatiality may be the most urgent condition of the refugee camp (Hailey, 2009). Through it the camp may form a resistance to occupation or to settling (*tawtin*) so as not to undermine the right of return (Hilal and Petti, 2018; Hilal and Petti, 2013); it may serve as a segregatory mechanism of contemporary apartheid, fulfilling older partitions in land through structures made to behave as ephemeral (Siddiqi, 2020); and in enacting those resistances and partitions, it forms the temporal and spatial basis of history and heritage (Hilal and Petti, 2021; Siddiqi, 2022a). The refugee camp fundamentally brings time and space into a new collusion. Through this it produces new meaning.

The institutionalised space of the camp on the other hand freezes space, as it were, in a non-time condition of nowness, an exceptional statue. The brute present, a temporality of uniformity yet of replication, then seems to be out of place and time, commemorating no past and anticipating no future. Such spaces of displacement, however, are constantly encountered, negotiated and (re)arranged—they are inhabited (Chitchian, Momić, Seethaler-Wari, 2020), drawing the past and the future into an ephemeral experience: subjects of time, subjects of space, moving in and out, connecting and building bridges, blurring the defined boundaries of the camp and its supposed negative, the non-camp.

Bringing together the timespace and codification of the camp with that of the non-camp bridges the timespace and codification of displacement with that of habitation. In sheltering in place, the sometimes intense and unruly materiality of the camp space (Abourahme, 2015) is inhabited temporally in an elsewhere, its arrival put on hold. Even in refugee camps inhabited by a third, fourth or fifth generation of residents, which are ostensibly beyond emergency—though the ontology of 'camp' can hardly be segregated from the emergency condition—this constant temporal negotiation defines the space of the camp. It defines not the material dimension alone, but the territorialisation and demarcation, in which the inhabitation and arrangement of space—the building of *an otherwise* into existence—actively constructs agents and architects, psychically, socially and materially. These processes of spatial (re)arrangement continually create, pulling in and altering that which surrounds them, a malleability that makes tangible the accompanying liquidity of time, of pasts, presents and futures.

Furthermore, the timespace of an otherwise allows us to move away from a politics of recognition alone. It supersedes labels such as 'camp' or 'refugee', and instead recentres inhabitation of space and time together, a space that goes beyond the confines of the camp and a time and subjecthood which goes beyond that of the refugee. It is simultaneously of here and there, of then and now, of that which is yet to come. As "vanishing point", referring to Ananya Roy and Chantal Mouffe, it constitutes "an outside that by being inside introduces a 'radical undecidability'" to the analysis of displacement and spatial relations (citing Mouffe, Roy, 2011; Mouffe, 2000, p. 12). These incommensurate and indeterminate vanishing points constantly navigate back and forth between the timespace of the 'camp' and the non-camp, the 'refugee' and the non-refugee;

in other words, they are "vanishing points at the limits of itineraries of recognition" (Roy, 2011, p. 235). Such a reckoning of an inhabitation of otherwise begs a closer look at the more familiar urban spaces of displacement (Sanyal, 2014; Sanyal, 2016) to ask if seemingly disparate geographies of city and camp are in fact in connection in a complex time-space continuum.

Questions remain. What are the possibilities and limits of architecture in helping us to unlearn, to rethink the boundaries and parameters of its predefined authorship, and to orient towards a different epistemological approach altogether? The first step would be to recast the author, finding her in a different figure: "the inhabitant" (Seethaler-Wari, Chitchian, Momić, 2021).

To shelter in place

To dissect the temporality of the camp and connect to not only the *before* but also the *after* (an after which could also be the *no*—repeated, endured, awaiting) and to think through this framework of both the past *and* the future we take in hand the idea of an otherwise, a yet-to-come condition, a state of incommensurability and unpredictability. The making of an otherwise during the duress of emergency is another language for 'inhabitation', of dreaming of a life beyond emergency. This is the root of life in the camp. It is, more precisely, to shelter in place for a time beyond.

We examine this inhabitation, the making of an otherwise, through the analysis of a serial exhibition of photographs posted on Instagram during the early days of the COVID-19 pandemic of 2020, a period of intensive sheltering-in-place around the world. *Life Beyond Emergency* (#lifebeyondemergency), curated by Anooradha Iyer Siddiqi (@iyersiddiqi), gathered her photographs taken in refugee contexts in East Africa and South Asia. The collection was hosted by *Warscapes* (@warscapes) and Jackfruit Research and Design (@jackfruitlive), and was included in the series *Urbanism Beyond Corona* (#UrbanismBeyondCorona) hosted by Urban Works Agency (@UrbanWorksAgency) and the Experimental History Project at the California College of the Arts Architecture Division. The discursivity of *Life Beyond Emergency* was dependent upon a community of followers engaging in a timespace of temporary and progressive assembling around image events. This discursive space was thus also a form of conceptual inhabitation, of dwelling in spaces that enabled multiple perceptions of time. The exhibition and its accompanying text are republished below in full. The exhibition panels perambulate through each landscape vis-à-vis the critical process of inhabitation, as a way to think beyond emergency and the camp, to imagine an otherwise.

Life Beyond Emergency

#lifebeyondemergency
@iyersiddiqi @warscapes @jackfruitlive

Life Beyond Emergency 0. How do we shelter in place and dream of life beyond emergency? This series turns to those who have crafted this theory in our time. @iyersiddiqi @warscapes @jackfruitlive #lifebeyondemergency #shelterinplace

Life Beyond Emergency 1. Aw Bare refugee camp, Ethiopia. This boy is being chased by one of his older brothers and a friend. He outpaces his pursuers, stops and whips around to calculate his lead, squeals with excitement, and runs off again. The house behind him was designed by a family of Somalis, one of whom lost his leg in the war. The UNHCR shelters refugees with physical disabilities in Zone 1 in its camps, the area closest to the food distribution centre and hospital. Living in Zone 1 in a UNHCR refugee camp minimizes the extra costs and risks involved with transporting food home. In Aw Bare, these savings translated into enhancing the design of the built environment. The sundried brick walls of this house supported a corrugated aluminium roof and satellite antenna. The plot was bordered with live Commiphora fencing, with an integrated gate built from found wood and reclaimed USAID packaging material.

The family living here was in the queue to be resettled to the United States. Their preference was to move to Australia. Photo: Anooradha Iyer Siddiqi. @iyersiddiqi @warscapes @jackfruitlive #lifebeyondemergency #shelterinplace #blacklivesmatter #somalilivesmatter #afrofuturism

Life Beyond Emergency 2. Shimelba refugee camp, Ethiopia. This painting is by Pietro Fernando, an artist and art trainer, who worked for the International Rescue Committee to establish a fine arts school in Shimelba. He instructed young people living in the camp to become teachers of visual arts and of traditional handicraft. For Fernando, instruction in the school of art served the purposes of expression and documentation. His aims were not toward therapeutic art practice, but toward the establishment of an institution, which would encourage students to comprehend their memories of a past culture, place, and time as well as their present identities as refugees. His paintings (of everyday scenes) and the artifacts he made (for storing, carrying, sifting, measuring) hung on the walls of the school's gallery. This oil on canvas shows a newlyweds' procession. It attends to the pervasiveness of the UNCHR in daily life in Shimelba. Photo: Anooradha Iyer Siddiqi. @iyersiddiqi @warscapes @jackfruitlive #lifebeyondemergency #afrofutures #refugeelife

Life Beyond Emergency 3. Shimelba refugee camp, Ethiopia. Shimelba is in Ethiopia's northern region, some hours' drive from Aksum. Refugees in Shimelba mostly came from Eritrea: either Tigrinya men from the cities, who had had fled conscription into militarized combat against the Ethiopian army, or Kunama farmers who perceived the Eritrean/ Ethiopian/ South Sudanese lands as home. The first group brought urban sensibilities into the camp, running coffeehouses and cinemas. The second group brought agrarian sensibilities into the camp, maximizing a small water supply to grow staples, harvesting and stockpiling grains, and raising each storehouse and domicile as a community. This café is in Little Asmara, in the commercial heart of the camp. Photo: Anooradha Iyer Siddiqi. @iyersiddiqi @warscapes @jackfruitlive #lifebeyondemergency #afrofutures #refugeelife

Life Beyond Emergency 4. Cox's Bazaar, Bangladesh. The UNHCR established a sub-office in Cox's Bazaar to shelter Rohingya refugees in 1991. For decades before the recently renewed genocidal actions of the Myanmari state and military, these migrants had become integral to a booming tourist economy in Cox's Bazaar. One of the most frequented holiday destinations in Bangladesh, Cox's Bazaar has hosted visitors from Chittagong, or points farther, such as Dhaka, on its long expanse of uninterrupted habitable sandy coastline, with vacation residences, high-rise apartments, restaurants, and hotels such as those in this photo from the early days of the beachfront's radical and often unregulated transformation. A day labour force, often comprised of Rohingya refugees trying to survive, lay behind the explosion in the development of the built environment. For centuries, Arakanese/Rakhine people have lived in the region that became Cox's Bazaar, to the north in the Chittagong hill tracts, and in Tripura state in India's northeast. The influxes of refugees and asylum seekers in recent decades has accompanied a radical capitalistic urbanization that has concentrated and enhanced a luxury industry in this border region between the nations of Bangladesh and Myanmar. Within this landscape, environments constructed by and for the Rohingya extend far beyond the refugee camps. Photo: Anooradha Iyer Siddiqi. @iyersiddiqi @warscapes @jackfruitlive #lifebeyondemergency #shelterinplace #Rohingyalivesmatter #Rohingya #Rakhine #Arakan #Bangladesh #Coxsbazaar #Chittagong #Dhaka

Life Beyond Emergency 5. Kebri Beyah refugee camp, Ethiopia. When the state structure and civil infrastructures of the Somali Democratic Republic began to break down in the late 1980s and early 1990s, armed conflict and water and food insecurity forced large populations in the southern region of the country to migrate. People fled from rural areas to the coast. They sailed southward to Kenya, or found emergency relief camps in Mogadishu. People also fled westward to Kenya, where a relief camp called Ifo was established near the town of Dadaab, or to Ethiopia, where they were sheltered near the town of Kebri Beyah in the Somali Region. Refugees have lived continuously in Kebri Beyah since then, and still do, three generations later. There is no fence around the camp, nor much material or aesthetic difference in the built environment inside and outside it. The architectural landmarks in the camp are those marking the administration by the UNHCR, the Ethiopian government, and contracted NGOs, the mosques and schools established by the refugees, and community and commercial centres, like London Shop, in this photo. A London Shop employee spoke at length about life in the camp while we watched several camels pass by, walking toward the main road. A Marehan Somali born in the Jubaland, he was twenty-one years old, and had arrived in Kebribeyah at age one. He attended secondary school in Kebri Beyah. He lived with several members of his clan, near the shop. He had never been to Somalia. Photo: Anooradha Iyer Siddiqi. @iyersiddiqi @warscapes @jackfruitlive #lifebeyondemergency #shelterinplace #blacklivesmatter #somalilivesmatter #afrofutures #refugeelife

Life Beyond Emergency 6. Shimelba refugee camp, Ethiopia. Eritrean Kunama farmers have formed a significant constituency in Shimelba, even if they have numbered far fewer than the majority Tigrinya urbanites from Asmara. Kunama dwellings and grain silos, as they appear in this photo, would only be situated so densely in a refugee camp. As explained by a young Kunama woman who owned a popular tea stall, each of the houses was built collectively by members of the community for each other. For days, she recalled, many hands went into forming the clay walls and thatching the roof of her two-room home, while she labuored over the stove in her kitchen, cooking meals for the group. She had lost her husband in Eritrea. Unmarried, with small children, she didn't move much throughout the camp. Her children went to school and came straight home, escorted by her brother. On the way home from school each afternoon, they stopped at the tea stall for a meal. In her words, in Kunama society, the community provided support to unmarried women. The men in this camp, many from different communities who had all fled violence and conscription in Eritrea, far outnumbered the women. This is not typically the case in refugee camps. In a new life with little protection, many women in Shimelba married quickly upon arrival, for the sake of security. She was an anomaly. Photo: Anooradha Iyer Siddiqi. @iyersiddiqi @warscapes @jackfruitlive #lifebeyondemergency #shelterinplace #Ethiopia #Shimelba #Kunama #africanlivesmatter #blacklivesmatter #refugeelife

Life Beyond Emergency 7. Dagaheley refugee camp, Dadaab, Kenya. Emergency environments are often understood as zones of space, less as zones of time. People who live in emergency camps know that there are many species of time. There is time regulated by a series of markers across a daily span, between the moments the sun rises and sets, or between the morning and evening curfews (thresholds at which the people and activities shift). There is time stretched into spans of days, which undulates with the seasons. There is time punctuated by holidays, festivals, weddings, and funerals. There is the suspension of time, with no capitalistic metronome, irregular work and school, and no habits of mass participation and mobility. Dagaheley refugee camp emerged from a nine-section grid drawn in 1992 by a German urban planner working for the UN-HCR, and was settled by 30,000 refugees, a population that tripled after twenty years, crowding the densely built environment. Dagaheley also emerged from time out of joint, from the regular sounds of the muezzin, the rhythm of the scents of bread and meat appearing in the market pictured here, the tread of shopkeepers sweeping the path in front of their shops, tailors requiring just so many hours to stitch a dress. As we shelter, emerge, re-shelter, and re-emerge, imagining #UrbanismBeyondCorona, we might start by imagining how time shapes space. This post is part of an Instagram series called #UrbanismBeyondCorona and hosted by @UrbanWorksAgency and the ExperimentalHistoryProject at the California College of the Arts Architecture Division. Architects and urbanists are invited to offer a prediction, warning, gift, hack, instrument, prompt, or question that reflects on the role designers and urban actors can play in shaping cities after Covid-19. Photo: Anooradha Iyer Siddiqi. @iyersiddiqi @warscapes @jackfruitlive @UrbanWorksAgency #lifebeyondemergency #shelterinplace #blacklivesmatter #africanlivesmatter #refugeelife #urbanismbeyondcorona

For a time beyond

To shelter in place for a time beyond is to live within paradoxes. It is to throw into question the presumed stabilities and instabilities of architecture, on the one hand, and displacement, on the other. Both terms—architecture and displacement—suggest specific iterations of refugee camps and also organising principles of shelter. They are ends and also structuring concepts through which to understand historical continuity and change, heritages lost and gained.

What is to be called *temporary*? And what is to be called *permanent*? In the camp, a temporariness evolves into permanence while a permanence never really remains. Both are ephemeral in their manifestation, yet constantly in transformation. Durations (spans of time) create illusions of difference as they stretch across time and space. The materialisation of this *timespace* creates two paradoxes.

Architecture and displacement refer to the actualised and the schematic simultaneously. This is the first paradox. Looking closely at the instantiation of time into space, in the form of the camp, illuminates a form both exceptional and ordinary. This is the next paradox. That exceptional, ordinary, actualised, schematic form is the kernel of inhabitation in emergency. Inhabitation is a negotiation of timespace, invoking a past while anticipating a future yet to come, within the materialities of built worlds, multiple perceptions, an imaginal existence. While the future of an elsewhere is anticipated for some, the recurrence of the past is the futurity for others. It is an otherwise awaited in the present, an elsewhere of the *there* in the here and the now. It is the temporality of moments, of distances, and durations without an end, distances yet to arrive, in which the past, present and future collide in a complex interplay, freezing one while diligently anticipating the other.

Inhabiting these paradoxes is the everyday fine grain of the camp, the core practice in making *an otherwise* by dreaming of a time beyond. Without the timeness of that time—both the time of dreaming and the time of making—there would be no space of the camp. There would be no holding still, stilling time, being *in situ*. An exhibition or series of image events may allow a small glimpse into the ways in which time becomes suspended, held, contained. But in the camp it is that initiative of making thought, that alternative productivity, that way of knowing, against the forces of containment which give rise to the capacity to shelter in place. For the camp, producing knowledge and living it are not separate.

References

Abourahme, N. (2015). Assembling and Spilling Over: Towards an 'Ethnography of Cement' in a Palestinian Refugee Camp. *International Journal of Urban and Regional Research*, 39: 200-217.

Oxford Refugee Studies Centre, Department of International Development. *Architectures of Displacement* (2017) [Research project]. 2017-2018 [Online]. Available at: https://www.rsc.ox.ac.uk/research/architectures-of-displacement [Accessed: 1 November, 2019]

Beeckmans, L., Singh, A., & Gola, A. (Forthcoming, 2021). Rethinking the Intersection of Home and Displacement from a Spatial Perspective. In L. Beeckmans, A. Gola, A. Singh & H. Heynen (eds.), *Making Home(s) in Displacement: Critical Reflections on a Spatial Practice*. Leuven: Leuven University Press.

Chitchian, S., Momic, M, & Seethaler-Wari, S. (2020). Architectures of an 'Otherwise': Inhabiting Displacement. In D. Cuff and W. Davis (eds), *Contingency: Ardeth. A Magazine on the Power of the Project*. 6: 249-255.

Hailey, C. (2009). *Camps: A Guide to 21st-Century Space*. Cambridge, MA: MIT Press.

Heynen, H. (1999). *Architecture and Modernity: A Critique*. Cambridge, MA: MIT Press.

Hilal, S., & Petti, A. (2013). *Architecture after Revolution*. Berlin: Sternberg Press.

Hilal, S., & Petti, A. (2018). *Permanent Temporariness*. Stockholm, Sweden: Art and Theory Publishing.

Hilal, S., & Petti, A. (2021). *Refugee Heritage*. Stockholm: Art and Theory Publishing.

Katz, I., Martin, D., & Minca, C. (eds.) (2018). *Camps Revisited: Multifaceted Spatialities of a Modern Political Technology*. London, New York: Rowman & Littlefield.

Mamdani, M. (1996). *Citizen and Subject: Contemporary Africa and the Legacy of Late Colonialism*. Princeton, NJ: Princeton University Press.

Morrison, T. (1997). Home. In W. Lubiano (ed.), *The House That Race Built: Black Americans, U.S. Terrain*, 3-12. New York: Pantheon.

Morrison, T. (2012). *Home*. New York: Alfred A. Knopf Inc.

Mouffe, C. (2000). *The Democratic Paradox*. New York: Verso.

Naimou, A. (2018). Preface. *Humanity* 8(3), Available at: http://humanityjournal.org/issue8-3/preface/ [Accessed: November 10, 2020].

Pieris, A. (ed.) (2019). *Architecture on the Borderline*. New York: Routledge.

Povinelli, E. A. (2011). Routes/Worlds. *e-flux journal*, Nr. 27 [Online]. Available at: https://web.archive.org/web/20111013071516/http://www.e-flux.com/journal/view/244#_ftn15 [Accessed: November 10, 2019]

Povinelli, E. A. (2012). The Will to Be Otherwise/The Effort of Endurance. *The South Atlantic Quarterly*, 111(3), 453-475.

Povinelli, E. A. (2014). Geontologies of the Otherwise. *Society for Cultural Anthropology*: Theorizing the Contemporary, *Fieldsights*, January 13 [Online]. Available at: https://culanth.org/fieldsights/geontologies-of-the-otherwise [Accessed: November 6, 2019]

Povinelli, E. A. (2017). Geontologies: The Concept and Its Territories. *e-flux Architecture*, 81 [Online]. Available at: https://www.e-flux.com/journal/81/123372/geontologies-the-concept-and-its-territories/ [Accessed: November 6, 2019]

Roy, A. (2011). Slumdog Cities: Rethinking Subaltern Urbanism. *International Journal of Urban and Regional Research*, 35(2), 223–238.

Sanyal, R. (2014). Urbanizing Refuge: Interrogating Spaces of Displacement. *International Journal of Urban and Regional Research*, 38(2), 558–572.

Sanyal, R. (2016). From Camps to Urban Refugees: Reflections on Research Agendas. *International Journal of Urban and Regional Research*.

Seethaler-Wari, S., Chitchian, S., & Momić, M. (eds.) (Forthcoming, 2021). *Inhabiting Displacement: Architecture and Authorship*. Basel: Birkhäuser.

Siddiqi, A.I. (2017). Architecture Culture, Humanitarian Expertise: From the Tropics to Shelter, 1953-1993. *Journal of the Society of Architectural Historians*.

Siddiqi, A. I. (2018). Writing With: Togethering, difference, and feminist architectural histories of migration. *e-flux Architecture*: Structural Instabilities [Online]. Available at: https://www.e-flux.com/architecture/structural-instability/208707/writing-with/ [Accessed: December 10, 2018]

Siddiqi, A. I. (2020). Ephemerality. *Comparative Studies of South Asia, Africa, and the Middle East* 40 (1), 24-34.

Siddiqi, A. I. (2022). Humanitarian Homemaker, Emergency Subject: Questions of Housing and Domesticity. *Architecture and the Housing Question*. London: Routledge.

Siddiqi, A. I. (2023). *Architecture of Migration: The Dadaab Refugee Camps and Humanitarian Settlement*. Durham: Duke University Press.

CHAPTER 2

Towards Dwelling in Spaces of Inhospitality

A Phenomenological Exploration of Home in Nahr Al-Barid

Ashika Singh
KU Leuven, Belgium

Introduction

In 2017, *Decolonizing Architecture* (DAAR) – a prominent architectural studio and art residency located in Palestine fronted by the architects Sandi Hilal and Alessandro Petti – produced a dossier entitled 'Refugee Heritage'. This dossier was the culmination of a series of workshops, lectures and a course hosted by the Royal Institute of Art in Stockholm which concluded with the nomination of Dheisheh, a Palestinian refugee camp in Bethlehem, for UNESCO recognition. This was a call to recognise and, indeed, redefine refugee heritage by "tracing, documenting, revealing and representing refugee history beyond the narrative of suffering and displacement" (Petti, 2017). The assertion of a 'Refugee Heritage' is part of a broader set of cultural, academic and political initiatives to represent refugee camps in terms other than violence and deprivation, "to imagine and practice *refugeeness* beyond humanitarianism" (DAAR, 2017). Building upon DAAR's radical rethinking of Palestinian refugee camps as sites of sociocultural and political heritage, the following will critically explore the concept of home in relation to refugee camps.

Refugee camps do not make for conventional heritage sites, but rather are artefacts of the 20th and 21st Centuries as sites of exclusion, exception and exhaustion (Agamben, 1996; Hailey, 2009; Welander, 2020), and represent a global failure to protect those most severely marginalised by our juridical and political paradigms of state nationalism. In the specific context of Palestine, the refugee camp represents what is often referred to as *al nakba* (the disaster or catastrophe) of 1948, when the state of Israel declared independence and nearly one million Palestinian people were forced to flee their homes. Refugee camps were a stopgap measure by NGOs and the newly-created UN Relief and Works Agency (UNRWA) to shelter the people forcibly displaced by war and collective expulsions. Many of these camps still exist today and endure as monuments to British imperialism and contemporary Israeli settler colonialism, as well as evidence of the inadequacy of multilateral humanitarianism (Weizman, 2011; Hanafi & Long, 2011). As Khaldun Bshara (2017) writes, "Palestinian refugee camps are the living testimony of suspended dreams".

What would it mean, then, to reconceive the affective possibilities of refugee camps in terms other than violence and deprivation, but something more akin to a site of endurance, resilience and resistance? Although they are complex and ambivalent architectures of care, do refugee camps not represent how dominant social and political systems seek to alienate asylum seekers and refugees? Is it really possible to conceive of such spaces as homes? By assuming space and the built environment as a product of socioeconomic, cultural and political production (Lefebvre, 1974) and by challenging romantic idealisations of the home, which can manifest itself in analyses of the camp as a space of exclusion and exception, I seek in a more theoretical capacity, as opposed to directly empirical one, to qualify what is more often than not an overtly geopolitical analysis of camp spaces. With the insights provided to me as a philosopher, specifically, a phenomenologist, and not as an empirical scientist, I propose prefatorily to sketch a critical phenomenological approach to dwelling, one that is arguably more open to and thus better at capturing the ambiguous reality of inhabiting spaces in such extreme and highly politicised conditions.

Phenomenology, as the study of lived experience, already has a longstanding tradition of reflection about what it means to be 'at home' or to dwell (Heidegger, 1954; Bachelard, 1958; Seamon & Mugerauer, 1985; Casey, 2009). As such, it has the potential theoretically to substantiate empirical investigations that endeavour to shed light on notions of home and home-making in refugee camps (Harker, 2009; Dudley, 2011; Trapp, 2015). However, phenomenology, even though it is a discipline that emphasises the implications of being in the world, tends to operate within a rather limited and often privileged scope of experience (namely European, middle-class, male and white), and therefore it rarely considers in any particular depth what it actually means to be in and to inhabit spaces beyond what is dominantly seen as convention. While I advocate for the need for a more detailed theoretical reflection on making home from a phenomenological perspective, the relationships between space, building and dwelling would yield greater insight only if complemented by a more practical and so already *spatialised* approach to refugee camps as found in, say, human geography and architectural studies (Katz, 2010; Ramadan, 2013; Katz, Minca & Martin, 2018, 2019; Handel, 2019). This is what I intend here by an intervention – or, more precisely, *intermezzo* – which looks in more detail at the concrete example of the Palestinian refugee camp, Nahr Al-Barid.

Nahr Al-Barid, which was established in 1949 in Northern Lebanon, offers a particularly interesting illustration of making homes in displacement. While the refugee camp has had nearly sixty years in which to develop into a more urbanised landscape, one which prior to its destruction was deemed socially and economically buoyant, its identity as a temporary Palestinian "camp" remains important to its residents. Following its destruction in 2007, which was the result of the conflict between the Islamist militant group, *Fatah Al-Islam*, and the Lebanese Armed Forces (LAF), scholars and activists alike have drawn attention to the significance of the spatial and built environment in shaping meaningful lives in an environment of displacement. Although it is not the first Palestinian refugee camp to have suffered the effects of systematic destruction, nor has it been the last, it is one that still exists in an extremely hostile context within the geopolitical context of the Arab League. Housing demolitions are often indiscriminately performed within Lebanese-Palestinian camps as a form of collective punishment (Sayigh, 2004), but the situation in Nahr Al-Barid has exposed and highlighted a number of conflicting issues regarding the Palestinian people's desire to improve their current housing conditions and rebuild their homes, and their desire to return to the national home of Palestine. This situation is perhaps due to how the hostile context of the space contrasts with the unprecedented scale of the reconstruction effort – in which both men and women participated. In this case the refugee camp has become more than a temporary place in which to subsist, but rather a symbol of Palestinian cultural heritage – that is, I propose, a place of 'dwelling' in a phenomenological sense.

The goal of this chapter is ultimately to show how a critical reflection on such examples can mediate and simultaneously benefit from a critical phenomenological approach to the concept of home, one that accommodates a greater plurality of voices, spaces and spatial practices. My interpretations of Nahr Al-Barid refugee camp are here ascertained at an epistemological distance, and so they exclude personal or direct experience of the camp space itself. Although somewhat unique in the framework of camp studies, my position as a 'philosopher' (as opposed to, say, a sociologist, anthropologist or ethnographer) arguably allows me critically to assess the multiple positions of field research and of field researchers (Gupta & Ferguson, 1977), who are more often than not themselves outsiders to and occasional visitors of a camp's context. A more critical phenomenology of dwelling can in turn, I propose, with respect to empirical insights, problematise assumptions about home and making homes that are constituted through a western, Eurocentric symbolic and material hegemony. It would then potentially revitalise how *we* see the activities of people who live in refugee camps in a way that supports the life-worlds and, indeed, the perspectives of inhabitants and their visions *for* the geopolitical world that *we* share and have in common. It should not be forgotten, however, that behind this expression of 'we' more often than not stand scholars, activists, law-makers, policy-drivers and politicians whose authority on such matters, including my own, bears relation to the part that they play in affirming the power of Western and Eurocentric institutions.

A phenomenological reading of home in situations of forced displacement

The refugee camp, more often than not, brings to the public imagination an aggregation of tents, composed in a grid-like formation and of structures which are easy to demolish. Their temporary nature, born of their emergency context, implies that these are spaces built ultimately to be forgotten; as such, these spaces can exploit a politics of ephemerality (Siddiqi, 2020). For over a century, camps have undermined and even compounded the western principle of a civic space in which the rights of citizens are inscribed and recognised, and their continued existence thereby represents a political failing of current legal systems to ascribe universal rights (Malkki, 2002; Diken & Laustsen, 2006). In this respect, the history typically attributed to refugee camps is one of violence, humiliation and deprivation linked to territorial exclusion, juridico-political exception and a politics of exhaustion. DAAR's 'Refugee Heritage' dossier therefore raises a rather timely, albeit controversial, question: how are we to understand the life and culture that people bring with them to, and develop in, refugee camps along with the suffering and marginalisation built into these spaces?

The tradition of phenomenology, at least of the Heideggerian variety, might provide an initial clue, given its emphasis on heritage or historicity as an ontological matter of dwelling and building. Dwelling, according to his now famous essay 'Bauen Wohnen Denken' (1954), relates not only to how people live day-to-day in terms of practices and sociocultural habits, but also to what *undergirds* that living and that particular way of life, which includes the spatio-temporal contingency of history and a collective relation to an origin – the 'history of being'. Proper dwelling concerns a particular mode of being in the world, one that underscores how our multiple relations to and our embeddedness in the world – what some phenomenologists call our 'situatedness' (Costello, 2014; Hünefeldt & Schlitte, 2018) – cannot be extricated from how we are and what is proximate and familiar to us in that world. Dwelling thereby *reveals* something about our world which building then manifests. Indeed, it is the activity of building that has the task and possibility of *"opening* a world" (Mugerauer, 1992, p. 216). A site of (proper) building is established in a landscape through a mutual collaboration between the natural environment and human culture, leaving neither unaffected by the encounter. Seen from this perspective, life and culture develop in relation to a built environment as people who have a history relative to a place or to a series of places become actively attuned and responsive to what is already (structurally) given.

Linking expressions of cultural and lived heritage to dwelling certainly aligns with my present effort to understand refugee camps in terms of home. Dwelling is often conceived as fundamental to the manifestation of home-like affectations, such as a sense of familiarity, security and belonging. Built environments in turn, insofar as they endure, can affirm and even reinforce these affectations. The phenomenological notions of dwelling and building do not, however, easily accommodate lived experiences of displacement, which are quickly and all too often pathologised in relation to bodily disorientation and a loss of "identity" (Casey, 1993, p. 37). Heidegger (1946/1993), in particular, often relates the experience of homelessness to the 'oblivion of being' (p. 257). Yet, this line of thought risks reinforcing the idea that humans are essentially bound to one particular dwelling-place of their origin, which is not dissimilar to the rhetoric of ethnonationalism. I argue that, although displacement, especially forced displacement, can result in trauma involving severe mental states of anxiety, doubt and fear, and even in probing questions of self and of one's relation to the world, this phenomenon is not somehow distinct from or alien to the processes of dwelling and building themselves. In fact, displacement can very often be the event that stimulates reflection on home and on the homeplace, whether this be in relation to one's needs and desires or to the ideals and functions of such a space.

For this reason, migrants' and forced migrants' everyday lives have become the laboratory for the investigations of the social sciences to make sense of home as a set of emotions, practices and of living arrangements (Boccagni, 2017; Boccagni & Brighenti, 2017; Ralph & Staeheli, 2011). More importantly, human displacement reveals that questions of dwelling and building are not necessarily bound either to a single location or to a place of origin. In this regard, Sara Ahmed's (2000) own phenomenological approach is significant for her ambition to reconceive home in relation to experiences of migration. As she notes, "[t]he journeys of migration involve a splitting of home as place of origin and home as sensory world of everyday experience" (p. 90). That is to say, provided the insights of literary articulations and empirical research on the matter, there are clearly *multivocal* significations of home.

Home is a condition, a space, a flow of time; it is neither sedentary, nor is it absolute; even as home can be used to signify one thing, a site or identity, it can connote another and be host to a number of conflicting sentiments, affects and associations. This makes home a particularly ambiguous term, yet it retains much power over our lives. The feminist phenomenologist Iris Marion Young (2006) argues not to reject the emotional and existential value of home, like some feminist thinkers, but rather to resist the idea of home that would reject its apparent conflicts, eradicate social differences and render it a 'safe space' in contrast to being not 'at home' (pp. 282-283). Home is, for Young, a site of oppression, specifically that of her mother who failed to conform to the idea of white American suburban femininity, motherhood and domesticity imposed upon her while also suffering from the loss of her husband and single-handedly raising her children. But it is also, as she conceives it through the writings of bell hooks on the matter, a site of restoration – a place where oppressed communities can seek personal and social affirmation. Without eliminating these contradictions, perhaps home could be better understood, as Hilde Heynen and Andre Loeckx (1999) suggest in relation to the question of modernity, as "a scene of ambivalence", which is to say as a spatial concept of multiple realities and tensions. It is in this sense of 'ambivalence' that home would better reflect the valued *ambiguity* of a modern world and modern spaces that are subject to various, and at times extreme, forms and forces of gendered, sexual, neoliberal, racialised and imperialist displacements.

Home, like cultural heritage, while ambivalent and not to be romanticised, still contains deep meaning in its invocation and attribution to a place or to places, which can lend power to or, indeed, be exploited for legal and political purposes. One way of looking at this is, as Cathrin Brun and Anita Fàbos (2015) propose, in terms of the multiple "constellations of home". Due to their focus on the experiences of refugees and other forced migrants, they note how dwelling appears "rather like a dialogue that spans place and time" (p. 12), incorporating both practical and idealised notions of home in relation to everyday practices, the homeland, including aspirations to one day 'return home', and desires to achieve a more stable existence in 'exile'. The metaphor of constellations proves useful here to highlight how the meanings of home can vary even as they overlap at different axis points contingent on the material and social conditions of a locale or spanning across a number of locales, prompting trans-local and transnational identifications.

Brun and Fàbos (ibid.) give a more coherent shape to these constellations of home by identifying three key significations, coded as 'home', 'Home' and 'HOME'. While 'home' refers to those day-to-day practices necessary for the sustaining of life and for the habitation of an environment, which can be situated in either the domestic space or shared public spaces, 'Home' emerges in relation to the social and cultural representation of "values, traditions, memories and subjective feelings of home" (pp. 12-13). The latter reflects an ideal which can stimulate social and material investments in the more practical sense of 'home'. It can also, however, foster a sense of idealism and nostalgia, implying that the 'home' can be seen to fall short of some notion of 'proper' dwelling. 'HOME' refers to the institutionalisation of certain ideals and practices of homemaking, thereby acknowledging the impact of the concept on a societal and political scale. This signification refers and endeavours in turn to bind spatial activities which help to improve, familiarise and create more lasting foundations in a place to *"the geopolitics of nation and homeland* that contribute to situations of protracted displacement" (ibid., p. 13). The dominant use of home and home-making in public discourse often employs 'HOME' in order to distinguish between who is *welcome*, and belongs somewhere, and who is considered 'foreign' or 'alien', and presumably then *unwelcome*.

Although pertinent and insightful, what this brief account of the multivocal and plural meanings of home cannot show is how exactly such constellations are *spatialised* in the world; the question of, say, how 'HOME' implicates the ideals of 'Home' which then inform and guide the spatio-temporal makings of a homeplace, and *vice versa*, may become clear only through local empirical investigations (as in fact follows in the particular issue of *Refuge* that Brun and Fàbos' article introduces). After all, very often these constellations are deeply embedded in, and thereby implicitly experienced through, what we do and how we see the orientation of things and the allocation of spaces around us. Ultimately, what is important to unpick and to represent clearly is how "hometactics", construed here as a decentred praxis of home-making and belonging, are operative (Ortega, 2016, p. 201). It is therefore by looking to the concrete, albeit liminal, example of refugee camps that such constellations can arguably become visible, as the political and cultural paradigms and systems implicate not only the causes for forced displacements, but also, as I will argue, the responsive processes by which displaced persons attempt spatially to accommodate and transform their situations of homelessness.

Intermezzo: Nahr Al-Barid refugee camp, Northern Lebanon

Refugee camps in Lebanon were first built in 1949 by UNRWA and other humanitarian organisations quickly and temporarily to shelter the first wave of forcibly displaced Palestinians from the appropriated territories of the newly established State of Israel. Over seventy years later, Palestinian camps in Lebanon endure as part of the Lebanese urban and rural landscape, and as Palestinian symbols of both a right to return to Palestine and a right to stay. The camps, whose separation from broader Lebanese life can in some cases consolidate top-down government policies of socio-economic segregation and disenfranchisement, do in many ways function as spaces of political control and police surveillance, and some have since become potential enclaves of religious fundamentalism as well as political dissidence (Peteet, 2005; Hanafi, 2008). At the same time, many now reflect the tendency towards camp urbanisation whereby what was once a series of tents has developed into a cityscape, organised by a complex regime of governance whose power is concentrated neither singularly in the hands of UN-RWA, nor in the hands of the host state, nor in those of the popular committees.

The Palestinian refugee camp of Nahr Al-Barid follows much the same pattern, and was well-known for having some of the largest souks in rural North Lebanon, which made it a prosperous and comparatively peaceful camp. The

Figure 1. Aerial image of Nahr Al-Barid refugee camp; aerial photo sourced from DAAR (online).

Figure 2. An illustration by Apurba Podder of the gradual developments in the camp's private and public structure, submitted for KU Leuven's Urban Analysis and Concepts Studio, 'The Nahr el Bared Studio'; image sourced from Hassan (2015) and reproduced with permission.

camp thus embodied for many a 'success story' of sorts, even the revival of a Palestinian city in exile, in spite of the especially hostile environment in which it took place. For these reasons, and especially in light of its 2007 destruction, Nahr Al-Barid constitutes a particularly interesting illustration of the complexities of home and dwelling in displacement.

Nahr Al-Barid was first built as a tent site, but, by the turn of the century, it consisted of two built-up sections: the original Old Camp, which housed the majority of the population (circa 20,000 people) and which was still under the mandate of UNRWA, and the New Camp (Fig. 1.). The Old Camp consisted of the original allocated space, rented by UNRWA, in which tents were erected and which soon became too small to house the second and third generations of residents. Inevitably, albeit under top-down scrutiny, people began to expand on the spaces available to them: first by building up, and then by buying land in the immediate vicinity of the settlement (Fig. 2.). The New Camp is a non-camp extension to the original camp, but it remains under Lebanese jurisdiction with a mixed Palestinian and Lebanese population. This overspill of the camp provided more space for informal investment, urban expansion and affordable housing for Palestinian refugees, among others. As Ismae'l Sheikh Hassan (2015) explains, the New Camp "allowed camp residents who were seeking to improve their living conditions by moving out from the overpopulated UNRWA camp, while remaining intimately part of the Nahr el Bared community" (p. 199).

In 2007, Nahr Al-Barid refugee camp was destroyed by one of the largest conflicts since the end of the Lebanese civil war in 1990, resulting in the displacement of most of its 27,000 Palestinian residents as well as several hundred Lebanese civilians. The near levelling of parts of the camp by heavy shelling and

Figure 3. The main road of the New Camp that used to connect Tripoli with the Lebanese-Syrian border in 2007. Before the conflict, this road was lined with hundreds of shops that serviced not only the camp residents, but also those in the adjoining villages of Akkar; photo sourced from Murphy (2007).

arson was claimed to be the collateral damage from battles between the LAF and *Fatah al-Islam*, which was then an Islamist militant group based in Nahr Al-Barid, even though much of the damage seemed excessive and intentional (Fig. 3.). Although the siege lasted only forty days, it resulted in the destruction of more than half of the camp's premises – the houses, the streets and common spaces – the difficult reconstruction of which continues to this day. Adam Ramadan (2009) records how residents found "houses smashed first by shells and bombs, then by vandalism and arson, possessions stolen and broken, offensive graffiti daubed on walls" (p. 153).

The conflict brought up again a number of painful, collective memories of the destruction and flight from the Tel al-Zaatar refugee camp (1976), the massacres of Sabra and Shatila (1982), and the brutal War of the Camps in the 1980s (Knudsen, 2018, p. 142). Palestinians had already faced decades of legal discrimination, marginalisation and forced displacement; they had been denied many basic civil rights, barred from ascertaining property and from working in white-collar professions, a fate that has engendered systemic poverty (Sayigh, 1995; Halabi, 2004). Therefore, even though few residents actually supported *Fatah al-Islam*'s campaign, the LAF's role in the camp's destruction was perceived by most as a continuation of the attack on the Palestinian people and on Palestinian camps in Lebanon.

In this context it is striking to read how one resident describes Nahr Al-Barid as a "second homeland […] my little paradise" which attests to the meaning of the camp space (Ramadan, 2010, p. 55). Following the siege, many residents compared their experience to the *nakbah*, and thereby to a re-living of exile from a dwelling place. The loss of the camp in this sense constituted the loss of decades of "hard work" which created a sense of stability and investment in a future (ibid., p. 57). Such investments, as a basic phenomenological reading would show, incur personal and social attachments to the camp, which became more than a temporary shelter but was a locus of familiarity, security as well as of meaning for a social and private life. However, most of these investments were, as is the case with so many 'informal' developments, never documented in archives or on official maps prior to the reconstruction effort (Halkort, 2013). What is more, the reconstruction of the camp has given rise to a number of political issues; most prominent among these are questions of the association of material development with permanence, what constitutes the identity of 'the camp', and the role of the Lebanese state and military in redevelopment.

Even though the Palestinian inhabitants were and continue to be well aware of the precarious geopolitical context in which they live and of their particular socioeconomic and political situation, Nahr al-Barid was not simply to be abandoned in favour of moving to another camp or city, but rather its reconstruction was seen as a political movement and a statement of resilience. Over the first fifty years of the camp's existence most residents acquired their land via power of attorney (Al Natour, 1997). Power of attorney is the common legal format used by Palestinians to obtain effective use-rights without being formally registered as owners of pieces of land. Although not definitive proof of ownership, this was one of the few ways in which Palestinians could register property claims in Lebanon; its tenuous link to the user made it almost impossible, however, for refugees to reclaim title deeds for their private homes and businesses after the camp's destruction. There would be no easy way, then, for them to retrieve the historically grown spatial structure of the camp. It was this risk of losing the camp for good that led a team of young architects to propose undertaking a geographical mapping exercise at a level of detail that sought to ensure that Nahr Al-Barid could be rebuilt just as it was before.

While the Lebanese military did not permit 'formal' reconstruction to take place directly after the conflict, a team of activist architects and planners was urgently assembled to formulate a master plan and thus to mobilise residents to engage in discussions regarding the rebuilding process (Hassan, 2015, p. 113). It took more than two years to collect raw data on property and business assets, and a similar amount of time to verify all losses reported by the refugees. Nonetheless, with the support of UNRWA and other relief agencies, the unprecedented grassroots initiative by the Nahr Al-Barid Reconstruction Commission for Civil Action and Studies (NBRC) to reconstruct the camp began to unfold. The centrepiece of this ambitious project was a property database that recorded the households, business and public buildings that had been constructed in and around Nahr Al-Barid. What the grassroots master plan could in turn provide was multiple illustrations of what according to its residents the refugee camp looked like prior to its destruction (Hassan, 2015, pp. 131-149; Archnet, 2013). Among the contributors of the plan, as John Whyte (the UNRWA project manager) points out, there was clearly a desire "to recreate the social geography of the camp, reproducing the original streets and public space" (cited in Knudsen, 2018, p. 143).

The master plan could moreover anticipate the putatively more 'official' plans for the camp's reconstruction which prioritised the army's access to the camp space. It was clear that the model sought to remove the urban-like maze of unnavigable alleys, now typical of Palestinian camp typologies, and to replace them with low-rise apartment blocks, separated by streets of ten to fifteen metres in width, indeed enough space for a tank to pass (Hassan & Hanafi, 2010, p. 38). The final master plan may have had to acquiesce to a number of top-down changes, especially given that consideration of how the project would be funded was a priority, but it continued to reflect the memories and perspectives of Nahr Al-Barid's residents. For many residents it was integral that the rebuilding of Nahr Al-Barid was seen as a rebuilding of a Palestinian camp, and not as a modern cityscape. Thus the popular slogan that emerged in the early days of the reconstruction effort: "Reconstructing Nahr el Bared is the first step towards returning to Palestine" (Hassan, 2015, p. 110). The Nahr Al-Barid refugee camp cannot in this sense be disentangled from the camp as a political symbol for eventual return to Palestine and, at the same time, for claims to social and political recognition. It is for this reason that we need to reassess how refugee camps figure in both the global and local imagination.

Despite the utopian language often applied to home-spaces or, indeed, to the progression of urban development, making home and urbanism need not imply some quixotic project. While the English concept of home cannot simply be transposed into an Arab milieu (Sayigh, 2005), the Arabic distinction between *beit* and *watan* provides its own opportunities for phenomenological reflection. While *beit* refers to the house or home of lived experience, not distinguishing between the material environment or shelter and the family unit or the local community, *watan* refers to the home of origin, namely, what is perceived as one's primary homeland. *Beit* implies something concrete to which a sense of security and permanence is attached; the Palestinian villager's *beit* was built to last forever. The material and social fibres of the settlement, however, including neighbourhood layouts based on groupings of families and their close affiliations, were not exclusive to one place and could be reconstructed in alternative locations if need be. That many camps bear the names of former Palestinian villages or of prominent families seeks to affirm this (Sanyal, 2014). Even though a refugee camp might not be the *watan* of Palestine, it may still become *beit*, and so be structured and built up to reflect historical symbols, providing a space for socio-economic and cultural investment by both men and women (Latif, 2012; Salih, 2017).

Figure 4. Rebuilt areas of Nahr Al-Barid. As of 2017, only 45 per cent of the camp's population has been able to return to the site; photo sourced from Starr (2017).

While home signifies a special relationship to place, it is one built upon a constellation of multiple conditions – spatial practices, ideals and geopolitical context – which are always capable of changing. As Hassan (2015) notes, the initial project to rebuild the refugee camp was never intended as the formulation of a closed architectural object: "[i]t was envisioned as a bridge between multiple 'past realities' and future/emerging refugee dynamics that would inevitably transform and appropriate the camp in both expected and unexpected ways" (p. 152). Like the spatial and socio-material fabric of the camp then, the notion of home is also always in transition and in development (Fig. 4.).

Spaces of in/hospitality: making homes of camps in the national geographic

By acknowledging in concrete terms the ambivalence of home and how it functions as a constellation in relation to practices, ideals and political hegemony in actual spaces over time, the question then follows: who is *not* at home in this world? When employed in public discourse, the politics of dwelling (or HOME) seek to reconfigure the relationship between state, people and territory in an effort to solidify it as some kind of natural category. The result is a "rooting of peoples" by way of a territorialisation of national identity, and hence the creation of a "national geographic" (Malkki, 1992). Personal memory of one's 'native' country, which can have deep emotional resonance especially in situations of displacement, is thereby constituted through a collective history of 'the homeland' and through what is perceived as native to a nation state. People who have been forced to leave their homeland and are unable to return in any near future may take refuge in a neighbouring state, but in principle there is nowhere else for them to go and make a new home. Therefore, in the context of post-World War II Europe, Hannah Arendt (1958) wrote that "[w]hat is unprecedented is not the loss of a home but the impossibility of finding a new one" (p. 293).

Arguably, despite multilateral conventions and the growth of humanitarian organisations, little has since changed: the initial violence of forced migration prevails in the processes of claiming asylum, strenuous systems of rejection and appeal, and the ever-present threat of deportation, all of which can involve detention in specific centres, prisons or refugee camps. The existence of refugee camps highlights that, even in cases when asylum is granted, refugees are not automatically eligible for the same rights as national citizens or even migrant workers. Many refugees in host nations, including Palestinians in Lebanon, do not have the right to rent, to acquire or to build property and, more often than not, their existence is merely tolerated within the physical parameters of the UNHCR's or UNRWA's governance. The space of the camp thereby carves out a place in a particular country and in the world for those deemed 'unassimilable' within the nation state paradigm of citizenship (Soguk, 1999). Although the humanitarian apparatus brings relief and aid, it has also become a system of power, bureaucracy, governance and regulation (Agier, 2011; Feldman & Ticktin, 2010). It is perhaps for this reason that many who study the spaces of camps find it hard to contemplate that people dwell therein.

It could be said that refugee camps provide structure and shape to 'refugeeness' that estranges forced migrants from living with meaning and legitimacy in the 'national geographic'. To live in a refugee camp is, in this sense, to inhabit a place (or zone) of social life deemed in a number of ways inhospitable and thereby uninhabitable, a place in which refugees merely wait in a limbo-like state to return to their place of origin (Hyndman & Giles, 2017). Neil Vallelly (2018) depicts this in phenomenological terms as a lived experience grounded in "an interminable present", whereby "the future ceases to exist as an imagined or even embodied possibility [...] only as a repetition of the present" (p. 217). Vallelly goes on to argue that this temporal collapse engenders a flattening of one's spatial apprehension and thereby denies forced migrants "from truly 'inhabiting' place in any meaningful way" (ibid.).

It is perhaps not surprising that, given my earlier apprehensive remarks on the matter, this phenomenological reading appears far removed from the experiences of Palestinians in the Nahr Al-Barid refugee camp, wherein decades of rebuilding culture and livelihoods have taken place, seeking to empower economic development, political claims to recognition and rights and, at the most basic but fundamental level, existential legitimacy (Peteet, 2005; Bshara, 2009; Feldman, 2015; Maqusi, 2017). Yet, it does reflect how, even in distinct settings wherein refugee camps have developed, such that they appear more like cities than the bare skeleton typically envisaged of camps and instead demonstrate a presence of cultural heritage, the practice of dwelling remains hostage to a political context of a host state that does not support the claims such day-to-day practices and its cultural artefacts make on a particular place. At the same time, such claims are complicated by the future ambitions of refugees who find their settlement in a new place antithetical to the return to their place of origin. In this way, similarly to Ahmed's notion of "strange bodies" (2000), refugee camps constitute refugees' bodies according to the economies of difference that organise their lives and their restricted and marginalised relation to the world. Strange bodies function as the "constitutive outside" and "the condition of possibility for" the subject "who determines the formation of home – the space one inhabits as liveable" (p. 52). Dwelling in the 'national geographic' implies being a citizen, and therefore being able and, more so, having the legitimacy – or right – to live in and to engage with the world. The relegation of refugees' bodies to inhospitable spaces thereby seeks to affirm the ease with which those fortunate enough to be considered citizens feel at home in the nation state.

Yet, as the construction and reconstruction efforts of Nahr Al-Barid refugee camp continues to illustrate, the experience of displacement is not symptomatic of an absolute loss of identity or potential for home-making, but rather of the much more dynamic and ambivalent process of dwelling. The experience of dwelling is a process that is sometimes achieved vis-à-vis day-to-day experiences of security, familiarity and community, all of which are subject to the material needs and the social processes of gradual inhabitation; indeed, another way to put this is to say that *beit* is as culturally and historically potent as *watan* (the homeland) in the interpretive process of coming to grips with what it means to be at home. At the same time, dwelling is conditioned by the sphere of socio-cultural and political meaning in which lies the political imperative for Palestinians to return to Palestine and remain temporarily in Lebanon, that is, in a state of displacement. As Mariana Ortega's concept of "hometactics" proposes, building on the work of Michel De Certeau (1984) and Maria Lugones (2003), such dwelling cannot easily be traced or mapped but it nonetheless produces a "sense of familiarity" in the midst of an environment or world to which one cannot fully belong (Ortega, 2016, p. 203). Dwelling in this sense is a tactical strategy – a process of making as well as unmaking – that goes beyond merely 'making do' (as per De Certeau) in order to develop a spatial context that reveals new possibilities within it. In line with Nasser Abourahme (2014), one could say that experiences of dwelling and of displacement in refugee camps can both diverge and converge at the junction of the 'material-lived' and the 'symbolic-political' (p. 4). And so, living between such conditions of dwelling is the everyday, even if not straightforwardly desirable, matter of spatial politics.

Nahr Al-Barid's destruction was so devastating in both effect and affect that it most certainly constitutes an act of 'urbicide', which means 'violence against or killing of the city'. This implies the destruction not only of material structures and social spaces but of a notion of rights and recognition (or existential legitimacy) which emerges from the cityscape. In the case of Nahr Al-Barid Ramadan (2009) writes, "[t]he seemingly unrestricted destruction of homes, the theft of possessions and arson, went well beyond any possible military necessity and became *the deliberate and systematic erasure of the camp*" (p. 153). Urbicide refers to the intentional eradication of any material evidence of a specific group's cultural heritage (Weizman, 2005; Abujidi, 2014) and, therefore, is fundamental to the project of genocide as it seeks to eliminate "the conditions of possibility of heterogeneity" (Coward, 2004). On the the other hand, for urbicide to occur the perpetrator must *assume a history and a socio-material heritage* as long as it seeks to destroy the embedded traces of that presence. The destructive actions of the Lebanese military in this respect underscore that Nahr Al-Barid had become a site of culture and heritage, one that continues to reflect personal, social and political attachments.

Conclusion

As homes, refugee camps are not necessarily conceived as places of comfort, or even as spaces of inherent stability or belonging. Home is, as Gaston Bachelard would say, "a place to daydream in" (Bachelard, 1958/1994, p. 6). These dreams, however, are not necessarily the dreams of a European, white and male dweller of Paris, but rather those of a group of Palestinian people who have long inhabited and fought for survival and justice in Lebanon. Palestinian refugee camps, in general, have existed for decades: generations have been born, lived and died in them; they have been sites of extreme conflict, armed resistance and everyday persistence. If we can recognise that refugee camps do have a history, as put forward by Alessandro Petti and Sandi Hilal of DAAR, then we can further acknowledge that they are places, not just of systemic estrangement, but also of immense activity – an activity that is orientated, not merely towards survival, but also towards rebuilding lives and establishing existential legitimacy. Such activity, which might also be conceived of as a multitude of "microtechniques of lived experience" (Ortega, 2016, p. 206), provides new everyday possibilities of making homes in a location or situation where the idealisation of home and home-making is not (ever or easily) granted.

Given such inhospitable conditions on a geopolitical scale, it is important to understand refugee camps in more concrete spatial terms so as to reflect better on the processes of home-making actually manifest in such spaces. What the above has sought to show is how a phenomenological exploration of home in contexts like that of Nahr Al-Barid can illuminate the multiple and often contradictory attachments to humanitarian and state technology in a manner that does not seek to eschew, but instead embrace, the tensions between various temporalities and the materiality of the space. In so doing, phenomenology, as the study of the spatio-temporal facets of lived experience, can further highlight that home is an everyday negotiation between the dynamism of built life and that of the human subject.

Certainly, the constellations of home are not specific or confined to experiences of forced displacement; nor, indeed, is the Palestinian refugee camp, as home, representative of all refugee camps worldwide or of other institutional settings (e.g. asylum seeker reception centres or refugee camps in southern African countries). Yet, in looking to such experiences and the multiple ways in which forcibly displaced people relate to living in a refugee camp, there is an opportunity to broaden our understanding of home and thereby to reflect critically on current discourses which intersect questions of home (and housing) only with those of citizenship and the nation state as well as with the top-down practices of humanitarianism and development (Salih, 2014). What my examination of a phenomenology of dwelling and of its potential for spatial application ideally provides, in this respect, is a glimpse into rethinking the discourse attached to refugee camps, and so a better understanding of these spatial technologies in their specific contexts and in relation to the people who build and dwell in them.

References

Abourahme, N. (2014). Assembling and Spilling-over: Towards an 'Ethnography of Cement' in a Palestinian Camp. *International Journal of Urban and Regional Research*, *39*(2), 200-217.

Abujidi, N. (2014). *Urbicide in Palestine: Spaces of Oppression and Resilience*, London and New York: Routledge.

Agamben, G. (1998). *Homo Sacer: Sovereign Power and Bare Life*. Tr. by Daniel Heller-Roazen. Stanford: SUP.

Agier, M., (2011), *Managing the Undesirables: Refugee Camps and Humanitarian Government*. Cambridge, UK: Polity Press.

Agier, M. (2002). Between War and City: Towards an Urban Anthropology of Refugee Camps. *Ethnography*, *3*(3), 317–41.

Ahmed, S. (2000). *Strange Encounters: Embodied Others in Post-coloniality*. Abingdon and New York: Routledge.

Al-Natour, S. (1997). The Legal Status of Palestinians in Lebanon. *Journal of Refugee Studies 10*(3), 360-377.

Archnet. (2013). Reconstruction of Nahr el Bared Refugee Camp Presentation Panels. Available at https://archnet.org/sites/6875/publications/9533 [Retrieved 4 August 2020].

Arendt, H. (1978, orig. pub. 1958). *The Origins of Totalitarianism*. New York: Meridian Books.

Bachelard, G. (1958/1994). *The Poetics of Space: The classic look at how we experience intimate places*. Translated by Maria Jolas. Bost, MA: Beacon Press.

Brun, C. & Fàbos, A. (2015). 'Making Homes in Limbo? A Conceptual Framework.' *Refuge: Canada's Journal on Refugees*, *31*(1), 5-17.

Bshara, K. (2017). 'Camp as Heritage.' *e-flux magazine online*. Available at https://conversations.e-flux.com/t/refugee-heritage-conversations-khaldun-bshara-camps-as-heritage/6772 [Retrieved 19 December, 2019].

Boccagni, P. (2017). *Migration and the Search for Home. Mapping Domestic Space in Migrants' Everyday Lives*. London: Palgrave.

Boccagni, P., & Brighenti, A. M. (2017). Immigrants and home in the making: thresholds of domesticity, commonality and publicness. *Journal of Housing and the Built Environment* 32, 1–11.

Casey, E. (2009). *Getting Back into Place: Toward a renewed understanding of the Place-World*. Second Edition. Indiana: Indiana University Press.

Costello, M. (2014). Situatedness. In: T. Thomas (ed.), *Encyclopaedia of Critical Psychology*. New York: Springer, 1757-1762.

Coward, M. (2004). Urbicide in Bosnia. In: S. Graham (ed.), *Cities, War and Terrorism: Towards an Urban Geopolitics* (pp. 154-171). Oxford: Blackwell.

De Certeau, M. (1984). *The Practice of Everyday Life*. Translated by Steven Rendall. Berkley, CA: University of California Press.

Decolonizing Architecture Art Residence (DAAR). (2017). 'Introduction'. *Refugee Heritage*. DAAR website. Available at http://www.decolonizing.ps/site/introduction-4/ [Retrieved 19 December, 2019].

Diken, B. & Laustsen, C. (2006). The Camp. *Geografiska Annaler*, 88(4), 443-452.

Dudley S. (2011). Feeling at home: Producing and consuming things in Karenni refugee camps on the Thai-Burma border. *Population, Space and Place 17*, 742-55.

Feldman, I. (2012). The Humanitarian Condition: Palestinian Refugees and the Politics of Living. *Humanity: An International Journal of Human Rights, Humanitarianism, and Development*, 3(2), 155-172.

Feldman, I. (2015). What is a camp? Legitimate refugee lives in spaces of long-term displacement. *Geoforum 66*, 244-252.

Feldman, I., & Ticktin, M. (eds.). (2010). *In the Name of Humanity: The Government of Threat and Care*. Durham, NC: Duke University Press.

Gupta, A. & Ferguson, J. 1977. 'Discipline and Practice: "The Field" as Site, Method, and Location in Anthropology'. In Akhil Gupta and James Ferguson (eds.), *Anthropological Locations* (pp. 1-46), Berkeley: University of California Press.

Hailey, C. (2009). *Camps: A Guide to 21st-Century Space*. Cambridge, MA: The MIT Press.

Halabi, Z. (2004). Exclusion and identity in Lebanon's Palestinian refugee camps: a story of sustained conflict, *Environment and Urbanization*, 16(2), 39–48.

Halkort, M. (2013). 'Rebuilding Nahr el Bared'. 12 December. *Open Democracy*. Available at https://www.opendemocracy.net/en/opensecurity/rebuilding-nahr-el-bared/ [Retrieved 4 August 2020].

Hanafi, S. (2008). Palestinian refugee camps in Lebanon: laboratories of state-in-the-making, discipline and Islamist radicalism. In Lentin, R. (ed.), *Thinking Palestine* (pp. 82-100). London: Zed Books.

Hanafi, S., & Long, T. (2010). Governance, Governmentalities, and the State of Exception in the Palestinian Refugee Camps of Lebanon. *Journal of Refugee Studies*, 23(?), 134-159.

Handel, A. (2019). What's in a home? Toward a critical theory of housing/dwelling. *EPC: Politics and Space 37*(6), 1045-1062.

Harker, C. (2009). Spacing Palestine through the Home. *Transactions of the Institute of British Geographers 34*(3): 320-332.

Hassan, I. & Hanafi, S. (2010). (In)Security and Reconstruction in Post-Conflict Nahr al-Barid Refugee Camp. *Journal of Palestine Studies 40*(1), 27-48.

Hassan, I. (2015). *On Urbanism and Activism in Palestinian Refugee Camps: The Reconstruction of Nahr el Bared*, PhD thesis, Leuven: Arenberg Doctoral School.

Heidegger, M. (1954/1993). Building Dwelling Thinking. In: David Farrell Krell (ed.), *Basic Writings: Ten Key Essays, plus the Introduction to Being and Time*. New York: HarperCollins Publishers.

Heidegger, M. (1946/1993). Letter on Humanism. In David Farrell Krell (ed.), *Basic Writings: Ten Key Essays, plus the Introduction to Being and Time*. New York: HarperCollins Publishers.

Heynen, H. & Loeckx, A. (1998). Scenes of Ambivalence: Concluding Remarks on Architectural Patterns of Displacement. *Journal of Architectural Education 52*(2), 100-108.

Hünefeldt, T. & Schlitte, A. (2018). *Situatedness and Place: Multidiscplinary Perspectives on the Spatio-temporal Contingency of Human Life*. New York: Springer International Publishing.

Hyndman, J. & Giles, W. (2017). *Refugees in Extended Exile: Living on the Edge*. London and New York: Routledge.

Katz, I. (2010). Spaces Stretch Inwards: Interactions between Architecture and Minor Literature. *Public Culture 62* (3), 425-432.

Katz, I., Minca, C. & Martin, D. (2018). The Camp Reconsidered. In Irit Katz, Claudio Minca & Diana Martin (eds.), *Camps Revisited* (pp. 1-14). London: Rowman & Littlefield.

Katz, I., Minca, C. & Martin, D. (2019). Rethinking the camp: On spatial technologies of power and resistance. *Progress in Human Geography XX*(X), 1-26.

Knudsen, J. (2018). Decade of Despair: The Contested Rebuilding of the Nahr al-Bared Refugee Camp, Lebanon, 2007-2017. *Refuge, 34*(2), 135-149.

Latif, N. (2012). Belonging and Un-Belonging: Home in Bourj al-Barajneh Refugee Camp. In S. Kanafani et al. (eds), *Anywhere But Now: Landscapes of Belonging in the Eastern Mediterranean*, Beirut: Heinrich Böll Stiftung Middle East, 25-36.

Lefebvre, H. (1991/1974). *The Production of Space*. Translated by Donald Nicholson-Smith. London: Wiley-Blackwell.

Lugones, M. (2003). *Pilgrimages/Peregrinajes: Theorizing Coaltion Against Multiple Oppressions*. Rowman & Littlefield.

Malkki, L. (1992). National Geographic: The Rooting of Peoples and the Territorialization of National Identity among Scholars and Refugees. *Cultural Anthropology 7*(1). Special Issue: Space, Identity and the Politics of Difference, 24-44.

Malkki, L. (2002). News from Nowhere: Mass Displacement and Globalised 'Problems of Organisation. *Ethnography 3*(3), 351-360.

Maqusi, S. (2017). Space of Refuge: Negotiating Space with Refugees inside the Palestinian Camp. *Humanities 60*(6).

Mugerauer, R. (1992). Architecture as Properly Useful Opening. In: A. Dallery, C. Scott & P. Roberts (eds.), *Ethics and Danger: Essays on Heidegger and Continental Thought* (pp. 215-226). New York: State University of New York Press.

Murphy, M. (2007). Everything they couldn't take they destroyed. 26 October. Electronic Intifada. Available at https://electronicintifada.net/content/everything-they-couldnt-take-they-destroyed/7195 [Retrieved 4 August 2020].

Ortega, M. (2016). *In-Between: Latina Feminist Phenomenology, Multiplicity, and the Self*. Albany, New York: SUNY Press.

Peteet, J. (2005). *Landscape of Hope and Despair: Palestinian Refugee Camps*. Philadelphia: University of Pennsylvania Press.

Petti, A. (2017). Refugee Heritage. *e-flux magazine online*. Available at https://www.e-flux.com/architecture/refugee-heritage/ [Retrieved 19 December, 2019].

Ralph, D., & Staeheli, L. A. (2011). Home and migration: Mobilities, belongings and identities. *Geography Compass, 5*(7), 517–530.

Ramadan, A. (2009). Destroying Nahr el-Bared: Sovereignty and urbicide in the space of exception. *Political Geography 28*(3), 153-163.

Ramadan, A. (2010). 'In the Ruins of Nahr al-Barid: Understanding the Meaning of the Camp.' *Journal of Palestine Studies, 40*(1), 49-62.

Ramadan, A. (2013). Spatialising the Refugee Camp. *Transactions of the Institute of British Geographers*, 38(1), 153-163.

Salih, R. (2014). Palestinian refugees: homes in exile. *OpenDemocracy*. Available at https://www.opendemocracy.net/en/5050/palestinian-refugees-homes-in-exile/ [Retrieved 19 December, 2019].

Salih, R. (2017). Bodies that walk, bodies that talk, bodies that love. Palestinian women refugees, affectivity and the politics of the ordinary. *Antipode (49)*3, 742-760.

Sanyal, R. (2014). Urbanising Refuge: Interrogating Spaces of Displacement. *International Journal of Urban and Regional Research 38*(2), 558–572.

Sayigh, R. (1995). Palestinians in Lebanon: (Dis)solution of the Refugee Problem. *Race and Class, 37*(2), 27-42.

Sayigh, R. (2005). A House is not a Home: Permanent Impermanence of Habitat for Palestinian Expellees in Lebanon. *Holy Land Studies* 4(1), 17-39.

Sayigh, R. (2004). Insecurity of Habitat for Palestinian Refugees in Lebanon. *Forced Migration Review*. Special Issue: House: loss, refuge and belonging, 8-9.

Seamon, D. & Mugerauer, R. (1985). *Dwelling, Place and Environment: Towards a Phenomenology of Person and World*. Dordrecht: Martinus Nijhoff Publishers.

Siddiqi, A. (2020). Ephemerality. *Comparative Studies of South Asia, Africa, and the Middle East 40*(1), 24-34.

Soguk, N. (1999). *States and Strangers: Refugees and Displacements of Statecraft*. Minneapolis: University of Minnesota Press.

Starr, S. (2017). UN Struggles to rebuild Palestinian refugee camp. 4 Feb, Last Accessed: 4 August 2020. Aljazeera. Sourced from https://www.aljazeera.com/indepth/features/2016/12/struggles-rebuild-palestinian-refugee-camp-161231140142502.html.

Trapp M. (2015). Already in America: Transnational homemaking among Liberian refugees. *Refuge, 31*(1), 31-41.

Weizman, E. (2011). *The Least of all Possible Evils: A Short History of Humanitarian Violence*. London and New York: Verso Books.

Weizman, E. (2005). Walking through Walls: Soldiers as architects in the Israeli/Palestinian conflict,' Conference Lecture: Symposium "Archipelago of Exception. Sovereignties of extraterritoriality. CCCB, 10-11 November. Available at https://www.publicspace.org/multimedia/-/post/walking-through-walls-soldiers-as-architects-in-the-israeli-palestinian-conflict [Retrieved 19 December, 2019].

Welander, M. (2021). The Politics of Exhaustion and the Externalization of British Border Control. An Articulation of a Strategy Designed to Deter, Control and Exclude. *International Migration*, 59, 29-46.

Vallely, N. (2018). "The Place that is Not a Place": A Critical Phenomenology of Forced Displacement. In Erik Malcolm Champion (ed.), *The Phenomenology of Real and Virtual Places*, London: Routledge.

Young, I. M. (2006). House and Home: Feminist Variations on a Theme. In N.J. Holland & P. Huntington (eds.), *Feminist Interpretations of Martin Heidegger* (pp. 252-288). University Park, PN: Pennsylvania State University Press.

CHAPTER 3

Who/What Is Doing What?

Dwelling and Homing Practices in Syrian Refugee Camps
– The Kurdistan Region of Iraq

Layla Zibar, Nurhan Abujidi & Bruno de Meulder
Brandenburg University of Technology, Germany, KU Leuven, Belgium
| Zuyd University, The Netherlands | KU Leuven, Belgium

"This is your home, and we welcome you with open arms"

In November 2019, the Turkish government initiated the 'Peace-Spring' military operation against Kurdish forces in Rojava, controlling the north-east parts of Syria.[1] Consequently, this attack produced waves of forcibly displaced populations crossing nation-state borders to seek refuge in adjacent countries. These waves, preceded by many since the Syrian conflict erupted in 2011, landed in the autonomous Kurdistan region of Iraq (KR-I)[2] and many displacees found shelter in camps in Duhok governorate.[3] In his official visit to this Bardarsh camp[4], Masrour Barzani, the Prime Minister (PM) of the Kurdistan Regional Government (KRG), announced a commitment to "providing humanitarian aid and everyday needs": he emphasised the 'international partners' whose 'responsibility' it is to 'support' his regional government's efforts to 'shelter' people in need in this 'global crisis'. PM Barzani addressed the newly displaced Kurds on Twitter following the visit: "This is your home, and we welcome you with open arms" (RUDAW, 2019). This official statements, promising a 'welcoming home' to the extended families to 'shelter' and to aid the vulnerable, signify perplexing 'hospitability' policies of the KRG regarding these arrivals: how do these temporary camps become homes for refuges recently ruptured from another?

Historically tracing this specific geographic zone on a map, one can trace the (dis)appearance of interconnected geopolitical narratives of the Kurdish inhabitants' continuous presence in regions of departure and destination. The (imagined)Fatherland:[5] Kurdistan (Homeland of the Kurds), '[t]rapped be-

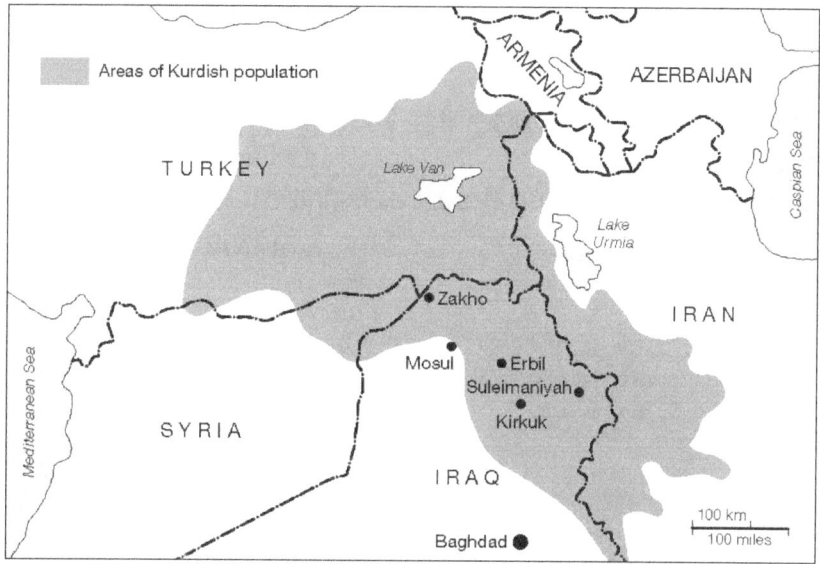

Figure 1. Kurdistan identified by population distribution. Source (Stansfield, 2003, p. 28).

tween the map and reality' (O'Shea, 2004) since 1900s, has been heavily fuelled by (re)assertions of and conflicts of nationalist ideas (Syrians/Iraqis (Arabs)/Turkey(Turks) vs Kurds) linked to territory (King, 2014; McDowall, 2004; Tejel, 2009). Such (re)assertions of home (re)created strong "sentiment [that] dwells at the very heart of a generation's identity" (Davis, 1979), forming a sense of collective identification ascribed over what many perceive as Kurdistan's territory. Hence, a sense of Kurdish nationalism, of what counts as home for the Kurds, follows Edward Said (1994) statement: "Nationalism is an assertion of belonging in and to a place, a people, a heritage. It affirms the home created by a community of language, culture, and customs, and, by so doing, it fends off exile, fights to prevent its ravages." (Said, 1994, p. 139).

For the Kurds, such assertions spring from the collective experiences embedded in territorial and generational presences of (up)rootedness and fight for national citizenship rights and against the various practices of marginalisation exercised upon them by the (territorial) nation-states (Gunes, 2019; McDowall, 2004; Tejel, 2009), resulting in a collective and territorial sense of unfulfilled nationalism and territory to call HOME. In other words, HOME for the Kurds becomes entangled with demarcated geographical boundaries infused with generationally transmitted tangible and intangible bonds. In this respect, despite the rupture of refugeehood – enacted by the involuntarily dislocation from ones' customary home- the case of being in KR-I for the Syrian Kurd may not portray the 'full elimination' or 'homelessness', but represents falling out of

Syrian citizenship into a (presumed) longed-for sense of 'Kurdishness' (once claimed in time and space). This specific geography seems to become, for these refugees, a hybrid form of 'home' and an 'exile' of some sort. It is a journey of returning to 'a lost home in the future', a chance for (re)foundation that conveys multi-layered future expectations, or this is what it appears to be.

Viewed from a distance, the idea of 'the refugee' often brings to mind the links between territorial dispossession(s) and the elimination from what was supposedly a fixed home into an endless exile. Such eliminating experiences – defined as rupture in this text- covers the uprooting of the habitual geographical belonging to citizenship rights, former social ties generational time-space continuity and a familiarized sense of belonging(s). Cut off from their *habitus*, refugees' experience of 'being' – in the Heideggerian sense – becomes unanchored (Heidegger, 1971). Refugee camps appear in the rifts of liminalities as materialised forms of this unanchored being: to safeguard the un-homed 'shelter provision' becomes the immediate response. Rendering the image of a 'refugee' as an abnormality insofar as s/he, 'all', fall outside the "national order of things" (Malkki, 1992), the generic media mainstream exhibits them 'everywhere' experiencing this 'unanchored being' as homelessness, enfolded with temporariness and uncertainty. In these generic images of homelessness the forcibly displaced are "exiled from the home they have known for centuries" (Sennett, 2017). Intellectuals, such as Said, Homi Bhabha, Gloria Anzaldúa, Eva Hoffman and Mourid El-Bargouthi depict uprootedness and rupture of home as "the unhealable rift between a human being and a native place, between the self and its true home" (Said, 1994). Home is, for them, the rooted identity, violently pulled up and thrown into exile, consequently, the 'banished' rupture from home are trapped in an endless heroic search, crave return to a utopia that they may never have experienced beyond stories and 'the good old world' (collectively) recalled.

Nevertheless, other academic and intellectual voices challenge this generic understanding of home as a smooth continuity from past to present in place. Devika Chawla (2012), for example, moves beyond this geographically rooted home in the past, differentiating between the move as coercive circumstances or choices. For her, "[h]ome has never been about returning, but about moving ahead. It was not an absence, but a search" (Chawla & Rodriguez, 2012, p. 5). Thus the mundane everyday phrase of 'going home' is related to a present experience of reaching and aspiring a place where one can be oneself, at ease, fulfilling (basic human) needs, in (supposed) sanctuary from the everyday stresses, and a stable ground to support the future. Thus, by having the choice to change and relocate home and contextual conditions, the former home becomes perceived as childhood home, a home-town and for many, the motherland.

Intriguingly, for Syrian refugee camps' dwellers in KR-I after years of displacement, sentiments of home surface in their descriptions of their presence in KR-I camps as *"here is somehow home too"*, while Syria *"is a burned mark on the heart"* and *"will be forever longed for*[home]*"*.

But then, what if the rupture from one home results into an 'enactment of homecoming' towards another? What if, in leaving and seeking refuge, one returns to one's roots? Where and what is home then? Coming closer to our case, how does the particular socio-spatial formation of supposedly 'temporary' refugee camps develop and evolve into homes in the making?

This chapter explores these questions and sheds light on the material manifestation of the perplexity of 'home' and the process of homing refugeehood in KR-I Syrian refugee camps. By developing a conceptual framework based on the ethnographic fieldwork of the first author between 2018 and 2019 and a series of semi-structured interviews with camp dwellers and humanitarian aid workers, the authors endeavour to understand homemaking processes and agency(ies) of/through the (re)production of the camp spaces and their significance in this particular case.

In search of a definition of home

> Home is the place where, when you have to go there, they have to take you in.
> (Frost, 1914).

Depicted in literature, the idea of home has been correlated with an assumed continuous state of a positive (emotional) condition. It is portrayed as "[t]he safe place where we can go as we are and not be questioned" (Angelou, 1987), and "where you find light when all grows dark" (Brown, 2015). It is a place "[t]o awaken from sleep, to rest from awakening, to tame the animal, to let the soul go wild, to shelter in darkness and blaze with light, to cease to speak and be perfectly understood" (Solnit, 2007): as such home renders unconditional forms of belonging and freedom. Home also represents – for many – an aspiration as a future project, a place to lay down new roots where prospects of warmth and continuity take shape and grow. T. S. Eliot writes "[h]ome is where one starts from" (Eliot, 2009 [1943]), that is, where the turn of an old life leads to a new beginning; it is a smooth transition of an undisrupted self-continuity.

Reading home as such, in the absence of it, one experiences *algos* (suffering) in an endless desire for *nostos* (homecoming). Illustrated beautifully in Homer's epic Odyssey, Ulysses suffers the pain of rupture from his wife, home, people and native land. In this rupture experience, nostalgia, generally defined as homesickness, develops and "invokes home in its very meaning" (Blunt, 2016). Being without a home for Ulysses seems to become an "irrevocable condition" experienced individually (Baldwin, 1956), where parts of the self are left behind (Mercier, 2007).[6] To recollect the fragments, Ulysses sets out on a sacred future quest to return, enduring all kinds of suffering, and puts all manner of effort into going back home, regardless of its greyness. Home becomes – for the ruptured – an endless search for the condition to be 'at ease' again.

Through this search for a definition of home in literature, nested descriptions bombard the researcher: of what, when, where and with whom it could be: the entanglement of relations between location, people, action and time keep (re)surfacing. Home situates in continuously interwoven tangible and intangible bonds. The tangible is the home embedded in the spaces and the people, rooted in multiscale temporal and geographical trajectories, while the intangible bonds are saturated by connecting the (former) self with the (positive) emotional condition embodied in the (former) home. In questioning what home is, nostalgia – and its scales – can hardly escape questions of self-continuity[7] (Diagram. 1.): the identity and belonging interlocked with space and time.

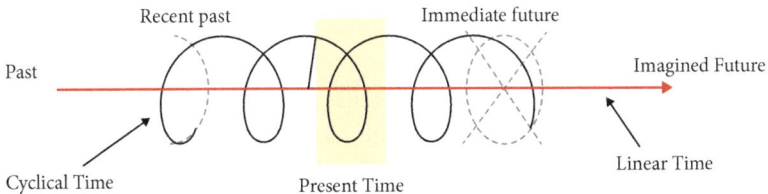

Diagram 1. Self-continuity between cyclical and liner time undisrupted. (authors, 2020).

Homelessness of refugeehood: The camp

Coming closer to refugeehood's particularity, being a refugee is – in its essence – a partial or full (violent) uprootedness from 'home'. This essence brings to mind Stegner's (1971) description:[8] "Home is a notion that only nations of the homeless fully appreciate and only the uprooted comprehend." This uprootedness ruptures the relational position of self-continuity of 'home' with time, space, political and collective belonging(s). Creating a form of self-discontinuity, which becomes an unbridgeable rift between life as it was and the uncertainty of where, with whom and how it will be. Indeed, 'home' is fully realised only when one leaves it. Through the rupture, a sense of homelessness surges in what Jaspers calls "conscious of the lack" (Jaspers, 1971): the refugee camp's spatiality and the refugees' bodily emplacement in 'alien geographies' represent the material manifestation of such 'lack' and irrevocable 'homelessness'.

A wealth of refugee scholarship juxtaposes refugee camps' spaces with waiting zones of 'limbo' (Dunn, 2018) and spatial forms of 'exception' (Agamben, 1998). These spaces represent the danger of being 'crime-ridden zones' and spatial arenas for 'power and control' (Hassan & Hanafi, 2010). In such spaces refugees are 'out of place' (Hyndman, 2000), experience a severe loss of familiarity (Said, 2000) and are looked upon with suspicion as a threat to the security of the people and the state. Their homes (metaphorically and territorially) exist somewhere only in the past. Therefore, studies as such juxtapose 'temporariness' and 'homelessness' with 'permanence' and 'home' seen in terms of territorial and nation-state belonging (Rajaram, 2002; Malkki, 1992).

Unlike in former juxtapositions, other scholars, including ones of migration, transnational and refugee studies, heavily criticise this binary thinking, questioning the assumption "that boundedness, rootedness, and membership in a single national, ethnic, or religious group are the natural order of things" (Levitt, 2012). Instead, they shift to the "emphasis on the fluidity of home, on the prevalence of 'routes' over 'roots' in shaping its experience, or even on its de-territorialization" (Boccagni, 2017, p. 108). Various scholars indeed believe that camps may constitute islands where forms of support and hospitality are present (Ramadan, 2010), time machines preserving heritage for (refugee) generations to come (Bshara, 2014), and localities where refugees are in the process of (re)inventing and (re)formation of their identity (Malkki, 1995).

These conservative tendencies of conflicted debates invited empirical academic research to emphasise the dynamic processes of refugees' attempts to revoke this loss of worldly anchorage(s). Several scholars emphasise that homing processes can materialise within temporariness and alienation, and camps become accidental cities in the making (Betts, Bloom, Kaplan, & Omata, 2017; Brun, 2001; Brun & Fábos, 2015; Herz, 2013; Jansen, 2018). Associating the concept of 'homing' with practices exercised on/within the physical space, scholars link homing to socio-spatial personalisation that contributes to security and identity (re)assertion recognised by the group (Porteous, 1976), place-making (Easthope, 2014), as well as demarcation(s) of spaces of domination (Somerville, 1989). By (re)articulating the given (humanitarian) structures of 'care and control', various actors initiate a transitional process from a 'shelter' to 'home', and from a 'space' to a 'place'. This 'homing' process becomes a form of (re)producing familiarity, (re)activating various forms of agency and reclaiming power over the self through space (Bshara, 2014; Ramadan, 2013). Still, fragments of the making/(re)production of given space, being in a place, being 'at home', the time factor and the agency that activates them do not fully align together: who/what is doing what? it is essential to demist the entanglements of human agential powers and the spatial agency(Awan, Schneider, & Till, 2011) in the camp in order to understand the ways in which homing processes occur in refugeehood's materiality.

Revisiting frames of home between sheltering and homing in refugeehood

In order to understand and answer the questions posed in the sections above, we use he relational entanglements of tangible and intangible bonds of home as the main frame of thinking. The tangible bonds are located in the embeddedness of home within spaces and people, rooted in multiscale time-geography trajectories, entangled with the intangible bonds which are saturated by connecting the (former) self with the emotional condition embodied in the (former) home. The recent uprootedness of the previous habitual homeland is this chapter's point of departure: the rupture from an 'earlier home' setting in motion a chain of events that link refugeehood to homing. To illustrate our point we use the following developed diagram of the 'homing' process (Diagram 2).

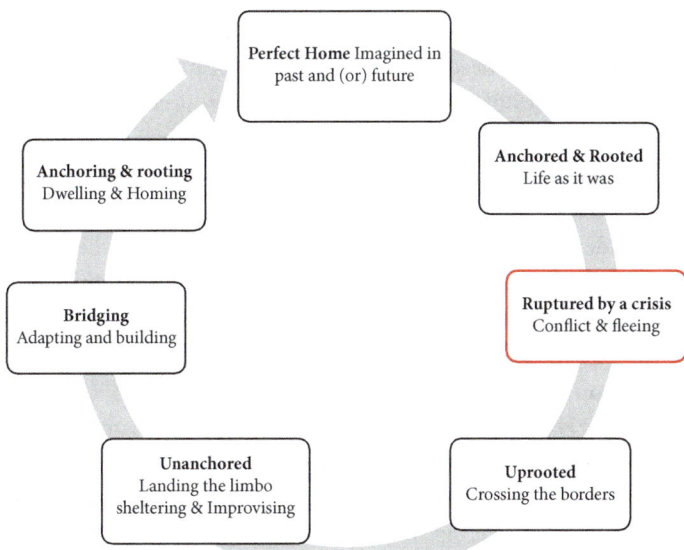

Diagram 2. Proposed Refugee Camp Homing Cycle diagram from a past home to an imagined one. (Authors, 2020).

The Refugee Camp Homing Cycle explains how homing is (theoretically) reached in a refugee camp. It starts with violent disruption from 'life as it was', followed by dispossession from multi-layered belonging to a territory, group and expected continuity. Then, by the act of moving and crossing nation-states' borders, refugees became subject to two dramatic changes: political status (citizen to a refugee) and alienation, which is caused by their partial (if not full) separation from earlier social networks embedded in locality. However, the severity of the rupture's impacts depend mainly on the mood of displacement and the international and local humanitarian regimes' attitudes towards the displaced within the host environment.

Consequently, by being pushed to cross state borders to seek sanctuary, refugees become unanchored floating fragments created by such uprootedness some arrive and land to wait in the camp. In the emergency phase, refugees temporarily disembark, addressing their basic need for shelter and protection, relying on provided and improvised structures (e.g. tents, camp, aid), living in the eventuality of 'making do'. With prolonged displacement needs extend in prolonged temporariness, and the floating fragments start to familiarize and relate (physically and emotionally) in attempt to bridge the rifts between the time-space past's fixities and present/future uncertainties within the 'alien' surroundings. Refugees start to bond with situational groups and adapt to 'longer stay' probabilities. As time goes by, the temporariness becomes ever more permanent; life in the camp descends into the (new/camp) ordinary and refugees exploit the possibilities of dwelling in its fixity. They become more anchored and rooted in this stable uncertainty. Homing, as an action, then emerges within the possibilities yet is rarely accomplished; however, the final 'home' seems to be fixed in an improbable future and recalled from the lost past.

First, to understand the spatial progression and the agency behind it from 'landing' to 'homing' we borrow two conceptual frameworks: the frame proposed by Handel (2019) and the one proposed by Brun and Fábos (2015). Handel's work allows us to move the act of provision beyond the humanitarian arena of care and to exercise control of "regimes of exception" (Agier & Bouchet-Saulnier, 2004), to incorporate the spaces as a homing canvas. In his work Handel delineates 'house' and 'home' concepts through two layers: a housing regime with broader institutional/state planning actions and active dwelling as an engine for homemaking. By substituting housing with sheltering, this understanding brings the agency of humanitarian regime services (Hilhorst & Jansen, 2010) at the material level (i.e. the camp's set-up in terms of planning, infrastructure, shelter provision, upgrade, etc.) into the equation.

The second step is to link scales/meanings of home to the homing process in forced displacement. This triadic constellation of home in Brun and Fábos's (2015) work introduces the following:
- 'home' as the meanings prompted by and the routinisation of day-to-day living experiences, done and undone by everyday practices (see also De Certeau, 1980).
- 'Home' represents feelings and intangible dimensions based on memories, traditions and an ideal dream exercised collectively at a group level.
- 'HOME' to include Nostalgia and the 'lost homeland' in the protracted displacement debate.

Although Handel's and Brun and Fábos's respective works can cover multiple aspects of homing at individual and group levels, few gaps remain. First, the temporary forms of adaptations after sheltering and prior to homing: using the camp as a performative space habitually negotiated on individual and collective levels (Connerton, 1989). Second, spatial references to the ways in which meanings are (re)attached to the material in order to familiarise oneself with the space-time alienation experience of the shelter/camp before becoming a 'home'. Third, the mental stimulation of a depiction of home to be imagined, expected and pursued (De Brigard, 2017) and the gap of a spatio-temporal understanding in terms of cyclical and linear time comprehension (i.e. everyday cycle, past-oriented and future-directed) in the protracted waiting are still missing.

To cover the first gap we expand on Handel's (2019) and Brun and Fábos's (2015) frameworks to incorporate and expand on 'dwelling' as a form of occupancy: a stage that follows the act of making/building and predates homing. Although a 'dwelling' – as a noun – refers to a physical condition beyond a temporary shelter, a stable structure, when read as a verb dwelling brings the time factor into the equation: live, stay, continue and linger in a particular physical setting and/or a condition to initiate another action or result. In our perception dwelling asserts a form of agency over the routinised habits and exploring the probabilities of 'moving along', a transitional period between sheltering and homing.

For the second and third gaps we include the work of Wildschut et al. (2019) in experimental social psychology. In their work with Syrian refugees in Saudi Arabia they examine the positive attributes of Nostalgia (past-oriented and future-directed) as coping mechanisms with present stresses of displacement. Furthermore, as memories carry the material characters of the surrounding, recent studies assert the mental simulation of possible scenarios of future events and 'what could have been', as a form of Nostalgia (De Brigard, 2017). We use their framework of the psychological functions of Nostalgia mentally to initiate and stimulate the process of 'homing' in refugeehood and reset the perception of time from cyclical loops frozen in limbo towards a linear future. They organise these functions in four general domains:

(a) Existential: (re)triggers self-continuity, meanings, core values and identity (re)formation.
(b) Self-oriented: (re)activates a sense of self-worth by revisiting positive self attributes and increasing self-esteem.
(c) Social: fosters connectedness, attachments, feelings of security, support, empathy and openness towards others.
(d) Future-directed: the evocation of better possibilities and ideas, and motivation to enact (homing) innovative ideas.

In the following section we explore the case of Syrian refugee camps in Iraqi Kurdistan at the intersection of the proposed and borrowed frames; we aim, in this respect, to unfold the complexity of home and homing in this particular case.

Syrian Kurds in Iraqi Kurdistan: The (up)rooting of home

Since the Syrian conflict erupted in 2011, 11.6 million have been displaced, with 5.5 million registered as refugees (UNHCR, 2020). Syrian refugees crossed nation-state borders and followed networks of help and support regarding shelter and protection in urban areas or camps. In the case of the Syrian Kurds in KR-I, these networks were embedded in ethnic similarities, political aspirations, territorial belonging and the concentrations of opportunities that paved the way for a more particular situation to arise.

Despite the violent character of the conflict portrayed in the mainstream media, Syrian Kurds in the North-East experienced the displacement slightly differently. By mid-2012 non-state actors had seized control over Rojava (Allsopp, 2015; Harling, 2013), while flows of internally displaced Kurds from other rural and urban areas clogged the region's towns and cities. The existing safe and stable home, at that time known to them, was damaged: increasing poverty, contestation, non-state militarisation; all adding to the escalating threat of the Islamic State of Iraq and the Levant (ISIL) and ever-latent danger escalating and approaching from the Turkish borders. All these factors added to the existing challenges for the historically marginalised ethnicity in Syria (Tejel, 2009).

With the generationally rooted fear of being persecuted by the ambiguous tides of power as enemies of the sovereign, waves of Syrian Kurds crossed the borders to KR-I to arrive at their imagined fatherland's realised part: 'KURDISTAN'.

Spatialising Refugeehood in Iraqi Kurdistan: The Camps

Rupture(s) and Camps

The geographical axis between the Syrian and Iraqi parts of Kurdistan has always had its share of violent events since World War I (WWI), with hundreds of sites of destruction and tales of coercive movements, uprootedness and collective loss of homes (King, 2014; McDowall, 2004; Tejel, 2009). The spatio-temporal pattern of chronic conflict and tides of forced displacements have asserted the prolonged humanitarian presence. These tides of forced displacements have simulated active coordination processes between KRG and the United Nations (UN) since the 1980s. This continuous presence and coordination led to the development of humanitarian actors' strategies and governmental bodies' creation, with the (conditional) blessing of the Iraqi Central Government[9], constituting the local humanitarian regime in the KR-I.

Upon arrival, the United Nations High Commissioner for Refugees (UNHCR) and the KRG registered people crossing borderers from Syria (without official entry permits) as refugees. With the registration document, refugees became officially entitled to humanitarian protection rights and various aids and support modalities. These modalities included setting up camps and developing institutional synergies to facilitate them. Many of these refugees' routes, therefore, ended in these settings. Indeed, camps were mushrooming their way up to becoming the spatial representation of this arrival and locality of the support. Today (2021), nine planned refugee camps[10] are scattered throughout KR-I's urban landscape, housing more than 40 per cent of the Syrian refugee population in Iraq, mostly Kurds.[11] These humanitarian support modalities also held extended tolerance for 'Brothers and Guests': in addition to the rights to shelter, free access to health service and education, Syrian Kurds also have minimum labour restrictions, freedom of movement in KRI, and are permitted to seek work (Etemadi)[12] (Khan et al., 2020; Yassen, 2019).

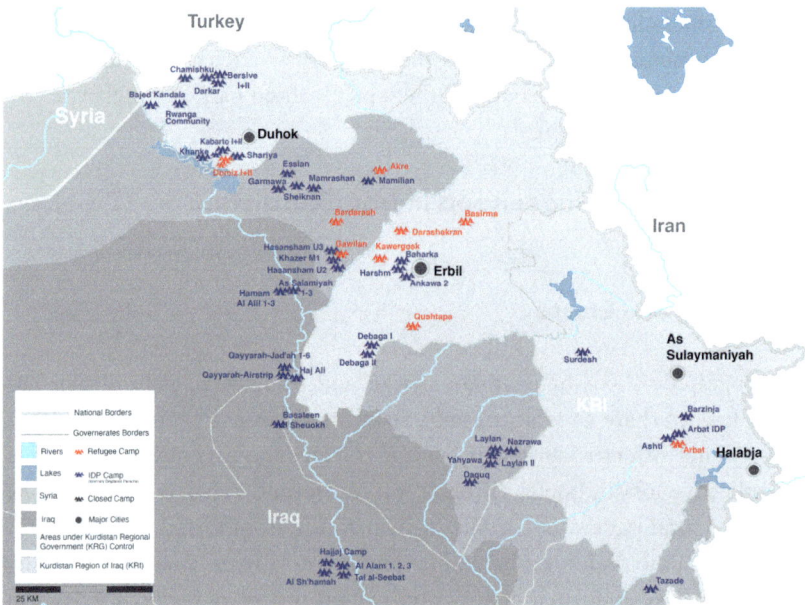

Figure 2. Displacement Camps in the Kurdistan Region of Iraq. Redrawn based on maps by UNHCR (2017), Reach (2019) (authors, 2019).

Setting up camp spaces in the (chronic) state of crisis

With the Syrian conflict and the rise and fall of ISIL since 2011, KR-I has been acting as the substantial humanitarian operation arena for the masses displaced.[13] The humanitarian regime in KR-I utilised 'the masterplan approach for refugee settlements' (UNHCR, 2016) as an emergency response in order to set up camps (whether for refugees or internally displaced persons or IDPs).[14] The approach has proven effective in the peak moments by providing the necessary infrastructure and sheltering units, and acting as a spatial apparatus to cope with sheltering the massive influxes (Middle East Research Institute, 2015). The response's strategy momentarily blends elements of emergency with overall development intentions, that is, with long-term initiatives to strengthen existing systems. The use of the 'masterplan approach' to set up temporary camps is clear evidence of this strategy. Furthermore, to coordinate humanitarian tasks, on the one hand, the KRG in 2014 established an institutional body for coordination and management, called the Joint Crisis Coordination Center (JCC) (JCC, 2016), which was followed later, in 2015, by the Board of Relief and Humanitarian Affairs (BRHA) as there were non-stop waves of displacement of both refugees and IDPs pouring into Duhok governorate (BRHA, 2015). On the other hand, the UNHCR shelter sector works closely with other Interagency Standing committees represented by clusters' (shelter cluster, wash cluster, etc.), which work as Inter-Agency Standing Committees, developing contextual strategies together and with the host governments (GSC, IFRC, & UNHCR, 2018).[15]

During the (pre-)emergency phase, setting up the camp included clearing the land to 'plant' camps: more than 50 standardised modular grids covered the region and served a primary urban function: sheltering. After being processed, each family (6 people) is assigned a single plot, tent and access to communal washing facilities. The 'conceived space' (Lefebvre, 1991) of the fenced modular grid[16] is (mostly) tiled with communities each of 16 shelters. Blocks are groups of communities with fluid spaces in between to allow movements and become future roads. A break in the grid is subject to site characteristics (topography, flash flood, etc.) or to accommodate parallel (urban) structures dedicated to serving the recipients of aid exclusively (administration, schools, primary health centres, etc.). Adult camp dwellers have access to (Sorani) Kurdish and English classes, a form of support to help them be integrated into the labour market (Middle East Research Institute, 2015), including local and international NGOs.[17] At the same time, their youngsters also receive the similar linguistic education at schools in order to become 'qualified' later to enrol in the region's universities (Khan et al., 2020).

Nevertheless, the camps' future scenarios, socio-spatial progression and meanings are closely related to occupant groups' possibilities to be integrated according to the host preference of the hosted group (refugees or IDPs). In different reports, 'sustainable solutions' are described as the IDPs' systematic return to their pre-displacement geographical locations, in contrast to the promotion of integration policies for the Syrian refugees. This contrast manifests itself through the decommissioning of IDP camps while upgrading refugee ones (physical and socio-economic components) (Khan et al., 2020; UNHCR, 2018).

Unanchored: Refugees arriving at the camp

Domiz refugee camp was the earliest Syrian refugee camp in KR-I, followed by seven planned ones within a year. UNHCR and KRG worked together to set up the camps at the same time as 'processing'[18] refugees to grant the registration document (forma). For Domiz, the designed capacity was only for 30,000 refugees., however, with the refugee influx, the camp's population peaked at 80,000 refugees in 2013. Within a year, the opening of the other camps and the redistribution of refugees, the number decreased and stabilised at about 31,000 registered individuals in 2020, most of them coming from the same geographic region in Syria (UNHCR Iraq, 2020).

In all camps, administration and services have prefabricated units acting as 'field offices' for the patchwork of international, regional, national and local bodies present (Holzer, 2013; Wilde, 2008), to ensure an 'optimum' performance in aiding the refugees.

Regardless of the 'home-welcoming' treatment, refugees arrived at the camp as 'occupational groups' in the early emergency phase, and many zones of the camp were as chaotic as the conditions that had produced them. In early days of Domiz camp in 2012, aid workers supported refugees set up their fabric tents after being allocated to a plot. The distributed tents occupied only part of the plot, leaving space for household activities, such as cooking and cleaning. Later after in the newly set camps[19], the strategy to shelter provision is the use of the improved shelter typology: each unit consists of plot with a concrete base, attend, and brick built kitchen, latrine and the bathroom.

One of the interviewees described his first memory of his arrival at Domiz camp in 2012: "*I could not understand, I felt thrown naked in the middle of nowhere*" as "*Our women were exposed to the public*". Such statements emphasised the unfamiliarity of the physical structures. Upon their arrival, the camp space seems to be a "fluid and strange setting totally lacking familiar reference points" (Halbwachs, 1950) and refugees, still in shock, can hardly recognise and navigate round their surroundings. The camps' 'provisional' and 'fluid' settings heightened the reality of the loss and the associated homelessness. Furthermore, it demonstrated the fundamental mismatch of expectations and norms between the provider and the provided. Hence, in this arrival to the nowhere, the refugees experience the rupture as being out of sync with space, time continuity limited to waiting and the loss of power, as their needs became exposed and reduced to basic survival.

These estrangement notions catalysed the need to recreate a sense of privacy, security and familiarity through different improvised making and unmaking practices exercised upon the physical setting provided. Swinging "between vulnerability and agential power" (Brun & Fábos, 2015), these needs mentally stimulated many refugees to "take the matter *with* their own hands" (Bshara, 2014). By evoking the role of the self-oriented and social domains of nostalgia, (spatial) memory became the reference to introduce familiarity to the alien surroundings.

The refugees began with the 'walling up' of plots by patching them with various materials: wooden poles, metal frames, sheets from ruined tents, (corrugated) metal sheets. Whether these materials were distributed, exchanged, bought or found, they were put to use, creating a rigid demarcation between the public/common and the private domains (Porteous, 1976; Raglan, 1964). Refugees followed and (or) paralleled this demarcation with internal articulations of the unit: they mainly set these divisions to facilitate the separation the everyday activities domains. These articulations included: setting private latrines, chaning the kitchen's size and location, and separating the living/guest room from and the 'other room', which was used depending on the family size and need (sleeping, storage, girls' room, etc.). These improvised material forms are assembled to 'endure', and 'make do for now' (Simone, 2018). However, 'now' at that stage has an uncertain endpoint in the immediate future.

Figure 3. Improvised structures at Domiz camp for Syrian refugees in Duhok, KRI. Caption from Video (https://refugeerepublic.submarinechannel.com/, 2013)

Bridging: Building the 'tent-free' camp

The harsh environmental conditions and the uncertain end-date of the Syrian conflict have encouraged setting more permanent structures. Consequently, moving into 'more durable shelters' became the general strategy for Syrian refugee camps in KR-I. With the blessing of the camps' management, many NGOs[20] provided materials and cash for refugees to upgrade their shelters. This upgrade was conditioned within guidelines that mainly ensured a degree of permanence within the plots' boundaries (brick walls, temporary roofs of either corrugated sheets or sandwich panels). Within a few months the humanitarian regime adopted 'improved shelters' instead of mere tents, adding brick-built latrines, bathrooms and kitchens for each plot[21].

Figure 4. Tents stretch into the distance at Domiz camp for Syrian refugees in Dohuk governorate. (UNHCR/J.Seregni, 2012)

Early camp arrivals saw this material provision of shelter and protection, combined with other forms of aid, as an opportunity. With access to internet connections and social media on both sides of the border, information travelled fast. Many refugees recommended their relatives (especially single males or newly married couples) to "*seize the existing opportunity instead of waiting*" or "*come and wait here*". As a result, fragments of the former social networks started arriving at the camps and filling the spatial structures, and new networks developed through 'being in it together, camp bonds started interweaving with the fixed grid and through socio-spatial (re)articulations. Evoked by the collective retrieval of former social codes, Nostalgia turned into a positive driver to bridge former spatial memories with the alien spaces in camps.

Figure 5. Tent Free Camp Campaign. PWJ Process of Shelter Upgrading Source: (PWJ, 2019)

In 2015 the UNHCR initiated the "tent-free camp"[22] campaign for the refugee camps in the KR-I. According to the PWJ report, the 'self-building' project's main goal was to "ensure that refugees live in more durable, semi-permanent shelters" (PWJ, 2019),[23] which came with built-in livelihood and participation components. Whether the standardised plots included partially built shelter forms (as the improved ones do) or not, the modular grid became a foundation for infrastructure and public works to follow camp upgrades later (such as pavements, water and sewage systems, electricity networks, street lights, etc.). Acting as a particular form of John Turner's sites and services, the modular grid pre-forms as a canvas that supporting self-generated semi-permanent shelter forms.

In similar projects, the NFOs' personal (PWJ in the tent-free project) provide technical guidance on and supervision of the building process and develops skilled labourers to "help refugees help themselves" as a form of self-reliance. Through giving the participants 'know-how', these skills are presumed to be useful in the labour market and to qualify these candidates to be available for other job opportunities. Using 'cash for work' as a strategy, the majority of NGOs hire and pay the participants for shelter construction (whether as beneficiaries or as labourers). In addition, the presence of the displacement camps with such projects generate 'well-paid' employment majority opportunities for host communities: locals are either contracted by INGOs, hired by them or they form their own local NGOs.

Combining these (re)generated socio-spatial bonds and various actors steered the camp's active building processes that spread virally. The interdependencies between camps and surroundings formed economic socio-spatial flows with urban centres (labourers, humanitarian aid, volunteers…). These flows accelerated an urbanisation process in the areas adjacent to the majority of the camps as well. In a short time, camps started to resemble many existing urban areas in the region, gradually shaking down their 'temporary' facades.

Anchoring

As stated above, different projects aspired to 'upgrade' the spatial conditions in refugee camps to ensure better living conditions and ease the hand-over to the KRG. These upgrades with socio-economic models of 'self-reliance' having been embedded, access to various employment models activated the refugees' agency. Through their engagement with (re)shaping their material realities (i.e., building, investing, working), refugees (partially) transitioned from passive recipients of care to active participants.

Nevertheless, the degree of refugees' investment in physical adaptation varies according to their personal projects. In the interviews, these projects varied between planning to start a family, staying until things were resolved, or waiting until a better opportunity (of resettlement) arose. The waiting stretches to a further point in the uncertain future in the camp. As a result, advanced (spatial) needs came forward, and refugees responded in having near-future prospects, and refugees responded by adjusting the basic amenities provided/altered in the post-emergency phase to suit these planned prospects.

Refugees with access to capital seem to experience more comfortable living conditions, reflected in investing in upgrading their dwelling units. Extra rooms are added to the standardised shelter designs, kitchens relocated, new connections to the existing sewage networks are made, and, if possible, internal courtyards are fashioned; in other words whatever the plot size allowed to accommodate the occupant's extended needs. The degree of this personalisation seem to relate to what it is '*desired to have*' and/or '*wanted to have back*' in such temporary settings. Hence, the internal makeshift re-alignments with these statements reflect the resurgence of a former spatial memory (embedded with cultural norms) in a poor attempt to claim an equivalent settings of how 'dwelling' is supposed to be despite the shadows of temporariness. These nostalgic memories become existential and future-oriented; they help populations come to terms with displacement and to move forward, although their homes in Syria are, in their view, 'something else' compared with the provisional present. Many refugees consider their dwellings to be spaces in which to "*just get by till things are clear*".

For Um Ibrahim, the end of her single life in Syria and becoming a refugee and a wife in the KR-I was indeed a new beginning (Eliot, (1943)2009). In late 2016 she crossed the border as a new bride to join her husband in Domiz camp through an arranged marriage. The camp management assigned the new family a plot together with the UNHCR forma and marriage certificates. Arriving in winter and becoming pregnant, the tent hardly accommodated the new circumstances. Um Ibrahim and her husband moved in with her in-laws for three months in a rented residence just outside the camp. It was 'crowded' at her in-laws', and they could no longer wait for the *mounzamt* (NGOs) to help them. During this period her husband and his brothers (camp dwellers now) constructed brick walls so that the space would become 'habitable'. To finance this construction, her husband borrowed money from 'here and there' and worked as an 'ordinary construction labourer' in Duhok city:

> We are still in debt, but we are paying it gradually. [...] I like it here more. I sleep when I want; wake up when I want; and cook (or not) whenever I want [...] You know, the female feels more comfortable in

her place. Soon, we will paint the walls. I also want to buy a wardrobe.
(Um Ibrahim, Interview, 2018).

When asked to draw or describe her former 'home', she asked if the 'home' was that belonging to her in-laws or her childhood one.

This form of arrival and the change of where home is/with, represent the overlaps and (partial) transitions between temporary waiting (tent) and anchoring in laying roots in the (presumed) continuity of marriage, children (brick built rooms, furniture). "Homing [acts] as a way of managing the distance between real and aspired homes in the biographical field(s)", argues Boccagni (Boccagni, 2017). Indeed, in Um Ibrahim story, these spatial readjustments of the camp's material surroundings became indistinguishable part of her family's autobiography. Thereby seeking betterment through personalising one's unit (i.e. appropriation by addition), one can retrieve and fulfil a desire based on the 'now' and on 'being' in the camp which goes beyond dwelling there, so that homing starts.

Figure 6. Interior shot of Um Ibrahim's living room. Aid agencies gave them the mattresses, while they bought the tv and ceiling fan from the market in the camp. Photo Credits: Layla Zibar, 2018.

Homemaking started with (re)rooting and anchoring in the camp: new arrivals building their 'new lives' despite the temporariness. The anchoring extends to the group levels through: the engagement of social activities performed together, such as hosting guests or cooking together. The social use overspills into units' threshold areas. Many families use their front porches as gathering places resembling their former habitual places. Um Ibrahim and her neighbour sit outside *"like we used to in Syria"* while their children play together. These uses extend to the roads on special occasions to host more prominent collective activities, such as celebrations or funerals, (usually) overlooking the formal multi-purpose hall, mimicking how these activities took place prior displacement (in their hometowns). Consequently, refugees keep 'their' outdoor spaces maintained and clean, and even furnish them with chairs and plants. Such practices – imported from past contextualised practices – (re)introduce welcome threshold zones as spatial cues other camp dwellers recognise. Therefore, the fluid space becomes a container for fragments of cultural habits restored from the past through these spatial adaptations; a more fluid culture reshaped by refugeehood seems to emerge (Hannerz, 1992).

Figure 7. The use of wiring and greenery to define boundaries and multi-thresholds. Kawergosk Refugee Camp, KR-I. Photo Credit: Layla Zibar, 2018

Figure 8. Use of outdoor spaces for group activities. Domiz Refugee Camp. KR-I. Photo Credit: Layla Zibar, 2018

Furthermore, other refugees have more entrepreneurial-oriented ideas for their living spaces. Based on the unit location, a room with an opening facing towards the public space could be used as a shop to generate income. According to many interviewees, one can still 'sell' his upgraded shelter to camp dwellers looking for one in which to start their married life or other refugees on the waiting list, and '*the list is long*'.

Um Ibrahim's story (similar to many others) represents the transition from the refugees' experience of vulnerability to "recognising individual and social accomplishments" (Boccagni & Brighenti, 2017). In anchoring and the statutory gradual shift within the humanitarian status to hybridize with a social one (Brun, 2015), a camp community(s) rises in the rearticulation of material settings and spatial upgrades. The inclination to meet group expectations, past recollections and possible future aspirations (guest rooms, welcoming porches, …) trigger the need for points of reference retrieved from spatial memories, hence directing Nostalgia's positive function in (re)anchoring refugees in time-space after disruption (Wildschut et al., 2019). in anchoring and remembering together. Homing, starts in cracking the time-frozen waiting linked to temporariness of the camp and refugeehood, and allowing cyclical time to relate with 'today', bridge it with yesterday and connect it to a possible tomorrow.

Where is HOME now?

In the previous sections we have examined the 'family-welcoming' KRG integration policies for the Syrian Kurds in camps, weaving a canvas of enabling structures and programs to drive camp refugees' soilless roots more deeply into the territory. With individual and collective acts which patch fragments of now and then, the 'temporary' physical structures convert from mere physical containers to a meaningful socio-spatial reality in the making (Thompson, 1978).

In arriving in Kurdistan, the imagined 'fatherland', a longed for 'landing' is (partially) achieved for the ethnically marginalized Syrian Kurds. In the interviews, examples of refugees responses to describe this landing are *"finally arriving at the real home"*, one which *"brought tears to the eyes"*. This generational dream of an improbable future to be free in one's fatherland became a reality only as a result of the violent displacement from the former reality. The thirst for belonging becomes, for many, a driver to reassert and rearticulate the Kurdish identity in the newly constructed space. When one visits these refugee camps, Kurdistan's flags[24] and pictures of its leaders cannot go unnoticed, thereby showing loyalty and gratitude to the generous hosts. Whether in the dwelling unit or public spaces, through forms and symbols, refugees verbally express their Kurdish belonging: *"we are home here too"*. This expression also extends to include the active engagement in learning the written language (Sorani Kurdish), enlisting with the Peshmerga, the official Kurdish Army, proudly serving to fulfil the 'duty' in protecting the fatherland.[25] In camps many Syrian Kurds started practising their 'Kurdishness publicly', without fear of persecution, by voting for the Kurdish referendum in 2017, thereby exercising what they believed to be their political right to decide the fatherland's future.

Nevertheless, it is not only about 'where' one lands but also 'how' it happens. Even under what seems to be one unifying identity, that of being 'Kurds', differences are omnipresent; after all, Syrian Kurds are still, legally speaking, refugees in KR-I. They are not 'legal' citizens, and they may never become such. Furthermore, when walking through the camp spaces one still can recognise temporary roofs, upside-down UNHCR logos on reused tent sheets, and the blue UNICEF logo on water tanks. An array of 'donor' logos adorns the signboard of every primary health care centre, school and even sanitary bag. These ever-repeated patterns and never-completed settings, combined with continuity of the humanitarian programmes, (re)assert notions associated with refugeehood and a situational sense of temporariness and camp-belonging.

Moreover, the non-conformities of historical trajectories between the host and the guest articulate sub-group cultural and habitual differences. They are the '*Syriakan*' (Syrians in Sorani Kurdish), as the host community calls them with non-conformities of Kurdish dialects (*Kurmanji* for the refugees and *Sorani* for the hosts). These factors, adding to many, appear to be limitations on the 'integration process' (Khan et al., 2020).

These (legal) ambiguities and embedded non-conformities render the Syrian Kurds again the 'other' in their 'imagined' land, and "*the memory of the life in Syria is becoming an irrevocable pain, they* [the Iraqi Kurds] *cannot comprehend*", as one of the interviewees stated. This situation, coupled with the economic hardship, creates push factors leading to in-camp migration[26].

Refugees seem to (re)construct versions of small Kurdish Syria(s), a Rojava Island(s) in camps' spaces. People visiting or living there compare it to "going back to Syria" (UNHCR, 2012) without leaving Kurdistan. Correspondingly, the camp spaces represent the crystallisation of the hybrid forms of political citizenship and ethnic memberships materialise. The political borders refugees crossed gradually become attached to the camp's physical boundaries. Regardless of their temporal permeability, these boundaries convert into socio-cultural ones. Mohammad and his brother-in-law, for example, moved back to the Domiz camp from Duhok city despite their steady job there. "*We know how to walk and talk here* [in the camp]. *We invested much money to build this unit. It is better to be here; we know each other [...] It feels right*", Mohammad noted.

Figure 9. Using the symbolism by painting Kurdish Flag to mark an entrance – Darashakran Refugee Camp, KR-I – Photo Credit: Layla Zibar, 2018

Fragments of a recent past in Syria still find their way to the present reality. Most of the camp shops have banners that explain their services in Arabic[27] side by side with Sorani Kurdish. External cues such as businesses and stores named after famous Syrian TV shows and locations (*Bab El Hara, Deriek, ...*), the Syrian food shops offering Shawarma and Syrian Bread, and Arabic and Kurdish[28] music streaming from shops all blend together in the street and are hardly noticed by camp dwellers; it is just another feature if an 'ordinary' day. In other words, these visual and sensual cues become "emanations of [a] reality" and "fabricated representations of it" (Anderson, 2016). These different retrieval forms appear to (re)foster a sense of connectedness, a reformation of identity that dwells in Nostalgia's existential and social domains; to borrow Levitt's (2004) term, it is a matter of "redefining the boundaries of belonging". The refugees are homing the camp by bringing to it positive security attributes, (re)fostering former and new attachments, and bringing forward what they identify with culturally from the past and ascribe it to this fragile present. It appears that a broader sense of belonging to a homeland and a nation-state crystalises physically: an 'us' that (re)asserts familiarity and homes the camp.

To conclude: Syrian-Kurds' Refugee Camps in KR-I – Homes and Towns in the making

This chapter aimed to reveal the complexity of 'home' meanings and their material manifestation of homing refugeehood in KR-I Syrian refugee camps. First, the chapter introduced the perplexing multi-layered belonging of the displaced group in the host territory: nation-belonging and arrival in the longed-for 'fatherland' embodied in the Kurdistan Region of Iraq by the violent rupture from Syria, the former homeland and the country of citizenship. Second, it endeavoured to unfold this perplexity and understand the homing process; in this case, the chapter revisited the meaning of home in forced displacement by reframing it in relation to space and time. In doing so, it expanded on the borrowed conceptual frameworks of 'what is home' by Handel (2019) and on 'making home in displacement' by Brun and Fábos (2015) by adding to them the notion of 'dwelling' as using the camp's physical structure as a performative space. Furthermore, the chapter built on Wildschut et al.'s (2019) work on 'psychological functions of Nostalgia' to understand (re)anchoring and (re)rooting: in its existential, self-oriented, social and future oriented aspoects that catered identity (re)formation when practised spatially.

In the case of Syrian-Kurdish refugee camps in the KR-I, the author followed the Refugee Camp Homing Cycle introduced earlier and linked it to the expanded conceptual frameworks to examine this cycle and the (re)articulation of home. This started by examining the refugee camps' case after the rupture by a crisis and crossing the nation-state borders from customary home and the former socio-political bonds. The uprooted groups act like floating fragments which land unplanned in a limbo of (new-set) temporary camps and tents as shelters. Temporary camp, provisional structures and unfamiliar physical surroundings reflect this unanchored arrival. The idea of bridging between the traces of former homes and the new alien realities appeared in the socio-spatial practices of re-assembling/re-uniting the former and new networks within the camp fixed grid and (re)form its material structures. Refugees involvement with camp upgrades and self-development programmes repeated in periodic rhythms plays a significant role in helping refugees to 'rest' their ruptured roots in the given space. Material vocabularies, symbols and personalised components reflect this resting and encourage the previous floating fragments to start to root. The bridging notion defined earlier is widened in this particular case to include bonding with the host through various forms of interlocking interdependencies and an (imagined) belonging tied to refugees' arrival to camps seeded to this specific geographic context.

Figure 10. Kawagosk Refugee Camp, KR-I – Photo Credit: UNHCR, 2019

The transition to anchoring in the camp is a result of spatial (re)calibrations processes enacted by the humanitarian regime, camp dwellers and the enabling material structures and programmes catalysing and conditioning these processes. As time goes by, re-setting everyday refugees' cyclical perception through work, near-future prospects and routinised activities, refugees start to recapture 'today' and 'tomorrow'. Indeed, by reconnecting with ones' past and (the immediate) future, being in the place and engaged in the act of building breaking the temporally frozen loops of waiting, this active forms of dwelling and laying roots reflect such anchoring. These (re)calibrations appear to be associated with references to spatial memory, recalled with different domains of the psychological functions of Nostalgia (in each (re)adjustment): what it should be, what it was, and what it could be. Refugees recalibrate the meaning of home, a lost one and one on the way back to another. On the individual level, it relates closely to the autobiographical story, the need to retrieve what was lost or to construct what could be.

Anchoring and homing in camps seem to expand for this particular group to (re)identify their -collective – belonging in the camps' locality within KR-I: the multi-layered generationally inherited belonging of being a Kurd; the situational one of being a Syrian refugee in KR-I; and the final home which has always existed 'somewhere else' and never 'here'. It is true that 'finding home' is the 'natural' reaction to uprootedness (Baum, 1900); the separation from home opened up the opportunity for an improbable future of an active belonging in Kurdistan to come forward. When asked about the future, camp refugees reply with answers varying between *'we are here now'* and *'we belong here', 'I am at home somehow'*. However, this identification with a possibility for a home in the KR-I locality could not blur the camps' temporary reality of refugees' status: home could have been here and there, but it is never fully here or there.

Started as temporary built environments to host the vulnerable, these planned camps appear to be taking steps towards permanence for the Syrian Kurds inhabiting and homing them. Indeed, these towns in the making are products of the KRG's willingness to accept 'brother and sisters'. These (re)productions ascribe to: the humanitarian actors spatial (upgrading) projects embedded with livelihood components, and the dwellers' efforts in participating in the spatial (re)production process. Nevertheless, the long-term scenarios for these seeds of urbanity still linger in the unpredictable future for both the refugees and the host region. Becoming permanent in occupancy and physical structures does not hide their fractured forms of urbanity (Agier, 2002). These unfinished projects are susceptible to political statutes, funding flotations/declines, unfolding crises within geopolitical chronic instability, unsurprisingly, resulting in the reproduction of exhausted and fragile realities. Regardless of the efforts to promote resilience, most of these settlements' dwellers are still heavily aid-dependent, while other extensive funds and resources are committed to constructing temporary camps doomed to closure.

Acknowledgments

This work would not have been completed without the kindness of the camp dwellers, who opened not only their homes but also their hearts, and shared their stories, past/present struggles and their future aspirations. In addition, we appreciate the generous support of UNHCR-Iraq, the Barzani Charity Foundation (BCF), KRG personnel and BORDA-Iraq for facilitating interviews, information, field visits to various camps, and their financial and logistical support in conducting field visits. Field Interviews, desktop research and the general framework are based on the first author's current Ph.D. research entitled "Refugee Camps as Urban Seeds: From Camp to Town; The Case of Kurdish-Syrian Refugee Camps in Kurdistan Region of Iraq", with a view to obtaining a dual Ph.D. degree from Brandenburg University of Technology (Germany) and KU Leuven (Belgium). This Ph.D. is being supervised by Prof. Heinz Nagler (BTU), Prof. Bruno de Meulder (KU Leuven) and Prof. Nurhan Abujidi (KU Leuven-ZUYD). Student scholarships have been supporting this Ph.D.'s progress (pre-doctoral and doctoral): BTU ArcHerNet-Ausschreibung (Jan. 2017-Dec. 2019), BTU Zentrale Gleichstellungsbeauftragte (Jan. 2020-Sept. 2021), and recently the Studienstiftung des deutschen Volkes (Dec. 2020-Dec. 2021).

Notes

1. Syrian Kurdistan is often called Western Kurdistan or Rojava. Today, the name Rojava is commonly used to refer to the de facto autonomous parts in north-eastern Syria.
2. The Kurdistan Region of Iraq (KR-I) is an autunoms region of the Federal Republic of Iraq, established in 1991. It has state-like status with broad authority over administrative and internal affairs and reports to the Iraqi central government. The region has four governorates (Duhok, Erbil, Sulaymaniyah and Halabja), and the majority of its population is of Kurdish origin.
3. This movement led to the reopening of the decommissioned Bardarash IDP camp to house refugees and the setting up of an extension to the Gawilan camp (OCHA, 2019; UNHCR, 2019a).
4. Baradarsh was at first an IDP camp. The KRG and UNHCR decommissioned the camp with the return and relocation of its IDPs in 2017. It was opened again later in 2019 to become the ninth refugee camp for the Syrian Kurds.
5. In this article, motherland refers to the geography of citizenship and birthplace and early life memories and experiences, while fatherland refers to the geography of ancestral and clan belonging generationally transmitted. Although both might fall into what many define as the homeland, the differentiation is crucial as part of (re)identifying the self with geographies, memories and meanings of belonging at individual and group levels as part of (re)identifying the self with geographies, memoires and meanings of belonging at individual and group levels.
6. "We leave something of ourselves behind when we leave a place, we stay there, even though we go away. And there are things in us that we ca find again only by going back there." (Mercier, 2007)

7. "Self-continuity, defined as the perceived connection between one's past and present, is considered a prerequisite of identity formation" (Wildschut, Sedikides, & Alowidy, 2019).
8. Pulitzer Prize-winning novel, 'Angel of Repose'.
9. Iraq is not a signatory state of The Convention Relating to the Status of Refugees 1951 and its 1967 protocol.
10. These camps are Domiz 1, Domiz 2, Gawilan and Bardarsh in Duhok governorate; Kawergwesk, Dara Shakran, Queshtapa and Basirma in Erbil governorate; and Arbat in Sulaymaniyah governorate.
11. Syrian Refugees in KR-I are Kurds and Arabs. Almost all Syrian Arab refugees stay in urban areas. Hence, this percentage in the existing data does not accurately reflect the concentration of Syrian-Kurdish refugees (camps and urban areas).
12. Although Syrians receive refugee status in KRI, their status in Iraq is considered 'illegal'. There were 135 IDPs Camps scattered in the region by the end of 2019 (Khan, Mansour-Ille, & Nicolai, 2020).
13. In November 2020, the Iraqi Government announced the closure of all camps outside the Kurdish-governed and -controlled territories. According to NRC, IOM and BBC News, this eviction started in August 2019, and was interrupted 'temporarily' by the outbreak of the COVID-19 pandemic (BBC, 2020).
14. Shelters and settlements are interrelated and need to be considered as a whole. 'Shelter' is the household living space, including the items necessary to support daily activities, whereas 'settlement' is the wider location in which people and community live (Sphere Association, 2018).
15. These clusters serve as coordination mechanisms and as a platform to support multilateral agencies' different field efforts on the ground. Governmental agencies, such as the Department of Sewage, Electricity Department (connection to the leading electricity, water supply and sewage networks), also contribute to the provision of services. At the same time, other departments on the governorates' level play a role in the provision of more intangible services in terms of security (Police and Asayish Office), health, education (Department of Education) and labour (Department of Labour and Social Affairs) (UNHCR Iraq, 2019).
16. In the Kurdistan Region of Iraq the modular unit is labelled a community: a standardised 16 plots (plot size 7 m*14 m built-up area). To begin with, each plot has a concrete slab for the standard UNHCR tent, in addition to brick walled kitchen, bathroom, and toilet. All these are connected to one septic tank per community. All the roofing materials are temporary and removable (sandwich panels, corrugated sheets).

17. "Basic and secondary education in [refugee] camps are mainly provided through schools operated by Kurdistan's Ministry of Education, complemented in some cases by facilities run by international NGOs. The government provides for the curriculum as well as the necessary funding for running the facilities and for teachers, who are frequently Syrian refugees with the right skills" (Middle East Research Institute, 2015).
18. This includes detailed information (including biometric data) about the household and the individual family members; reviewing and authenticating documents issued by the country of origin, identify vulnerabilities.
19. The exception to this rule is Basirma refugee camp, which was made up of caravans which have since been systematically replaced by improved and upgraded shelters.
20. For example, the Norwegian Refugee Council (NRC), Peace Winds Japan (PWJ).
21. This model is present in newly set-up camps (IDPs & Refugees).
22. Funded by the US Department of State's Bureau of Population, Refugees, and Migration BPRM and approved by the humanitarian regime (UNHCR, KRG), these shelter upgrade projects are also being undertaken to this day (2021) in other Syrian refugee camps. Peace Winds Japan is the leading implementation partner (IP) in this project.
23. The 'self-building project' in Erbil camp included providing orientation sessions to the self-builtprocess, standardised shelter layout, bills of quantity (BOQ) and labourer payments (phased into eight stages). While the participation component includes informing sessions and focus group discussions with beneficiaries, it intersects with the livelihood one by adding incoming generating opportunities for refugees (PWJ, 2019).
24. Including flags of the Kurdish Democratic Party.
25. This army is recognised only by the Iraqi central government. It is a source of pride among families if they have a member in the Peshmerga, not to mention the financial and other privileges that come with it.
26. The economic crisis became severe in relation to the war with ISIS, along with economic siege and the penalties executed by the Iraqi central government in the background related to the referendum enacted by KRG in September 2017.
27. In Syria, Arabic is the official language taught in mandatory schooling, because the government banned Kurdish (Tejel, 2009).
28. In the field work, the first author, being a Syrian Kurd, recognised songs by Fairouz, Um Kalthom (Arabic), Ciwan Haco and Zakaria Abdullah (Syrian-Kurdish).

References

Agamben, G. (1998). *Homo Sacer: Sovereign Power and Bare Life* Stanford, Calif: Stanford University Press.

Agier, M. (2002). Between War and City. *Ethnography, 3*(3), 317-341.

Agier, M., & Bouchet-Saulnier, F. B.-S. (2004). Humanitarian Spaces: Spaces of Exception. In F. Weissman & f. Médecins sans (Eds.), *In the shadow of 'just wars': violence, politics, and humanitarian action*. Ithaca, N.Y: Cornell University Press.

Allsopp, H. (2015). *The Kurds of Syria: political parties and identity in the Middle East* (New paperback edition ed.). London; New York: I.B. Tauris & Co. Ltd.

Anderson, B. R. O. G. (2016). *Imagined communities: reflections on the origin and spread of nationalism* (Revised edition ed.). London New York: Verso.

Angelou, M. (1987). *All God's Children Need Traveling Shoes*. Vintage Books.

Awan, N., Schneider, T., & Till, J. (2011). *Spatial Agency: Other Ways of Doing Architecture*. Routledge.

Baldwin, J. (1956). *Giovanni's Room*. Paris: Dial Press.

Baum, L. F. (1900). *The Wonderful Wizard of Oz*. Chicago, Illinois: George M. Hill Company.

BBC. (2020). Iraq camp closures 'could leave 100,000 displaced people homeless'. Retrieved from https://www.bbc.com/news/world-middle-east-54873830

Betts, A., Bloom, L., Kaplan, J., & Omata, N. (2017). *Refugee economies: forced displacement and development* (First edition ed.). Oxford: Oxford University Press.

Blunt, A. (2016). Collective Memory and Productive Nostalgia: Anglo-Indian Homemaking at McCluskieganj. *Environment and planning. D, Society & space, 21*(6), 717-738.

Boccagni, P. (2017). *Migration and the Search for Home: Mapping Domestic Space in Migrants' Everyday Lives*: Palgrave Macmillan US, New York.

Boccagni, P., & Brighenti, A. M. (2017). Immigrants and home in the making: thresholds of domesticity, commonality and publicness. *Journal of Housing and the Built Environment, 32*(1), 1-11.

BRHA. (2015). *IDP Camps in Duhok*. Retrieved from http://www.brha-duhok.org/

Brown, P. (2015). *Golden Son*: Hodder & Stoughton.

Brun, C. (2001). Reterritorilizing the relationship between people and place in refugee studies. *Geografiska Annaler: Series B, Human Geography, 83*(1), 15-25.

Brun, C. (2015). Active Waiting and Changing Hopes: Toward a Time Perspective on Protracted Displacement. *Social analysis, 59*(1), 19-37.

Brun, C., & Fábos, A. (2015). Making Homes in Limbo A Conceptual Framework. *Canada's Journal on Refugees, 31*(1).

Bshara, K. (2014). Spatial Memories: The Palestinian Refugee Camps as Time Machine. *Jerusalem Quarterly*(60).

Chawla, D., & Rodriguez, A. (2012). *Liminal Traces: Storying, Performing, and Embodying Postcoloniality*: Rotterdam: Sense Publishers.

Connerton, P. (1989). *How Societies Remember*: Cambridge University Press.
Davis, F. (1979). *Yearning for Yesterday: A Sociology of Nostalgia*: Free Press.
De Brigard, F. (2017). Nostalgia and Mental Simulation. In A. Gotlib (Ed.), *The Moral Psychology of Sadness*: Rowman & Littlefield International.
De Certeau, M. (1980). *The practice of everyday life*. Berkeley, Calif.: Univ. of California Press.
Dunn, E. C. (2018). *No Path Home: Humanitarian Camps and the Grief of Displacement*: Ithaca: Cornell University Press.
Easthope, H. (2014). Making a Rental Property Home. *Housing Studies, 29*(5), 579-596.
Eliot, T. S. ((1943)2009). *Four Quartets: read by Ted Hughes*: Faber & Faber.
Frost, R. (1914). *North of Boston*: Henry Holt.
GSC, IFRC, & UNHCR. (2018). *GSC Strategy 2018-2022*. Retrieved from https://www.sheltercluster.org/strategy-2018-2022/documents/gsc-strategy-2018-2022
Gunes, C. (2019). *The Kurds in a New Middle East: The Changing Geopolitics of a Regional Conflict*. Cham: Springer International Publishing.
Halbwachs, M. (1950). *On collective memory*. Chicago: University of Chicago Press.
Handel, A. (2019). What's in a home? Toward a critical theory of housing/dwelling. *Environment and Planning C: Politics and Space*.
Hannerz, U. (1992). *Cultural complexity: studies in the social organization of meaning*. New York, NY: Columbia Univ. Press.
Harling, P. (2013). *Syria's Kurds: A Struggle Within a Struggle* (136). Retrieved from Brussels: https://www.crisisgroup.org/middle-east-north-africa/eastern-mediterranean/syria/syria-s-kurds-struggle-within-struggle
Hassan, I. S., & Hanafi, S. (2010). (In)Security and Reconstruction in Post-conflict Nahr al-Barid Refugee Camp. *Journal of Palestine Studies, 40*(1), 27-48.
Heidegger, M. (1971). *Poetry, language, thought* (A. Hofstadter, Trans.): New York (N.Y.): Harper and Row.
Herz, M. (2013). *From camp to city: refugee camps of the western Sahara*: Zürich: Lars Müller.
Hilhorst, D., & Jansen, B. J. (2010). Humanitarian Space as Arena: A Perspective on the Everyday Politics of Aid: Humanitarian Space as Arena. *Development and Change, 41*(6), 1117-1139.
Hyndman, J. (2000). *Managing displacement: refugees and the politics of humanitarianism*. Minneapolis: University of Minnesota Press.
Jansen, B. J. (2018). *Kakuma Refugee Camp: Humanitarian Urbanism in Kenya's Accidental City*: Zed Books.
Jaspers, K. (1971). *Philosophy of Existence* (R. F. Grabau, Trans.): University of Pennsylvania Press.
JCC. (2016). About Joint Crisis Coordination Centre – JCC. *Joint Crisis Coordination Centre – KRG*. Retrieved from https://jcckrg.org/en/page/about-joint-crisis-coordination-centre-jcc-31

Khan, A., Mansour-Ille, D., & Nicolai, S. (2020). *Strengthening the knowledge base for education in emergencies practitioners and partners: Iraq Case Study*. Retrieved from https://www.odi.org/sites/odi.org.uk/files/resource-documents/200428_iraq.pdf

King, D. E. (2014). *Kurdistan on the global stage: kinship, land, and community in Iraq*. New Brunswick, New Jersey: Rutgers University Press.

Lefebvre, H. (1991). *The production of space* (Nachdr. ed.). Malden, Mass.: Blackwell.

Levitt, P. (2004). Redefining the Boundaries of Belonging: The Institutional Character of Transnational Religious Life. *Sociology of Religion, 65*(1), 1-18.

Levitt, P. (2012). What's wrong with migration scholarship? A critique and a way forward. *Identities (Yverdon, Switzerland), 19*(4), 493-500.

Malkki, L. (1992). National Geographic: The Rooting of Peoples and the Territorialization of National Identity Among Scholars and Refugees. *Cultural Anthropology, 7*(1), 24-44.

Malkki, L. (1995). *Purity and exile: violence, memory, and national cosmology among Hutu refugees in Tanzania*: Chicago: University of Chicago press.

McDowall, D. (2004). *A modern history of the Kurds* (3. revised and upd. ed., repr ed.). London: Tauris.

Mercier, P. (2007). *Night Train to Lisbon*: Atlantic Books.

Middle East Research Institute. (2015). *Pathways to Resilience: transforming Syrian refugee camps into self-sustaining settlements feasibility study for resilience-building in Syrian refugee camps and their neighbouring host communities in the Kurdistan Region of Iraq*. Retrieved from Erbil, Kurdistan Region, Iraq:

O'Shea, M. T. (2004). *Trapped between the map and reality: geography and perceptions of Kurdistan*. New York: Routledge.

Porteous, J. D. (1976). Home: The Territorial Core. *Geographical Review, 66*(4), 383-390.

PWJ. (2019). [Iraq] 801 Shelters Upgraded: End-of-Year 1 Report | peace winds JAPAN. Retrieved from https://peace-winds.org/en/news/1979

Raglan, L. (1964). *The Temple and the House*: Routledge and Kegan Paul.

Ramadan, A. (2010). In the Ruins of Nahr al-Barid: Understanding the Meaning of the Camp. *Journal of Palestine Studies, 40*(1), 49-62.

Ramadan, A. (2013). From Tahrir to the world: The camp as a political public space. *European Urban and Regional Studies, 20*(1), 145-149.

RUDAW. (2019, November 11, 2019). 'This is your home': PM Barzani to northeast Syria refugees after camp visit. *Rudaw*. Retrieved from https://www.rudaw.net/english/kurdistan/09112019

Said, E. W. (1994). Reflections on Exile. In M. Robinson (Ed.), *Altogether elsewhere: writers on exile* (pp. 137-149). Winchester, MA: Faber and Faber.

Said, E. W. (2000). *Reflections on exile and other essays*. Cambridge, Mass: Harvard University Press.

Sennett, R. (2017). *The Foreigner: Two Essays on Exile*: Notting Hill Editions.

Simone, A. M. (2018). *Improvised Lives: Rhythms of Endurance in an Urban South*: Wiley.

Solnit, R. (2007). *Storming the Gates of Paradise: Landscapes for Politics*: University of California Press.

Somerville, P. (1989). Home sweet home: A critical comment on Saunders and Williams. *Housing Studies, 4*(2), 113-118.

Sphere Association. (2018). *The sphere handbook: humanitarian charter and minimum standards in humanitarian response* (P. Sphere Ed. Fourth edition ed. Vol. 3). Geneva, Switzerland: Sphere Association.

Stansfield, G. R. V. (2003). *Iraqi Kurdistan: political development and emergent democracy*. London; New York: Taylor & Francis e-Library.

Stegner, W. (1971). *Angle of Repose*: Fawcett Crest.

Submarine Channel. (2013). Refugee Republic Retrieved from https://refugeerepublic.submarinechannel.com/intro_en.php?o=o

Tejel, J. (2009). *Syria's kurds: history, politics and society*. London; New York: Routledge.

Thompson, P. (1978). *The voice of the past: oral history* (3rd ed ed.). Oxford [England]; New York: Oxford University Press.

UNHCR. (2016). Settlement folio. In UNHCR (Ed.). Geneva, Switzerland: Shelter and Settlement Section, UNHCR

UNHCR. (2018). SETTLEMENT STRATEGY FOR REFUGEES IN THE KURDISTAN REGION OF IRAQ 2018 – 2021. from UNHCR Offical Database Website

UNHCR. (2020). Syria Regional Refugee Response. Retrieved from https://data2.unhcr.org/en/situations/syria#_ga=2.16598902.1742755276.1589970978-446417775.1589970978&_gac=1.62021982.1589970978.CjwKCAjwqpP2BRBTEiwAfpiD-8h6Uj0dehBdKQp-aslcAxQ7TWu_AogbSwCJDxBVeaQn50GSm-zBwx-oCTsoQAvD_BwE

UNHCR Iraq. (2019). *IRAQ FLASH UPDATE NO.3*. Retrieved from Online: https://reporting.unhcr.org/sites/default/files/UNHCR%20Iraq%20Flash%20Update%20%233%20-%2022%20October%202019.pdf

UNHCR Iraq. (2020). *Iraq: Syrian Refugees Statistics – March 2020*. Retrieved from Erbil, Iraq: https://data2.unhcr.org/en/documents/details/75248

UNHCR/J.Seregni. (2012). Tents stretch into the distance at Domiz camp for Syrian refugees in northern Iraq's Dohuk governorate. Retrieved from https://www.unhcr.org/news/stories/2012/10/5085491d6/thousands-syrian-refugees-arrive-iraq-special-needs.html

Wildschut, T., Sedikides, C., & Alowidy, D. (2019). Hanin: Nostalgia among Syrian refugees. *European journal of social psychology, 49*(7), 1368-1384.

Yassen, A. O. (2019). The Prospects for Durable Solutions for Syrian Refugees in the Kurdistan Region of Iraq: A Case Study of Erbil Governorate Camps. *Refugee Survey Quarterly, 38*(4), 448-469.

CHAPTER 4

In the Name of Belonging

Developing Sheikh Radwan for the Refugees in Gaza City, 1967-1982

Fatina Abreek-Zubiedat
ETH Zürich, Switzerland

> If we seek to anchor the refugee to his place of residence and keep him occupied there, we must construct things so that eventually they will become his home [...] [T]he more his home is dearer to him, the more he is anchored to the place and the more attached to the place he is, the less interest he takes in factors which might require him to move once again.
> Engineering Services in Israel LtD Planning team (1971)[1]

Introduction

This candid statement of the objectives of Israeli planners appears in the opening remarks to the 1972 *Gaza Strip and Northern Sinai (GSNS) Master Plan*, a government planning document devised and published by a team of professional Israeli architects and planners that lays the foundations for an Israeli policy of rehabilitating the Palestinian refugees in the Gaza strip. The quotation reflects the belief among the Israeli team that the Palestinian refugees' 'right of return' could be ended if the Israeli government were to succeed in constructing another home for them in exile which would "anchor" them to their new place. The right of return was embodied in the UN Resolution 194 (III) of 11 December 1948, to ensure the repatriation of or compensation for the refugees, who believed they would eventually return to their homes in what became the State of Israel.

Because Israeli architects and planners were given broad leeway to define the issues, come up with solutions and create facts on the ground, this testament to their beliefs is significant in understanding Israeli development policy in the Gaza Strip. Architecture played an active role in determining the way in which the Israeli government addressed one of the most difficult issues in the Israeli-Palestinian conflict: the Palestinian refugees' right of return. The professionals of the *GSNS* master plan believed that the "refugee problem" could be solved by economic stimuli paired with a forced emptying of the refugee camps and the provision of new housing in the Strip cities. The planners' humanitarianism, expressed in their rhetorical support for refugees' civil rights and their equality to Gazan locals, did not lead to misgivings about the morality of their proposals. In guaranteeing the intensification of the Israeli settler colonial project and its expansion into the recently occupied Gaza Strip, it soon emerged that the two not only were not at odds, but also that they were, in fact, surprisingly compatible.

This chapter uses public and private archival documents produced by Israeli planners and military officials between 1967 and 1982 to trace how the distinction between refugees and local citizens expressed itself in Israeli deliberations about the physio-spatial layout of the city of Gaza. Israeli development in Gaza is read here not as a homogenous vortex of knowledge/power, but rather as an arena where contradictory interests and agendas clashed. As the first part of the chapter establishes, very little is known about how the logic and objectives of Israeli settler colonialism played out in the unique socio-urban fabric of Gaza. Exploitative development, I argue, rather than destruction or attrition (Abujidi, 2014; Graham, 2002; Weizman, 2011), took centre-stage in Israeli attempts to establish control over Gaza.

A rewarding approach to this question is to conceptualise architecture as cultural production (Celik, 2008; King, 2004; Prakash, 2002; Wright, 1991) and examine its colonial hue. The chapter follows daily urban life to understand how developmental architecture, a cultural production that is permeated by scientific justifications and embedded in universalism (Muzaffar, 2007; Pyla, 2013; Siddiqi, 2017), intervenes in the camp-city relationship. This effort potentially helps us better to understand the materiality of the camp-city as a form of "colonial urbanism" (Wright, 1991, p. 6), where urban design is wedded to economic development. In this way, the GSNS can be compared in turn with French colonial architecture in North Africa that treated the region as a frontier of experimental modernism.

The second part of this chapter critically examines the Israeli planners' ostensibly progressive desire to ensure equal urban citizenship for Palestinian refugees. At the centre of this argument stands an analysis of the intervention in the delicate relationship between camp and city by the Israeli military government and its representative in the field – the Public Works Department (PWD) – through the construction of Sheikh Radwan. The neighbourhood was designated as a permanent housing solution for the inhabitants of the nearby Shati refugee camp (Fig. 1). The urban historical perspective allows us, then, to revisit the enactment of an Israeli development project in the Strip until its abrupt termination with the implementation of the peace accords with Egypt, and to explore its lasting effects on the permanence of the Palestinian refugee camps in the Strip.

Figure 1. Map of Gaza City with Shati Refugee Camp and Sheikh Radwan with its basic infrastructure, 1973 (Tel Aviv Survey Department, University of Haifa. English subtitles were added by the author).

Camp-city relations in development discourse

In the aftermath of 1948 Gaza became a major sanctuary for the war's refugees from across Palestine. Some 250,000 refugees from central and southern Palestine were forced to flee to the Gaza strip and were barred from returning to their homes by the new State of Israel. Bereft of national citizenship and robbed of whatever property and possessions they owned, most refugees were reduced to bare subsistence in the makeshift camps on Gaza's margins established by the United Nations Relief and Works Agency for Palestine Refugees in the Middle East (UNRWA).

Like the refugees, the locals of the towns and cities of the Gaza Strip – Rafah, Gaza, Dayr al-Balah and Khan Yunis (together with a population of around 200,000) – were not given citizenship rights under the Egyptian regime. Unlike the refugees', however, much of locals' social and economic status remained intact in the aftermath of the war. Under Egyptian law they did have access to, and a say over, state resources managed through their local municipalities (Bauböck, 2003; Holston, 1999; Isin, 2002; Purcell, 2002; Varsanyi, 2006). Wealthy and privileged residents continued to enjoy economic opportunities and political levers uniquely available to the landowning and propertied classes. Apart from their officially unequal urban citizenship status, a material and spatial gulf divided locals of all varieties from refugees.

This difference was etched into the built environment. Physically set apart from the city's neighbourhoods, the refugee camps were visibly flimsier and more crowded than even the poorest quarters of the city. The sense of urgency to resolve the Palestinian refugee crisis was aggravated by the camps' squalor, their poverty, and the endemic lack of opportunities for refugee youth. Soon after the Nakba (the 1948 catastrophe), the camps became symbolic sites of the Palestinian national struggle for political liberation and return, wherein refugees turned from peasants to 'freedom fighters' (Abourahme, 2018, p. 35; Sayigh, 1979, p. 166). The camps thus also served as a reminder to non-refugee Palestinians of the urgency of materialising the Palestinian refugees' right to return.

Notwithstanding the extension of urban citizenship rights exclusively to locals, some researchers of urbanism recorded the informal processes of development and urbanisation in the camps and focused their analytical attention on the everyday practices and domestic life in the camps. The result was the conceptualisation of "camp as city" (Agier, 2002) and an analytical exploration of the relationship between the camps' spatiality and the refugees' citizenship (Abourahme and Hilal, 2009; Abreek-Zubiedat, 2014; Hanafi, 2009, 2010; Martin, 2015; Ramadan, 2013; Sanyal, 2014). Sanyal (2014), for instance, combined these two parts of the debate on the refugee camp, claiming that it "could be seen as the site from which new urban citizenships emerge that may lay claims to national citizenship [...] or to alternate visions of life, community and rights" (p. 570). The distinction between the camp and the city, or between the 'urban periphery' and the 'city', to use Holston's terms (2009, p. 246), is thus blurred by those 'insurgent citizens' who fight for their right to security which was a prerequisite to leading a dignified life in the city.

In the historical period we are concerned with here, however, the demand for equal rights in the municipal sphere was spearheaded by the Israeli occupier, not the camp dwellers themselves. Israeli occupation forces promoted 'normalisation' as an instrument of control and a way to end 'the refugee problem' of 1948. In so doing, they put forward colonial architecture and economic development planning as two primary modalities through which to redefine the boundaries between the camp and the city.

Several researchers pointed out how development planning was formed by the desire more effectively to exploit local resources and populations and how it served historically to facilitate the colonial takeover of territories and make them more profitable (Bissell, 2011; Comaroff, 1997; King, 2004; Legg & McFarlane, 2008; Robinson, 2006). Development, as an object of inquiry, however, was given a scientific seal of approval after World War II (WWII). Development invokes 'economic stewardship' – the proper control and deployment of resources. This means that the coloniser of yesteryear was given the mantle of the developer, which lent him the power to direct and control the developed (the former colonial 'native') as a subject temporarily suspended within the dynamic of tutelage (Ferguson, 1990; Sachs, 1992; Escobar, 1995). Architecture and engineering "improvement" projects form a core part of the development agenda, where economic progress is often conflated with humanitarian aid. For the coloniser the humanitarian premise is the "triumph of civilization over barbarism" (Celik, 2008, p. 248), covered in the "development syndrome" (Beeckmans, 2017), that is, the use of development slogans to modernise the city and simultaneously launch new forms of social engineering, such as housing projects. Pyla (2013) writes that whether led by international institutions, corporate interests, national governments of the post-colonial world or post-imperial western governments, the drive towards development has been envisaged in the built landscape through competing conceptions of economic and social change (p. 7).

These projects, which lent impetus to the humanitarian legacy of the architecture of development, become more complicated when they are discussed as settler-colonial state projects, as in the case of Israel. As it is a settler colonial state, development logic becomes part of the structural land-centred project expanded through the elimination of indigenous society (Veracini, 2006; Wolfe, 2006). The alignment of urban trends in cities with the modalities of settler colonialism compelled scholars to read the conflict through a binary opposition of coloniser\developer and colonised\developed, as a process of ethnic cleansing, in which the former ultimately replace the latter (Yiftachel

& Yacobi, 2003; Hepburn, 2004; Dumper, 2005; Pullan, 2011). The empirical materials in the following segments of the chapter are meant to show how architectural conventions were used to diffuse politically charged issues with a casual problem-solving attitude. They thus shed new light on neglected aspects of settler colonialism. As discussed in the following sections of the chapter, Israeli rhetoric drew on the vocabulary of development in an attempt to reframe the city-camp divide in the Gaza strip away from the national and towards a broader international framework of humanitarian and economic development.

Israeli development policy

In the aftermath of the 1967 war the Israeli government appointed a committee of economists and social scientists and tasked them with finding 'constructive solutions' to the Palestinian refugee problem. The committee, colloquially called "the Rehovot Group", analysed Israel's military and economic interests regarding possible outcomes for the refugee problem and sought to use professional expertise in planning to adapt them into workable action plans. Among its members were representatives from the Ministry of Defence, headed by the economist Pinhas Sussman, from the Ministry of Housing, headed by the architect Yehuda Drexler, and professionals from the Israeli Office for Engineering Services Ltd., a government consortium that brought together private architectural and urban planning firms and other professionals in related fields, including Rafael and Edna Lerman (co-founders of Lerman – Architects and Planners Ltd.), who were selected to serve as lead architects. Development, for Drexler, Sussman and the Lermans, was the correct way to establish control over the newly occupied lands and peoples without requiring large expenditure.[2]

The group's working assumption was that Israel would be forging long-term ties with Palestinians in the Gaza Strip and in the West Bank. Still, the Gaza Strip represented a considerable challenge. Given its lack of exploitable natural resources, the planners treated the Strip's economic development as a zero-sum game.[3] The committee opted for a strategy of hands-on involvement, whereby politically charged issues were tackled as daily issues requiring sensible problem-solving solutions, particularly through humanitarian intervention.[4] One clear example of this approach relates to the refugees' economic rehabilitation. The absorption of refugees into existing towns and cities was a step towards making them dependent on Jewish settlements, which were to become the new economic hubs of the area.[5] In their master plan of 1972, entitled "The Gaza Strip and Northern Sinai", the committee recommended that the administrative jurisdiction be entirely redrawn and, first, that the refugee camps outside the new municipal jurisdictions be demolished and their inhabitants resettled inside the Strip's cities. At the same time Israel was to establish a brand new all-Jewish port city to the south-west of Rafah – Yamit – which would provide employment and services to all the Israeli southern Mediterranean seaboard, including the Gaza Strip. There was political capital to be made from adopting its plan, committee members pointed out: a good-faith attempt on Israel's behalf to resolve a tangled humanitarian problem of great urgency would play out well in the international arena.[6]

The extent to which the planning of Yamit was integral to refugee rehabilitation schemes in the minds of Israeli planners is recorded in contemporary correspondence between Israeli government ministries and development bodies. In a letter to the Chief of the National Planning Desk in the Ministry of Interior, a district officer for internal affairs in the Israel Defence Force (IDF) in Gaza and Northern Sinai Headquarters explained how:

> [Planners] assumed that housing the refugees shall be done by means of expanding existing Arab settlements rather than establishing new ones […] one must strive to pull refugees southwards and thus weaken Gaza's claim as the Strip's capital […] a port is to be established to the south of Khan Younis […] a Hebrew city will be established to the south of Rafah in a safe driving distance of some 8-10 KM from the proposed port.[7]

This led to the decision to construct new housing for refugees and to elevate them to an equal municipal footing in addition to building Yamit. The initial experimental stage for rehousing plans for refugees was implemented in the cities of Rafah and Khan Younis (Abreek-Zubiedat & Nitsan-Shiftan, 2018) (Fig. 2). These housing experiments have accelerated the building of Sheikh Radwan – the focus of the chapter. In this context, the Shati camp was considered as an ambitious housing project for refugees that was in practice characterised by low infrastructure and construction standards and was seen as a "slum". The Sheikh Radwan neighbourhood, therefore, was part of a development plan which sought broadly to recalibrate the power relations in the area. In the first instance, Israel's plan for Sheikh Radwan undercut the protected national distinction between the camp and the city, that is, by undermining the temporariness forms embedded in the camp as separate entity from the city. The Israeli PWD was the expert agency put in charge of carrying out the plan's ambitious social engineering goals in Gaza.

Figure 2. "Brazilian neighborhood" near Rafah city, refugees' evacuees from Jabalia camp, 1975 (National Photography Collection, photo by Moshe Milner).

Self-built housing as a means of assimilation

The systematic implementation of the GNSA master plan began immediately after its publication in 1972. The leading architects of the master plan team ('Office for Engineering Services, Ltd.' by Rafael and Edna Lerman) determined the initial scheme. The Lermans originally intended to build Sheikh Radwan as a 1,000-housing unit complex for 7,000 residents on 12-metre-wide plots of 250-300m² (Ministry of Labour 1973; Eldad Sagiv, interview with author, 4 May 2012). The conceptual development of the residential units and their design and construction was overseen by the PWD and its main Engineer of the Southern District, Dov Eizenberg (Fig. 3).

The PWD's, and specifically Eizenberg's, appearance on the scene was not coincidental. The department has long served the Israeli executive branch as an instrument for carrying out such technical projects. Its new chief architect, Mordechai Shoshani, sought to upgrade the department from a serviceable public works department that worked adequately in technical design and development to one that would specialise in architectural design and whose projects would display the cutting edge of architectural and urban discourse, especially in its more technological aspects. For years, starting in the British mandatory period, the PWD's work pattern was one of hasty construction of large-scale projects of

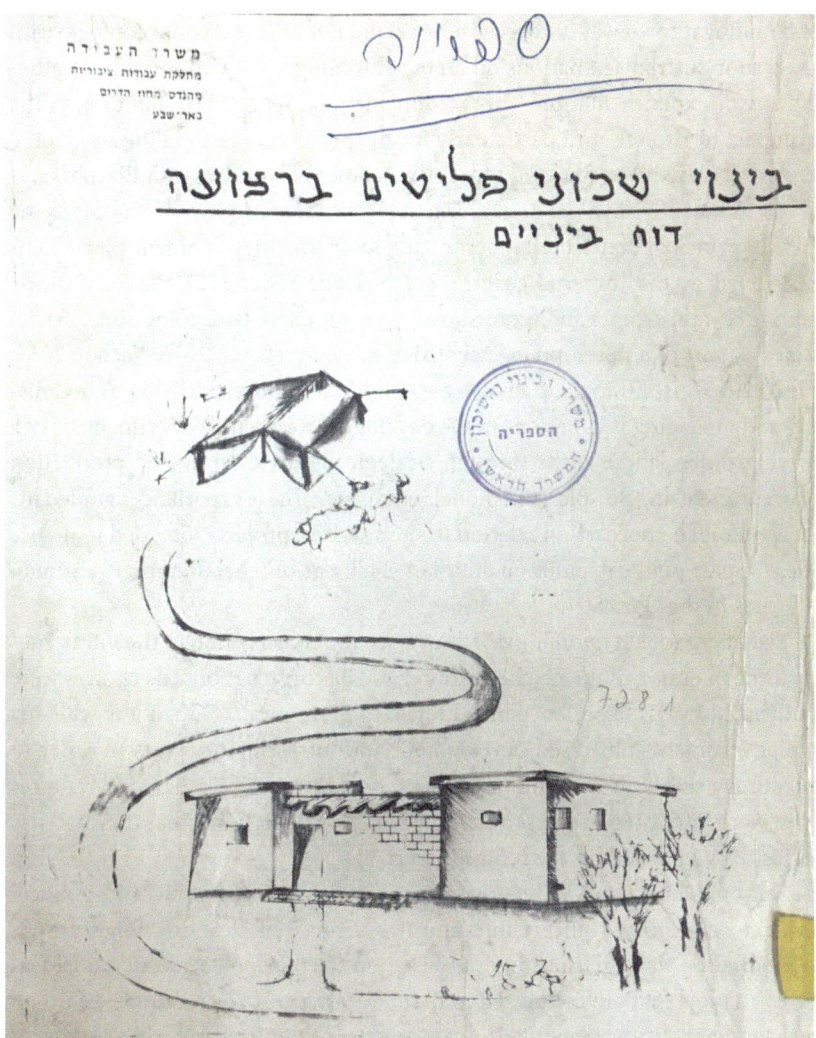

Figure 3. Cover of the booklet "Building Refugee Housing in the Strip: Interim Report", published by the Public Works Department (PWD)'s Southern District to summarise the rehabilitation project in the Strip in 1971-1973 (Israel Architecture Archive [IAA]).

buildings and infrastructure (Fuchs, 2000; Hashimshoni, 1997, pp. 101–122). Shoshani (1967) wrote that, during the 1960s, architecture in Israel was mired in an ideational discomfiture, occupying an ill-defined space between science and art. In keeping with the professional Zeitgeist, Shoshani placed man at the centre, preferring "good technical work over art" as the best way to meet daily needs.[8] Shoshani was aware of the role of the PWD in exporting architectural knowledge to developing countries. However, because architecture in Israel was still finding its own way and because Israel did not believe it could compete with western industrialised nations on an equal footing, Shoshani sought out other arenas for experimentation. This accounts for his approach to building in the occupied territories, and particularly for his position regarding the residential project at Sheikh Radwan and thus for his choice of working with Eizenberg.

As an executive in Solel Boneh, Eizenberg was sent in 1960 to Ethiopia as the PWD's principal construction contractor to oversee development plans commissioned by the Imperial government of Haile Sellasie. Eizenberg was one among several experts and professionals who were sent to decolonising African states as part of a development "civilising mission" (Levin 2016; Yacobi, 2015; Efrat, 2015). In Ethiopia, Eizenberg gained first-hand experience in organising and managing populations in the developing world and experimented with driving down labour costs through strategically dividing up the production process and using pre-planned models en masse.[9] These experiences guided his heavy-handed approach in relation to the sensitive projects intended to defuse the complex political and humanitarian challenge of rehabilitating Palestinian refugees in the Gaza Strip.

Eizenberg took it upon himself to oversee the construction of the infrastructure, the planning of the neighbourhood and its construction. His choices were influenced by his experience in Ethiopia, in granting developed lots whereby the government subsidised development and infrastructure costs in order to encourage self-built housing projects. In order to receive a new lot, refugees who were interested in the programme would have to prove that they had demolished their house in the refugee camp.

Self-built housing was seen as appropriate in the economic and political context of territorial uncertainty and the absence of clear sovereignty. Self-rehabilitation through housing was based on the "site and service" model featured in plots that are connected to basic infrastructure was a model of urban development that was popular in some western countries suffering from economic depression during the 1930s and 1940s due to its perceived strength in mitigating the lack of capital on the part of the tenants and the economic difficulties faced by municipal governments and the state (Harris, 1999; Kwak, 2015). From 1949 onwards, the need for immediate and considerable improvement to living standards in developing countries plagued by high rates of unemployment became a cornerstone of the Truman administration's American-led 'age of development' (Muzaffar, 2007; Turner, 1976).

This global model was adapted in Gaza as a workable compromise between refugees who lacked capital and the Israeli state which sought to avoid being saddled with the costs of constructing a neighbourhood for refugees and was generally averse to investing too heavily in the Strip's development. Still, self-built housing met the most important of the Israeli goals at relatively low cost (Fig. 4). It would officially make the refugees residents of the cities and towns, sever them from UNRWA support and render them dependent on Israeli aid and loans. Thus, the construction and development of self-built housing neighbourhoods functioned as a programme of normalisation that would eventually replace claims to the right of return or to national independence with a claim to a kind of confederative autonomy. The implementation of the model was by accelerating forms of global spatial culture embodied in the Mediterranean architecture.

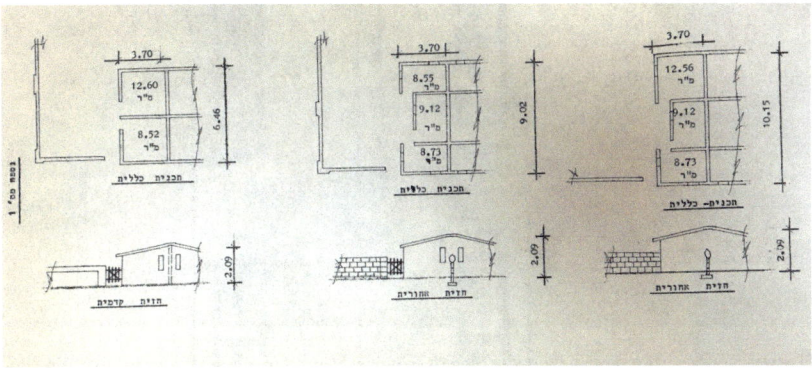

Figure 4. Arch. Shimon Margolin Housing drawings in the "Brazilian Project" in Rafah, modified and executed in Sheikh Radwan by Dov Eizenberg (IAA archive).

Mediterranean housing in the name of belonging

In working on the housing layout plan, Eizenberg combined the "traditional Gazan" inner courtyard house with the self-built housing model – a singular model with which he had had experience in Ethiopia. Incorporating certain elements of vernacular aesthetics and appropriating local ways of life in the built environment is a well-known practice to legitimise and streamline the exercise of colonial power. Indeed, these practices of "conquering the hearts of the natives" were designed to pacify local resistance to foreign rule (Wright, 1991, p. 1).

Eizenberg's residential types fitted his strategy of "building construction in self-management while deepening production".[10] This allowed him and the PWD to revert to the most cost-effective model, saving both time and expense. Eizenberg himself patented this method of construction and its use of materials which he called the "Growing House" (Ministry of Labour, 1973): modular, industrial, and monotonous "boxes" that served as basic structures which ostensibly allowed for later expansion by the residents themselves and saved as much as 50 per cent of the time typically required for the initial construction of a residential unit (Shoshani, 1973) (Fig. 5).

Figure 5. Wooden model illustrates the "Growing House" precast concrete structure designed by Dov Eizenberg and registered as a patent (IAA archive).

To Eizenberg the benefits of the "Growing House" exceeded the saving of money and time. They allowed residents to populate the residence quickly and expand it according to their own needs, independently of any external professional help (Ministry of Labour, 1973). The initial "core unit" provided the refugees with a crude shelter and anchored them to their places by encouraging them to 'make it theirs' by initiating subsequent expansions and completing the construction themselves (Fig. 6). These arguments associate Eizenberg with a contemporary dominant architectural culture experienced mainly in North African (post-)colonial cities, where western architects such as Alison and Peter Smithson, Aldo van Eyck, Georges Candilis, Shadrach Woods and others tried to ground a sense of community and belonging by creating a sense of 'home' to counter the threat of vulnerability and temporality (Van der Heuvel, 2015; Avermaete, 2010; Goldhagen & Legault, 2000).

Eizenberg's initiatives and ideas were warmly received by his superiors. According to the Main Architect of the PWD, Mordechai Shoshani, "The ideas presented [by Eizenberg] provide the PWD with a great opportunity to plan Mediterranean housing for refugees" (Shoshani, 1973). Mediterranean housing

Figure 6. PWD during the construction works at Sheikh Radwan Neighbourhood, 1976 (National Photography Collection, photo by Moshe Milner).

enjoyed widespread popularity in architectural circles and practitioners after WWII (Herzfeld, 2005). Still, researchers point out that the timelessness and universality that the Mediterranean style adopts were often thin veneers for imperial ambitions and nationalist politics (Fuller, 2006; Lejeune & Sabatino, 2010; Crane, 2011). Thus, the Mediterranean growing houses allowed the PWD to mediate between economic development and cultural-political assimilation in the name of belonging.

Eizenberg chose to place the houses at the fronts of the plots, so that they formed a continuous façade towards the street and residents enjoyed a degree of domestic privacy stipulated by custom. The back yards, divided by low walls, bordered each other. This was meant to assure that at least the façades of the houses would be uniform, while the rest of the built environment would be eclectic, defined by renovations that residents would undertake themselves, each according to their financial and material means. This, he argued, would minimise Israeli investment without compromising the quality of the housing (Eizenberg Blog). Eizenberg offered three main types based on the idea of the growing house: (a) a basic structure, designed as a "seminal" unit, 42m^2 in size; (b) the planning and construction of houses sized 81-85m^2; or (c) the construction of double-unit maisonettes with one unit on top of the other. He also earmarked a portion of the plots for fully fledged "self-built" housing (Fig. 7).

Figure 7. "Growing House"-Type B residential building in Sheikh Radwan, designed and executed by Dov Eizenberg (IAA archive).

Choosing an aesthetic form of expression that evoked the cultural heritage of the Mediterranean was perhaps a crude way to instil a sense of belonging in these hastily constructed neighbourhoods. It depended on making the refugee an active agent and was attempted under the promise of standardising and rationalising parts of the city of Gaza for the purpose of incorporating them in a broader development plan. The experimental neighbourhood was inhabited by a thousand families from Shati camp between 1973 and 1980. The economic development projects that included the planning of permanent neighbourhoods for Palestinian refugees were terminated in 1982 following the peace treaty signed with Egypt in 1979, with the Israeli withdrawal from Rafah Salient and the Sinai desert, the evacuation of Jewish settlements from the area and the demolition of Yamit.

Conclusion

As a contested arena of colonial development, Gaza was a place where professional scientific knowledge in architecture, fashioned through professional experimentation throughout the Global South and fused with the promise of the right to the city, served the political ends of Israeli settler-colonialism. Gaza's urban history offered the opportunity to explore the city materiality in line with northern and southern African cities' colonialism, and in the intersection of the global, post-World War II criticism and socio-spatial transformations.

Sheik Radwan's residential neighbourhood in Gaza city demonstrates the complexity of dissolving the refugees' claim to the right of return. This was achieved through the implementation of a housing project invested in professional development discourse as a means of control. Architects and engineers revealed their participation in critical aspects of the Israeli settler colonialism and, at the same time, conveyed their architectural discourse to redraw the national and spatial boundaries that set the camp apart from the city. Israeli development and humanitarian aid were connected to the geo-strategic move that would have seen Yamit – a Jewish city – become an economic engine to replace Gaza as the central city of the Strip. It also reshaped Gaza's urban fabric by undermining the national-political spatial organisation that preserved the camps. The development programmes would make refugees dependent on Israeli government loans, housing programmes and employment opportunities. Israeli developers thus replaced separation between different groups of Palestinians with separation between Palestinians and Jewish settlers, thus imposing its own logic of separation on a cityscape marked by the politics of Palestinian nationalism.

The Israeli development project reached an impasse in 1979 as a result of the signing of a peace agreement between Israel and Egypt. This abruptly ended the development project with the destruction of Yamit and the evacuation of the Jewish settlers from the Sinai desert. The Israeli withdrawal was part of a peace deal with Egypt, but not with the Strip. With the economic motivation to develop the Strip gone, Israeli rule limited itself to the exclusively Jewish settlements of Gush Qatif and, after the end of the disengagement process and the final withdrawal from the Strip in 2005, to nothing but military surveillance and an effective siege policy. Gaza became an object of violence in the name of the first and only aspect left – security, and the Palestinian refugees continued to be held captive by the conflicting goals of Palestinian nationalism and Israeli occupation. The siege deprived locals and refugees of any basis of economic development and worsened the situation when the fundamentalist organisation, Hamas, rose to power. Hamas leaders, as Gazans describe, are themselves often refugees from Shati camp, many of whom resided in Sheikh Radwan. Today, not only has the urban fabric of Sheikh Radwan integrated into the nearby neighbourhoods, but the socio-economic situation of some of the refugees has also surpassed that of the locals, since the Gazan elite have left the city. Thus, class struggle, as one could conclude, is converted from local\owner-refugee\stranger, to Fatah-Hamas activist.[11]

Notes

1. Gaza Strip and Northern Sinai command centre, the masterplan taskforce, planning teams – Engineering Services in Israel LtD, 'Plan for family residential unit in the Gaza Strip', The Avie and Sarah Arenson Built Heritage Research Center Archive, the Faculty of Architecture and Town Planning, the Technion.
2. ISA, "Refugee issues and more": SA-Privatecollections-MichaelBruno-000o7u9.
3. Israeli State Archives (hereafter: ISA), Prime Minister's Office, "Proposition to develop industry in Israel and in the held territories through rehabilitation", file ISA-PMO-PrimeMinisterBureau-001145v, report and correspondence with board of directors of the Economic Development and Refugee Rehabilitation Trust.
4. ISA, Michael Bruno collection – public activities, "Rehovot Group in the Weitzman Science Institute", 1969-1970. ISA-Privatecollections-MichaelBruno-000lb2k, working plans and memoranda of the "Rehovot Group" regarding the refugee problem and proposals for refugees' rehabilitation.
5. ISA, Michel Bruno Collection– public activity, articles on the held territories' economy et cetera. 1972-1973, "Background materials for work group of deputy committee for territories' affairs", ISA-Privatecollections-MichaelBruno-000ln1r.
6. ISA, Rehovot Group from the Weizman Institute for Science, "Rehovot Plan on the Refugee Question". ISA-mfa-UNInterOrg2-000ah1y.
7. Yizhak Gvirtz to Eliezer Brutzkus, 6 Febuary 1972. ISA, "Planning in held territories, 1967-1976", The National Planning Department (Brutzkus) – planning in held territories. ISA-MOIN-InteriorPlans-0003vyl. See also: Brutzkus to Chief Economic officer in the Interior Ministry of 4 September, 1972 and 25 January 1973, ISA, "Planning in Sinai", The National Planning Department (Brutzkus), 1970-1973. ISA-MOIN-InteriorPlans-0003j3s.
8. ISA, Ministry of Economy and Industry, 1967-1970, "PWD execution policy – November 1968", ISA-moital-moital-0010r08.
9. See Dov Eizenberg's online blog: https://sites.google.com/site/doveizenberg/ (retrieved: 03/10/2019). Eizenberg was mainly influenced by Israeli architect, Zalman Enav, who worked closely with Emperor Haile Selassie and has specialised in tropical architecture. For further discussion see Levin (2016) and Yacobi (2015).
10. Yair Kotler, "Untitled." *Haaretz (suppl.)*, 19 December 1975; Eizenberg Blog.
11. From correspondence with Gazans: Essam A-Shawa; Salem al Qudwa and Aziz Fara, September 2020.

References

Abourahme, N. (2018). 'Nothing to Lose but Our Tents': The Camp, the Revolution, the Novel. *Journal of Palestine Studies, 158*(1), 33-52.

Abourahme N. & Hilal, S. (2009). The Production of Space, Political Subjectification and the Folding of Polarity: the Case of Deheishe Camp, Palestine. In J. Holston & T. Caldeira (eds.), *Peripheries: Decentering Urban Theory*. Berkeley: University of California Press. Link: http://www.campusincamps.ps/wp-content/uploads/2012/12/Nasser-Abourahme-and-Sandi-Hilal_Deheishe-Paper.pdf.

Abreek-Zubiedat, F., & Nitzan-Shiftan, A. (2018). 'De-Camping' through Development: The Palestinian Refugee Camps in Gaza, 1967–1982. In I. Katz, D. Martin & C. Minca (eds.), *Camps Revisited: Multifaceted Spatialities of a Modern Political Technology* (pp. 137–157). New York: Rowman and Littlefield Publishers.

Abreek-Zubiedat, F. (2014). The Palestinian Refugee Camps: The Promise of 'Ruin' and 'Loss'. *Rethinking History Journal, 19*(1), 72–94.

Abujidi, N. (2014). *Urbicide in Palestine: Spaces of Oppression and Resilience*. Abingdon: Routledge.

Agier, M. (2002). *On the Margins of the World: the Refugee Experience Today*. Cambridge: Polity Press.

Avermaete, T. (2010). Nomadic Experts and Travelling Perspectives. In T. Avermaete, S. Karakayali, & M. von Osten, (eds.), *Colonial Modern: Aesthetics of the Past, Rebellions for the Future* (pp. 130-149). London: Black Dog.

Beeckmans, L. (2017). The 'Development Syndrome': Building and contesting the SICAP housing schemes in French Dakar (1951–1960). *Canadian Journal of African Studies / Revue canadienne des études africaines, 51*(3), 359-388.

Bissell, W. (2011). *Urban Design, Chaos, and Colonial Power in Zanzibar*. Bloomington: Indiana University Press.

Comaroff, J. (1997). Images of Empire, Contests of Conscience: Models of Colonial John L. Domination on South Africa. In A. L. Stoler & F. Cooper, *Tensions of Empire: Colonial Cultures in a Bourgeois World* (pp. 137-163). Berkeley: University of California Press.

Crane, S. (2011). *Mediterranean Crossroads: Marseille and Modern Architecture*. Minneapolis: University of Minnesota Press.

Dumper, M. (2005). *The Politics of Jerusalem Since 1967*. New York: Columbia University Press.

Efrat, Z. (2015). Proxy Colonialism: The Export of Israeli Architecture to Africa. *Herz,* 487-95: http://ispada-archive.com/pdf/Pages_from_African_Modernism_essays.pdf [Retrieved: 16 March, 2020].

Escobar, A. (1995). *Encountering Development: The Making and Unmaking of the Third World*. Princeton: Princeton University Press.

Ferguson, J. (1990). *The Anti-Politics Machine, "Development," Depoliticization, and Bureaucratic Power in Lesotho.* Cambridge: Cambridge University Press.

Fuchs, R. (2000). Public Works in the Holy Land: Government building under the British Mandate in Palestine, 1917-1948. In L. Campbell (ed.), *Twentieth-Century Architecture and its Histories* (pp. 275-306). Special Millennial Issue of the Society of Architectural Historians of Great Britain.

Fuller, M. (2006). *Modern Abroad: Architectures, Cities, and Italian Imperialism in the Mediterranean and East Africa.* London and New York: Routledge.

Goldhagen S., & Legault R. (eds.). (2000). *Anxious Modernism, Experimentation in Postwar Architectural Culture.* Montreal: Canadian Centre for Architecture; Cambridge, Mass.: MIT Press.

Graham, S. (2002). Bulldozers and Bombs: The Latest Palestinian–Israeli Conflict and Asymmetric Urbicide. *Antipode, 34*(4), 642–649.

Harris, R. (1999). Slipping through the Cracks: The Origins of Aided Self-Help Housing, 1918-1953. *Housing Studies, 14*(3), 281-309.

Hashimshoni, T. (1997). *Memoires, 1904-1972: On the Path I walked.* Tel-Aviv: Studio-Dolev-Altuvia.

Hepburn, A. C. (2004). *Contested Cities in the Modern West.* London. U.K.: Palgrave Macmillan.

Holston, J. (1999). Spaces of Insurgent Citizenship. In J. Holston (ed.), *Cities and Citizenship* (pp. 155-173). Durham: Duke University Press.

Holston, J. (2009). Insurgent Citizenship in an Era of Global Urban Peripheries. *City and Society, 21*(2), 245–267.

Isin, E. (2002). *Being Political: Genealogies of Citizenship.* Minneapolis: University of Minnesota Press.

King, A. (2004). *Spaces of Global Cultures: Architecture Urbanism Identity.* New York: Routledge.

Kwak, N. H. (2015). *A World of Home Owners: American Power and the Politics of Housing Aid.* Chicago: The University of Chicago Press.

Legg, S., & McFarlane, C. (2008). Ordinary Urban Spaces: Between Postcolonialism and Development. *Environment and Planning A 40*(1), 6-14.

Lejeune, J., & Sabatino, M. (eds.). (2010). *Modern Architecture and the Mediterranean: Vernacular Dialogue, Contested Identities.* Oxon: Routledge.

Levin, A. (2016). Haile Selassie's Imperial Modernity: Expatriate Architects and the Shaping of Addis Ababa. *Journal of the Society of Architectural Historians, 75*(4), 447-468.

Martin, D. (2015). From Spaces of Exception to 'Campscapes': Palestinian Refugee Camps and Informal Settlements in Beirut. *Political Geography, 44,* 9-18.

Ministry of Labour, Public Works Department (PWD) [Israel]. 1973. "Building Refugee Housing Projects in the Strip: Interim Report". Jerusalem: Ministry of Labor, Department of Public Works. Israeli Architecture Archive (IAA). [Hebrew]

Muzaffar, I. M. (2007). *The Periphery within Modern Architecture and the Making of the Third World*. Ph.D. Diss, Massachusetts Institute of Technology.

Pullan, W. (2011). Frontier Urbanism: The Periphery at the Centre of Contested Cities. *The Journal of Architecture*, 16(1), 15-35.

Pyla, P. (ed.). (2013). *Landscapes of Development: The Impact of Modernization Discourses on the Physical Environment of the Eastern Mediterranean*. Cambridge: Harvard University Press.

Ramadan, A. (2013). Spatialising the Refugee Camp. *Transactions of the Institute of British Geographers*, 38(1), 65-77.

Robinson, J. (2006). *Ordinary Cities: Between Modernity and Development*. London: Routledge.

Sachs, W. (1992). *The Development Dictionary: A Guide to Knowledge as Power*. London: Zed Books.

Sanyal, R. (2014). Urbanizing Refuge: Interrogating Spaces of Displacement. *International Journal of Urban and Regional Research*, 38(2), 558–572.

Shoshani, M. (1967). Architecture in the Public Works Department. *AA – The Architects' Monthly Publication – The Architects' and Engineers' Society in Israel*, Issue 'B', 6-12. [In Hebrew]

Shoshani, M. (1973). I am disappointed by the profession, many Architects are willing to be Sell-Swords. *AA – The Architects' Monthly Publication – The Architects' and Engineers' Society in Israel*: 8-11. [in Hebrew]

Turner, J. F. C. (1976). *Housing by People: Towards Autonomy in Building Environments*. London: Maryon Boyars.

Van der Heuvel, D. (2015). The Open Society and its Experiments: The Case of the Netherlands and Piet Blom. In Mark Swenarton, Tom Avermaete and Dirk Van der Heuvel (eds.), *Architecture and the Welfare State* (pp. 133-152). Oxon: Routledge.

Varsanyi, M. (2006). Interrogating 'Urban Citizenship' vis-a-vis Undocumented Migration. *Citizenship Studies*, 10(2), 229-249.

Veracini, L. (2006). *Israel and Settler Society*. London: Pluto Press.

Weizman, E. (2011). *The Least of All Possible Evils: Humanitarian Violence from Arendt to Gaza*. London and New York: Verso.

Wolfe, P. (2006). Settler Colonialism and the Elimination of the Native. *Journal of Genocide Research*, 8(4), 387–409.

Wright, G. (1991). *The Politics of Design in French Colonial Urbanism*. Chicago: Chicago University Press.

Yacobi, H. (2015). *Israel and Africa: A Genealogy of Moral Geography*. Abington: Routledge.

Yiftachel, O., & Yacobi, H. (2003). Urban Ethnocracy: Ethnicization and the Production of Space in an Israeli Mixed City, *Environment and Planning D: Society and Space*, 21(6), 673–693.

PART 2

SHELTER

CHAPTER 5

At Home in the Centre?

Spatial Appropriation and Horizons of Homemaking in Reception Facilities for Asylum Seekers

Paolo Boccagni
Università di Trento – ERC StG HOMInG, Italy

Introduction

This chapter aims to advance the study of the lived experience of asylum reception facilities in Europe by discussing the determinants, potential and impact of homemaking practices in the everyday life of people 'in waiting', like asylum seekers. Understandably, refugee reception is mostly addressed in terms of humanitarianism, exceptionalism and surveillance of (undesired) human mobility. However, there is a promise to investigate it also as a matter of homemaking and space appropriation, even in unhomely and temporary infrastructures.

The recent debate on refugees' housing needs covers a variety of accommodation options, arrangements and strategies. Temporary or even protracted emergency shelters are the most widespread and debated (Couldrey & Herson, 2017; Albadra et al., 2018; Scott-Smith, 2020). In the aftermath of the so-called refugee crisis in Europe, however, research has increasingly been done on less emergency-driven housing arrangements, primarily in the form of state-funded accommodation. Innovative case studies have illuminated, particularly in Northern Europe, the influence of infrastructural housing quality on residents' wellbeing (Hauge et al., 2017), on their residential satisfaction (including that of families and minors) (Archambault, 2012; Karlsson, 2019), and on the possibility for them to feel "at home" in typically unhomely places (Gronseth & Thorshaug, 2018). Throughout this literature the focus on the lived experience of asylum seekers is paralleled with an emerging interest in "what buildings do" (Gronseth et al., 2016): the variety of "affective and emotional states" that the built environment "triggers" among residents (Zill et al., 2019), given their social and legal predicament, but also as a reflex of different views and practices about the functions and aims of asylum centres.

While the development of accommodation for asylum seekers is rather variable and context-specific due to its path-dependency with national welfare and immigrant policies, there are good reasons to revisit it through home studies (Blunt & Dowling, 2006; Brun, 2012). In this optic research has been done on the (un)intended consequences of the ways of designing, allocating and using reception facilities (Willems et al., 2020), but also on their potential contribution to refugees' recovery of a sense of home or, at least, of domesticity (e.g. Rainisio, 2015). Both questions may seem hardly relevant wherever far more basic sheltering needs are disregarded in the first place. Yet, their significance as an ideal aim for asylum reception and the very real need of refugees – as much as anybody else – to make themselves at home (Brun, 2012; Boccagni et al., 2020) are enough for a critical conceptual inquiry. Even in inhospitable housing arrangements refugees tend to assess their conditions, including what is lacking or missing there, through the metrics of what 'home' means to them and of the aspiration to achieve it (van der Horst, 2004; Hauge et al., 2017).

Particularly at the early stages of the status determination process asylum centres have a relatively narrow mandate (Kreichauf, 2018): to control forms of (unwanted) mobility, ensure residents' basic social protection and, at best, facilitate their socialisation into the rules and language of the receiving society. Yet, asylum centres may end up also being sites, and possibly co-producers, of forms of homemaking from both "above" and "below", which I systematically explore in this chapter.

Following an overview of the recent literature on asylum seekers' residential trajectories and on the elusive meaning of home inside them, I analyse, first, how reception facilities can assume relatively home-like contours, whether by design or – more often – following the spontaneous initiative of their residents; second, the constraints to which homemaking in asylum centres is subject, but also the need for a non-essentialised and processual view of home, in order to appreciate both refugees' agency and the influence of the built environment. The temporal, spatial and relational bases of their "struggles for home" (Jansen & Lofving, 2008), parallel to their housing trajectories, are critically discussed along these lines. As I conclude, the opportunities for asylum seekers to cultivate and reproduce a sense of home on the move matter as much as, or more than, the abstract and disembodied home-like features of the built environment in which they are hosted.

Home, homing and asylum reception centres

Being forced to leave what used to be home and having to reconstitute it anew under conditions of more or less protracted uncertainty is an all too obvious fact at the root of forced migration. Likewise, the absence of a single and fixed place

Figure 1. A drawing behind a bench in front of the entrance to a refugee centre, taken by author.

suitable to be called home in the here and now is recurrently emphasised in refugee studies. However, the very notion of home can be problematised and conceived as disjointed from its subtext of ascription and fixity (Malkki, 1992), with critical awareness of the over-idealised imaginaries associated with it. Following this reflexive exercise, a space for conceptual reframing emerges: one which I propose to fill with the concept of *homing* (Boccagni, 2017). This is an invitation to see home as an ongoing need and attempt to attach a sense of security, familiarity and control to the place(s) in which people live. Reframed along these lines, home retains all of its existential significance for the forcibly displaced. At the same time it operates as a category to make better sense of their potential to interact with the places, built environments and material cultures they encounter over time. Home, then, is no longer just a matter of loss or domicide – even for those forcibly on the move. It is rather an assemblage of meaningful

materialities, emotions and relationships; a battlefield in which refugees' attempts at home*making* are negotiated; a question of complex interactions between refugees' countries of origin, present living conditions and ideals about belonging, inclusion and self-achievement (Brun & Fabos, 2015).

At all of these levels home may not be one place, but is definitely a matter of relations with places – including those at odds with people's own ideals or memories of home and, most critically, those where they end up "in waiting" (Rotter, 2014; Bendixsen & Eriksen, 2018). Such places have an influence of their own, which is more ambiguous than the mainstream representation of refugee camps would entail. Even the most unhomely of asylum centres has something to say on the constructions and negotiations of home among the forcibly displaced. Indeed, the lived experience of refugee centres can be better understood by reading into the intersection of home and forced migration studies (Boccagni, 2017; Hart et al., 2018; Dossa and Golubovic, 2019).

Following this premise, at the core of this chapter is a conceptual investigation into asylum seekers' "struggle for home" (Jansen & Lofving, 2008; Gronseth & Thorshaug, 2018) from within reception centres. A more or less extended stay there is just one step in the "complex and life-long process of recreating home" of the forcibly displaced (Neumark, 2013: 244). Living in a centre provides a degree of material safety, but it also reproduces a sense of protracted, potentially traumatising uncertainty about residents' future life prospects, directions and locations (Thorshaug & Brun, 2019). It demands, therefore, a conceptual inquiry – and then more empirical research – as a social setting in itself.

While the housing careers of forcibly displaced people are fragmented and discontinuous, an analytical continuum can be traced between all ranges of housing provision: from informal settlements to first-reception shelters and camps for more or less protracted displacement (Turner, 2015), to more structured and "autonomous" housing facilities, including ordinary dwellings. Each of these arrangements can be explored in the light of the interaction between infrastructural qualities and the possibility, ability and interest of residents to draw more than a sense of basic protection from it.

Against a background of "uneven geography of asylum accommodation" all over Europe (Zill et al., 2019), the focus of this chapter is on formal, state-funded reception centres, where asylum seekers are hosted and entitled to some basic assistance while their applications are assessed. Major differences exist between and within countries regarding the "architectural, functional and socio-spatial determinations" of asylum reception infrastructures (Kreichauf, 2018, p. 18). Yet, their commonalities in social organisation, institutional mandate and target populations are enough to form a conceptual framework around notions of domesticity and homemaking, preliminary to comparative analysis.

Exploring the experience of home in formal reception centres for asylum seekers in Europe is obviously not the same as discussing home in refugee camps (e.g. Dudley, 2011; Hart et al., 2018) or in makeshift accommodation in poorer countries (e.g. Kellett, 2002) or in Europe itself (Giorgi & Fasulo, 2013). Although there are functional equivalents between "camps" and "asylum centres", the former category tends to be used mostly for the Global South and the latter is more used for state-funded reception structures in the Global North. Certainly, the distinction (as much as the single labels) is politically contentious (Kreichauf, 2018). It has to do less with geography than with a broad difference in infrastructural quality, and possibly in the degree of separateness or interaction with the surrounding environments.

Even in the most inclusive and supportive of refugee centres the remit of reception initiatives remains limited. Exogenous factors, such as status recognition (and then integration and labour market policies), and endogenous factors, such as the dislocation of refugees' kin ties and of their life projects over time, shape their future life chances far more than housing as such. Even so, exploring the subjective experience of an asylum centre is not a pointless or irrelevant effort. There is a merit in investigating how infrastructural variables, location and interaction (or lack thereof) with the surrounding environment affect residents' wellbeing (Hauge et al., 2017), and under what conditions such an infrastructure, or particular sections of it, can be invested with the "positive" meanings, values and emotions that the word "home" evokes (van der Horst, 2004; Archambault, 2012). A case can then be made for the homemaking capacity of reception facilities to affect newcomers' wellbeing and their ability to "navigate" the steps of their mobility trajectories (Vigh, 2006).

No one *chooses* to live in an asylum reception centre. While staying there is generally not compulsory, it is still a requirement for asylum seekers to obtain assistance while their applications are under scrutiny, and possibly in the subsequent stages (e.g. the appeal process). As the literature shows (Zill et al., 2019), refugee reception and housing facilities are generally made out of "leftover", poorly maintained old and vacant buildings, originally devised for different purposes and target populations (e.g. barracks, motels, hospitals, schools, etc.). Already by way of appearance these structures exhibit an institutional aim of deterrence – asylum seekers should not feel welcome or encouraged to stay unless they really need to – and embody the expectation of a provisional and conditional stay. Temporariness and conditionality, that is, the time and effort needed to "check" whether an application is "legitimate", are instrumental in justifying the use of sub-standard accommodation for what is treated as a sub-standard population, confined in a spatial and legal "permanent state of exception" (Agamben, 1998, p. 168).

Nonetheless, the infrastructural and spatial organisation of an asylum centre is neither a neutral background, nor one with a function of pure surveillance and differential treatment – were it even Whyte's (2011) "myopticon", an arrangement instrumental to "keep[ing] temporality on hold" in residents' everyday life (Thorshaug, 2019). While the *raison d'être* of these buildings rewards inertia and militates against any substantive investment to improve them, this is not always the whole story. As some recent case studies have shown, these infrastructures are sometimes readapted, and ideally made more "domestic", in terms of infrastructural maintenance, but also through organisational aspects:

the use of semi-public space for gatherings, the availability of cooking facilities for residents, or the possibility for them to decorate space in meaningful ways (Gronseth et al., 2016; Vandevoordt, 2017; Willems et al., 2020). As or more important is that the scope for refugees to cultivate meaningful ways of dwelling is shaped by the relative control on their life routines and use of day-to-day spaces, as well as by the possibility of sharing them with family members, friends or other people with a similar ethnonational, language or cultural background. From the viewpoint of local authorities and service providers there is then some scope for *homemaking from above,* involving both housing quality and "home-like qualities". This has constitutive limitations, and yet deserves more attention in an optic of residential "satisfaction". Moreover, while individuals or families live in a centre for a more or less extended (and sometimes undefined) time span, they may develop an emotionally meaningful, if ambiguous, relationship with the built environment in which they live. This also depends on a variety of influences: everyday interaction with other guests, the social inclusion programmes (if any) in which they take part, and the broader scope for interaction with the surrounding local communities.

The point, then, is not whether an asylum centre can ever be called home in an emotionally 'thick' sense as opposed to a merely descriptive one. Instead, the point is to see whether and how temporary reception infrastructures, which by definition conflate control and care work, can facilitate meaningful forms of homemaking under circumstances of provisionality (Thorshaug & Brun, 2019), liminality (Ghorashi et al., 2018) and marginality (Boccagni et al., 2020) for their guests-as-residents.

The challenge of housing quality and the lures of home-like qualities

Even in generally unhomely places, housing conditions have their own influence on the well-being of residents. This holds for spatial and infrastructural aspects like the maintenance of a building, its relative overcrowding, its location, but also the private space available in it. In principle, relatively decentralised and small-scale housing options seem to "provide more homely qualities than institution-like buildings" (Hauge et al., 2017, p. 12; Thorshaug, 2019). Yet, infrastructural variables tell only part of the story of housing quality. Equally important is the lived experience inside: how, if at all, a centre acknowledges and is adapted to the routines, needs and tastes of the residents; how open and flexible it is to the use of semi-public space for informal gathering, playing, praying, and so forth. In all of these respects, purposeful attempts can be made to make semi-public spaces intelligible, meaningful and accessible, rather than leaving them as a neutral backdrop or a provisional area of transit.

In essence, the perceived quality of housing has to do with the degree of privacy and autonomy embedded in reception facilities and in their organisational cultures: all that residents are allowed to do there on their own and the physical and symbolic room for manoeuvre they have in doing so (Willems et al., 2020). Cases in point involve the possibility for them to cook by themselves, possibly recovering their traditional ways of doing so (including the kind of food), or to invite outsiders – "guests" of the "guests" – into their own rooms (van der Horst, 2004; Rainisio, 2015; Vandevoordt, 2017). This resonates with the literature on home studies, which emphasises the importance of privacy, autonomy and control for residents to develop some sense of home even in unconventional settings (Dovey, 2005; Giorgi & Fasulo, 2013; Easthope et al., 2015). Achieving a balance between "privacy" and "connectedness" (Willems et al., 2020) is then a key challenge for asylum centres, whenever they aim to be something more than the functional equivalent of a car park for people "in waiting" (Bendixsen & Eriksen, 2018).

Of course, a participatory and user-sensitive approach is not without its contradictions. This is not only because it runs counter to the engrained practice of most reception facilities. More fundamentally, it is utterly irrelevant for the essential counterpart of reception – the institutional apparatus in charge of the legal processing of asylum applications, which is hardly intelligible from within the centre itself (Whyte, 2011). Moreover, any top-down attempt to improve reception spaces beyond a basic standard may end in zero-sum games: what makes some residents feel more at home might make others less so. Housing itself, let alone feeling at home, is generally constructed by residents as far less of a priority than getting "the papers" and "a job". Indeed, discussing with them "the distance between their current condition and a desirable housing situation, trying to give to this latter a concrete and intelligible form" (Rainisio, 2015, p. 12) may end in tokenism or in wishful thinking. Residents' consultation without empowerment tends to reproduce disorientation and frustration whenever people articulate housing aspirations that are utterly incompatible with the place they live in; or, more critically, when they fail (or are not in a position) to articulate any positive and focused desire. In turn, residents' ability to use and interest in "actively" using these degrees of freedom is highly variable, depending also on their socio-demographics, legal conditions and position in the life course and across migration networks.

All these critical remarks, however, should not obscure another empirical fact: as a number of ethnographies have illustrated (Boccagni et al., 2020), microforms of homemaking "from below" do take place and demand more attention, even within the constitutive limitations of everyday life in reception centres.

Resident homemaking and beautification from below

Over time, as residents find out that their stay, while being temporary, may be less short-lived than expected, there is an increased likelihood that they will engage in active, albeit "reluctant", forms of homemaking (Gronseth & Thorshaug, 2018). Under the label of *homemaking* I group different sets of practices that articulate an endeavour to bring the lived environment closer to a sense of normality, by adapting it to one's needs, interests or tastes. These practices make up a pragmatic field of politics of the everyday, out of the micro ways in which people approach their residential circumstances as more than instrumental affordances – indeed, as something they expect to bear the mark of their own use, presence and possibly appropriation.

Homemaking involves all "attempts" – whether successful or not – "to make spaces 'ordinary' through the processes… that try to reclaim 'normal' life and create a 'home'" (Sanyal, 2014, p. 570). Within an asylum centre this results in a highly constrained, variable and context-dependent process, which still goes some way beyond a simple habituation – the sense of familiarity people gain out of virtually any environment, out of the extended time spent there. The point, then, is not only that residents take initiatives to "fill their days with meaningful activities" rather than surrendering to their structural emptiness (Ghorashi et al., 2018). The question is also how, in doing so, they rely on the built environment and reshape it by carving out some niche of more or less ephemeral and exclusive domesticity. I propose to group these practices, which can be negotiated on all scales from close corporeal proximity up to an entire infrastructure, into four heuristic categories:

- Ways of *improving* space, thereby making it more comfortable and suitable to the preferences, tastes and needs of one particular resident or a group of them;
- Ways of *enabling cultural reproduction* and *biographical continuity* (Archambault, 2012), wherever residents shape their everyday activities – eating, dressing, cultural consumption – in ways or through materials that mirror their lifestyles prior to migration;
- Ways of *privatising* space, as they try to earmark, in terms of functional or emotional value, some portion of anonymous, impersonal or at best collective spaces by creating thresholds of privacy and intimacy inside them. This may be done with the aim of gaining more space for oneself and one's belongings, for purposes of sociability and prayer, or anyway to "make the space say something about you" (Cresswell, 2004, p. 2);
- Ways of *beautification,* out of any attempt aesthetically and sensorially to improve the everyday living space by bringing it closer to one's tastes and domestic cultures (Neumark, 2013). Wall decorations, curtains, carpets, par-

ticular objects being displayed in particular ways are cases in point. In fact, beautification is worthy of more elaboration, if only because the bulk of research on it has been done on mainstream middle-class households (Miller, 2001; see also, on immigrant house interiors, Dibbits, 2009; Levin, 2014). Yet, there is no reason to exclude from its remit more marginal and marginalised housing environments, including refugee centres (van der Horst, 2004), squats (Giorgi & Fasulo, 2013) and improvised informal settlements (Mavrommatis, 2018), not to mention large refugee camps (Hart et al., 2018).

Acts of spatial appropriation, such as ordering one's personal objects in a purposeful sequence or attaching a picture or an image close to one's bed place, provide valuable hints for the study of the residents' struggles for home. They reveal the resilience of a need to exert some control over everyday space and time in order to draw from it a sense of predictability and security (Douglas, 1991; Neumark, 2013). Moreover, spatial appropriation points to people's attempts to personalise a place by infusing it with their own sense of identity and taste, including references to their biographies. This is less a matter of aesthetics than of the retention of some ability and desire to make oneself at home, or of a need and desire for "homing", no matter where.

Figure 2. A prayer rug hanging on the balcony of a refugee centre, taken by author.

In fact, refugees' attempts to bring their day-to-day life environments closer to their own tastes and desires are severely constrained by their living conditions. Furthermore, any micro-attempt to improve a shared and communal space in aesthetic and value-laden terms can turn out to be contentious. It articulates different and potentially contrasting aesthetics and tastes, but also habits and lifestyles. Research into the fine-grained texture of these micro forms of homemaking reveals symbolic and identity tensions that have latent political implications in everyday interactions within and between groups of residents.

More fundamentally, space appropriation has no single and obvious interpretation (Boccagni & Duyvendak, 2021). The absence of any visible form of beautification in a room does not merely articulate a sense of estrangement and alienation from that place. It can also be an expression of active resistance to accepting it as *one's place*, hence as an ordinary living setting that "deserves" to be beautified (Thourshaug & Brun, 2019). It is, in other words, a form of unhoming in the here and now, whereby all that has to do with home is projected in an aspired future that should take place elsewhere. Following this critical point, homemaking in an asylum centre does not necessarily mean that residents are reconciled with it, nor that they draw much wellbeing out of it, even while it is the less worse option available.

While studying homemaking in a centre does illuminate people's identifications, agency and aspirations, it cannot exhaust the field of what home means to them, nor of their efforts and opportunities to achieve it. After all, there is no need to reduce the emotional and practical scope of home to anybody's living place – even less to a temporary and disadvantaged one. Neither the temporality nor the spatiality of homemaking can be reduced to the qualities of even the best of refugee housing facilities.

Homemaking and fragmented temporalities: Fixed artefacts vs. shifting life trajectories

It is important to appreciate, first of all, the intersection between the temporality of refugee housing and life trajectories (Fontanari, 2017) and the temporality of home itself. There is a tension between any attempt to make asylum facilities home-like, including those enacted by residents themselves, and the temporariness of their stay. Fragmentation in housing pathways, legal indeterminacy and temporal suspension all militate against emotional investment in an asylum centre – although mere habituation may result in people leaving more "traces" than they perhaps would admit (Thorshaug & Brun, 2019).

As extensive literature shows, feeling at home in a place has to do not only with the life conditions and opportunities available, but also with the sheer amount of time spent there (Blunt & Dowling, 2006; Boccagni et al., 2020). Making oneself at home takes time, even more so under new and disadvantaged circumstances (Gram-Hanssen & Bech-Danielsen, 2012). There is no inherent reason why people who are or perceive themselves as "on the go" – for instance, newcomer asylum seekers, and those who aim at secondary mobility trajectories (e.g. from South or

East Europe to North Europe) – should cultivate a strong attachment to any place in particular. Even if they did, this would not necessarily be in their own interest. In this sense, feeling at home is an irremediably long-term aim – one that fundamentally depends, in the case of asylum seekers, on obtaining a legal status. In the short term, people with mobile and fragmented life trajectories, and often traumatic past experiences, may see little point in cultivating a meaningful attachment to any place in particular, let alone 'beautifying' it. Home in the here and now may even be a source of distress which is coped with by means of recollections from the past and projects (or dreams) for the future (Kabachnik et al., 2010).

Having said this, there is no reason to reduce the discussion on homemaking in reception facilities to this basic point. Rather than reading refugee life circumstances as a matter of lack-of-home (following their initial loss-of-home), there is a promise in reframing them along a continuum of *degrees of homeliness*. This leads us to explore whether, how and when a place or parts of it are "homely enough" for different users, with different purposes, on different occasions. Temporary hosting facilities can then be revisited as more or less hospitable venues for rehearsing a variety of homemaking practices, potentially transferable elsewhere over time, parallel to refugees' housing careers.

Once in a 'homing' perspective we shift from an essentialised vision of home as full and stable achievement to the study of the conditions that make for a good enough home experience at least intermittently, we are in a position to appreciate 'homely bubbles': that is, the circumstances to which residents attach a sense of security, familiarity and control, as discussed above. Even inside refugee centres, people produce some form of home as "an ontologically secure microsphere in the here and now, whilst nourishing bonds with a life that was left behind. Home is not so much a place, but a situation where people, objects, scents and tastes feel familiar, safe and warm" (Vandervoordt, 2017, p. 616). However, any 'bubble' rests on boundaries being marked, and possibly on forms of home un-making being enacted, towards other residents or groups of residents. A reasonable aim to be pursued in running reception centres, then, is facilitating meaningful opportunities of homemaking, but also mediating between them. And, indeed, the aim should be less homemaking in itself than cultivating the capability to enact and transfer it elsewhere and in the future.

Beyond Protection and Privacy: Home as a Matter of Social Relationships, Recognition and Participation

Along with the temporality of homemaking it is important to appreciate its multiscalarity. The constellation of circumstances people associate with home need not overlap fully with their private or domestic space, if any. There is an aspect of feeling-at-home that exceeds domestic life and even the achievement of better housing conditions (Blunt & Dowling, 2006; Boccagni & Duyvendak, 2021). Home as a social experience can embrace different social, spatial and territorial scales of reference, including – and most ambivalently for asylum seekers – the country of origin, or some parts of it, as the only "real home" (Brun & Fabos, 2015).

If making oneself at home rests on decent housing but is not reducible to it, pursuing this ideal aim by focusing only on reception centres would mean over-emphasising the private and individualised aspects of home, relative to its social and public side. Having access to some private space in an asylum centre is little solace if asylum seekers have no meaningful relationships outside it, ending up stuck in their own "thoughts" night and day (Fontanari, 2017; Thorshaug, 2019). Feeling somewhat at home in an alien context depends on cultivating relationships that reach beyond the walls of a reception place; indeed, on gaining recognition, rights and, increasingly, the ability to navigate through the public sphere of the receiving community.

Many case studies of refugee reception tell about centres that are purposely isolated or invisibilised from the surrounding neighbourhoods. While this has to do with well-known external pressures and constraints, a major point remains: the success of service providers in facilitating refugee interaction with the receiving communities is critical to the residents' chances of making themselves at home over time. Investing in community work and development is as (or perhaps more) central to this aim as user-led adaptations in asylum facilities. Even inside the latter, after all, the chances of embedding some sense of home are strongly dependent on the social relationships being cultivated there. It is not by chance that, for instance, the refugee informants of Archambault (2012), who had recently been moved from an asylum centre to an "ordinary" dwelling, deemed it essential to keep in touch with those who had remained there. As the author points out, "feelings of 'home' are more closely associated with the meaningfulness of social relationships than the physical environment, in similar quality housing" (p. 45).

Managing reception centres along inclusive lines, therefore, should ideally enhance their connections with the local community, thus paving the way for the residents' social inclusion over time (Zill et al., 2019). The potential of asylum facilities as "home-makers" has to do not only with infrastructural aspects, but also with their positive contribution to the homemaking capabilities of residents *in* and *out* of them.

Certainly, making oneself at home in the public sphere of multi-ethnic societies under the mounting pressure of nativist or utterly racist politics is no easy endeavour. More fundamentally, it is conditioned by asylum seekers' legal indeterminacy, which reduces both the scope of and the incentives for their civic participation (Boccagni & Righard, 2020). Nonetheless, there are all sorts of pragmatic, no less than normative reasons for the pursuit of refugees' home-making to transcend housing, while necessarily being based on it in the first place. Their 'real' home, if ever there will be a semi-permanent one, will not be a reception centre anyway. Cultivating their capacity to project new realistic *routes* after it may be more of a priority for their own wellbeing than investing in their *roots* in a particular local context.

Conclusion: Home as a place and as a capability to be transferred across places

A research focus on the lived experience of guests in asylum centres cannot be dissociated, of course, from a broader understanding of the international refugee regime and of people's chances to navigate internal borders in the countries where they claim asylum. Over time, obtaining and then retaining formal protection status marks the main threshold for asylum claimants to be able to make themselves at home anyway. It is the attachment to a sense of *hope* to a place that informs and nourishes a sense of *home* to grow up there, as research in migration and refugee studies has illustrated (Brun, 2015; Boccagni et al., 2020). That said, what happens in between is far more than empty waiting – even inside asylum centres – and deserves in-depth analysis in its own right. The argument in this article has been precisely meant as a framework for comparative research along these lines.

Such a framework invites us to study the interplay between three subtexts of homemaking in asylum centres: a *pragmatic* one, related to people's ordinary need to improve the places where they happen to live on their own terms (at least if their habituation is enough to acknowledge that, for the time being, these are *their* places); a *policy-relevant* one, since the dialectic between perceived homeliness and estrangement of the built environment facilitates a better understanding of housing quality and residential satisfaction, as a matter of emplaced wellbeing (or lack thereof); and an *existential* one, for everyday life in a reception centre marks a significant transition, although not necessarily a durable improvement, in the housing pathways and in the long-term homing concerns of forcibly displaced people.

In all these respects, writing about asylum centres in general terms is clearly a heuristic simplification. Empirical and comparative research needs to take account of national and local specificities regarding legal frameworks, mandates, infrastructures, educational purposes (if any) and degrees of openness to the broader communities. However, there is no reason to look only at refugees' lives *within* a centre. Rather, the relative accessibility of the surrounding urban or rural communities, in terms of infrastructures no less than interpersonal and group networks, in itself requires attention. This also calls for stronger collaboration between research on housing, home and social welfare in order to understand and facilitate refugees' orientation to the local communities of settlement and, over time, their life projects and trajectories. That said, and as long as the existential question of home can be addressed within a refugee centre, this should be with a long-term purpose – not only making a place home-like, which is bound to be a partial and contentious endeavour anyway, but also empowering people to make (any) place more home-like, as part and parcel of their homing trajectories over time and space.

Acknowledgements

Research for this chapter was done within the scope of HOMInG-The Home-Migration Nexus, a project funded by the European Research Council (ERC-StG 678456, 2016-2021), and of HOASI, a MIUR-funded project on home and asylum seekers in Italy. Both projects are based at the University of Trento, Italy. More information is available at homing.soc.unitn.it.

References

Agamben, G. (1998). *Homo sacer*. Stanford: Stanford University Press.
Albadra, D., Coley, D., Hart, J. (2018). Toward healthy housing for the displaced. *The Journal of Architecture, 23*(1), 115-36.
Archambault, J. (2012). 'It can be good here too': Home and continuity in refugee children's narratives of settlement. *Children's Geographies, 10*(1), 35-48.
Bendixsen, S., & Eriksen, T. (2018). Time and the Other: Waiting and Hope among Irregular Migrants. In M. Janeja & A. Bandak (eds.), *Ethnographies of Waiting: Doubt, Hope and Uncertainty* (pp. 87-112), London: Bloomsbury.
Boccagni, P. (2017). *Migration and the search for home*. New York: Palgrave.
Boccagni, P., & Duyvendak, J. W. (2021). Homemaking in the public. On the scales and stakes of framing, feeling, and claiming extra-domestic space as "home". *Sociology Compass, 15*(6), 1-14.
Boccagni, P., Pérez-Murcia, L. E., & Belloni, M. (2020). *Thinking Home on the Move: A Conversation across Disciplines*. London: Emerald.
Boccagni, P., & Righard, E. (2020). Social work with refugee and displaced populations in Europe. *European Journal of Social Work, 23*(3), 375-83.
Blunt, A. & Dowling, R. (2006). *Home*. London: Routledge.

Brun, C. (2012). Home in temporary dwellings. In S. Smith (ed.), *International Encyclopedia of Housing and Home*. London: Elsevier.

Brun, C. (2015). Active waiting and changing hopes. *Social Analysis, 59*(1), 19-37.

Brun, C., & Fabos, A. (2015). Making homes in limbo? *Refuge, 31*(1), 5-17.

Couldrey, M. & Herson, M. (eds.). (2017). Shelter in displacement. *Forced Migration Review, 55*.

Cresswell, T. (2004). *Place*. London: Blackwell.

Dibbits, H. (2009). Furnishing the salon: Symbolic ethnicity and performative practices in Moroccan-Dutch domestic interiors. *International Journal of Consumer Studies, 33*, 550-57.

Dossa, P. & Golubovic, J. (2019). Reimagining home in the wake of displacement. *Studies in Social Justice, 13*(1), 171-86.

Douglas, M. (1991). The idea of a home. *Social Research, 58*(1), 287-307.

Dovey, K. (2005). Home as paradox. In G. Rowles, H. Chaudhury (eds.), *Home and identity in later life: International perspectives* (pp. 361-369). New York: Springer.

Dudley, S. (2011). Feeling at home: Producing and consuming things in Karenni refugee camps on the Thai-Burma border. *Population, Space and Place, 17*, 742-55.

Easthope, H., Lui, E., Judd, B., & Burnley, I. (2015). Feeling at home in a multigenerational household. *Housing, Theory and Society, 32*(2), 151-70.

Fontanari, E. (2017). It's my life. The temporalities of refugees and asylum-seekers within the European border regime. *Etnografia e Ricerca Qualitativa, 1*, 25-54.

Giorgi, S. & Fasulo, A. (2013). Transformative homes: Squatting and furnishing as sociocultural projects. *Home Cultures, 10*(2), 111-34.

Gram-Hanssen, K. & Bech-Danielsen, C. (2012). Creating a new home: Somali, Iraqi and Kurdish immigrants and their homes in Danish social housing. *Journal of Housing and the Built Environment, 27*, 89-103.

Gronseth, A. S. & Thorshaug, R. (2018). Struggling for home where home is not meant to be. mimeo.

Gronseth, A., Stoa, E., Thorshaug, R., & Hauge, A. (2016). *Housing Qualities and Effects on Identity and Well-being: Theoretical perspective for interdisciplinary research on asylum seeker reception centres*. Lillehammer University College, Research Report no. 169/2016.

Hart, J., Paskiewicz, N. & Albadra, D. (2018). Shelter as home? Syrian homemaking in Jordanian refugee camps. *Human Organization, 77*(4), 371-380.

Hauge, A. L., Stoa, E. & Denizou, K. (2017). Framing outsidedness: Aspects of housing quality in decentralized reception centres for asylum seekers in Norway. *Housing, Theory and Society, 34*(1), 1-20.

Jansen, S. & Lofving, S. (eds.). (2008). *Struggles for home: Violence, hope and the movement of people*. Oxford: Berghahn.

Kabachnik, P., Regulska, J. & Mitchneck, B. (2010). When and where is home? *Journal of Refugee Studies, 23*(3), 316-36.

Karlsson, S. (2019). You said 'home' but we don't have a 'house': Children's lived rights and politics in an asylum centre in Sweden. *Children's Geographies,17*(1), 64-75.

Kellett, P. (2002). The construction of home in the informal city. *Journal of Romance Studies, 2*(3), 17-31.

Kreichauf, R. (2018). From forced migration to forced arrival. *Comparative Migration Studies, 6*, 1-22.

Levin, I. (2014). Intersectionality in the migrant house. *Journal of Intercultural Studies, 35*(4), 421-41.

Malkki, L. (1992). National Geographic: The Rooting of Peoples and the Territorialization of National Identity among Scholars and Refugees. *Cultural Anthropology, 7*(1), 24-44.

Mavrommatis, G. (2018). Grasping the meaning of integration in an era of (forced) mobility. *Mobilities, 13*(6), 861-75.

Neumark, D. (2013). Drawn to Beauty: The practice of house-beautification as home-making among the forcibly displaced. *Housing, Theory and Society, 30*(3), 237-61

Rainisio, N. (2015). These places do not understand us: Environmental psychology of the refugee centers. In E. Giunta, A. Rebaglio (eds.), *Design research on temporary homes. Hospitable places for homeless, immigrants and refugees* (pp. 72-89). AADR.

Sanyal, R. (2014). Urbanizing Refuge: Interrogating Spaces of Displacement. *International Journal of Urban and Regional Research, 38*(2), 558-70.

Scott-Smith, T. (2019). Beyond the boxes: Refugee shelter and the humanitarian politics of life. *American Ethnologist, 46*(4), 509-521.

Thorshaug, R. O. (2019). Arrival In-between: Analyzing the Lived Experiences of Different Forms of Accommodation for Asylum Seekers in Norway. In B. Meeus, K. Arnaut & B. van Heur (eds.), *Arrival infrastructures: Migration and Urban Social Mobilities* (pp. 207-227). London: Palgrave.

Thorshaug, R. O., & Brun, C. (2019). Temporal injustice and re-orientations in asylum reception centres in Norway. *Fennia, 197*(2), 232-48.

Turner, S. (2015). What is a refugee camp? *Journal of Refugee Studies, 29*(2), 139-148.

Vandevoordt, R. (2017). The politics of food and hospitality. *Journal of Refugee Studies, 30*(4), 605-21.

Van der Horst, H. (2004). Living in a reception centre: the search for home in an institutional setting. *Housing, Theory and Society, 21*, 36-46.

Vigh, H. (2009). Wayward migration. *Ethnos, 74*(1), 91-109.

Whyte, Z. (2011). Enter the myopticon: Uncertain surveillance in the Danish asylum system. *Anthropology Today, 27*(3), 18-21.

Willems, S., De Smet, S., & Heylighen, A. (2020). Seeking a balance between privacy and connectedness in housing for refugees. *Journal of Housing and the Built Environment, 35*, 45-46.

Zill, M., van Liempt, I., Spierings, B., & Hooimeijer, P. (2019). Uneven geographies of asylum accommodation. *Migration Studies,* mny049.

CHAPTER 6

Bare Shelter

The Layered Spatial Politics of Inhabiting Displacement

Irit Katz
University of Cambridge, U.K.

Introduction

It could be a sleeping bag hung around a bunk bed, forming a more intimate space in a shipping container shared by a group of refugees in a state-created camp. It could also be an improvised kitchen added by a family of forced migrants to their prefabricated timber emergency shelter, so they could cook their own meals. It might be an ad hoc business, such as a grocery shop opened in a shack previously used only for accommodation in a makeshift refugee camp. Or it could be a mural which was carefully drawn to decorate the external walls of a shared ephemeral shelter. These, and many other forms of spatial adaptations which change prefabricated or makeshift shelters, are part of the variety of ways in which displaced people shape and alter their intimate spaces in institutional and makeshift camps around the world. These shelters are often created as temporary structures of protection in transitory and often precarious sites which are expected eventually to disappear. Their inhabitants, however, who have already experienced losing their homes at least once in their country of origin, invest time, effort and sometimes capital in transforming their shelters into more habitable spaces, even if their spatial endeavours will exist for only a short period of time.

While displaced people live in a wide range of shelters from squats in abandoned buildings to rented apartments, emergency shelters are often created as part of designated and in many cases temporary institutional or makeshift 'sites'. Whether they are called 'refugee camps', 'hospitality centres', 'hotspots' or 'humanitarian facilities', such confined sites are connected to the world around them only through particular and often strictly controlled human and material infrastructures. They supply the basic necessities for their residents, such as food and basic shelter, while at the same time disconnecting their residents from the everyday environments, economies and forms of living around them. These sites and the shelters within them form dehumanising spaces in which the residents are seen as objects of control and conditioned care (Katz, 2019). In many cases, however, the inhabitants of these sites and shelters immediately and substantially act to change their anonymising and dehumanising environments through various forms of spatial adjustment and re-appropriation.

In camps in Northern France, created primarily during the so-called migration 'crisis' between 2015 and 2017, either for or by those attempting to cross the Channel to the UK, residents began to improve their temporary homes as soon as they moved in (Katz, 2019). In the La Linier camp in Grande-Synthe near Dunkirk the repetitive prefabricated timber shelters created for the refugees by Médecins Sans Frontières (MSF) were significantly expanded upon on the first day they were occupied (Katz, 2017, 2020; Gueguen-Tiel & Katz, 2018). Not far from there, in the makeshift Calais 'Jungle' camp, shelters were carefully built, repurposed and decorated inside and out by their inhabitants. In both camps, importantly, shelters were re-appropriated to create ad hoc businesses such as barbers' shops, grocers' shops and restaurants, while they were also used for habitation (Turner, 2016; Guguen, 2017). With the alterations of these shelters, their sites were transformed too, turning from camps composed of identical prefabricated units, or from camps of scattered tents and shacks, into more defined spaces of human living.

What is the meaning of these and other spatial actions conducted by displaced people to re-appropriate their emergency shelters? Should they be dismissed as a collection of random material and spatial adaptations born out of bare necessities, or could they be considered as a set of actions which together accumulate a profound political meaning? This chapter critically engages with the work of the political theorist, Hannah Arendt, to examine the possible political meaning of the spatial alterations of emergency shelters by the forced migrants who inhabit them. Arendt's work is for a number of reasons particularly relevant for questions on the political meaning of spaces of displacement. First, Arendt is deeply engaged with critical studies on refugees, related to her own personal experience of refuge. In addition, her work imaginatively rethinks the meaning of the political sphere in the modern world while also conceptualising politics spatially. Her work is also concerned with the relationship between the private and public realms in the creation of the political sphere, a topic which is especially relevant for understanding spaces of displacement. Arendt's work had a substantial influence on thinkers who are concerned with displacement, including its political and spatial meanings, amongst whom are the philosopher Giorgio Agamben (1998) and others (e.g. Rancière, 2004; Krause, 2008;

Staeheli et al. 2009; Schaap, 2011; Dikeç, 2013; Katz, 2015; Bialasiewicz 2017; Beeckmans 2019; Singh, 2020), and this chapter aims to add to these interventions.

The chapter discusses the political meaning of inhabiting emergency shelters in three main parts. The first discusses the political meaning of the emergency shelter as a 'bare shelter', i.e., a minimal space created either for or by forced migrants only for their basic and temporary protection. The next part examines the meaning of 'bare shelter' in relation to Arendt's work, with particular emphasis on her reflections on the private and public realms, the modern state and stateless people. The last part critically discusses Arendt's thought to gain a political understanding of the spatial transformations of emergency shelters by their inhabitants. The chapter argues that spatial actions of building and re-appropriation conducted by displaced people on their emergency shelters may be considered as political actions even if they were not initially conducted as such and are visible only to those inside the camp. These actions, in which forced migrants add layers to their bare shelters, actively transform their dehumanising environment into places that are more suitable for human habitation. These spatial actions, through which forced migrants take control over their exposed spaces of refuge by actively transforming them according to their particular needs, preferences and habits, including enhancing the distinction between the private and public realms, also enable them to re-establish their agency together with their political subjectivities.

Bare shelter

A house or a home is usually considered to be a permanent dwelling which is connected to broader everyday human environments. Both are also inherently linked to dwelling as a human activity associated with inhabiting a place which we feel belongs to us and to which we feel we belong. The geographer Maria Kaika (2004), in her investigation of 'the modern western home', argues that bourgeois dwellings "became constructed not only as a line separating the inside from the outside (a house), but also as the epitome, the spatial inscription of the idea of individual freedom, a place liberated from fear and anxiety, a place supposedly untouched by social, political and natural processes, a place enjoying an autonomous and independent existence: a home" (p. 266). While this is only a naïve image of home, which is quite different from many actual homes across the globe where people suffer from many kinds of insecurities such as domestic violence and precarious living conditions, this ideal image is still important in the cultural, symbolic, emotional, social and political economies of 'the home' and its meaning. Dwelling could be acknowledged, as Ingold (2005) argues, as the Heideggerian "way of being at home in the world", but at the same time "home is not necessarily comfortable or pleasant place to be, nor are we alone there" (p. 503). Not only should the actual home therefore be considered in relation to the idealised home, exposing the inherent gap between the two, but, as we always live among other people, the home should also be considered in relation to the material worlds, histories and power relations in which it is embedded and should be perceived as part of a broader political milieu. Creating a home within often complex associations and environments, especially in contested and exclusionary contexts such as refugee camps and other spaces of displacement, could be a substantial act of world-making, and such an act, as Brickell (2012) argues, could have deep political meanings.

Forced displacement could be considered as one of the most complex contexts for home-making. In situations of displacement the feeling of home is further compromised by the often precarious and temporary shelters displaced people inhabit while they are on the move or are provisionally settled as temporary guests by often reluctant host countries. These shelters are often erected in designated 'sites' or camps which have become, as noted by Arendt and later by Agamben (1998) and many other scholars, "the routine solution for the problem of domicile" (Arendt, 1962, p. 279). If the excluding space of the camp, depicted by Agamben as the paradigmatic space of modern (bio)politics, is the inadequate replacement of the abandoned homeland, we can say that the emergency shelter is the inadequate replacement of the lost home. In the precarious and uncertain realities of displacement the role of the home as a place of belonging is often stripped down in favour of the thinner space of the mere functional minimal shelter, defined here as 'bare shelter'.

'Bare shelters' could be created in different forms and materials, whether as repetitive mass-produced prefabricated units or as makeshift shacks. What is common to these forms is that they provide only the basic protective envelop, a 'shell' that shields their residents from the elements and provides only minimal and compromised privacy from the outside world (Katz, 2020). In the container camp near the Calais Jungle (Fig. 1.) each unit was shared by twelve people who were often strangers to one another yet did not have a private space of their own and suffered as a result of what were described as "impossible living conditions" (Gueguen-Tiel & Katz, 2018). In the makeshift Jungle camp, minimal shelters were also mostly shared by inhabitants, while they were sometimes further developed to be used for additional functions such as grocers' shops (Fig. 2.). In the MSF camp near Dunkirk each of the small identical prefabricated shelters was shared by a family or by a group of people, providing no more than basic protection.

Figure 1. The container camp within the Jungle camp; photo taken by author in April 2016.

Figure 2. A grocers' shop in the Jungle camp; photo taken by author in April 2016.

All the other basic necessities of the residents of these bare shelters are usually located in other facilities in the camp (e.g. shared toilets and showers, shared kitchens or dining halls), which often lack privacy or are not provided at all. In the case of mass-produced prefabricated shelters, these are often designed for a categorical and anonymous universal place and user, with standardised and rationalised features which enable their production process to be industrialised, yet do not answer the needs of particular people in specific environments (Katz, 2020). However, when these shelters are inhabited in a particular space and by actual users with specific needs, resources and capabilities, they may be re-appropriated by their residents who change their 'bare shelter' into a temporary home.

Spatial actions related to homemaking happen very differently in camps around the world. In some contexts, such as in camps for Syrian refugees in Jordan and Iraq, prefabricated and makeshift bare shelters have been transformed into homelier spaces in environments which are sometimes deliberately created to be uninhabitable (The Refugee Republic, 2012; Doraï & Piraud-Fournet, 2018). A counter-example could be found in some Palestinian refugee camps, where inhabitants sometimes object to the improvement of their dwellings to underline their refusal to accept them as potential permanent homes, while inhabiting these spaces nevertheless with the use of particular spatial articulations (Abourahme, 2015). These actions of dwelling and the refusal to dwell, in some of these contexts, could mean a symbolic political gesture that goes well beyond the arena of the shelters in these camps, while they could also be understood as everyday spatial actions that "spill over" (ibid.) to the political in a variety of ways.

Actions of habitation often not only influence the more intimate personal spaces in the camp, but also reform the subjectivities of their inhabitants from dependant recipients of help to people who can act and change their physical and sometimes also their social and economic realities. The timber MSF shelters near Dunkirk, nicknamed 'chicken houses' by their residents to indicate their dehumanising nature and appearance, were quickly given additional ad hoc extensions and layers, some almost doubling their size. Porches and decorations were added, kitchens were constructed, storage spaces were created to support the small retail stalls placed outside, and symbols, graffiti and flags indicating the countries of origin or destination of their dwellers were drawn and attached to the shelters (Fig. 3.).

Figure 3. The prefabricated shelters in the MSF camp near Dunkirk where the reappropriation could already be seen; photo taken by author in April 2016.

How can we interpret these spatial processes of habitation as actions which are meaningful beyond the personal adaptations of private spaces? Could we account for them as political actions that not only functionally and aesthetically change the specific space of the shelters but also recreate the political subjectivities of their dwellers? In order to answer these questions I will examine the meaning of the relationship between space, displacement and the political sphere through Arendt's work. In particular, I will examine the relations between the private space and the political sphere in order to understand how the often-depoliticised meaning of the home can be politicised in precarious situations of forced displacement.

The political sphere and the private/public realms

Politics, for Arendt, are the realisation of freedom and of a fully human life. While the *raison d'être* of politics is freedom, without which "political life as such would be meaningless" (2006, p. 145), freedom itself is inherently related to the ability to begin anew. In strict contrast to Heidegger's significance of human *mortality*, Arendt focuses on *natality* as an emphasis on the human capacity for new initiatives and beginnings, a capacity that is the essence of politics and freedom, as it emphasises the distinctiveness of each human being and the ability of people to change the world accordingly. Arendt's actors are reborn when they act, and political action, like every birth, is about the unknown. The ability to begin anew is "unexpected, unpredictable, and ultimately causally inexplicable" (Arendt, 2005, pp. 111–112) and is possible "only because each man is unique, so that with each birth something uniquely new comes into the world" (Arendt, 1998, p. 178). Political action is about the gathering together of individuals who create a new human world for themselves by radically changing the old one through acting together in performative and agonistic manners (Honig, 1992), while recreating themselves through this action.

Acting in concert is fundamental to freedom and to the creation of a political sphere, as freedom and the political sphere exist only in the presence of others. "We first become aware of freedom or its opposite in our intercourse with others, not in the intercourse with ourselves", writes Arendt (2006, p. 147), emphasising that the condition of acting politically is *plurality*, and politics could happen only through action and speech in the public realm. 'Public' for Arendt signifies the enduring human world; whatever appears in public can be seen and heard by everyone and therefore constitutes a human reality. Political action "corresponds to the human condition of plurality" as it is established on our equality as unique humans: "[p]lurality is the condition of human action because we are all the same, that is, human, in such a way that nobody is ever the same as anyone else who ever lived, lives, or will live" (Arendt, 1998, p. 8). Plurality, here, is not only a numerical matter; it means that who we are is distinct, while at the same time we are always more than one. When people act politically, they act in concert as unique and free individuals and create what Arendt defines as the 'space of appearance' in which they reveal themselves to one another in their distinctness. The political space of appearance is the temporary actuality of the movement of distinct people coming together in the public realm, and it disappears when the political activities cease to exist. It is through the performative production of action in the public realm that people together create who they are, and at the same time it includes their distinctiveness and togetherness.

While for Arendt the appearance of the political sphere is dependant in the existence of the public realm, the public realm and its political potential are dependent on the existence of a separate private realm where the political has no place. This separation between the public and the private has been grounded in political thought since antiquity, as it can be seen in Aristotle who already excluded the private realm of the household from the political sphere. The household or *oikos* – the family or the home and its *oikonomia*, in which our word 'economics' as the proper place for the activities related to the maintenance of life is rooted – is established "for the supply of men's everyday wants", and was put forward in direct opposition to the *polis*, that is "the state or political community" created "for the sake of good life" (Aristotle, ca. 350 B.C.E./1999, pp. 3-6). Arendt reinforces the Aristotelian-based division between the domestic and the political, while also uncovering their actual interdependencies. Only if the household is a separate site where people live together based on their "[biological] wants and needs", can the *polis*, as the public sphere which is based on "the mastering of the necessities of life in the household" (Arendt, 1998, pp. 30-32) and where people could engage in political action as unique and equal individuals who are free from these necessities and needs, thus be created.

While the separation between the private and public political realms was, according to Arendt, fundamental to the existence of the latter, further interdependencies reveal the public realm as the 'proper' place for politics as conditioned by certain attributes of the private realm. These attributes include the household as a place with a *fixed location* of familial belonging recognised by others; "Without owning a house", writes Arendt (1998), "a man could not participate in the affairs of the world because he had no location in it which was properly his own" (pp. 29-30). Having land, property, a stable location, a privately-owned 'home base' was a means to facilitate freedom. The ability to move in the world as a free and equal individual was conditioned by the domestic realm, with *domestic* referring to one of the senses of the term *demos* in Greek, that of the *deme*, meaning a location. These separations and interdependencies between the private and public realms were reinforced both legally and spatially. The *wall* which surrounded the household was seen as vital to the *law* of the city, "which originally was identified with this boundary line" (ibid., p. 63). The separation between the private and the public also had a profound meaning for our complex existence as humans who inhabit both realms. "Privacy was like the other, the dark and hidden side of the public realm", notes Arendt, "and while to be political meant to attain the highest possibility of human existence, to have no private place of one's own (like a slave) meant to be no longer human" (ibid., p. 64).

We can identify four attributes that establish the separations but also interdependencies of the public realm and the political sphere in the private realm of the household: the provision of one's bare necessities through the economy of the household; the existence of the household as a permanent location; the household as a wall that physically and legally creates the public realm, and the existence of a private place as an intimate 'place of one's own' as a basic human need. But what happens to the private/public division and to the related political sphere when these spatial and social separations and interdependencies collapse, such as in exposed situations of forced displacement?

If we consider the 'bare shelter' of the camp, we can see the absence of all four aspects noted by Arendt as distinguishing the private realm from the public which are important for the creation of a political sphere and for human existence. Firstly, the bare shelter does not provide for the necessities of its residents, but only for their minimal physical protection from the elements, with other necessities such as food and hygienic facilities provided elsewhere in the camp. Secondly, as a temporary and anonymised space, the shelter in the camp does not provide a permanent location (*demos/deme*) but only a provisional one. Thirdly, as the shelters functioning more as scattered 'rooms' in the 'household' of the camp rather than as distinguished private realms firmly separated from the public, they do not together constitute the real or symbolic 'wall' that creates the public space outside them. Lastly, because the bare shelter is often shared by family members or individuals and its complementary units (e.g. toilets, showers, dining halls) are also shared by other people in the camp, they do not create proper private spaces 'hidden' from the public.

In these spaces of displacement and refuge the distinction between the household and the public space that Aristotle and Arendt describe as fundamental for political life is replaced by what Agamben (1998) describes as a "zone of indistinction", where "city and house became indistinguishable" (p. 188). With the camp itself produced as a major 'household' with no outside, where only mere biological life is maintained while the possibility for external political life is taken away, and the 'bare shelter' itself is perceived not as a home but only as a 'room' in the space of the camp, in which other bodily needs are being provided by 'rooms' placed separately (for hygiene and dining), this detached 'camp-household' often does not even create its own *oikonomia*, but is dependent on the humanitarian economy provided by international aid organisations supported by donor states. This 'camp-household' is also based not on freedom and equality but on confinement and hierarchy, with the displaced being produced as dependant people relying on the goodwill of the main 'provider', taking away their possibility of becoming autonomous, free and equal political actors.

What, then, is the meaning of the reappropriation of shelters in the camp? If these 'rooms' are further developed by the displaced to create 'homely' spaces, which sometimes encompass their own minor informal economies in the camp (such as grocer's and the barber's shops), how could we relate these actions in the private realm to the creation of a political sphere?

The refugee is a central figure in Arendt's thought, and her reflections on the legal and political situation of statelessness and the lived experience of the uprootedness of refugees from everyday reality followed her own experience as a Jewish refugee escaping Nazi Germany, her home country; "We lost our home, which means the familiarity of daily life", writes Arendt in 'We Refugees' (1994 [1943], p. 110). Yet, the modern situation of statelessness also means being banished from the tightly-knit political world of "the trinity of state-people-territory", which for Arendt means exclusion from the human world. "Only with a completely organized humanity", Arendt (1962) states, "could the loss of home and political status become identical with expulsion from humanity altogether" (p. 297). In such a global order, those who are displaced outside not only suffer from 'the loss of their homes', which is "the loss of the entire social texture into which they were born and in which they established for themselves a distinct place in the world" (ibid., p. 293). More significantly, for Arendt, people who are displaced from their homeland lose their "place in the world which makes opinions significant and actions effective", a world acknowledged by a political community of citizenship which guarantees their "right to have rights" (ibid., p. 296). This dual loss of *home* and *homeland*, together with the state's protective political sphere of citizenship rights, is what for Arendt altogether disconnects refugees from the human world. It is indeed the camp, according to her, that has become "the only practical substitute for a nonexistent homeland", and "the only 'country' the world had to offer the stateless" (ibid., p. 284).

The camp, then, is not only where private and public realms dissolve into one another, cancelling a division needed for the political sphere to appear. The camp, for Arendt, is where the figure of the refugee, who is ejected from the political realm of national citizenship, is stored; a 'country' which is in itself detached from enabling political frameworks, where people are deprived of the ability to be part of a political community that will ensure their basic rights and freedom.

Where politics reside

Arendt's understanding of the political, especially in relation to the private/public realms and to stateless people, is important to the analysis of the meaning of the spatial changes made by refugees to their shelters in the camp as it relates to their specific position both as outsiders in the world of nation states and in relation to the spatial realm of the shelter in which they act. Yet, we can identify two ontological assumptions in her work on certain conditions that are required for the political sphere to appear and that might limit the ability to analyse the possibility of the bare shelter to become a space of political action. The first is Arendt's insistence on public/private separation as a condition for the appearance of the political in the public realm, while the second is the rendering of stateless people incapable to act politically. Both these limitations to the political posed by Arendt might support the assumption that people who are appropriating their shelters in the camp are doing so solely as individuals in need, rather than expressing a political call by doing so.

The responses to these complexities and contradictions in Arendt's work are the subject of ongoing academic debate, concerning both the political status of the refugees and private/public separation. Some scholars adopt Arendt's notion of statelessness in interpreting the situation of displaced people as victims deprived of rights and therefore subject to total domination (Krause, 2008). Yet, it could be argued that such accounts fail to register the refugees' political mobilisation and agency (cf. Dikeç, 2013). Others observe that there is a conceptual difficulty that emerges from Arendt's 'constraints' on the political, including both the understanding of stateless people as deprived of politics and her public/private distinction as the basis for the political (e.g. Schaap, 2011; Dikeç, 2013; Rancière, 2004).

Rancière (2004) sees Arendt's conceptualisation of politics, in which political life is not contaminated by social or private life, as 'pure politics' which is limiting the political to certain ways of life and to particular realms. Schaap (2011) also maintains that Arendt's view of stateless people as deprived of political life separates "those who are qualified to participate in politics and those who are not" (p. 23), limiting politics to only those who are 'authorised' for political action. "If statelessness corresponds not only to a situation of rightlessness but also to a life deprived of public appearance", asks Schaap, "how could those excluded from politics publicly claim the right to have rights, the right to politics?" (ibid., p. 33). Or, as Mustafa Dikeç (2013) puts it, if rightlessness for Arendt "equals deprivation from politics – from speech, action and appearance in the public realm" (p. 86), how do we then account for the actions and political claims of those who are stateless and undocumented?

Arendt's own approach to politics, however, offers ways to untangle these claims. As Bonnie Honig (1992) notes, Arendt's separation between the private and public realms is quite tenuous because, as shown earlier in this chapter, these realms constantly permeate and cross-fertilise one another in her work, and the resources for the politicisation of the private/public distinction could be found in Arendt's own account of politics. Reading Arendt in a way that "grounds itself in the agonistic and performative impulse of her politics", argues Honig, "must, for the sake of that politics, resist the a priori determination of a public/private distinction that is beyond augmentation and amendment" (p. 100). On the other hand, Gündoğdu (2012) answers Rancière's claims regarding Arendt's approach to human rights and the political meaning of statelessness by engaging with her *aporetic* thinking as a way of creating possibilities to rethink key concepts, particularly during a crisis, using her form of critique to show how human rights could be rethought and reinvented.

These approaches enable one to consider the spatial reappropriation of the bare shelter by its inhabitants as potentially political, gradually restoring an intimate and functioning private realm while also gradually reshaping its relationship to what is becoming, following these actions, a better-defined public realm. By adding kitchens to their units refugees restore their capacity to cater for themselves, and by transforming their shelters into small businesses they also establish a modest *oikonomia*, a way to earn a living. Such actions rebuild the ability of displaced people to have their necessities provided by their own re-created private realms rather than by the camp and its supporting agencies. By spatially transforming their shelters while adding decorations and symbols to them, inhabitants create an individualised place rather than an anonymised one to localise themselves in the world, creating their domestic space as *deme*. By adding these specific layers to their embodied shelters they also reveal themselves as unique individuals who together create articulated public spaces in their once anonymised camp while attentively defining the separation between their public and private realms. By dividing their shelters internally and adding rooms to them they also create their own intimate private places in them, answering a basic human need. By these spatial actions the refugees in the shelters carefully separate a private realm from a public one and localise themselves in the previously abstract space of the camp where these private/public realms were produced as indistinguishable. By creating these spaces the refugees in the camp also actively change their subjectivities as people who can act and change their world rather than being passive and dependant recipients of aid as they were thought of by those creating the camp and shelters for them.

Indeed, Honing (1992), as a feminist theorist who engages with Arendt's political theory by looking for the possibility to act in the private realm, maintains that "the distinction between public and private is seen as the performative product of political struggle, hard-won and always temporary" (p. 111). The spatial changes to the camp's shelters by the camp's inhabitants could be seen as their performative action, which transforms a highly compromised private space and at the same time politicises it as an uninhabitable space that must be altered.

The stripped space of the camp and the bare shelters bring people together, but as unified objects of control and provision and not as free, equal and unique subjects. In such spaces they are 'bodies' gathered and managed together because of *what* they are – displaced people who need to be provided for – and not because of *who* they are – distinct people who are inherently different from one another. Arendt (1962) writes on human creativity as "the capacity to add something of one's own to the common world" (p. 475). In their creative spatial actions, which add internal and external layers to their once bare shelter, inhabitants not only add to a common world but significantly recreate it together through their power and spatial agency, together restoring their 'who-ness' as distinct individuals who not only share a space and a situation of displacement, but also creatively influence and change this reality or this 'world' for themselves and for others. Such an "urge to make a home as a way of finding a place in the world", as Handel (2019) argues in relation to a different contested and abused reality of the creation of a Palestinian home in the occupied territories, where a home as a place in the world is being denied, "exposes the everyday dwelling as an inherently political experience" (p. 4).

Although, as Arendt notes, forced migrants have lost their political community and their national citizenship that protected their rights, we could argue that the spatial actions of those inhabiting the bare shelters in the camp recreate a different kind of political participation and citizenship. Indeed, as Isin (2000) points out, "globalization have challenged the nation-state as the *sole* source of authority of citizenship" (p. 5), and citizenship increasingly displays a volitional quality as a dynamic political constellation and practice. The adaptation of the bare shelter, and with it the space of the camp, produces new social relations within such spaces that, with the reworked private/public division, might not only create an environment to the political to appear but in themselves, in their accumulated value, be a spatial-political act which adjust a dehumanising space to an environment more proper for human habitation. Nyers' (2015) concept of 'migrant citizenship', entangled with autonomous mobility and the political agency and subjectivity of migrants, could be considered a term which adequately illustrates how the re-appropriation of spaces such as the bare shelter forms "a creative process that is generative of new worlds, identities, and modes of belonging" (p. 34).

As suggested by Singh (2020), spatial actions in the camp could be interpreted as Arendt's notion of 'world building' connected more broadly to all fundamental activities of the human condition that bring about the creation of a habitable human world through which and in which politics could be enacted. For Singh, these actions could be registered as political because of their visibility "to a wider, common world" which ensures that they will be seen by others (through newspaper articles and artwork) and thus appear in public, and therefore will be registered as political actions. However, the world created by the camp's inhabitants, even if this world appears only to those inhabiting it, should nevertheless be considered political. By their material recreations of their bare shelters the displaced people in the camp reject and resist the place designated to them as anonymous objects of care and control with no real place in the world. By restoring their private realm they create for themselves such a private place in the world in an act which, in the dehumanising environment of the camp, could be seen as inherently political, especially when it is done in concert by many of those inhabiting these shelters.

Conclusion

By theoretically analysing the meaning of the reappropriations of prefabricated and makeshift emergency shelters by their inhabitants through critically engaging with the work of Hannah Arendt on politics and space, this chapter reflects on the transformations of the stripped 'bare shelter' by its inhabitants as inherently political. Arendt's political and spatial theory is used to comprehend what is lost in a dehumanising situation of displacement located in the anonymising and objectifying camps and emergency shelters, and how these same spaces could be recruited to rebuild anew the world that was lost to their inhabitants, even if temporarily and precariously. With this approach the political action in the camp is created not only when people are acting together in public as unique individuals. Rather, it starts at an earlier stage, when people are beginning physically to reconstruct their private world in a way that will create the conditions for them to live in it as subjects, that is, as distinct human beings rather than as unified objects of care and control. If, in Arendt's thought, one needs a human world to act politically, we could consider these spatial actions of displaced people as ones which create such a world that is deliberately denied to them as already political. They not only together create a world in which they could act in concert, but they also together create a new physical world which they might call their own.

References

Abourahme, N. (2015). Assembling and spilling-over: towards an 'ethnography of cement' in a Palestinian refugee camp. *International Journal of Urban and Regional Research*, *39*(2), 200-217.

Agamben, G. (1998). *Homo Sacer: sovereign power and bare life*. Stanford: Stanford University Press.

Arendt, H. (1962/1951). *The Origins of Totalitarianism*. Cleveland and New York: Meridian Books.

Arendt, H. (1998/1958). *The Human Condition*. Chicago: Chicago University Press.

Arendt, H. (2006). *Between Past and Future*. New York: Penguin Books.

Aristotle. (1999). *Politics* (Benjamin Jowett, Trans.). Batoche Books. https://socialsciences.mcmaster.ca/econ/ugcm/3ll3/aristotle/Politics.pdf (Original work published ca. 350 B.C.E)

Beeckmans, L. (2019). Mediating (in)visibility and publicity in an African church in Ghent: African religious place-making and solidarity outside the urban regularity. In L. Bialasiewicz & V. Gentile (eds.), *Spaces of Tolerance: The Changing Geographies of Religious Freedom in Europe* (pp. 180-198). London: Routledge.

Bialasiewicz, L. (2017). 'That which is not a mosque': Disturbing place at the 2015 Venice Biennale. *City*, 21(3-4), 367-387.

Brickell, K. (2012). Geopolitics of home. *Geography Compass*, 6(10), 575-588.

Doraï, K. & Piraud-Fournet, P. (2018). From tent to makeshift housing: a case study of a Syrian refugee in Zaatari camp (Jordan). In Fawaz, M., Gharbieh, A., Harb, M., & Salamé, D. (eds.), *Refugees as City-Makers* (pp.136-139). Beirut: American University of Beirut.

Dikeç, M. (2013). Beginners and equals: political subjectivity in Arendt and Rancière. *Transactions of the Institute of British Geographers*, 38(1), 78-90.

Gueguen-Teil, C. & Katz, I. (2018). On the Meaning of Shelter: Living in Calais's *Camps de la Lande*. In I. Katz, C. Minca & D. Martin (eds.). *Camps Revisited: Multifaceted Spatialities of a Modern Political Technology* (pp. 83-98). London: Rowman and Littlefield.

Gündoğdu, A. (2012). 'Perplexities of the rights of man': Arendt on the aporias of human rights. *European Journal of Political Theory*, 11(1), 4-24.

Guguen, G. (2017). 'Interior Itineraries': Paris photo exhibition shows migrants at home. France 24, 7 January. Available at https://www.france24.com/en/20170107-paris-photo-exhibit-itineraires-interieurs-migrant-homes-fert [Retrieved 29 June, 2021].

Handel, A. (2019). What's in a home? Toward a critical theory of housing/dwelling. *Environment and Planning C: Politics and Space*, 37(6), 1045-1062.

Honig, B. (1992). Toward an agonistic feminism: Hannah Arendt and the politics of identity. In J. Butler and J. W. Scott (eds.), *Feminists Theorize the Political* (pp. 215-235). New York: Routledge.

Ingold, T. (2005). Epilogue: Towards a politics of dwelling. *Conservation and Society*, 3(2), 501.

Isin, E. F. (2000). Democracy, citizenship and the city. In E. F. Isin (ed.), *Democracy, Citizenship and the Global City*. London: Routledge.

Kaika, M. (2004). Interrogating the geographies of the familiar: Domesticating nature and constructing the autonomy of the modern home. *International Journal of Urban and Regional Research,* 28(2): 265–286.

Katz, I. (2017). Between bare life and everyday life: Spatialising the new migrant camps in Europe. *Amps: Architecture_Media_Politics_Society 12*(2), 1–21.

Katz, I. (2019). En Route: The Mobile Border Migrant Camps of Northern France. In Pieris, A. (Ed.). *Architecture on the Borderline: Boundary Politics and Built Space* (pp. 119-138). London: Routledge.

Katz, I. (2020). Adhocism, Agency, and Emergency Shelter: On Architectural Nuclei of Life in Displacement. In Scott-Smith T. & M. E. Breeze (Eds). *Structures of Protection* (pp. 235-246). New York: Berghahn Books.

Kotef, H. (2010). Bai't (home/household). *Mafteakh: Political-Lexical Review,* 1: 1–22.

Krause, M. (2008). Undocumented migrants: an Arendtian perspective. *European Journal of Political Theory,* 7, 331–48.

Nyers, P. (2015). Migrant citizenships and autonomous mobilities. *Migration, Mobility, & Displacement,* 1(1).

Rancière, J. (2004). Who is the subject of the rights of man? *South Atlantic Quarterly,* 103, 297–310.

Schaap, A. (2011). Enacting the right to have rights: Jacques Rancière's critique of Hannah Arendt. *European Journal of Political Theory,* 10, 22–45

Singh, A. L. (2020). Arendt in the refugee camp: The political agency of world-building. *Political Geography,* 77, 102-149.

Staeheli, L., D. Mitchell, & C. Nagel. (2009). Making Publics: Immigrants, Regimes of Publicity, and Entry to 'the Public', *Environment and Planning D: Society and Space* 27: 633–648. doi:10.1068/d6208; see: The Refugee Republic: Jumpstarting a new existence in an emergency city – everyday life in a refugee camp (2012). Available at https://refugeerepublic.submarinechannel.com/ [Retrieved 29 June, 2021].

Turner, M. (2016). Inside the homes of the Calais Jungle camp – in pictures. *The Guardian,* 27 February. Available at https://www.theguardian.com/world/gallery/2016/feb/27/homes-inside-the-calais-jungle-camp-in-pictures [Retrieved 29 June, 2021].

CHAPTER 7

Refugee Shelters done Differently

Humanist Architecture of Socialist Yugoslavia

Aleksandar Staničić
Delft University of Technology, The Netherlands

Introduction

> [...] there are no [too] big or [too] small themes in architecture, the size of buildings has no influence on architectural experience, building traditions are inexhaustible source of inspiration for new designers, landscape is the prime factor in artistic determination of work of architecture. (Mitrović, 1971, p. 6).[1]

"Architectural miniatures", to use the words of Mihajlo Mitrović himself, which are similar to miniatures in music, painting or sculpture, can send powerful messages and have far-reaching cultural impact. There is no idea too pertinent, nor ideology too grand that cannot be conveyed through the smallest of architectural forms, prudent materialisation or carefully designed detail. This chapter is dedicated to one such example; in it I will demonstrate how big ideologies, global geo-political aspirations and, by no means less important, an innovative approach to humanitarian architecture all manifested themselves in the design of one single building: the United Nations' shelter for foreigners in Banja Koviljača, formerly in the Socialist Federative Republic of Yugoslavia, today in the Republic of Serbia. It is certainly a unique example that is a product of its time and unrepeatable set of circumstances, so much so that, it can be argued, it cannot be classified as a refugee *shelter* at all.[2] The most recent refugee crisis, however, unequivocally confirmed that it is one. But instead of presenting this building as an anomaly among refugee shelters, in this chapter I will present it as an exemplar of successful international cooperation and a humane approach to homemaking for displaced people from which many lessons for the design of refugee shelters can be drawn. In terms of the chapter's structure, I will start with the local (i.e. nation-building in Socialist Yugoslavia) and global (i.e. cultural exchange between the "three worlds") geo-political contexts in which the building came to be set, the motivation and reasoning for its construction, followed by the discussion of the design itself and the impact it made, before I conclude with the most resent developments – namely, its being part of the Eastern Mediterranean refugee route – and lessons for the future.

In Yugoslavia, just as in the rest of the world, modernism, modernisation and, by extent, modern architecture had a powerful political agenda. From the dawn of its days at the end of the Second World War, Socialist Yugoslavia's nation-building was supported by the intense spatial production that was supposed to be the face of the new modern state (Blagojević, 2007; Kulić, Parker & Penick, 2014). The country's new capital, New Belgrade, was built from scratch according to the principles of CIAM, reflecting the ambition of the Yugoslav Communist Party to assume one of the leading roles in the newly established world order. The decades-long project followed a well-established pattern of construction of new capital cities – the erection of new ministries, governmental institutions and other "representative" buildings – in an effort to break the link with the ideologically inappropriate past (Vale 1992), echoing similar processes that were happening in many African countries at the time following their newly gained post-colonial independence (Avermaete, 2010; Beeckmans, 2014, 2018).

The architectural and political nation-building gained a completely new dimension following the political rift between Josip Broz Tito and Joseph Stalin in 1948 which led to the expulsion of Yugoslavia from the communist bloc under the dominion of Soviet Union (Lampe, 2000; Ramet, 2005). This historic event, as it turned out, opened the door for a young socialist nation politically and culturally to reinvent itself on its own terms. In the decades that followed the country developed a unique system of self-management (in Serbian, '*samoupravljanje*'), branded by many modern-day historians as "soft" socialism or even "socialist democracy" (Stojiljković & Ignjatović, 2019), which also had substantial ramifications for architectural and urban production. The totalitarian rule by the Communist Party of Yugoslavia, with Tito as its undisputed leader, intertwined self-managing industrial production with a lavish lifestyle that drew its inspiration from the capitalist West (Kulić, 2009a). This state of "in-betweenness" required, and indeed produced, an architectural style that was "capitalist in form and socialist in nature": in its formal appearance it had to be distant from the aesthetics of socialist realism, traditionally associated with the Soviet Union, while simultaneously embodying the "progressive ideology" of the Party (Kulić, Mrduljaš & Thaler, 2012).

A solution was found in the creation of a specific kind of "Yugoslav" modernism characterised by a high level of professional independence, individualism and creative freedom to search for original architectural expression. Architects drew inspiration from the local building traditions, often modernising and re-interpreting elements of vernacular and religious architecture (Grabrijan & Neidhardt, 1957; Alić, 2013a, 2013b). This alchemy may seem unnatural, given the unfavourable status of religion and nationalist determinants in the eyes of communist ideology, but, according to Stojiljković and Ignjatović (2019), it was allowed because

> The main concepts of [Yugoslav structuralist] architecture were seen to give a plastic and visible expression to the Yugoslav Marxists' ideas of socialism as completed naturalism, a dialectical relationship between the universal and the individual, between different pasts and unhistorical essences, and between society, nature, and culture. (p. 872)

These ideas were considered progressive even by the global standards of the time, which comes as no surprise considering how enthusiastically Yugoslav architects tried to be in sync with the global architectural scene by gorging on contemporary architectural literature coming from both Eastern and Western spheres of influence (Kulić, 2009b; Štraus, 1991).[3] At the same time, the social status of architects was so elevated that they were considered one of the main drivers of social change and economic growth, even to the point that the construction of modern forms at the expense of vernacular architecture was often used as a substitute for actual modernisation of the country (Herscher, 2010).[4]

Another defining historical moment for the development of the Yugoslav socialist project was the founding conference of the Non-Aligned Movement held in Belgrade in 1961, at the zenith of the Cold War. The movement was seen as a third, neutral alternative to the two confronting political and ideological paradigms, the Eastern and Western blocs (Avermaete, 2012). The Yugoslav political leadership quickly realised that non-alignment could be used as an opportunity to position itself as an unofficial leader of the "Third bloc", spread its international influence and even act as a cohesive element in a deeply polarised and divided world. Many socialist countries saw clear benefits to such an alliance, first of all, in conquering a huge, underdeveloped market that ranged from South America, through Africa, to far East Asia.[5] Łukasz Stanek (2020) underlines the economic logic of non-alignment by arguing that, far from being "an ideological smokescreen or a utopian vision", the world socialist system functioned primarily as "an existing reality of foreign trade". Architecture, large building corporations and architects who operated across the national borders played no small roll in achieving these ambitious goals.⁶ But, as shown in Stanek and Avermaete (2012), this engagement was far from unilateral and comprised solely of export-import projects. Instead, it created a "contact zone" where all sides involved were influenced by the reflexive cultural exchange, while the formation of large state-controlled construction firms, the exchange of expertise across disciplines, and the practicalities of micro- and macro-politics completely shattered and redefined the traditional dynamics of architectural practice.

In Yugoslavia, the formation of the Non-Aligned Movement started a series of events that had an enormous effect on economic, cultural and – by translation – architectural production in the country. Their high status within the Non-Aligned Movement gave Yugoslav construction firms such as *Energoprojekt* and *Mašinoprojekt* a privileged position when bidding for commissions in developing countries. This, in turn, gave the Yugoslav regime a convenient platform from which to spread and promote its political and ideological agenda of "brotherhood and unity" well beyond the state's borders (Sekulić, 2016; Mitrović, 1995). Architects who worked in those firms exported their idea of socialist modernist architecture all over the world, but at the same time were influenced by alien traditions, limitations of available resources and local know-how. All of this caused the cultural exchange to bloom, broke down the boundaries between European and non-European architectural traditions, and produced unique specimens of modern and postmodern architecture both in Yugoslavia and elsewhere.

But also, as recently argued by Herscher (2019), "modernism in architecture can be understood as, among other things, an attempt to reorganize architecture according to some of the imperatives that also organized humanitarianism" (p. 25). Yugoslavia, at the time, did not have systematically built, large-scale refugee shelters on its own territory and, to the best of my knowledge, it did not have much (if any) experience in building refugee shelters elsewhere, so it would be far-fetched to claim any systematic development of humanitarian architecture or its causal influence on the Yugoslav "modern(isation) project". However, Yugoslavia was surely aware of the "post-World War II emergence of an international humanitarian regime" (Siddiqi, 2017), and in this new political climate, one can assume, wanted to position itself as a part of the progressive world. This, of course, raises the question of the nature of the humanitarian aid Yugoslavia could offer at the time, as this aid was not rooted in any kind of actual necessity; rather, one could argue, it was the result of surplus resources caused by the stellar rise of Yugoslav GDP in the 1950s and 1960s.⁷ Reflecting on Hannah Arendt's (1951) assessment of the nature of humanitarian aid, Anooradha Iyer Siddiqi (2013) argues that there are two basic questions we should be asking: "[t]he first has to do with the political nature of the not-for-profit gesture. The second has to do with the political nature of gestures born of excessive abundance" (p. 14). She goes on to conclude that "both support the will toward the monumental, that is, a sublime response to crisis. These celebrations of – and memorials to – the humanity at the core of the aid gesture often result in built form" (ibid.).

The motivation to build a refugee centre in Yugoslavia in 1960s, and especially the monumental architecture of the building, would neatly fit this interpretation. First, it was not clear at that moment who exactly would be the refugees the centre would be hosting; the client was the United Nations, not any ethnic or national group in particular. In fact, instead of the urgency that usually accompanies the design and construction of refugee centres, this project was veiled from the start with a thin layer of elitist—architectural and political—prestige. In the same way that Yugoslavia was buying political relevance on the world map with this project, the architects involved were motivated by a desire "to operate with political relevance and thus realize the promise of modernism, expanding their remit into the realm of the social sciences […] in order to achieve its problem-solving potential" (Siddiqi, 2017, p. 369). The result is "a fiction of architecture as an art of equality in which 'the same design approach' subtends the shelters of refugees and the refuges of the tax sheltering class" (Herscher, 2019, p. 27).[8]

Refugee shelters done differently

As mentioned above, meaningful collaboration between Non-Aligned countries went far beyond the creation of a joint political platform and hollow promises of solidarity; from the economic perspective, non-alignment created a huge global market that awaited exploitation. This went hand-in-hand with high levels of cultural and educational exchange, such as large numbers of foreign exchange students who attended Yugoslav universities without paying fees and vice versa. It also became common practice to help allies in need by sending humanitarian aid or taking refugees from conflict areas into dedicated shelters.[9] These reception centres were built specifically for the purpose of hosting displaced people, refugees and asylum seekers. The quality of those places was exceptionally high, both in originality of architectural expression and applied building standards, such that it was not possible to distinguish them from social housing or even leisure facilities in whose vicinity they were usually situated. In all fairness, the number of refugee shelters built in Yugoslavia was not so high that their construction would impose a burden on the state budget, and the number of displaced people who found a home in those facilities was purely symbolic in the first years of (and even decades after) their opening.[10] What

Figure 1. Map of temporary reception centres and permanent (stationary) refugee centres in Serbia in 2018. Source: https://www.azilsrbija.rs/wp-content/uploads/2019/02/Mapa-izbeglickih-centara-u-Srbiji-2018-11-10.jpg)

was at stake here was not the disaster relief, but the international reputation of the state, so the architects who designed them did so with special care, seeing them above all else as places to display and promote local cultural heritage as a way of inciting transcultural exchange.

The United Nations' shelter for foreigners in Banja Koviljača (sr. *Prihvatilište za strana lica u Banji Koviljači*, or, *Stacionar OUN u Banji Koviljači*, Fig. 2.), as it was officially called, was designed in 1964, only three years after the Non-

Aligned Movement was formed.[11] As indicated by its name, it was financed by the United Nations, although specific details of this arrangement, at least at the moment, remain unknown. Yugoslavia was a founding member of the United Nations, highly regarded at the time, therefore it would not be so far-fetched to assume that this project served as part of the Yugoslav leadership's efforts additionally to strengthen straighten its international reputation, and position itself among the leaders of the new 'Free World'. Looking at the history of the UNHCR of that period, the 1960s (when this project was commissioned) was the time when "the institutionalization of humanitarian architecture and planning expertise occurred in multiple frameworks [...] By the mid-1970s, state-based, private, and academic initiatives together contributed the fine grain of analysis to a growing professional culture concerned with relief and disaster" (Siddiqi, 2017, p. 374).[12] Undoubtedly the United Nations' shelter for foreigners in Banja Koviljača can be interpreted as part of these efforts. Formally, the carrier of the project was the Federal Ministry of the Interior Affairs (in Serbian, *Savezni Sekretarijat za Unutrašnje Poslove*), which in all formal documents was called the "investor".[13] This was standard practice at the time as all refugee shelters and asylum centres were under the direct jurisdiction of this Ministry.

The architect of this particular edifice, Mihajlo Mitrović (1922-2018), was the founder and lead architect of the small architectural practice in Belgrade called "Projektbiro" (Fig. 3.). But, despite his abundant experience as a practising architect, he never worked for large construction firms on international commissions.[14] His only international experience came shortly after his graduation, in 1950, when he spent one year in France and Denmark as a fellow of the United Nations, which in hindsight might have helped him land this commission. In the 1960s, by the time he was in his 40s, he had proven his talent for

Figure 2. United Nations Refugee centre in Banja Koviljača. Architect Mihajlo Mitrović, 1964, a) in 1966 (source: *Mihajlo Mitrović: Izložba arhitekture, Muzej primenjene umotnosti Beograd, 13-25. april 1971*), and b) in 2018 (source: http://arhiva.kirs.gov.rs/docs/azil/Centar_za_azil_Banja_Koviljaca.pdf).

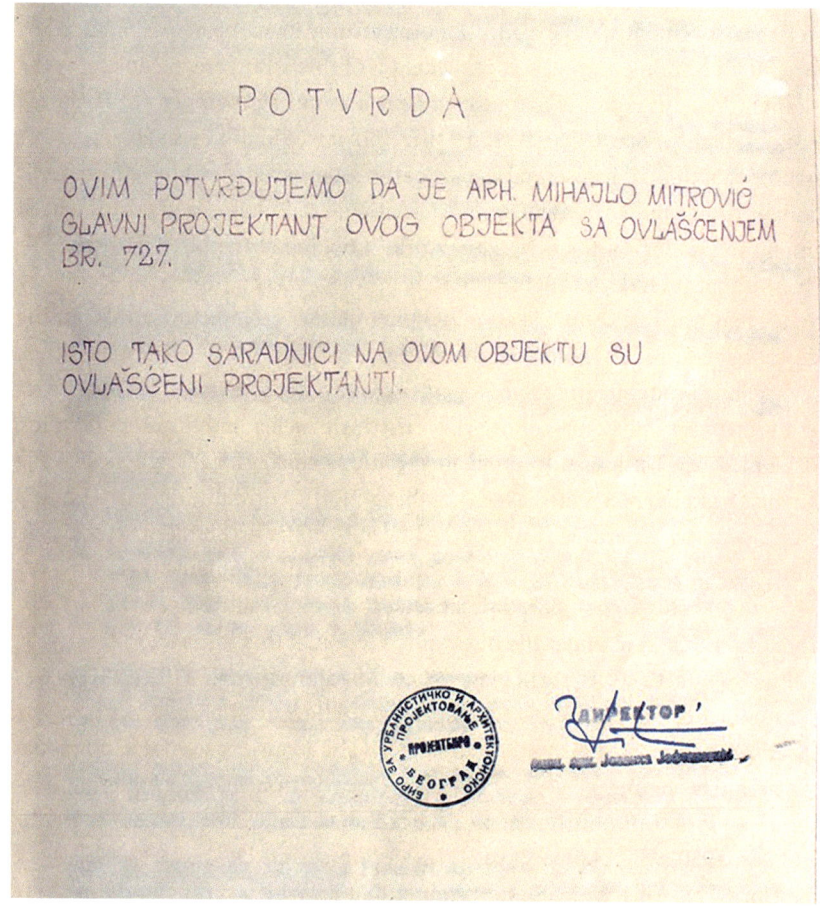

Figure 3. Official document from "Projektbiro" Belgrade stating that Mihajlo Mitrović is the main author of the building (source: Inter-Municipal Historical Archive in Šabac, Serbia).

designing architectural "miniatures" – as he referred to those buildings himself – tucked away in a natural setting and rich with traditional motives. Constantly playing with symbolic readings of sculptural and decorative elements in architecture, Mitrović possessed particular sensitivity for the power of architecture as a mediator in helping people in transit to become acquainted with an unfamiliar context. That same year he designed a customs house at the Gevgelija border crossing, a modern building with strategically placed sculptural motifs taken from local monasteries (Fig. 4.).[15] He saw this building primarily as a place where "tourists entering the country would get the first-hand information about cultural sites they are about to encounter just down the road" (Staničić, forthcoming).[16] In his work Mitrović aspired to transform those places of continuous stress and estrangement into places of meaningful cultural contact

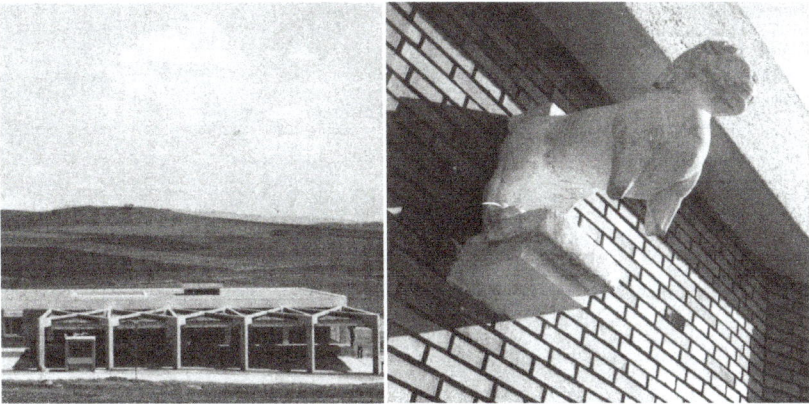

Figure 4. Customs house at Gevgelija border crossing, North Macedonia. Architect Mihajlo Mitrović, 1965 (source: Mihajlo Mitrović: izložba arhitekture, Muzej primenjene umetnosti Beograd, 13-25 April 1971).

Figure 5. Position of the refugee centre (at the map marked as "Asylum Center") next to the Banja Koviljača (source: Google Maps).

between the hosts and the people coming from abroad, whatever the reason for their visit might be. His inclination towards semiotics of folklore and traditional motifs (unlike that of his contemporary, Bogdan Bogdanović, whose symbolism was often described as too abstract and even surreal) was particularly useful for this, although in the late stage of his career this tendency often morphed into open nationalistic outbursts.[17]

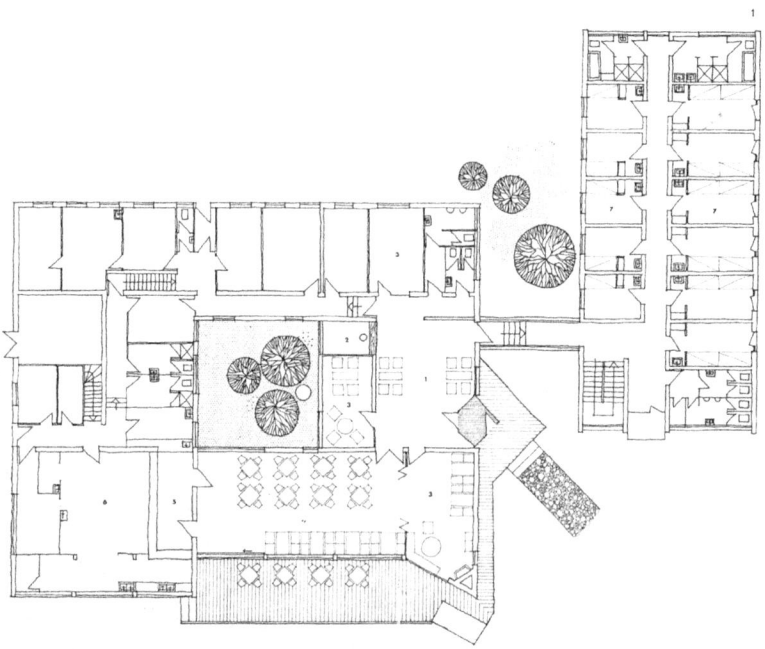

Figure 6. United Nations Refugee centre in Banja Koviljača. Architect Mihajlo Mitrović, 1964. Ground floor plan (source: *Mihajlo Mitrović: izložba arhitekture, Muzej primenjene umetnosti Beograd, 13-25 April 1971*).

Just as with the custom house in Gevgelija, the design of the shelter in Banja Koviljača draws its inspiration from the surrounding picturesque terrain from which it grows organically. Banja Koviljača is one of the most luxurious spas in Serbia, only a couple of kilometres from the Serbian-Bosnian border, and the refugee centre is at the very edge of the spa complex (Fig. 5.).[18] The architect himself vividly explained his key concepts by stating that "with its forms and materials, the edifice succumbs to the mighty colors and silhouettes of the beautiful park and the forest that hover above" (Mitrović, 1971, p. 8).[19] The small building of only couple of hundred square metres in area, and with only 120 available beds, consists of two tracts (dormitory and a restaurant) joined with a narrow and enclosed passage connection (Fig. 6.). These tracts are covered with low-slope twin roofs that lie on massive wooden beams (Fig. 7.). The use of intertwined wooden elements, and especially wide overhanging eaves, is reminiscent of Serbian old building traditions, most famously in the construction of medieval wooden churches and concurrent vernacular architecture. The façade is composed of large window surfaces combined with wall canvases coated in local 'broken' stone. In his monograph on the work of Mihajlo Mitrović, Aleksandar Kadijević writes that what gives this building its charm

Figure 7. United Nations Refugee centre in Banja Koviljača. Architect Mihajlo Mitrović, 1964. Detail of the façade (source: *Mihajlo Mitrović: izložba arhitekture, Muzej primenjene umetnosti Beograd, 13-25 April 1971*).

is precisely this "combination of contemporary industrial and natural materials" (Kadijević, 1999, p. 60). In a broader Yugoslav context, such traditional-to-modern transgressions were not rare occurrences; modern reinterpretations of elements of Oriental architecture, for example, were present in the work of Juraj Neidhardt and Dušan Grabrijan (1957) and Andrija Mutnjaković (Stojiljković & Ignjatovič, 2019), revealing the complexity and depth of the interconnection between the socialist political and architectural agendas. The dominant architectural motif, immediately visible from every possible angle, is the tall chimney with its open, pyramidal capital piece (Fig. 8.). It clearly marks the most important room of the entire complex: as in old, traditional Serbian houses, there is a large, multifunctional living and dining room with an enormous triangular hearth in its most protruding angle. This room is the epicentre where all day-to-day activities happen; where people gather, talk, play and dine. In the Serbian building tradition the hearth represents the inexhaustible spring

Figure 8. United Nations Refugee centre in Banja Koviljača. Architect Mihajlo Mitrović, 1964. Its appearance today (source: http://arhiva.kirs.gov.rs/docs/azil/Centar_za_azil_Banja_Koviljaca.pdf).

of (the building's) energy and life, so Mitrović invested a significant amount of attention in designing its details and in carefully collecting various natural and artificial materials (Fig. 9.).

The living/dining room is clearly the most important space in the entire complex, as it is the only one that receives natural light from both sides – because of a glassy and open atrium in the centre of the edifice (Fig. 10.). Although essentially modern in its architectural expression, the architect rooted this modernity in traditional elements that are abundant in this part of the country.

Mitrović's idea of homemaking for displaced people, therefore, was to recreate warm atmosphere of local traditional houses that, in his view, would invite displaced people to become familiar with indigenous culture and explore local "hidden treasures" even further. This approach, one could argue, lies in stark opposition to the modern-day design, organisation and positioning of refugee shelters, where shanty design is being implemented on purpose to prevent displaced people taking root or, at very least, feeling like at home (Akšamija, 2021). This was recently also pointed out by Siddiqi (2013), who noted that "camp architecture acts to communicate a fleeting existence in time. Architectural signs of permanence socially threaten host countries, signal a protracted state of displacement for refugees, and politically complicate the activity of humanitarian stakeholders" (p. 16). In the most extreme examples, such as the Al Azraq Refugee Camp in Jordan, refugees are even banned from planting any kind of vegetation on camp soil, as it is perceived as both figuratively and literally taking roots (Staničić, forthcoming). Even the most recent efforts to make the humanitarian architecture more *human* do not forego its essentially ephemeral character (Herscher, 2017; see also Laue, 2013).[20] The fact that

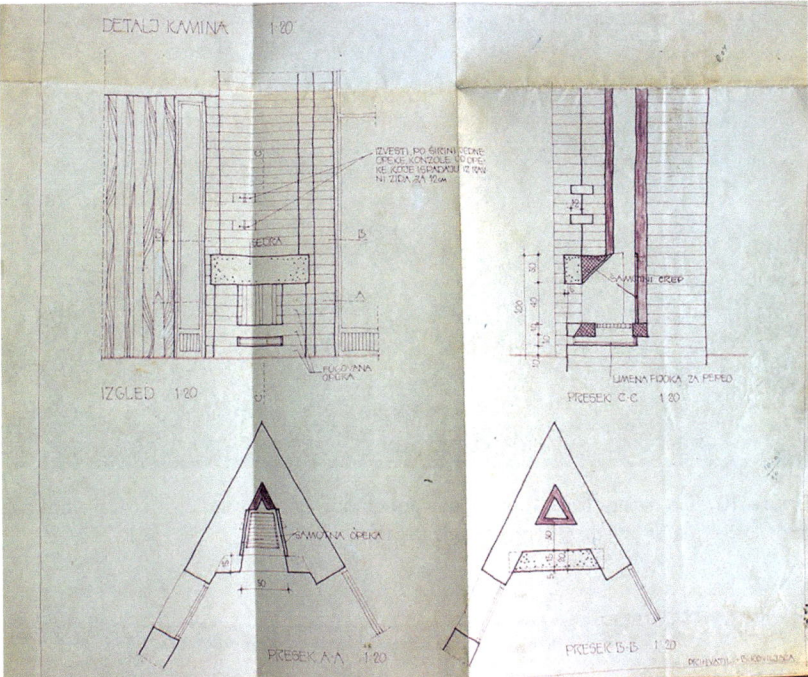

Figure 9. Detailed drawings of the fireplace/hearth, the centrepiece of the entire refugee centre. Architect Mihajlo Mitrović, 1964 (source: Inter-Municipal Historical Archive in Šabac, Serbia).

Mitrović's building managed to achieve the warmth of a home through quality design, while at the same time being a permanent, firm construction showcases the high standards of humanitarian architecture advocated by Socialist Yugoslavia and welcomed by the United Nations at the time.

The appraisals from both the local architectural guild and high UN officials the edifice got right after its inauguration further support this. An article published in the local newspaper, *Glas Podrinja*, stated that "the most beautiful building in this part of the country has been built", crediting designers and construction workers alike for its great success (Fig. 11.).[21] At the opening ceremony, Sadruddin Aga Khan, then the United Nations High Commissioner for Refugees (and not to be mistaken for Aga Khan IV, the founder of the prestigious Aga Khan Award for Architecture), acknowledged the unusual but rational architecture of the refugee centre (Mlađenović, 1983, p. 6). In a letter he personally received from Sadruddin Aga Khan (June 10, 1966), Mitrović testifies that Aga Khan "feared the possibility that refugees might decide to stay in this shelter voluntarily longer than they supposed to" (Ibid.), words that could be interpreted even as surprise at the shelter's hominess and high quality archi-

Figure 10. The dining/living room. The interior today (source: http://arhiva.kirs.gov.rs/docs/azil/Centar_za_azil_Banja_Koviljaca.pdf).

Figure 11. Scan of a newspaper article entitled "Završen hotel Ujedinjenih Nacija", *Glas Podrinja*, 22 September 1966 (source: Inter-Municipal Historical Archive in Šabac, Serbia).

tectural design. Mitrović was particularly proud of these words (in the interview I had with him he mentioned them several times), which proves that this was precisely the effect he was aiming for.

The building's unique design did not go unnoticed among Yugoslav planners and architects – although it appears that the function of the building was not relevant for them to evaluate. In 1967 the building won the prestigious *Borba* award for architecture on the level of Republic of Serbia (Alihodžić, 2015). The jury offered the following rationale for its decision:

> The Refugee Centre in Banja Koviljača [...] represents a significant contribution to our architecture. This building is characterised by well-balanced masses and expert usage of authentic materials, as well as by the emphasis put on the texture of wall surfaces. Mitrović uses local materials and, by exploiting their unique features for the design of external as well as internal spaces, achieves authentic architectural expression. The composition of basic volumes is skilfully embedded in the ambiance through terrain modelling and respect of the surrounding natural values. The simple but functional scheme is enriched by the [perceived] 'mobility' of volumes that accurately interpret the content of the interior. Mitrović achieves the particular and exceptional quality of the building through the artistic treatment of architectural details [...]. (Unknown, 1967, p. 15).[22]

The appraisal does not mention the humanitarian purpose of the building, nor does it try to raise its significance to the international level, which could have been expected considering the prominent investor. By winning the award on the Republic level, the project automatically won the nomination for the Federal (Yugoslav) *Borba* award on behalf of the Republic of Serbia. There it was again shortlisted but lost in the final round of voting by a narrow margin (the jury voted 5:6) to the elementary school building in Kočevje, designed by the architect Jože Kreger (ibid.). The *Borba* award brought national publicity to the project, whose design was later reproduced in many architectural books and journals, especially the ones that focus on the opus of Mihajlo Mitrović.

The construction of the Refugee Centre in Banja Koviljača marks the time when Yugoslav architects were undoubtedly aware of the potential and importance of an international presence and transcultural exchange. Just a few years earlier, Yugoslavia's participation in Expo 58 in Brussels with the pavilion designed by Vjenceslav Richter had demonstrated not only the richness of cultural production in Yugoslavia, but also its high regard in international circles (Kulić, 2012b). What followed were decades of prolific activity of Yugoslav construction firms abroad, when the international style in Yugoslav architecture sprouted. The exchange of expertise and exposure to diverse cultures quickly redefined styles and geographies of architectural production on both sides of the Iron Curtain (Avermaete & Stanek, 2012). Some of the well-known examples that later came about as a result of these activities include the House of Yugoslav-Norwegian Friendship (today, the House of Serbian-Norwegian Friendship) in

Figure 12. The House of Serbian-Norwegian Friendship in Gornji Milanovac. Architect Aleksandar Đokić, 1987 (source: *www.gornjimilanovac.rs*).

Figure 13. The residence of the Iranian ambassador in Belgrade (source: *www.beobuild.rs*).

Gornji Milanovac, designed by Aleksandar Đokić in 1987, wherein design elements of traditional Norwegian ships are combined with local building traditions (Fig. 12.), and the residence of the Iranian ambassador in Belgrade with its triangular concrete canopies (Fig. 13.). More or less successful, these buildings, in their effort to bridge different worlds, managed to redefine the concepts of local, regional, European and global architectural heritage, resulting in what Beeckmans called a "transnational housing vernacular" (Beeckmans, this volume, p. 7).

Figure 14. Asylum centre in Bogovađa (source: http://arhiva.kirs.gov.rs/docs/azil/Centar_za_azil_Bogovadja.pdf).

As for the refugee centres in Serbia, those that managed to come close to the high standards set by Mitrović's work are rare, but their quality and humanitarian approach to design are still much higher than in their global counterparts. The one that is worth mentioning is perhaps the refugee centre in Bogovađa, but the comparison between the two is hardly possible considering the lower quality of construction and basic usage of traditional elements in the latter case (Fig. 14.). In other cities in Serbia refugee centres are either adapted hotel buildings (such as hotel "Berlin" in Sjenica) or administrative buildings of former factories (such as former furniture factory "Dallas" in Tutin).[23] The Refugee Centre in Banja Koviljača showed that creativity and beauty are possible, even necessary, in this unseemly field of architectural production. Although the scale on which it operated is miniscule compared to refugee shelters close to actual conflict zones, it demonstrated the power of architecture to transform unfortunate social circumstances, such as displacement and segregation, into an opportunity for meaningful cultural contact. In the context of humanitarian architecture in Yugoslavia, Mitrović's design can be seen as trailblazing considering the fact that one decade later, in the 1970s, "organisations such as Oxfam and Care supported a rethinking of camp and shelter architecture to one which takes locally available resources and the refugees' origin into account" (Laue, 2013, p. 19). The Refugee Centre in Banja Koviljača also stands in stark contrast to the minimal architecture of modern-day refugee shelters that "limits the capacity of refugees to build their own spaces and their own lives" (Herscher, 2019, p. 27). By adopting the high-design approach to humanitarian architecture, Mitrović actually managed to resolve the tension between development and humanitarian relief which, in architectural terms, has pitted 'dwelling' against 'shelter'. According to Herscher, "each raises the stakes for expertise differently: the former by ennobling the shared mission of architecture and humanitarianism, and the latter by reducing it to functionalist, instrumentalized science" (*ibid*). By blurring the clear-cut distinction between dwelling and shelter, between refugee shelter and refugee camp, Mitrović actually managed, however intuitively, to bridge this gap.

Post scriptum

It should be noted that in this complex network of foreign and domestic actors, the one actor who did not play any role in the construction of the shelter is the "migrant-as-architect". The shelter was designed without any input from migrants themselves, without even knowing who the end-users or their actual needs might be, hence completely depriving refugees of their spatial agency. In the first few decades after its opening, the refugee centre in Banja Koviljača operated almost quietly, mostly by welcoming small numbers of asylum seekers from South America (Chile), Africa and, in the late 1980s, from Eastern Europe (namely, the Czech Republic, Slovakia and Romania). The current director of the Centre, Robert Lesmajster, testifies that, at some point, the centre was even used as a holiday resort for the employees of the Ministry of the Interior.[24] The centre was finally put to test in the 1990s during the Yugoslav wars and subsequent refugee crisis (Jovanović & Rudić, 2011). Between 1991 and 2006 it sustained a surge of refugees from neighbouring Bosnia, Croatia and Kosovo which exposed its most notable flaw—the lack of capacity to accept large numbers of people.[25] The structure, which was built to host no more than 120 residents, often hosted two to three times that number. Years of heavy usage left visible marks on the structure, such that it had to be refurbished in 2006 with the financial support of the UNHCR. The Serbian government decided to establish the Asylum Centre in Banja Koviljača on 6 December 2008, following the passage of the Asylum Act (Official Gazette of the Republic of Serbia no. 109/2007) and the Regulations on Housing Conditions and Provision of Basic Living Conditions in Asylum Centres (Official Gazette of the Republic of Serbia no. 31/2008).[26] The passing of these regulations was one of the preconditions for Serbia to join the "white" Schengen list.

During the most recent refugee crisis, Serbia was part of the so-called 'Balkan route' (that is, the 'Eastern Mediterranean Route') that saw refugees coming from the hot conflict regions of the Middle East, Africa and South Asia on their way to the European Union (Philippou, 2020). Different national politics on refugee acceptance and the subsequent erection of border fences created bottlenecks in some Balkan countries, most notably North Macedonia, Serbia and Croatia, forcing refugees to live unwillingly in one place for a longer period of time. According to Katz (2016), "the call 'No camp!' reflects the refugees' personal and political demand not to be stopped and suspended in dreadful conditions for unknown periods of time in places they did not wish to come to" (p. 19). At the peak of the migrant crisis in 2011 the refugee shelter in Banja Koviljača hosted somewhere between 1,000 and 2,500 people (depending on the source), more than ten times the capacity of the centre. People were sleeping outside the shelter's walls in the back yard, but also in the spa's public park and city bus station, which inevitably led to some friction with the local population (Rudić, 2014). It could be argued that the problem with the local population appeared when the migrants started "making homes in displacement", that is, when their effort to form an "infrastructural citizenship" (Lemanski, 2019) was recognised and made visible.[27] The reception of refugees among locals worsened after a series of incidents (in which only a handful of those refugees were *not* in fact the victims of crimes), inciting street protests organised by local citizens. Refugees were not happy about being transported here either, because it seemed like a huge detour from their usual route through to the North of Serbia and Hungary (although this perspective changed significantly when Hungary closed its border with Serbia, so that refugees had to take alternative routes through Croatia and Bosnia).

Since then, the situation has only slightly improved. The Commissariat for Refugees and Migration of the Republic of Serbia reports a steady inflow of refugees that go through the centre, about 1,000 per year (at the moment, only 38 people are living there), but still some local organisations demand the permanent closure of the refugee centre and its removal from the spa. The building, whose purpose was to welcome foreign friends in need and serve as a bridge between cultures in the overall national climate of hostility and bigotry, turned into the major source of intolerance and segregation. In today's climate of EU Member States' hostility towards refugees that include severe 'pushbacks' via the Balkan route (intercepting ships in the Mediterranean Sea, raising barbed wire fences along the Serbo-Hungarian boarder, police brutality exercised in Hungary and Croatia), it is questionable whether "the warmth of a home" can be achieved solely through one good shelter. I would argue that it is not (only) the quality housing that provides the sense of dwelling and home, but the social, political and cultural climate that makes refugees feel welcome.

Acknowledgements

I am grateful to Mihajlo Mitrović (1922-2018) for allowing me to consult his personal archives and getting the opportunity to interview him as a background for this chapter. Special thanks go to the editors of this volume and blind peer reviewers whose comments were invaluable in shaping the final version of the text.

Notes

1. Author's translation.
2. As we will see later in the text, in local literature this building is referred to as a 'shelter', 'centre', 'infirmary', 'station', 'accommodation', even a 'hotel'. This raises bigger questions of what a refugee shelter actually is, from both the functional and architectural/compositional points of view. The way this building was conceptualised, built and ultimately used does not help the discussion—it serves as temporary and emergency accommodation for displaced people, but the quality of construction and the sheer scale of the building make it clear that this is not a temporary structure. The shelter-centre dichotomy will resurface a few more times in this chapter, reinforcing the conclusion that the building actually belongs somewhere in between these two categories.
3. This was also confirmed to the author in several interviews with prominent Yugoslav architects, such as Mario Jobst (Belgrade, 31 August 2019) and Mustafa Musić (Belgrade, 3 January 2020).
4. This aggressiveness also had some negative effect on the overall social tolerance in ethnically diverse and historically charged society, which famously backfired in the Yugoslav wars of the 1990s through ethnic and territorial homogenisation. For the discussion of this see Staničić (2017).
5. The map of Non-Allinged Movement member states can be found here: https://en.wikipedia.org/wiki/Non-Aligned_Movement#/media/File:NAM_Members.svg
6. The literature on this topic has grown exponentially in recent years, with the already established opus of Łukasz Stanek, Tom Avermaete, Hilde Heynen, Haim Yacobi, Vladimir Kulić, Dubravka Sekulić, Luce Beeckmans and many others. Furthermore, specialised journals such as *Architecture Beyond Europe* (https://journals.openedition.org/abe/?lang=en) are particularly focused on transnational cultural exchanges in the field of architecture. Special thanks go to Luce Beckmans for this reference.
7. This was between 1948 and 1965, on average a whopping 8.5 per cent per year.
8. The architecture of this edifice, as we will see later in this chapter, closely resembles social housing built all over Yugoslavia at the time.
9. Yugoslavia was on both the giving and receiving ends of humanitarian aid. The most cited instance is the global effort to rebuild the city of Skopje (today in North Macedonia) after the 1963 earthquake.
10. Serbia alone today has five permanent (stationary) centres with a total capacity of 1,700 people (Fig. 1.), while Croatia and Slovenia have two (capacity 700 people) and four centres (429 people), respectively (source: https://www.asylumineurope.org/reports/country/serbia/types-accommodation). Despite all my efforts, I was unable to find out what the overall number of such shelters built in the the whole of Yugoslavia was, nor how many of them were financed by the United Nations.
11. Building permit No. 9204/64 was issued on 24 September 1964 by the Municipality of the local town of Loznica, but the submitted construction plans are missing. Ljubisav

Rašović, archivist of the Municipality of Loznica, suspects that they were lost during the 2006 reconstruction (interview with the author on 9 January 2020). I managed to locate later additions to the plan, such as building permits for a boiler-room auxiliary building (no. 06-1870/1) and a permit for the surrounding landscape (no. 06-4526/1-65) in the Inter-Municipal Historical Archive in Šabac, Serbia. Here, I want to thank local architect and activist Marko Gavrilović for all his help in gathering the data.

12. United Nations High Commissioner for Refugees and the Office of the United Nations Disaster Relief Coordinator (also known as the United Nations Disaster Relief Office, or UNDRO, the predecessor to the United Nations Office for the Coordination of Humanitarian Affairs). See Siddiqi, 2017.
13. The contractor was local construction firm "Zidar". All relevant documents that I managed to find in the local archive in Šabac in fact come from this firm. Very little—almost nothing—is preserved in the Municipality of Loznica archive. This actually points to the chronic problem in architectural scholarship in Serbia, which is the lack of a propper archivial culture and practice. The municipality of the city of Loznica which issued the construction permit is obliged by law to keep the project in its archives. However, at the time of my inquiry only a few pages remained, mainly installation drawings. Employees testify that the documentation was 'borrowed' by someone in 2008 during the reconstruction of the building and never returned. It was not possible to find out who 'borrowed' it. When it comes to private archives of architects, only recently did we start seeing signs of increased awareness regarding the preservation of original drawings. A systematic and institutionalised architectural archive on a national level, unfortunately, does not exist.
14. A short biography of Mihajlo Mitrović, in Serbian, is available here: http://aas.org.rs/mitrovic-mihajlo-biografija/.
15. Today, Gevgelia lies on the border between Greece and North Macedonia. Mitrović's custom house was destroyed in the early 1990s.
16. The sites he had in mind were primarily Serbian Orthodox monasteries; other religions and ethnicities were conspicuously absent. When, during our interview, I asked him about the motifs from mosques or catholic churches, having in mind the multiculturality of the Yugoslav population, he just waved his hand. Interview with the author held in Belgrade on 17 July 2014.
17. For example, after the NATO bombing of Belgrade in 1999 he designed a residential building on Takovska Street with a sculpture of an eagle above the entrance "looking" towards the ruins of the bombed Radio Television of Serbia building nearby.
18. The selection of this particular spot also remains a mystery. Although very picturesque, Banja Koviljača is relatively far (some 150 kilometres) from Belgrade, the administrative centre of the country, and reaching it by car is not an easy task.
19. Author's translation.
20. I wish to thank anonymous reviewers for this reference.

21. Interestingly, the title of the article is „United Nations *hotel* completed" (author's translation and emphasis). See N.M., "Završen hotel Ujedinjenih Nacija", *Glas Podrinja*, 22 September 1966.
22. Author's translation.
23. Source: http://www.kirs.gov.rs/wb-page.php?kat_id=205&lang=2
24. Interview with the author conducted on 9 January 2020.
25. Data available at https://www.asylumineurope.org/reports/country/serbia/conditions-reception-facilities
26. Source: http://arhiva.kirs.gov.rs/docs/azil/Centar_za_azil_Banja_Koviljaca.pdf
27. It should also be noted that this had not previously been a problem with refugees from the region (most of whom spoke Serbian) or, before that, with refugees from Eastern Europe who were white and came in much smaller numbers.

References

Akšamija, A. (2021). *Design to Live: Everyday Inventions from a Refugee Camp*. Cambridge: MIT Press.

Alić, D. (2013a). Designing for a Socialist Future: the Technology, Ideology and Meaning of Modern Architecture in Post-World War II Bosnia. *Centropa, A Journal of Central European Architecture and Related Arts,* 13(1), 83-94.

Alić, D. (2013b). Bosnian Islamic architectural heritage, Modernism and socialism. In A. Suartika (Ed.), *Vernacular Transformations: Architecture, Place, and Tradition* (pp. 169-197). Bali: Pustaka Larasan.

Alihodžić, R. (2015). *Arhitektura u Crnoj Gori 1965-1990.: (Kroz prizmu "Borbine" nagrade)*. Podgorica: Crnogorska akademija nauka i umjetnosti.

Arendt, H. (1951). *The Origins of Totalitarianism*. New York: Schocken Books.

Avermaete, T. (2010). Framing the Afropolis: Michel Ecochard and the African city for the greatest number. *OASE. Architectural Journal*, 82, 77–101.

Avermaete, T. (2012). Coda: the reflexivity of Cold War architectural modernism, *The Journal of Architecture*, 17:3, 475-477.

Beeckmans, L. (2014). The adventures of the French architect Michel Ecochard in postindependence Dakar: a transnational development expert drifting between commitment and expediency. *The Journal of Architecture*, 19:6, 849-871.

Beeckmans, L. (2018). The Architecture of Nation-building in Africa as a Development Aid Project: Designing the capital cities of Kinshasa (Congo) and Dodoma (Tanzania) in the post-independence years. *Progress in Planning*, 122, 1-28.

Blagojević, Lj. (2007). *Novi Beograd: Osporeni modernizam*. Beograd: Zavod za udžbenike i Arhitektonski fakultet Univerziteta u Beogradu.

Grabrijan D. & Neidhardt, J. (1957) *Arhitektura Bosne i put u suvremeno* (Architecture of Bosnia and the Way to Modernity). Ljubljana: Državna založba Slovenije.

Herscher, A. (2010). *Violence Taking Place: The Architecture of the Kosovo Conflict.* Stanford, Calif.: Stanford University Press.

Herscher, A. (2017). *Displacements: Architecture and Refugee.* Cambridge, MA: MIT Press.

Herscher, A. (2019). Designs on Disaster: Humanitarianism and Contemporary Architecture. In S. Chattopadhyay and J. White (eds.), *Routledge Companion to Critical Approaches to Contemporary Architecture.* London and New York: Routledge.

Jovanović, M. & Rudić, M. (2011, November 10). Panika u parku azilanata. *Vreme, 1088.* Available online at: https://www.vreme.com/cms/view.php?id=1019001

Kadijević, A. (1999). *Mihajlo Mitrović: projekti, graditeljski život, ideje.* Beograd: S. Mašić: Muzej nauke i tehnike: Muzej arhitekture.

Katz, I. (2016). A network of camps on the way to Europe. *Forced Migration Review,* 'Destination Europe', 51, 17-19.

Kulić, V. (2009a). *Land of the in-between: Modern architecture and the state in socialist Yugoslavia, 1945-1965.* PhD Thesis: Faculty of the Graduate School of The University of Texas at Austin.

Kulić, V. (2009b) 'East? West? Or Both?' Foreign perceptions of architecture in Socialist Yugoslavia, *The Journal of Architecture,* 14:1, 129-147.

Kulić, V., Mrduljaš, M. and Thaler W. (2012). *Modernism In-Between: The Mediatory Architectures of Socialist Yugoslavia.* Berlin: Jovis.

Kulić, V. (2012b) An Avant-Garde Architecture for an Avant-Garde Socialism: Yugoslavia at EXPO '58, *Journal of Contemporary History,* 47:1, 161-184.

Kulić, V., Parker, T. and Penick, M., eds. (2014) *Sanctioning Modernism: Architecture and the Making of Postwar Identities.* Austin, US: University of Texas Press.

Lampe, J. (2000). *Yugoslavia as history: twice there was a country.* New York: Cambridge University Press.

Laue, F. (2013). 'Shelter Architecture – Emergency Versus Innovation, Contextualisation and Flexibility.' *Trialog 112/113.* Special Issue: Camp Cities, 19-27.

Lemanski, C. (2019). *Citizenship and infrastructure: practices and identities of citizens and the state.* London: Routledge.

Mitrović, M. (1970). Zapis o tri moja dela, *Arhitektura Urbanizam,* 66, 6-11.

Mitrović, M. (1971). *Mihajlo Mitrović: izložba arhitekture, Muzej primenjene umetnosti Beograd, 13-25. april 1971,* exhibition catalogue. Zagreb: Sitotisak studentski centar Zagreb.

Mitrović, M. (1995). *At the Turn of the Century: the architecture of Energoprojekt between 1951-1995.* Belgrade: BIGZ.

Mlađenović, I. (1983). Arhitektura sa razlogom. *Gradac 50.*

N.M. (1966, September 22) Završen hotel Ujedinjenih Nacija. *Glas Podrinja.*

Philippou, M. (2020). The Spatial Extensions of the Right to Seek Asylum: The Eastern Mediterranean Refugee Route. *Footprint,* 14:2, 49-68, https://doi.org/10.7480/footprint.14.2.4486.

Ramet, S. (2005). *The three Yugoslavias: state-building and legitimation, 1918-2005.* Bloomington, IN: Indiana University Press.

Rudić, M. (2014, April 3). Netrpeljivost i šivaća mašina. *Vreme*. Available online at: https://www.vreme.com/cms/view.php?id=1187020.

Sekulić, D. (2016). *Constructing Non-alignment: the Case of Energoprojekt*. Belgrade: Museum of Contemporary Art: Publikum.

Siddiqi, A. (2017). Architecture Culture, Humanitarian Expertise: From the Tropics to Shelter, 1953-93. *Journal of the Society of Architectural Historians* 76(3), 367-384.

Siddiqi, A. (2013). Humanitarianism and Monumentality. *Trialog 112/113*. Special Issue: Camp Cities, 14-18.

Siddiqi, A. (2013). Emergency or Development? Architecture as Industrial Humanitarianism. *Trialog 112/113*. Special Issue: Camp Cities, 28-31.

Stanek, Ł. (2012) Introduction: the 'Second World's' architecture and planning in the 'Third World. *The Journal of Architecture*, 17:3, 299-307.

Stanek, Ł. (2020). *Architecture in Global Socialism: Eastern Europe, West Africa, and the Middle East in the Cold War*. Princeton University Press.

Stanek, Ł. & Avermaete, T. (2012). Cold War transfer: Architecture and planning from socialist countries in the 'Third World'. *The Journal of Architecture*, 17(4) [special issue].

Staničić, A. (2017, June 13-15). Modern architecture as the origin of ethnic homogenization of Yugoslavia: true or false? *EAHN 2017, Histories in Conflict: Cities | Buildings | Landscapes*, conference presentation at Van Leer Jerusalem Institute, Jerusalem.

Staničić, A. (forthcoming). Teaching Culturally Sensitive Design: Interview with Azra Akšamija. In Elisa Dainese and Aleksandar Staničić (Eds.) *War Diaries: Design After the Destruction of Art and Architecture*. University of Virginia Press.

Staničić, A. (forthcoming). Politics and architecture of border crossings: the case study of Gevgelija in North Macedonia. In Angeliki Sioli, Kris Palagi and Nishat Awan (Eds.) *Bordering On* (in preparation).

Stojiljković, D.M. and Ignjatović, A. (2019) Towards an authentic path: Structuralism and architecture in socialist Yugoslavia, *The Journal of Architecture*, 24:6, 853-876.

Štraus, I. (1991) *Arhitektura Jugoslavije: 1945-1990*. Sarajevo: Svjetlost.

Unknown. (1967, February 19). Nagrada SR Srbije: Stacionar u Koviljači. *Borba*, p. 15.

Vale, L. (1992). *Architecture, Power and National identity*. New Haven: Yale University Press.

https://www.asylumineurope.org/reports/country/serbia/types-accommodation
https://www.asylumineurope.org/reports/country/serbia/conditions-reception-facilities
https://www.azilsrbija.rs/wp-content/uploads/2019/02/Mapa-izbeglickih-centara-u-Srbiji-2018-11-10.jpg
http://arhiva.kirs.gov.rs/docs/azil/Centar_za_azil_Banja_Koviljaca.pdf
http://arhiva.kirs.gov.rs/docs/azil/Centar_za_azil_Bogovadja.pdf
www.beobuild.rs
http://www.kirs.gov.rs/wb-page.php?kat_id=205&lang=2
www.gornjimilanovac.rs

CHAPTER 8

Years in the Waiting Room

A Feminist Ethnography of the Invisible Institutional Living Spaces of Forced Displacement

Maretha Dreyer

University College Dublin, Ireland | Cape Peninsula University of Technology, South Africa | Hasselt University, Belgium

"Be careful, dear! And call me when you get home…" My mom is anxious on the other side of the phone. She's calling from South Africa while I'm on my way to volunteer for the first time at a skillshare evening at a Direct Provision centre, an accommodation centre in Ireland where asylum seekers[1] receive shelter and sustenance while waiting for their application for international protection to be processed.

Introduction

Changes in migration patterns, together with a global increase in the "securitization of migration" (Huysmans, 2000), have led to a growing number of people worldwide finding themselves in situations of forced immobility – waiting for indefinite periods of time. Asylum seekers who have sought international protection in a host country, but whose claims for refugee status have not been determined, are often caught up in the uncertainty of such prolonged conditions of displacement (Doná, 2015). Large-scale accommodation in camps and institutional settings provided by governments and humanitarian organisations are often intended as temporary measures to provide for an immediate need for shelter, but many asylum seekers end up in these settings for years. In these liminal spaces, displaced individuals are faced with the challenge of turning shelter into home (Boccagni, this book; see also Szczepanikova, 2012; Van der Horst, 2004; Vandevoordt, 2017).

Hyndman and Giles describe in their article, *Waiting for what? The feminization of asylum in protracted situations (2011)*, that asylum seekers on the move are viewed by governments in the global North as a potential liability or even a security threat. State policies aim to immobilise asylum seekers and fix them to place in refugee camps or institutional accommodation centres. In these spaces asylum seekers are feminised by rendering them as "passive, helpless, static" (p. 363) in order to reduce the threat that temporary status poses. While reception or "welcome" centres – as the institutional settings providing shelter for asylum seekers are also referred to – lack the iconic typological characteristics of the refugee camp, these more formal spaces of displacement, together with the experiences of their residents, are less frequently acknowledged and studied (Sanyal, 2019).

This chapter aims to provide insights into the socio-spatial regulation of the asylum applicants within one such institutional setting in Ireland and reflects on the relational aspects of space that shape each individual's subjective experience. The research focuses on Hatch Hall, an accommodation centre situated in Dublin, where I volunteered at a skill-share initiative between June and August 2016. Data generated during this time were in the form of a reflexive journal in which I documented my observations, thoughts, experiences and critical reflections as researcher. Instead of focusing on the physical features of space, extracts from my journal are employed throughout this chapter to initiate explorations into several theoretical themes and concepts I encountered within the space.

The Irish asylum application system

In Ireland the State fulfils its obligation towards basic subsistence for asylum applicants by providing board and lodging in several State-funded Direct Provision centres scattered around the country. Although Direct Provision was introduced in 2000 as a temporary measure to provide short-term shelter, the inefficiency of the asylum application process has led many applicants to wait for years in Direct Provision for a final decision on their applications (McMahon Report, 2015).

A host of rules regulate life in Direct Provision. Besides the routine expected from institutional living, "house rules" in Direct Provision centres include that residents are required to obtain permission to sleep out, decorate or make use of any electrical equipment in their rooms, or leave children in the care of another adult. Residents do not have a say about with whom they share a room and are expected to move when required by management – that could be to a different room or even a different centre altogether (RIA, 2019). All meals are served at specific times and many residents have complained that the food is not culturally appropriate (McMahon Report, 2015).

The majority of the centres are located in buildings that were originally intended for short-term accommodation, such as former hotels, hostels, convents, military barracks or mobile homes. Consequently, most residents do not have access to private living space or cooking facilities. The accommodation comprises mainly bedrooms, unable to house the activities that long-term living entails (McMahon Report, 2015).

Residents are not detained in these centres and are supposedly 'free' to come and go. However, several factors confine them mostly to the centre and its immediate surroundings, contributing to the marginalisation, social isolation and exclusion of Direct Provision residents from society in general:

- lack of finance and income due to regulations around joining the work force, insufficiency of the personal allowance provided by the state and being excluded from social welfare entitlements (O'Reilly, 2013);
- institutional regulations which prescribe the protocol for receiving visitors, meal times and rules regarding overnighting elsewhere (Reception and Integration Agency, 2019);
- spatial considerations such as the remote location of some centres and lack of facilities for inviting people to their homes (McMahon Report, 2015).

Unlike in other European countries, the accommodation centres are not operated by non-profit organisations and private operators have made a lucrative business of providing accommodation for asylum seekers (Thornton, 2014). Mounting public criticism of Direct Provision has highlighted the major issues of the system to be: uncertainty; lack of autonomy and privacy; marginalisation and isolation; negative impacts on emotional and mental health; and the extended period of time people spend in Direct Provision while their applications are being processed (McMahon Report, 2015).

Hatch Hall

> "*How bad can it be?*" I think to myself, looking up at the façade of the lovely old redbrick building. We sign in at security and follow one of the residents down the hallway to the communal lounge. There are security cameras everywhere! Am I really allowed to be here? A few women are waiting for us in the communal lounge. It's a large room with high ceilings, a brownish carpet, obscured glass panel doors on two sides and large sash windows lighting up the room. It looks as if it could have been beautiful in its days – maybe it used to be a ball room? The walls are now painted a bright custard yellow. There's an old box TV, a few coffee tables and chairs and a couch standing about incoherently. The furniture is too small for the size of the room, making the room feel empty – even with the people in it.

The first time I visited Hatch Hall, I was rather surprised to find that this accommodation centre for asylum seekers was situated in the heart of Dublin in – what was from my perspective – a lovely neo-Gothic building from 1912 (Fig. 1.). Until 2004, Hatch Hall was used as a student residence for privileged third-level male students, most of whom studied medicine at University College Dublin. In 2004 the property was sold to a developer and contracted out to the Department of Justice as a Direct Provision centre (RIA, 2016).

Figure 1. Street façade of Hatch Hall, Dublin, Ireland; photo taken by author.

During the second half of 2016, when I volunteered at the centre, the number of residents in Hatch Hall varied between 108 and 128, and included couples, single people and families. There were also about thirteen children, all living with at least one parent. Two thirds of the residents were men and one third women. Although the capacity of the centre was determined as a maximum of 200 residents, an outbreak of chickenpox temporarily prevented new residents being admitted (RIA, 2016, 2017). Due to the building's previous use as a student residence, asylum seekers were accommodated in shared bedrooms, some with *en-suite* bathrooms. Residents had no access to private living spaces or cooking facilities. Food or cooking was not allowed in the bedrooms. As far as I could establish, communal areas included the lounge where we met on skill-share evenings, a dining hall, a games room, laundry area and an outside children's play area. Single adults were accommodated in multi-occupancy rooms, sharing the space with several people from diverse cultures and backgrounds, often unable to speak the same language. Families were accommodated in one or more rooms, depending on the size of the family and the gender of the children (McMahon Report, 2015). This meant that for most of the residents personal space was limited to their bed and the area immediately surrounding it. This resulted in an extreme lack of privacy and autonomy.

In 2019 the Direct Provision centre at Hatch Hall was closed and the building sold with plans for it to be developed into a luxury hotel (Quinlan, 2019).

Methodology and method

> The women are surprised to hear that I'm from South Africa.
> "*You're too light!*" Precious[2] exclaims. We all laugh.

While in Ireland on a year-long research mobility, I came into contact with an ad hoc group of volunteers who had somehow obtained permission to host what they referred to as "skillshare evenings" at a Direct Provision centre. The sessions were arranged as weekly informal gatherings around an arts and crafts or physical activity in the centre's communal lounge – the only public area where visitors were allowed. As an architect and novice feminist scholar, I joined the group as a visiting participant with the intention of doing research into the living conditions of Direct Provision.

Typically, skill-share sessions were attended by a small group of four to ten women and children from the centre, and around six or eight volunteers. Some men living in the centre, especially the younger men, occasionally joined in if we were doing a physical activity such as dancing or learning how to *hula hoop*. They also stopped by regularly at the end of the session to socialise, always eager to share the story of how they ended up in Hatch Hall. In contrast, women rarely shared where they were from and never mentioned how they came to be in Ireland: our conversations were slow and interrupted while we were focused on making flowers out of toilet paper rolls or weaving mandalas; we limited our interactions to the weather, our families, how we miss the sun in Africa, but mostly to "please pass the scissors".

My choice of a data collection method for this research was predominantly determined by the limitations of my position as a guest participant/researcher within the group. Although several participatory and emancipatory methods could probably be considered more appropriate for doing research within a sensitive context such as Direct Provision, my options were restricted to observing and participating in whatever activity was planned for the evening. An ethnographic method such as participant observation thus seemed to be a feasible option.

Ethnography

Creswell and Poth (2018) define ethnography, in general, as a qualitative research method in which sensory observational techniques are employed to study, describe and interpret social organisation patterns of a group of people in a specific context. Ethnographic data collection often involves doing fieldwork whereby the researcher meticulously records observations while being immersed as a participant/researcher in the day-to-day lives of the group being studied. Collected data are analysed and interpreted by applying a theoretical lens, and finally written up and published as an objective account of the studied culture.

Standard ethnographic research methods have, however, proved to be problematic for many feminist scholars. In fact, Visweswaran (1994), Abu-Lughod (1990) and Stacey (1988) have even questioned whether it is worth pursuing a feminist ethnography at all while it may be impossible for this method to meet all feminist research aspirations. Feminist theories are typically based on a shared epistemological perspective that knowledge is situated (Haraway, 1988) and produced in encounters between an embodied self and other(s) (Davids & Willemse, 2014). This implies that what a researcher can come to understand or know is always subjective, partial, relational and thereby entangled with power hierarchies (Hesse-Biber, 2012). This foundation serves as an epistemological and methodological lens that guides both the selection of subject matter and how the researcher approaches a method (Pillow & Mayo, 2014). From a feminist perspective, the main concerns with ethnography are therefore frequently associated with a range of interrelated issues including the relationship between the researcher and researched, the authority of the researcher, representation and a claim to objectivity (Behar et al., 2011; Pillow & Mayo, 2014).

These factors could be particularly problematic within contexts where substantial power imbalances exist between the researcher and those researched. This is often the case in research focussed on displaced people, where power imbalances are regularly left unacknowledged by academics and aid organisations alike. In these circumstances, where ethnography is often used as a research method, ethnographers should be mindful that their research is not "perpetuating colonial control of 'distant' peoples and places" (Rosaldo, 1989, pp. 30-31). In other words, with the legacy of colonialism implicated in many contexts of displacement, *how* we do ethnographic and other research with displaced people is of particular significance.

Reflexive journal

Based on the considerations above, I made use of a reflexive research journal as a data collection tool for my ethnographic exploration into the space of Direct Provision. Instead of a linear research process, the "reflection-in-action" (Schön, 1983; 1987) that the use of a reflexive journal requires necessitates a continuous back and forth interaction between the different stages of the research. According to Schön (1987), the ability to "think about what you are doing while you are doing it" is particularly useful in situations of "uncertainty, uniqueness and conflict" (p. 16), as is often the case when doing research in a sensitive context such as Direct Provision. Thus, my journal became a written record of the evolution of the research.

While collecting data, I attempted to concentrate specifically on capturing the spatial qualities of my experience, while being aware of how space and social interaction influence each other. However, making use of a reflexive journal also provided me with an opportunity to respond to several feminist research goals – most of which are focussed on highlighting the researcher's subjective presence within the research. Etherington (2004) proposes that keeping a reflexive journal can develop the researcher's self-awareness by providing a platform for "reflecting and processing our internal and external responses and behaviours" (p. 128). She explains:

> We reflect on our roles, on the impact of the research upon our personal and professional lives, on our relationships with participants, on our perception of the impact we may be making on their lives and on our negative and/or positive feelings about what is happening during the research process. (ibid., p. 127).

Such a process of interrogation of feelings and emotions that takes place within the private space of a journal can lead to new insight as it provides a researcher with the opportunity to openly and honestly become aware of their biases. Dauphinee (2010) argues that conventional academic writing practices do not adequately provide a way for researchers to express and process the emotions they might experience while conducting research. Such experiences could, for instance, include emotionally loaded or compromising situations:

> [W]hat we end up doing is privately remembering, rather than publicly writing [such experiences] into our publications. This divides our experiences in the field into public and private and, quite predictably, results in a silencing of the private. (p. 805).

Figure 2. Surveillance in Direct Provision. Source: Asylum Archive, photos taken by and courtesy of Vukasin Nedeljkovic, 2007.

Consequently, personal experiences are often simply excluded from research, resulting in the "writing out" of the complexity of the author's involvement under the guise of objectivity. A reflexive research journal creates a space for the researcher to connect with the research process in a personal, authentic and multi-dimensional manner. Hence, in an attempt explicitly to demonstrate that my thoughts, decisions and actions regarding the study were not objective, but rather produced by my identity, assumptions and past experiences becoming interwoven with the research, I deliberately wrote my subjective self into the data from the outset. In addition to meticulously documenting my observations during each skill-share session, I also engaged critically with other more personal aspects of the research process. This was done by adding reflections on my actions as well as the thoughts, feelings and emotions I felt during and after each visit to Hatch Hall. Subsequently, data emerged as detailed narrative descriptions of people, events, emotions and spatial qualities within Direct Provision, interwoven with my personal reflections in the process of trying to make sense of my experience of doing the research.

Post-colonial perspectives on representation

Post-colonial theory advocates for an awareness of "who is speaking" in research. In *Can the Subaltern Speak?* (1987), Gayatri Spivak considers the role of agency involved in representation and problematises speaking on behalf of others. She suggests that those in positions of power or privilege should rather provide opportunities for marginalised groups to speak for themselves. Davids and Willemse (2014) question whether reflexive writing techniques are indeed capable of shifting power dimensions. Speaking about or on behalf of others always involves authority and privilege. This is supported by Pillow and Mayo (2014) who argues that "[…] no textual experimentation removes the fact that we are writing 'about'—whether it is about others or ourselves or ourselves and others" (p. 15). Therefore, while the reflexive techniques I implemented to write myself explicitly into the research might be an adequate reaction to the notion of seemingly "objective" research, they do little to resolve the problems involved with representation.

Further problematising the complexities of representation, Sara Ahmed argues in *Strange Encounters: Embodied Others in Post-Coloniality* (2000) that creating knowledge about cultural others in less powerful positions inevitably sets them up as "strangers" or someone who is different from "us" – an "Other". As she explains, through encounters between "us" and "others" in local contexts "the figure of the 'stranger' is produced, not as that which we fail to recognise, but as that which we have already recognised as 'a stranger'" (ibid., p. 3). Strangers are thus not people that we do not know; they become strangers exactly because of what we already know about them, and this, in turn, determines how we react to them. Encounters between embodied others are always shaped by historical encounters. "[C]ontemporary discourses of globalisation and multiculturalism involve the reproduction of the figure of the stranger, and the enforcement of boundaries, through the very emphasis on becoming, hybridity and inbetweenness" (ibid., p. 13). The knowledge produced about the stranger therefore also has spatial implications, as it ultimately enforces boundaries by determining who are included as "us" and who form the margins of the excluded "others".

In this way, the ethnographer is thus automatically implicated in the production of "the stranger" when creating knowledge about a group of marginalised people. The short introductory vignette shared in the opening paragraph of this chapter, where my mother expresses her concerns about my safety within the Direct Provision space, is testimony to the colonial history of what we think we know about asylum seekers. Even from another country, my mother senses the supposed threat – or "stranger danger" as Ahmed (2000, p. 78) refers to it – that these "bodies out of place" pose. What is "known" about asylum seekers sets them up as strangers, while my "knapsack of privileges" (McIntosh, 1989) positions me, a white South African in Ireland, as less of a danger. The legacy of colonialism that my identity represents places me in a position of power within Direct Provision that allows me to create knowledge about others. By producing knowledge about asylum seekers I am inevitably perpetuating the rhetoric of *them* as out of place "others" and ultimately reproducing colonial inequalities.

The theory discussed in this section on methodology and methods urged me to reconsider ways in which research is conducted within contexts of displacement. I questioned whether it was appropriate – or even possible – for me, as a privileged white South African woman, to do research based on ethical feminist values in Direct Provision. In an effort to navigate at least some of the complexities of representation and power imbalances inherent in ethnographic research methods within the constraints of the skill-share initiative, I focused my research on the *space* of Direct Provision in particular. However, as will be discussed in more detail in the following section, social behaviour and space are interdependent. An exploration of space will thus not be complete without a consideration of personal experiences and broader social dynamics.

A feminist interpretation of space and place

> "*Hatch Hall was a home from home [sic], a place where one could make friends for life. It was a place where one could test and discover who you were but, most of all, a place where you could be part of a piece of history. The building really was an institution [...]. It was a haven where great minds and talents came together at the dawn of their adult lives*", writes a former resident who lived in Hatch Hall during his student years (Dugdale, 2009).

My spatial investigation into Hatch Hall started by juxtaposing this description by a student during Hatch Hall's more privileged past with my own observations and what I had read about the experiences of asylum seekers in Direct Provision. From this, two observations emerged as a starting point: firstly, that the colonial – and from my initial perspective, *pleasant* – appearance of the building from the outside could contribute to feelings of disconnect and nullify the experiences of asylum seekers; secondly, I noted that if two groups of people could have completely different spatial experiences of the same place, this could not simply be attributed to physical space or the built environment alone. This insight supports Hilde Heynen's (2013) model of "space as stage" that allows for our experience of space to be determined by both the architecture and the social interactions within a space.

In her article, 'Space as Receptor, Instrument or Stage: Notes on the interaction between spatial and social constellations', Heynen (2013) proposes that multidisciplinary research is needed in order for one to acquire a more holistic understanding of the interaction between the built environment and social behaviour. She distinguishes between three different models that could possibly explain this interaction: firstly, architectural space is mostly understood in the social sciences as a passive *receptor* within which social interaction takes place. This method takes "the existence of actual architectural and urban space as a given background, rather than as an active factor that in itself is capable of producing such behaviour" (p. 344). Secondly, from an architectural perspective space is often believed to be *an instrument* with the ability to shape the social interactions that take place within it. "They focus on the capacity of space to impose certain desired behaviours on subjects, which effectuate a-symmetrical power relations between domineering and oppressed groups" (p. 346). However, both these models fail fully to explain the complex interaction between people and the built environment. My research therefore aims to investigate space as described by Heynen's third model – the multidisciplinary perspective she defines as 'space as a stage'. This conception proposes that space can, on the one hand, afford certain social constructs and disallow others, while on the other hand also being influenced and changed by the agency of its inhabitants. As stage, space can thus both "accommodate and condition social behaviour" (Heynen, 2013, p. 346).

Doreen Massey's work (1994; 2005), which applies gender theories to existing concepts and methods of theorising space and place, sheds further light on my observation that the same space can be experienced in completely different ways. Feminist theorists frequently argue that gender characteristics are not stable and attributable to a fixed essence, but rather socially constructed and relational (Butler, 1988). Massey (1994) draws on this concept to question the essentialist and stable conceptualisation of space and place. She maintains that the dichotomous nature of the dominant theoretical understanding of space and place supports the exclusivity and boundedness of place as well as the sentimental associations with place as *home* or *motherland*. Massey (1994) therefore suggests a feminist strategy to "thinking in terms of relations" (p. 7) in order to reconceptualise our understanding of space and place. She argues that both space and place should be conceptualised in terms of social relations such as class and gender. Massey (2015a) stresses that, "while space is socially constructed, the social is spatially constructed" (p. 254). In this way, space can be acknowledged as much more than a passive backdrop or container for social interaction, while the important role of social interaction in the subjective experience of space becomes evident.

All spaces therefore change depending on the identity of the occupants and obtain significance through social relations and interaction, and through this process of signification space becomes place (Tyner, 2012, p. 16). Space, when regarded as relational, can simultaneously hold different meanings for different individuals or, in other words, be a different place to several people. Rather than stable and definite, place is "a dynamic ensemble of people and environment that is at once material and experiential, spatial and social" (Dovey, 2010, p. 7). The particular combination of social relations which are part of what defines the uniqueness of any place is by no means included within that place itself. Therefore, places cannot exist without people; they are lived and embodied spaces (Tyner, 2012, p. 18). As it is constituted through "reiterative social practice, place is made and remade on a daily basis" (Creswell, 2004, p. 1). This draws attention to the important role that socio-political power relations play in our subjective experience of place.

> Such a view of place challenges any possibility of claims to internal histories or to timeless identities. The identities of place are always unfixed, contested and multiple. And the particularity of any place is, in these terms, constructed not by placing boundaries around it and defining its identity through counter-position to the other which lies beyond, but precisely […] through the specificity of the mix of links and interconnections to that 'beyond'. Places viewed this way are open and porous. (Massey, 1994, p. 5).

Instead of being linked to one demarcated geographical position, place thus stretches over several locations and incorporates physical, emotional, social, economic and cultural qualities. According to Brun and Fábos (2015), opening up the conventional conception of place as explained above can create new possibilities for understanding the interaction between displaced individuals, place and home.

Home

On several occasions one of the volunteers who was aware of my research and a former resident of Direct Provision himself, had asked some of the women in the group to show me their rooms. The question was always met with the same answer: "*It is not allowed. You know I will get into trouble*".

One evening, after the skillshare activity, Elijah offered to show me his room: Very conscious of all the security cameras [Fig. 2.], I follow him down numerous corridors and up several flights of stairs, into the part of the building that is restricted to visitors. I'm rather anxious, so I nervously chat along the way. "*If you don't take me back down, Elijah, I'll never get out of here,*" I comment, trying to hide my uneasiness with a feeble joke. I'm not supposed to be here. The hallways are clean and empty. It looks like hospital corridors with linoleum floors and light walls. No pictures, no curtains. *Nothing that says "home".*

Home is a much debated and contentious subject. Early western feminist debate problematised home as an institution of women's oppression in which gender norms and power relations are upheld (De Beauvoir, 1949; Friedan, 1963) by confining women to a life of endless housework. However, there are also feminist theorists who maintain that home could also be conceptualised in a more positive way. According to bell hooks (1990) the concept of home holds powerful political potential for change that should not be overlooked. According to her, home has the potential to be a place of healing, where one could recover to wholeness. Iris Marion Young supports this position in her article, 'House and Home: Feminist variations on a theme' (2005), by suggesting an alternative perspective on home and, more specifically, housework. She maintains that home is a place of "remembrance" where positive as well as negative experiences from the past are "preserved" and subsequently framed and reframed, through the mundane activities of everyday life. By enactment of often-gendered household tasks, home is created and recreated through the continuity of identities, families and cultures – irrespective of location. Young explains, for instance, that preparing food maintains culture and produces home: "She prepares the sauce according to her mother's recipe in order physically to nourish her children, but at the same time she keeps alive and old cuisine in a new country" (Young, 2005, p. 143). This leads to a more fluid and dynamic conception of home by introducing the idea that home does not need to be fixed to a specific place at all, but is rather produced by the everyday embodied actions of homemaking. For asylum seekers the continuation of such familiar household tasks could provide opportunities to reduce feelings of temporariness and dislocation by encouraging relational and emotional connection to place as open and dynamic, rather than attachment to a fixed location. Brun and Fábos (2015) propose that home in forced migration "focuses more on the relational and emotional perspectives of home rather than the territorial connections to a home" (p. 8). For asylum seekers home can thus consist of a complex trans-local system where both "place of origin and place of refuge" (p. 8) work together to create a sense of belonging. Home can as such incorporate far-reaching social and emotional connections that span several continents at once: "from the material and territorial to the imaginary and symbolic" (p. 9).

Intersectionality and embodiment

> *"This is my room,"* Elijah announces. A single bed and bunkbed are moved tightly together on one side of the room to create space for a small table with a computer and speakers, a wardrobe and some shelves with clothing. He explains that he doesn't have to share his room like the other men as he is not an asylum seeker anymore. He's just staying here while finding alternative accommodation in Dublin. "*The others don't have extra belongings such as shelves or computers*", he clarifies. I ask about privacy and lockable cupboard space. "*Privacy is good*". He has his own bedroom and bathroom.

Our experience of space relies to a large extent on our bodies. It therefore follows quite naturally that each person's experience of space will be unique, determined by their specific height, size, health, age and physical abilities. Other characteristics that make up each person's unique identity, such as gender, race, socio-economic position, motherhood, marital status, culture etc., also play a role in an individual's experience of space. Within the context of Direct Provision, space and place take on a particular significance as these concepts are complex – entangled with the politics of power, oppression and belonging.

In his book, *Discipline and Punish* (1977), Foucault explains that power can play out at microlevels of society. Minor incidents of power are expressed as complex layers of privilege within the space of Direct Provision, where some residents, such as Elijah, are treated as superior to 'the others'. This constitutes internal hierarchies amongst the residents, whereby privileges are determined by each resident's intersectional identity. "Intersectionality", a term coined by Kimberlé Crenshaw (1989; 1991), refers to an analytical framework that makes use of diversification in order to deconstruct collective identity and explains the multidimensional nature in which oppression, marginalisation and exclusion work. Building on this theory, Bürkner (2012) argues that identity categories that play a particular role in social inequality within the context of migration are class, gender, race and body, where 'body' includes features such as age, appearance and ability. This explains how power relations in Direct Provision are determined by the embodied experience of each person's unique combination of identity characteristics. Additionally, in Direct Provision asylum application status in particular plays a very important role in determining the level of autonomy individuals are granted. This is evident from Elijah being allowed to stay alone in his room and personalise it to a certain extent, while 'the others' do not have these privileges; by the women being unable to show me their rooms, while Elijah could do so; or the men spontaneously telling their stories, while women kept conversation to the minimum.

Young (1990) explains that oppression manifests itself in five different ways: through exploitation, marginalisation, powerlessness, cultural imperialism and violence. The space of Direct Provision subjects asylum seekers in varying degrees to at least marginalisation, powerlessness and cultural imperialism. The residents are not a homogenous group and experience different levels of oppression in Direct Provision based on their intersectional identity traits.

Figure 3. Children playing at a skill-share evening in Hatch Hall, photo taken by and courtesy of Marluce Lima (All We Need is Love), 2016.

Emancipatory power of making a home

> "*The other guys struggle with privacy, as they can't choose who they share a room with. Here, let me show you.*" He gets up, leads me outside to the next room. He knocks: "*Hi Somali, my friend Somali, open up. We have a visitor. She wants to see your room. Just cover yourself up.*" I feel mortified at just how inappropriate the situation is. I shouldn't be here…the door is opened cautiously from the inside. Except for the different arrangement of the furniture, the room is identical to Elijah's. Even the curtains and bedding look exactly the same. However, in this room it is obvious that there is not enough storage space, making it seem cramped and claustrophobic. "*See there's place for three single men in this room,*" Elijah explains. "*At the moment, the centre isn't full, so there's only two men sharing the room for now*". I cannot imagine that there could be space for another man and his belongings in here. "*The men are from different countries. They have different cultures and speak different languages. Sometimes there's conflict if one man wants to sleep and another wants to watch TV and they can't speak the same language…*"

Most of the everyday activities performed at home, such as cooking, eating, cleaning, sleeping, bathing, socialising and celebrating, are culturally determined and have spatial implications. The repetition of these tasks in a specific, familiar way has the potential to recreate home, irrespective of place or geographical location. In some cases space needs to be modified or personalised in order to accommodate the movements specific to an action.

Direct Provision is not an environment conducive to meaningful attachments and a feeling of belonging as the most intimate detail of residents' lives are controlled and scrutinised by the system. In Direct Provision bodily movement is determined and controlled through rules and surveillance, but also the affordances of the space. This creates additional disconnect as asylum seekers are unable to re-enact habitual embodied routines – such as eating, sleeping, religious practice and caring – in the familiar way they used to back 'home'. The supposedly 'neutral' space of the centre affords most residents few to no opportunities to modify and personalise their living spaces or to determine how they would want to carry out activities such as sleeping, for instance. This creates feelings of alienation. For an asylum seeker the colonial architecture of this centre thus becomes a "space of Otherness, which strip[s] her of her dignity and personal power" (hooks, 1990, p. 83). Although from an outsider's perspective it might look like a comfortable refuge and suitable solution to accommodate asylum seekers, the space of Direct Provision is so alien and impossible for most residents to connect or relate to that residents might never feel comfortable in the space. In this excessively controlled environment, forced assimilation into Western 'neutrality' transforms residents' lives into meaningless waiting, evident in the way one resident describes her day:

> "I sleep...I wake up, I eat breakfast, I go to my room, I wait for lunch, after lunch, I go to my room, I wait for dinner, after dinner, I go to my room. I sleep..."

Conclusion

Due to the increasing securitisation of migration, growing numbers of displaced people are currently forced to wait for long periods of time in environments intended to be temporary solutions. The most iconic spatial representations of such temporary spaces are refugee camps. However, forcibly displaced people find shelter, are accommodated or make their homes in a variety of different ways. Institutional contexts of displacement are less often studied and thereby even more obscured, further marginalising the inhabitants of these spaces.

One such context is the seldom researched spaces of institutional living that some countries provide for asylum seekers waiting for their refugee status to be decided. At face value, institutional living might seem to be a workable solution for a difficult situation. I argued, however, that spaces providing large-scale accommodation for asylum seekers such as Direct Provision in Ireland instead work to marginalise and alienate residents and to invalidate their experiences. Within the space of Direct Provision, the stringent control and surveillance of residents' everyday lives serves to segregate them from the rest of society. By providing culturally inappropriate accommodation with little to no opportunity to adjust space or to recreate home by doing homemaking activities, residents are stripped of their agency and it further engenders asylum seekers as docile, static and helpless.

Feminist theory on space, place and home can provide insights into spatial practices and making homes in situations of displacement. The act of making a home – be it constructing it, adjusting it, by homemaking tasks, or recreating home by doing and redoing seemingly simple daily acts such as sleeping and eating in a familiar way – has emancipatory potential for displaced individuals. It can counteract feelings of uncertainty, dislocation and unsettledness.

Domesticity, as the performance of everyday life, has the potential to transform abstract space into meaningful place or, ideally, even into home. Displaced people need the autonomy to make decisions regarding their own lives and the spaces they inhabit in order to recreate a sense of home. In Direct Provision, however, even the most trivial details of residents' lives are regulated to such an extent that forming any attachment to place is reserved for only a privileged few.

Intersectionality can be a useful framework for understanding how asylum seekers in situations of displacement might be affected in different ways or intensities. I considered the social regulation of the asylum applicants within a centre in Dublin and discussed the formation of internal hierarchies that uniquely shape each individual resident's spatial experience. Through this investigation it became evident that several identity characteristics – and in this case, asylum application status in particular – plays an important role in the level of autonomy or exclusion of residents.

Research on displaced people has a history founded in colonialism and is still often conducted by outsiders: academic researchers and humanitarian organisations who do not have first-hand experience of living the life of the researched group. Moreover, large power imbalances with regard to economic, cultural and political capital often exist within these contexts between the researcher and the researched. Feminist and post-colonial critiques of the authority of the author and representation in research argue that alternative approaches should be explored. I proposed the use of a reflexive journal as part of an ethnographical study that aspires to feminist research ideals. Keeping a reflexive journal assisted me to become aware of and critically reflect some of the complexities and contradictions that my personal identity as researcher within the Direct Provision space introduced into the research. By superimposing theory on displacement, space and power with the reflexive data from my personal experience within the Direct Provision centre during skill-share events, I came to acquire a better understanding of the relational qualities of space that shape each individual's unique experience.

In the light of this, and building on a recent article by Xue and Desmet (2019), who argue that introspection is a valid and powerful method in experience-driven design research, I propose that reflexive ethnographic methods should similarly be regarded as an effective approach in architectural research. Future research could include more mixed methods to simultaneously incorporate both visual and reflexive data in order to obtain a richer understanding of the ways in which space and social relations influence each other.

Acknowledgements

I am grateful to Dr. Aideen Quilty (University College Dublin), Prof. Dr. Ann Petermans (Hasselt University) and the editors and reviewers of this publication for valuable input into this research at various stages. Thank you to Vukasin Nedeljkovic and Marluce Lima for allowing me to include their photographs. I also want to thank the European Commission and Erasmus Mundus Programme for financial support, which enabled me to do this research.

Notes

1. In general terms, "refugee" refers to a person who flees their country of origin or fears persecution on the basis of race, religion, nationality, political opinion or membership of a social group (Thornton, Glossary of Terms: Irish Asylum Law, 2013). The term "asylum seeker" refers to a displaced individual who has sought international protection in a host country, but whose claim for refugee status has not been determined (UNHRC, 2015). Based on the Universal Declaration of Human Rights 1948 (UN General Assembly), the 1951 Refugee Convention and its 1967 Protocol (UN General Assembly, 1951), every asylum seeker is entitled to accommodation and subsistence while their application for international protection is being reviewed.
2. In order to protect participants' identity, data have been anonymised by removing direct identifiers and making use of pseudonyms.

References

Abu-Lughod, L. (1990). Can there be a feminist ethnography? *Women and Performance, 5(1)*, 7-27.

Ahmed, S. (2000). *Strange encounters: Embodied others in post-coloniality*. London: Routledge.

Behar, R., Ellis, C., Bochner, A., Kincheloe, J., McLaren, P., Richardson, L., & Visweswaran, K. (2011). Reflexive Ethnography. In N. K. Denzin, & Y. S. LIncoln, *The Qualitative Inquiry Reader* (pp. 2-4). Thousand Oaks: SAGE Publications.

Brun, C., & Fábos, A. (2015). Making Homes in Limbo? A Conceptual Framework. *Refuge, 31(1)*, 5-17.

Butler, J. (1988). Performantive Acts and Gender Constitution: An Essay in Phenomenology and Feminist Theory. (J. H. Press, Ed.) *Theatre Journal, 40*(4), 519-531.

Creswell, J. W., & Poth, C. N. (2018). *Qualitative inquiry and research design: Choosing among the five approaches (4th ed.)*. Thousand Oaks, CA: Sage Publications.

Creswell, T. (2004). *Place: A Short Introduction.* Malden: Blackwell.

Dauphinee, E. (2010). The ethics of autoethnography. *Review of International Studies, 36*(3), 799-818.

Davids, T., & Willemse, K. (2014). Embodied engagements: Feminist ethnography at the crossing of knowledge production and representation — An introduction. *Women's Studies International Forum, 43,* 1-4.

De Beauvoir, S. (1949). *The second sex.* New York: Vintage House.

Department of Justice and Equality. (2015, June 30). Final Report: Working Group to Report to Government on Improvements to the Protection Process, Including Direct Provision and Supports to Asylum Seekers. Retrieved [27 June, 2016] from http://www.justice.ie/en/JELR/Report%20to%20Government%20on%20Improvements%20to%20the%20Protection%20Process,%20including%20Direct%20Provision%20and%20Supports%20to%20Asylum%20Seekers.pdf/Files/Report%20to%20Government%20on%20Improvements%20to%20the%20Protection%20Process,%20including%20Direct%20Provision%20and%20Supports%20to%20Asylum%20Seekers.pdf

Doná, G. (2015). Making homes in limbo: Embodied virtual "homes" in prolonged conditions of displacement. *Refuge, 31*(1), 67-73.

Dovey, K. (2010). *Bocoming Places: Urbanism/Architecture/Identity/Power.* London: Routledge.

Dugdale, N. (2009, April 15). *Dugdale's Limerick.* Retrieved August 21, 2016, from Sic Luceat Lux Vestra: https://nigeldugdale.wordpress.com/2009/04/15/sic-luceat-lux-vestra/

Etherington, K. (2004). *Becoming a reflexive researcher.* London: Jessica Kingsley Publishers.

Foucault, M. (1977). *Discipline and Punish: The Birth of the Prison.* Guilford: Billing and Sons.

Friedan, B. (1963). *The feminine mystique.* New York: W. W. Norton & Company.

Haraway, D. J. (1988). Situated Knowledges: The Science Question in Feminism and the Privilege of Partial Perspective. *Feminist Studies, 14*(3), 575-599.

Hesse-Biber, S. N. (2012). Feminist research: Exploring, interrogating, and transforming the interconnections of epistemology, methodology, and method. In *Handbook of feminist research: Theory and praxis* (2nd edition ed., pp. 2-16). Thousand Oaks: Sage Publications.

Heynen, H. (2013). Space as Receptor, Instrument or Stage: Notes on the interaction between spatial and social constellations. *International Planning Studies, 18(3-4),* 342-357.

hooks, b. (1990). Homeplace: A Site Resistance. In *Yearning: Race, gender and cultural politics* (pp. 41-49). Boston, MA: South End Press.

Huysmans, J. (2000). The European Union and the securitization of migration. *Journal of Common Market Studies, 38*(5), 751-777.

Hyndman, J., & Giles, W. (2011). Waiting for what? The feminization of asylum in protracted situations. *Gender, Place & Culture: A Journal of Feminist Geography, 18(3)*, 361-379.

Massey, D. (1994). *Space, Place and Gender.* Cambridge: Polity.

Massey, D. (2005). *For Space.* London: Sage Publications.

McIntosh, P. (1989, July/August). White privilege: Unpacking the invisible knapsack. In *Peace and Freedom* (pp. 10-12). Philadelphia: Women's International League for Peace and Freedom.

McMahon Report. (2015). *See Department of Justice and Equality, 2015.*

O'Reilly, E. (2013). Ombudsman Emily O'Reilly: Asylum Seekers in Our Republic: Why have we gone wrong? Retrieved 21 October 2021, from Studies: An Irish Quarterly Review, Summer 2013, Vol. 102, No. 406, pp. 131-148: https://www.jstor.org/stable/23631159

Pillow, W. S., & Mayo, C. (2014). Feminist Ethnography: Histories, Challenges, and Possibilities. In S. N. Hesse-Biber, *Handbook of Feminist Research: Theory and Praxi* (pp. 187-205). Thousand Oaks, CA: Sage Publications.

Quinlan, R. (2019, September 11). Red Carnation Hotels buys former student digs at Hatch Hall for €20m. *The Irish Times* (p. 8).

Reception and Integration Agency. (2016). *Interim Figures: June 2016.* Dublin: Department of Justice and Equality.

Reception and Integration Agency. (2017). *Reception and Integration Agency: Annual Report 2016.* Retrieved from http://www.ria.gov.ie/en/RIA/Annual%20report%202016%20.pdf/Files/Annual%20report%202016%20.pdf

Reception and Integration Agency. (2019). *House Rules and Procedures for Reception and Accommodation Centres.* Dublin: Department of Justice and Equality.

RIA. See Reception and Integration Agency.

Rosaldo, R. (1989). *Culture and Truth: The remaking of social analysis.* Boston, MA: Beacon.

Sanyal, R. (2019, January 25). *Unsettling Architectural Narratives of Refuge: From Camps to Cities.* Retrieved December 16, 2020, from Max Planck Institute Open Lectures: https://www.mmg.mpg.de/332078/online-lecture-2019-01-25-siddiqi

Schön, D. (1983). *The reflective practitioner: How professionals think in Action.* Farnham, United Kingdom: Ashgate Publishing.

Schön, D. (1987). *Educating the reflective practitioner.* San Francisco, CA: Jossey-Bass Publishers.

Spivak, G. C. (1987). *In Other Worlds: Essays in Cultural Politics.* London: Methven.

Stacey, J. (1988). Can there be a feminist ethnography? *Women's Studies International Forum, 11(1)*, 21-27.

Szczepanikova, D. A. (2012). Between Control and Assistance: The Problem of European Accommodation Centres for Asylum Seekers. *International Migration*, 51(4).

Thornton, L. (2014, April 3). *More Asylum Seekers in Direct Provision than Prisoners in Jail*. Retrieved September 10, 2016, from http://www.irishtimes.com/news/education/more-asylum-seekers-in-direct-provision-than-prisoners-in-jail-1.1747679

Tyner, J. A. (2012). *Space, Place, and Violence: Violence and the Embodied Geographies of Race, Sex, and Gender.* New York: Routledge.

Van der Horst, H. (2004). Living in a reception centre: the search for home in an institutional setting. *Housing, Theory and Society, 21*(1), 36-46.

Vandevoordt, R. (2017). The Politics of Food and Hospitality: How Syrian Refugees in Belgium Create a Home in Hostile Environments. *Journal of Refugee Studies, 30*(4), 605-621.

Visweswaran, K. (1994). *Fictions of feminist ethnography.* Minneapolis (MN): University of Minnesota Press.

Young, I. M. (1990). Five Faces of Oppression. In *Justice and the Politics of Difference* (pp. 39-65). Princeton: Princeton University Press.

Young, I. M. (1997). *Intersecting voices: Dilemmas of gender, political philosophy, and policy.* Princeton: Princeton University Press.

Young, I. M. (2005). House and Home: Feminist Variations on a Theme. In *Female Body Experience: Throwing Like a Girl and Other Essays* (pp. 123-154). Oxford: Oxford University Press.

PART 3

HOUSE

CHAPTER 9

Gendering Displacement

Women Refugees and the Geographies of Dwelling in India

Romola Sanyal
London School of Economics, U.K.

Partition and gender

In 1947 India and Pakistan were divided into two sovereign nation-states and became independent from British colonial rule. The processes by which these states were cleaved were fraught and complex. Violence tore communities apart as bureaucrats drew lines that divided terrain and habitations of people (Chatterji, 2002). Spectacular violence by way of looting, rapes and killings and large-scale displacement of people took place between West Pakistan (today Pakistan) and India. Along the Eastern frontier too millions of people moved between what became East Pakistan (today Bangladesh) and Eastern India, including the states of Assam, Tripura and West Bengal. This was one of the largest mass migrations of people in modern history, with estimates of 10-15 million having moved to either side of the border (Daiya, 2011). Scholars argue that the partition has remained 'unfinished business' in the subcontinent as people continue to move in search of refuge, spurred on by the same communal logics that underpinned Partition many decades ago (Samaddar, 1999) (Fig. 1).

The history of Partition and the rehabilitation of refugees in India and Pakistan has a decidedly gendered element to it. Feminist historians have unpacked many aspects of it, from the violence that was gendered to the process of 'recovering' (tracing and bringing back 'home') women who had been abducted by the 'other' community and the ways in which they slotted into the national imaginary, particularly in India (Butalia, 1998; Daiya, 2011; Kaur, 2007; Menon & Bhasin, 1998; Zamindar, 2007). Women's bodies became the sites of contestation around family, community, nation, even though they were often cast aside once 'recovered' (Menon & Bhasin, 1998). The bureaucratic responses to rehabilitat-

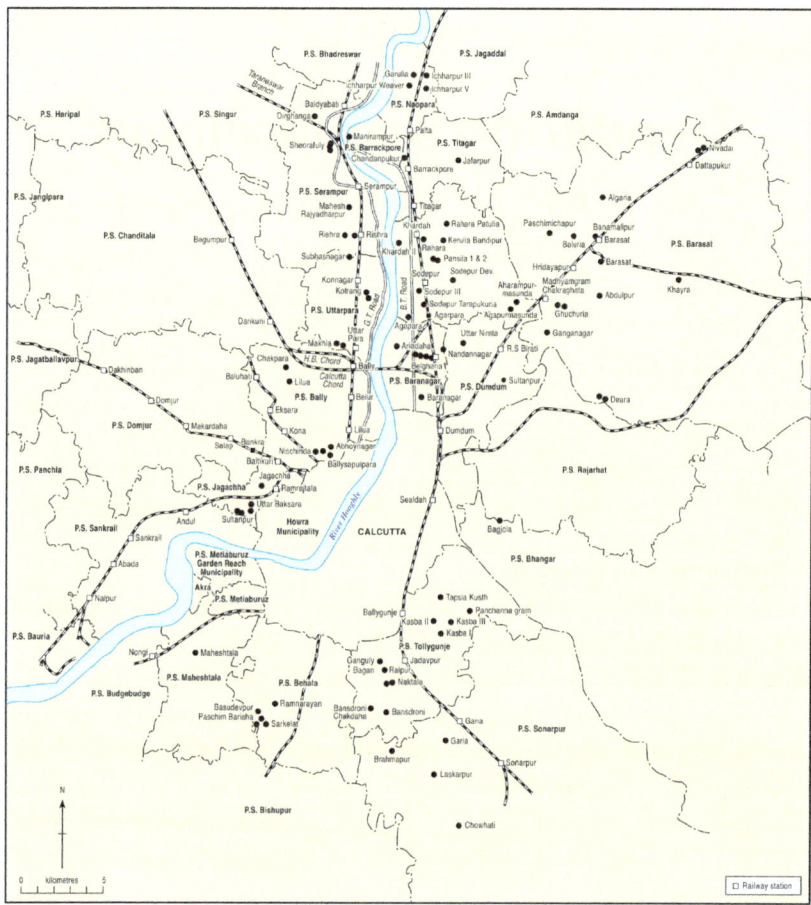

Figure 1. "A Map showing the govt schemes within a radius of 15 miles from Calcutta." Courtesy of the Department of Relief and Rehabilitation, Government of West Bengal (India).

ing and resettling refugees were equally gendered in their approach. 'Recovered women', for example, were often rejected by their families as they were seen to have become 'polluted' by having been in sexual relations with men outside the family. They, along with their children born through these relations, were often ostracised (Menon & Bhasin, 1998). Widows, single women, aged and infirm were also feminised by the Indian state. Uditi Sen (2018) notes that the state took on the role of the patriarch in the aftermath of Partition and assumed that 'unattached women' unsupported by a normative family structure were particularly vulnerable, and by virtue of their gender were unable to support themselves. The government therefore assumed the responsibility for providing particular forms of assistance such as the provision of shelter, basic amenities and services on a long-term and even permanent basis. Accordingly, a number of ashrams and

'Permanent Liability (PL) camps' for those 'unfit' for rehabilitation, such as abandoned women and children, widows and those too old, emerged in a number of sites in cities such as Delhi and in ex-military camps on the outskirts of cities such as Kolkata (see Fig. 1., for camps in the state of West Bengal of which Kolkata is the capital) (Chatterjee, 1994; Chaudhury, 2010; Dey, 2009; Sen, 2018).

There is of course a political economy of rehabilitation as well. Camps were originally set up in the east, in states such as West Bengal, to encourage refugees to 'go back', but bureaucrats soon realised that not only were refugees not returning, but instead, more were arriving. The management of return transformed into an apparatus of recovery and rehabilitation as these transit camps were replaced with Relief and Transit camps, Permanent Liability (PL) camps and colony camps. Within this classification system further distinctions were created. In the Permanent Liability category, those who were unattached women were placed in women's camps. Meanwhile, worksite camps were developed to keep able-bodied men engaged in useful works until a resolution could be found for them (Das, 2000). Even within the machinery of managing displacement, unevenness and inequality became entrenched as considerably more money was spent on refugees from the Punjab, whilst those from the East were given substantially less. Those housed in camps in West Bengal, for example, were given paltry sums of money to survive on, barely enough food, or money for cremation, and new clothes only twice a year. Children were provided with education, and there was some training provided as well for women to earn some income. Yet, although there are differences between the camps in terms of services, by and large, and especially within the context of Bengal, those housed within them are effectively impoverished. Most of those who ended up in the camps came from lower caste and poorer backgrounds and had limited means of resettling themselves (Chaudhury, 2010; Sen, 2018).

While there is much written on the history of Partition including gender, my intervention shifts away from this to engage in a geographical and spatial analysis of Partition, with a focus on place-making. I do this by undertaking a deeper analysis of the literature and methodology before delving into a brief discussion of empirics. Hitherto the study of Partition has largely been explored by historians, and to some extent by anthropologists. There has been little analysis, however, of Partition by geographers, planners, architects or those doing spatial research. The considerable body of writing on the effects of Partition on gendered relations also operates largely at a particular spatial scale – that of the nation state. Indeed the vast majority of literature tends to look at how the state -and in this case the Indian state – dealt with the 'Women's question' within the context of Partition and its aftermath. Even those writings that drew on policy responses at the sub-national scale – for example looking at the responses by the state of

West Bengal to East Bengali refugees – tack between state level and national level responses.[1] Some of the reasons for this are obvious, as regulatory and financial guidelines and provisions came from the national government, which ultimately guided the actual resettlement and rehabilitation processes at the state level. Partition historiography rarely, if ever, considers other scales, for instance the urban one or that of the home, even though many of the conflicts operated at the scale of the urban and over questions of remaking or establishing homes.

There is also very little meaningful analysis of refugees as agents of socio-spatial change. Prafulla Chakrabarti's analysis of refugees and the left movements in West Bengal, which is often trotted out as *the* seminal work on urban refugees, in fact focuses on the politics of refugees and not on the specifics of the city of Calcutta where this story unfolds (Chakrabarti, 1990). We learn little, if anything, about the governance structure of the city or its finances, its spatiality or history. The fact that the city only a few years ago received millions of migrants trying to find refuge from a devastating famine is ignored. The city is not really understood as a distinct built environment and geography, with a specific municipal government, its own sets of politics and a dynamic space with already existing socio-spatial relationships. There is limited engagement with the materiality of refugee spaces themselves. Passing references are made to the nature of the built environment of refugee squatter colonies or camps, and even less consideration is given to how the physical spaces were constructed, how they affected social relations, mental and physical health or relations between refugees and non-refugees. The idea of the home as a physical, material, social and emotional space that is constantly evolving, that both is emplaced and stretches beyond the confines of the structure of the dwelling itself, remains largely overlooked. This is not specific to Chakrabarti's work, but permeates the work of most historians of Partition, in that by and large they tend to elide critical analysis of space and geographical scale. Instead, they remain within what John Agnew refers to as the territorial trap of the state (Agnew, 1994).

Yet, geographers, planners and architects have continually drawn our attention to the importance of thinking critically about space and scale and considering how they are invented, contested, assembled and disassembled by various actors, expertise, materials and so forth (Marston et al., 2005; Massey, 1994; McCann & Ward, 2012; Painter, 2008; Robinson, 2013). In thinking about the politics of producing space, it is also useful to consider the relationship between domestic space and that of the city. Indeed, this is an intimate one, and calls for 'right to the city' to be anchored in people's demands to inhabit the city. Thus, scholars have shown how housing struggles, efforts by the poor communities to put down roots and to establish homes in informal settlements are fraught with difficulty and violence (Benjamin, 2008; Bhan, 2009; Datta, 2016; Ghertner, 2010). Refugees and migrants are further marginalised within these processes as they are often invisible and susceptible to violence and exploitation, given their precarious socio-legal status. Feminist scholars have also drawn our attention to the fact that Lefebvrian notions of 'right to the city' ignore questions of gender, race, ethnicity and so forth (Beebeejaun, 2017). Thus, despite progressive moves towards making the city a space to be shared by all, women and other gender and sexual minorities continue to be ignored as city-makers and as those who have particular issues with claiming rights to the city (ibid).

Geographers working on critical analysis of the home argue that home is a spatial imaginary made up of "a set of intersecting and variable ideas and feelings which are related to contexts, and which construct places, extend across spaces and scales and connect places" (Blunt & Dowling, 2006). Scholars note that home is a space that anchors people, that is imbued with social and emotional attributes. Equally, however, they can be oppressive, violent spaces, particularly for women and marginalised groups, sometimes becoming prison-like and oppressive for them (Blunt & Dowling, 2006; Meth, 2003). Drawing on Heidegger, Blunt & Dowling (2006) distinguish between dwelling and being at home, where the former refers to inhabiting a particular space, whilst the latter infuses space with meaning.

In architecture there has been rich scholarship on gender and homes, including on how house form reveals the social and sexual division of space within the home. Scholars have noted that the structure and location of houses and homes (suburbs for example) facilitate social reproduction, social and sexual division of labour, domestication and challenges to it (Boyer, 1986; Hayden, 1996; Heynen & Baydar, 2005). Heynen, for example, observes how the home became a contradictory site of modernity – on the one hand standing in opposition to it by symbolising tradition, and on the other hand being the site of experimenting with social and sexual relations and reproduction through design (Heynen & Baydar, 2005). While much of the scholarship on architecture and domesticity has centred on Western societies, there has also been critical scholarship examining similar issues outside 'the West', drawing our attention to how the home has been a space for experimenting with modernity and nation-building (Bozdogan, 2002; Karimi, 2013). These arguments, amongst others, are important in thinking about what the space of the home means, how that meaning is constructed through a gendered process and how in turn it constructs particular ideas of gender as well. These insights are invaluable as we unpack the idea of home in the context of displacement and exile. How does refuge operate as a space of safety but also as one of gendered oppression, violence and imprisonment? How does the detention and endless waiting forced on people within particular spaces feminise them (Hyndman & Giles, 2011)? How is home embodied not just within a physical structure, but within everyday objects that displaced people carry with them (Motasim & Heynen, 2011)? In other words, geography and place are critical to the understanding of displacement, and displacement in turn helps us to unpack the complex spatial transformations at different scales, and how spaces and places become infused with meaning.

Doing Partition research

In this section I wish to take up some of these aspects to reflect on the gendered forms of home-making and place-making that took place in the aftermath of Partition with a specific focus on the eastern side of India, and particularly the state of West Bengal. I contend that the making of homes is fundamental to how refugees survive displacement and rebuild their lives. For my argument I draw together architectural and geographical perspectives and focus on material and social aspects of building refuge that tend to be lacking in the analysis of refugee histories. As I was hard pressed to find any discussions about the material nature of spaces or even reflections on the nature of the urban environment itself, I rely here on oral histories, interviews and archival material that I did manage to gather on this. I had done fieldwork in refugee colonies in the city of Calcutta between 2006 and 2007, mainly in the colonies of Bijoygarh, Azadgarh and Netaji Nagar in the Tollygunge area, collecting oral histories and interviews with approximately 45 individuals and spending months visiting their homes and neighbourhoods and photographing those places. By then, most people who had directly migrated due to Partition were very aged, and memories had become somewhat unreliable. Conversations had to be delicate to account for the energy and comfort of interviewees.

Historians of Partition, particularly in relation to West Bengal, have noted the caste differences in terms not only of the temporality of migration, but also of the location where people went. Scholars have, for example, rightly pointed out the upper-caste, middle class nature of urban refugee squatters who were also among the first refugees to arrive in the state, who capitalised on their socio-cultural privilege to recover their class positions and also became politically active – in many ways reconfiguring the political landscape of the city for decades to come (Chatterjee, 1994; Chaudhury, 2010; Ray, 2002; Sen, 2018). On the other hand, lower caste refugees came in later waves of displacement and were disproportionately represented amongst the camp populations and in ex-camp sites (Chaudhury, 2010). They were subject to more draconian forms of state-led rehabilitation, and continue to struggle with poverty, marginalisation and invisibility (Chaudhury, 2010; Mukherjee, 2020).

The colonies in which I did my fieldwork were very much part of the upper-caste, middle class, privileged geography of displacement and rehabilitation. My interest was not to reconstruct a middle-class history of Calcutta, but rather to understand the ways in which refugees became city-makers through acts of land appropriation and building practices that we usually assign to subaltern groups such as squatters. Indeed, it is fascinating that a set of people who saw themselves as being middle class utilised practices of forcible acquisition of land, of building their own settlements in order to reclaim their class position and also urbanising the city in particular ways. I was interested in understanding how protracted urban displacement occupied a grey space between forced migration and urban poverty and what that could teach us about the politics of urbanisation. My aim, then, was to write against much of the prevailing Partition historiography that saw the city as an apolitical and static space against which the process of recovering agency and political voice took place. Rather, I was curious about how displacement underpinned the socio-spatial transformation of this sprawling metropolis. I am, however, conscious that intersectional oppression plays a key role in how and why upward mobility and celebratory accounts of success are available to only a select group of people.

When I was undertaking fieldwork I was well aware that there were distinct gender, class and caste aspects to my interviewees. Indeed, this became a feature, a snowballing exercise, and assumptions were made about my caste, class and marital status. I was simultaneously seen as *close*, as having had some ancestral ties to East Bengal, and *far*, as someone whose family was predominantly settled in the US and who was doing a PhD at the time in an American institution.[2] As a result, middle-class, upper-caste, educated once-refugees introduced me to their friends and colleagues who inhabited the same social space. While I managed very few interviews with people from lower socio-economic or caste positions in the colonies, my position as a woman did enable me to interview women. This was sometimes not easy, as male family members would aggressively demand why I needed to speak to them. At other times it was straightforward, as women themselves came forward to be interviewed and spoke frankly about the various challenges they faced as they grew up in these neighbourhoods. In other instances family members who were keen on reproducing certain histories of colonies would proudly introduce me to their mothers and sisters, yet be 'present' throughout the interview. On somewhat odd occasions I would interview women whose families would express surprise at their mothers' and grandmothers' involvement in refugee struggles and colony building.[3] Although much writing has been done on the history of refugee colonies in Calcutta, including by residents themselves, this is extremely male-centric, which is unfortunate as women played important roles in shaping these spaces, turning them into sites not just of rehabilitation, but also of reshaping ideas of home and belonging. I note all this to reflect on the fact that we embody subjectivity and difference, which in turn affects the research process – whom we meet, what they say, how they say it. Facts are therefore not neutral, but rather are mediated through the different positionalities of interviewer and interviewee. Pretending that one is a 'native informant' with an 'authentic voice' that can 'speak on behalf of others' is therefore a deeply problematic exercise, as Spivak reminds us (Spivak, 1999). The second is to remind ourselves that the role of women refugees cannot be collapsed into a singular narrative as victims or as heroes, but rather is highly contingent on their caste, class, education, social and family position and the ways in which state and society perceive them. I will draw on some of these interviews to discuss the role of women in making colony spaces.

Finally, as an urbanist, I am centrally interested in the city, but I am acutely aware that separating the urban from the rural is deeply problematic. Indeed, if we are to understand cities as being in topological relations with other spaces we need to understand how the camp and the city are intimately intertwined with each other. With this interest in mind, I had reached out to bureaucrats in the still functioning Department of Relief and Rehabilitation, Government of West Bengal to visit some of the camp sites outside Calcutta. However, as a young, single woman researcher having come from 'elsewhere', I quickly became acutely aware of the gendered nature of this access, particularly in relation to the gatekeepers for these sites. Due to that and to the scale of my fieldwork in Calcutta, I unfortunately gave up on these visits. I have thus focused predominantly on the particular colonies in Calcutta where I did my fieldwork, but I hope that the earlier discussions of the camps that are drawn from scholarly and archival material provide a glimpse into the significant differences that arose between different sites and how women slotted into different socio-spatial imaginaries in the post-Partition context.

Koshto aar Cheshta: Narrating the rebuilding of lives

I entitle this section *koshto aar cheshta* (suffering/hardship and struggle/endeavour) as these were the key themes that emerged in my fieldwork among refugees in the refugee colonies in Calcutta, including among women. The two terms lie in creative tension with each other – suffering and hardship (*koshto*) lay the foundation for hard work, struggle and endeavour (*cheshta*) lead to changes in life circumstances. They have a temporal element to them as well as the *koshto*, referred to here, harks to a bygone era and the *cheshta*, which it gave rise to, led to a recovery of class position. I will begin by discussing how these ideas go on to frame narratives of survival and recovery among refugees and how they permeate the shaping of domestic spaces themselves. I will then turn to critically unpacking how these terms can signal particular class positions and conceptions of 'deserving poor'.

As noted earlier, the first waves of refugees from East Bengal/East Pakistan were predominantly upper class, upper caste refugees with some prior exposure to urban life (Ray, 2002). However, despite their somewhat social and material privilege, they had also lost many of their possessions and social ties as a result of exile, and thus arrived in Calcutta in a more precarious situation. It is not a stretch to say that displacement had driven them into considerable poverty and one they had not experienced before (Chatterjee, 1994; Sur, 1997; Weber, 2003). In many interviews, respondents used the term *ek kapore* to describe how they left East Bengal. *Ek kapore* translates to 'with one cloth', and indeed some interviewees, such as a priest in a local temple claimed he came away wearing a *gamcha* or loincloth -not even proper clothes-, which again refers back to the notion of *ek kapor*. But the term is largely metaphorical as it not only captures the urgency and finality of departure, but also percolates into the foundational stories of the colonies themselves.

Like many other subaltern classes, refugees struggled to find a foothold in the city. Because many came from middle class backgrounds they refused to stay in camps, citing poor living conditions, but also because of their sense of pride. Instead, they chose to live elsewhere, often with relatives, in rented accommodation in different parts of Calcutta, hoping for government support for resettlement. The government in the meantime, burdened with limited resources and expertise, did little to adequately rehouse most of them. As a result, many refugees who realised that help for them might never arrive, decided to take matters into their own hands. Here is where the language of *koshto* frames the narratives of refugee squatters as they recollect the early days of colony establishment and survival. Groups of refugees decided to invade land on the fringes of the city and build their own homes and settlements through self-help squats. Many of these were located in the southern fringes of the city, including Tollygunge, Kashba, Jadavpur and Behala. The land that they occupied was sparsely populated, but was owned by a range of different landlords, both middle class and wealthy families. Many Muslim families also lived in these areas and were evicted by refugee communities as they settled there (Sanyal, 2014; Sur, 1997).

In their narratives the refugees claim responsibility for undertaking a number of tasks and spatial transformations including demarcating plots, digging and buildings ponds and roads and setting up communal services such as markets and schools (Sanyal, 2009; Sur, 1997). Most of the squats are seen to be headed by young men. The houses were made of easily available material like mud and bamboo; some had tiled roofs; most houses were small, consisting of one room or sometimes two; the houses were divided and developed over time (Weber, 2003). Flimsy materials also made for difficult times, especially during the long monsoon months when houses regularly flooded, soaking furniture and cooking stoves, bringing in snakes and other dangers. One respondent, who now lives in a three-storey brick house, explained her predicament in the early days of the colony this way:

> Even after the houses were built, wherever there was any open land, there would be a lot of water-logging. When it rained the water used to come inside my house and room. I used to put my stove on top of the chair or bed and cook my meals. Where else could you cook? How else could you light the stove? (Interviewee A).

As time passed and as people became more secure in their tenure and had some extra income, they were able to invest in developing their houses – upgrading them to tin structures with tiled roofs, sometimes adding a second floor (Ray, 2002; Sanyal, 2009).

For women, the descent into poverty had significant personal implications. As several scholars have noted, many had to step outside the home for the first time and come into contact with unrelated men. They had to balance domestic chores with work and support of a community building. The living conditions also made life difficult as they had to bathe and undertake toilet activities in public ponds that dotted the landscape (Chakrabarti, 1990; Sur, 1997; Weber, 2003). While much attention is given to the *koshto* becoming more secure and upwardly mobile, other forms of suffering that women may have encountered in the days of piecing their lives together in the colonies is overlooked. For example, there is limited discussion about the gendered inequalities within the household, though some of this creeps through as they discuss the sacrifices they had to make with regard to education or work. There is no discussion either of domestic violence or alienation amongst women and other members of their families within any of the literature relating to the refugees in Calcutta (Sur, 1997), even though, as noted earlier, many women, particularly those who were 'recovered', were ostracised by their families.

Finally, a sense of spatial alienation permeated the conversations with my interviewees. There was an acute sense of being 'othered' through distance, as interviewees reflected on the difficulties they faced in being 'far away from the city', the lack of transport connections between the colonies and the city of Calcutta, and, by extension, the difficulty in accessing basic services such as hospitals, offices and other places. The acts of squatting and self-help were thus anchored in this pervasive sense of isolation, a lack of development and a sense of abandonment.

Manas Ray's autobiographical work entitled *Growing Up Refugee* opens with an evocative scene where lampposts were erected and numbered in the Netaji Nagar colony in 1966, bringing with it a sense of feeling closer to Calcutta (Ray, 2002).

The language of *cheshta* permeates the heroic narratives of struggling against all odds to establish colonies, becoming successful and reclaiming middle class status. The role of women in all this is significant, if under-acknowledged. For example, they participated in colony-building in numerous ways. One was to guard plots at night against potential eviction by the state, thugs hired by the landlords on whose land they had squatted, or encroachment by fellow squatters. They claimed to defend these colonies against police evictions both by placing themselves bodily on the frontlines and by taking up arms themselves (Sur, 1997; Weber, 2003). A fascinating interview with a colony leader's wife brought up discussions about women's committees and solidarity work among women both in the nascent stages of colony formation and later, well after it was established. These narratives, however, failed to make the cut in her husband's memoirs. Another key part played by women was the actual construction of colony spaces. This is an understated aspect of their contribution to building colony spaces. Malini Sur's work on this is informative, as she notes that her interviewees who were women "recalled walking long distances to carry soil… women participated in carrying sacks and sacks of soil and building their homes with their husbands and sons" (Sur, 1997, p. 72). Yet, the dominant narratives of colony construction render it a predominantly male activity. As Pickerill (2015) points out, women's roles in the physical construction of structures have largely been marginalised. Rather, women are seen more as interior decorators. Construction, in contrast, is positioned as a profession that is seen to be male-centric, and indeed such assumptions of 'who builds' creep into how we view who has been involved in the physical construction of refugee spaces as well.

Finally, there was their engagement in waged labour to help finance their families's futures, including the building of homes. Many women I interviewed worked in a variety of professions – from teaching to secretarial work or other professions seen to be suited to women. Sur (1997) notes that the upheaval did little to upend gendered subject positions or labour and many women effectively occupied lower waged, feminised work, and were expected to maintain the home as well as do waged work. Unlike their male counterparts, who focused on the heroism of colony-building, women inevitably talked about the hardships of living under harsh conditions, making homes habitable despite enduring poverty. Their earnings would pay for the education of their siblings and/or the modernisation of their homes, but these often came at the expense of their own aspirations and educational pursuits. One interviewee talked about how displacement interrupted her studies so that she could not complete her schooling, and when she resumed them learning maths or other subjects was like throwing darts in the dark. Women's waged work was an important aspect of financing the upgrading of home and colony spaces. Manas Ray's evocative autobiography captures some of this:

> The bookshelf was lined with thick coloured papers bought from G.C Laha's; small curios were put on display. *Didi* one day came home with a large packet containing a Bombay Dyeing bedcover with temple-sculpture prints and some colourful drapery. Mother during her afternoon recesses dragged her old Singer machine on to the middle of the floor and started stitching curtains, her looking-glasses on her nose, wetting the broken end of the thread on her tongue to make it pointed for ease of entry into the eye of the needle-all the time thinking of the 'interior decoration' of father's younger uncle's flat next to Indira cinema in the heart of south Calcutta. (Ray, 2002).

Furnishing space with the remnants of what was brought over after Partition is mixed together with new purchases to signal arrival on the urban stage and to one's firm presence within the urban and national space as a permanent resident. Homes become hybrid spaces of what is left behind and what is imagined for the future. Women thus are key authors in the making of homes and home-spaces, and of the modernity that seeps into their spaces through their waged labour, which enables purchases to be made and through their sweat equity that builds/decorates these spaces. How do we write an architectural history of auto-construction in the context of forced displacement?

Sixty years later the neighbourhoods, which by now have been formalised and regularised, have transformed into brick and mortar structures and asphalted roads. Contemporary shops line the streets. Residents of the area who have not yet moved out point out with pride that their neighbourhoods are no different from other middle class neighbourhoods in Calcutta. They claim they have everything. As they secured formal titles to land many years later, their land has now increased in value, the city continues to expand and speculation abounds. Some have sold their properties to developers for tidy sums and have moved out, transforming the social makeup of these spaces. Now 'outsiders' have moved in and these are no longer really 'refugee colonies' (Fig. 2), but rather middle class suburbs of an ever-expanding city. In this transformation of colony space, its upgrading and insertion into the urban landscape, women have again been key authors. They have enabled the material transformation not only of their homes, but also of the city.

One can argue that in fact the terms of suffering and struggle that frame the process of claiming and building sites and lives signal not just entrepreneurial

Figure 2. Contemporary houses in the refugee colonies of Calcutta, photo by author.

spirits, but also a meritocratic, bourgeois notion of success. The underlying argument here is that it has been through hard work, suffering and determination that refugees have been able to rebuild their lives and reclaim their middle class status. But, in fact, as scholars have argued, this explanation is not so straightforward, as caste politics permeate the ways in which governments rehabilitated people and responded to activities such as colony-building (Chaudhury, 2010; Mukherjee, 2020; Sen, 2018). If these refugees succeeded it is because they had the social and cultural capital, the kinship ties, a level of education, assets that they could, to a degree, rely upon in order to stake their political claims and remake their lives after displacement. Yet it is interesting that, despite having this social and cultural capital, these refugees were compelled to engage in squatting – an act that is associated with 'subaltern' classes. Indeed the shame of 'descending' into a lower class position is something that appears in Partition historiography and literature (Chatterjee, 1994; Gangopadhyay, 1990).

I wish to expand on this discussion of *koshto* and *chesta* as straddling both deprivation and entrepreneurialism, and all their bourgeois trappings, to suggest that they signals a form of future-making. I argue here that refugees' nostalgic views of suffering and the hard road to 'success' carry within them the possibility of living for a future, of improving one's condition. This contradicts what many refugee scholars focus on – the constant waiting and uncertainty that refugees are subjected to, how they are forced to inhabit a present and how future-making may be impossible for them. How can refugees make homes when the present in fact is all they live in? What if for years they are subjected to endless uncertainty and a sense of temporariness as they are moved from one site to another? Refugee and migration scholars have turned increasingly towards thinking about the politics of time and how that shapes the lives and mental health of those considered undesirable migrants (Andersson, 2014; Conlon, 2011). However, forced migration is not a singular process with singular outcomes. Rather, very different situations may emerge even in protracted situations, informed very much by geopolitics. Cathrine Brun and Anita Fàbos (2015), for example, have argued in their work that although refugees may be forced to wait, they may still make plans and activities for futures, however limited these may be. Malini Sur shows how women's bodies play highly varied roles in geopolitics: on the one hand they are subject to violence, violation and patriarchal control, and on the other they are authors of nation-building, national security, and are also able to negotiate borders and thresholds by virtue of their gender. Women embody risk and threat differently, and are able to move and navigate through landscapes differently from men, thus having a different sense of time, place and possibility. We thus need to be attentive to how borders and places are gendered in their make-up (Sur, 2012; Sur, 2018). In the case of Partition refugees, the exceptionalism of the situation enabled a specific group of people to reclaim their lives. What these refugees in Calcutta demonstrate through their acts of land acquisition, colony building, protests against the municipal, state and national governments for their rights is the active construction of a future where they not only rebel against the state, but also seek its acknowledgement and their right to belong (Chatterjee, 1994).

Conclusions: Figuring women's space in Partition historiography

In this short chapter I have offered a brief glimpse into the ways in which women participate in the production of colony spaces – in the making of homes and, by extension, the making of the city. Their histories, and particularly their home lives, remain understudied even though their contribution to the physical, social and emotional construction of the home spaces is significant. Although these women come from privileged backgrounds, having had some education, being upper caste and middle class, their descent into poverty also had a considerable personal effect on them. Displacement and self-settlement meant that their home-making practices were stretched socially and spatially. Their 'work' extended beyond the confines of their physical homes, to the city where they were compelled to work in order to build, extend and solidify the houses they had produced through squatting. Little consideration is given to the sacrifices that these women made in the process of producing spaces and how their narratives capture both the despair of that present and the hope for the future. I have argued here that in fact these twin narratives of suffering and struggle capture both the deprivation and the hope that animated the lives of refugees. Through its entrepreneurial narrative and bourgeois positioning, it also signals the possibility of future-making for refugees.

Their future-making stands in contrast to what happened to the many women who were thrust into homes, ashrams and camps in India, and kept away from the public eye. Here, they were expected to remain wards of the state and effectively imprisoned within these so-called spaces of relief/refuge. Yet, here too, one cannot dismiss the agency of refugees, and despite their impossible conditions they also staged protests and laid claims to rights in a variety of ways. One could argue that what they were able to do was engage in active waiting, but the home-making in this process remained highly circumscribed.

Partition historiography has unearthed numerous aspects of the episode, including the effects on women, the relationship between the state and refugees, and, increasingly, close attention to questions of caste. While these endeavours are laudatory, it is also imperative to pay attention to the question of scale and consider how space plays a key role in mediating the relationship between the displaced and the emplaced, and within these groups as well. Delving into the space of the home and the household offers one way of understanding how these spaces are stretched across time and space, how they link pasts and futures, homes left behind and homes to be made. They stand in an uneasy tension with spaces secured for far less fortunate individuals. Thinking through the home with a gendered lens allows us to unpack quotidian processes that may be entirely overlooked in grand narratives of marginalisation.

Notes

1. See, for example, the work of Joya Chatterji and Uditi Sen.
2. I use terms like 'close' and 'far' by translating from Bengali where one would refer to someone as *apon* (one's own) or *por* (as someone who is a foreigner).
3. I note here that I am not alone in encountering these issues in the field. Indeed, others who have undertaken interviews and ethnographies with refugee communities have faced the same. See, for example, the work of Rachel Weber, Malini Sur and Nilanjana Chatterjee.

References

Agnew, J. (1994). The territorial trap: The geographical assumptions of international relations theory. *Review of International Political Economy*, 1(1), 53–80.

Andersson, R. (2014). *Illegality, Inc.: Clandestine Migration and the Business of Bordering Europe* (1st Edition). Berkeley, C.A.: University of California Press.

Beebeejaun, Y. (2017). Gender, urban space, and the right to everyday life. *Journal of Urban Affairs*, 39(3), 323–334.

Benjamin, S. (2008). Occupancy Urbanism: Radicalizing Politics and Economy beyond Policy and Programs. *International Journal of Urban and Regional Research*, 32(3), 719–729.

Bhan, G. (2009). "This is no longer the city I once knew". Evictions, the urban poor and the right to the city in millennial Delhi. *Environment and Urbanization*, 21(1), 127–142.

Blunt, A., & Dowling, R. (2006). *Home* (1st Edition). London and New York: Routledge.

Boyer, M. C. (1986). *Dreaming the Rational City: The Myth of American City Planning* (New Ed edition). Cambridge, M.A.: MIT Press.

Bozdogan, S. (2002). *Modernism and Nation Building: Turkish Architectural Culture in the Early Republic* (New Ed edition). Seattle, W.A.: University of Washington Press.

Brun, C., & Fábos, A. (2015). Making Homes in Limbo? A Conceptual Framework. *Refuge: Canada's Journal on Refugees*, 31(1).

Butalia, U. (1998). *The Other Side of Silence: Voices from the Partition of India* (New edition edition). Penguin Books India.

Chakrabarti, P. K. (1990). *The Marginal Men: The Refugees and the Left Political Syndrome in West Bengal*. Toronto: Lumière Press Publishers.

Chatterjee, N. (1994). *Midnight's Unwanted Children: East Bengali Refugees and the Politics of Rehabilitation*. Providence, R.I.: Brown University Press.

Chatterji, J. (2002). *Bengal Divided: Hindu Communalism and Partition, 1932-1947*. Cambridge: Cambridge University Press.

Chaudhury, A. B. R. (2010). Politics of Rehabilitation: Struggle of the Lower Caste Refugees in West Bengal. *Contemporary Voice of Dalit*, *3*(1), 61–82.

Conlon, D. (2011). Waiting: Feminist perspectives on the spacings/timings of migrant (im)mobility. *Gender, Place & Culture*, *18*(3), 353–360.

Daiya, K. (2011). *Violent Belongings: Partition, Gender, and National Culture in Postcolonial India*. Philadelphia, P.A.: Temple University Press, U.S.

Das, S. K. (2000). Refugee Crisis: Responses from the Government of West Bengal. In P. K. Bose (Ed.), *Refugees in West Bengal: Institutional Practices and Contested Identities* (pp. 7–31). Calcutta Research Group.

Datta, A. (2016). *The Illegal City: Space, Law and Gender in a Delhi Squatter Settlement*. London and New York: Routledge.

Dey, I. (2009). *On the Margins of Citizenship: Principles of Care and Rights of the Residents of the Ranaghat Women's Home, Nadia District*. Retrieved from: http://www.mcrg.ac.in/rw%20files/RW33/RW33.pdf.

Gangopadhyay, S. (1990). *Arjun*. London and New York: Penguin Books.

Ghertner, D. A. (2010). Calculating without numbers: Aesthetic governmentality in Delhi's slums. *Economy and Society*, *39*(2), 185–217.

Hayden, D. (1996). *Grand Domestic Revolution: History of Feminist Designs for American Homes, Neighbourhoods and Cities* (New Edition). Cambridge, M.A.: MIT Press.

Heynen, H., & Baydar, G. (eds.). (2005). *Negotiating Domesticity: Spatial Productions of Gender in Modern Architecture* (1 edition). London and New York: Routledge.

Hyndman, J., & Giles, W. (2011). Waiting for what? The feminization of asylum in protracted situations. *Gender, Place & Culture*, *18*(3), 361–379.

Karimi, P. (2013). *Domesticity and Consumer Culture in Iran: Interior Revolutions of the Modern Era* (1st edition). London and New York: Routledge.

Kaur, R. (2007). *Since 1947: Partition Narratives among Punjabi Migrants of Delhi*. Oxford: Oxford University Press.

Marston, S. A., Jones, J. P., & Woodward, K. (2005). Human geography without scale. *Transactions of the Institute of British Geographers*, *30*(4), 416–432.

Massey, D. (1994). A Global Sense of Place. In *Space, Place and Gender* (pp. 146–156). London: Polity Press.

McCann, E., & Ward, K. (2012). Assembling Urbanism: Following Policies and 'Studying Through' the Sites and Situations of Policy Making. *Environment and Planning A: Economy and Space*, *44*(1), 42–51.

Menon, R., & Bhasin, K. (1998). *Borders and Boundaries: Women in India's Partition: How Women Experienced the Partition of India*. New Brunswick, N.J.: Rutgers University Press.

Meth, P. (2003). Rethinking the 'domus' in domestic violence: Homelessness, space and domestic violence in South Africa. *Geoforum*, *34*(3), 317–327.

Motasim, H., & Heynen, H. (2011). At Home with Displacement? Material Culture as a Site of Resistance in Sudan. *Home Cultures, 8*(1), 43–69.

Mukherjee, A. (2020). Re-thinking protracted displacements: Insights from a namasudra refugee camp-site in suburban Calcutta. *Contemporary South Asia, 28*(1), 58–73.

Painter, J. (2008). Cartographic Anxiety and the Search for Regionality. *Environment and Planning A: Economy and Space, 40*(2), 342–361.

Pickerill, J. (2015). Bodies, building and bricks: Women architects and builders in eight eco-communities in Argentina, Britain, Spain, Thailand and USA. *Gender, Place & Culture, 22*(7), 901–919.

Ray, M. (2002). Growing Up Refugee. *History Workshop Journal, 53*(1), 149–179.

Robinson, J. (2013). "Arriving at" Urban Policies/ the Urban: Traces of Elsewhere in Making City Futures. In O. Söderström, S. Randeria, D. Ruedin, G. D'Amato, & F. Panese (Eds.), *Critical Mobilities* (pp. 23–50). Lausanne: EPFL Press.

Samaddar, R. (1999). *The Marginal Nation*. SAGE Publications India Ltd. Available at https://us.sagepub.com/en-us/nam/the-marginal-nation/book220547.

Sanyal, R. (2009). Contesting refugeehood: Squatting as survival in post-partition Calcutta. *Social Identities, 15*(1), 67–84.

Sanyal, R. (2014). Hindu space: Urban dislocations in post-partition Calcutta. *Transactions of the Institute of British Geographers, 39*(1), 38–49.

Sen, U. (2018). *Citizen Refugee: Forging the Indian Nation after Partition*. Cambridge: Cambridge University Press.

Spivak, G. C. (1999). *A Critique of Postcolonial Reason: Toward a History of the Vanishing Present*. Cambridge: M.A.:Harvard University Press.

Sur, M. (1997). *Relocating Gendered Identity: A Study of East Pakistani Women Refugees in Calcutta* [M.A Thesis]. Tata Institute of Social Sciences.

Sur, M. (2012). Bamboo baskets and barricades: Gendered landscapes at the India-Bangladesh border. In *Transnational Flows and Permissive Polities: Ethnographies of Human Mobilities in Asia* (pp. 127–150). Retrieved: https://researchdirect.westernsydney.edu.au/islandora/object/uws%3A37015/.

Sur, M. (2018). Asia's Gendered Borderlands. In A. Horstmann, M. Saxer, & A. Rippa (Eds.), *Routledge Handbook of Asian Borderlands* (pp. 30–41). London and New York: Routledge.

Weber, R. (2003). Re (creating) the home: Women's role in the development of refugee colonies in South Calcutta. In J. Bagchi & S. Dasgupta (Eds.), *The Trauma and the Triumph: Gender and Partition in Eastern India* (pp. 59–79). Kolkata: Bhatkal & Sen Press.

Zamindar, V. F.-Y. (2007). *The Long Partition and the Making of Modern South Asia: Refugees, Boundaries, Histories*. New York: Columbia University Press.

CHAPTER 10

Homing Displacements

Socio-Spatial Identities in Contemporary Urban Palestine

Alessandra Gola
KU Leuven, Belgium & Yalla Project, Palestine

Theoretical framing

Since the fall of the Ottoman Empire, Palestine has undergone repeated transformations of borders and governmental authorities. In the last century alone, the territory and people who comprise it have been variously reshuffled and partitioned under the British Mandate into the States of Israel, Egypt and Jordan, creating spots of extraterritoriality or ambiguous jurisdictions in turn, such as can be found in the case of Jerusalem and in the multitude of refugee camps. The conflicts that produced these changes were all-encompassing, affecting micro and macro geographies and economies, laws, communities and families, and, naturally, causing displacements and migrations. The less visible side of the geo-political shifts are the manifold experiences of displacement that have forged the everyday existence of Palestinians since 1948.

Displacement, in all its forms, is so endemic to the modern history of the Palestinian people that it has become a core aspect of their identity as a nation.[1] However, the different experiences subject to displacement contributed to fragmenting the Palestinians into quite diverse and sometimes distant communities and sub-cultures (Bhabha, 2013). Refugees, exiles, returners nomadic communities (e.g. the Bedouins), urbanised villagers, economic and educational migrants, and black-market labourers who must go back and forth from Israel and its settlements in the West Bank – each of these groups carries a remarkably different identity relative to legal status, conceptualisation of the home, temporariness, everyday practices and built structures.

A large body of scholarship recognises the relationship between displacement and the formation of the Palestinian national identity (Hammer & Schulz, 2003; Khalidi, 1997). With a focus on Palestinian refugeehood in camps (e.g. Bjawi-Levine, 2009; Bshara, 2012; Fincham, 2012; Halabi, 2004; Johansson & Vinthagen, 2015; Rosenthal, 2016; Sayigh, 1977) and/or on the transnational Palestinian diaspora (e.g. Abu-Saad, 2006; Azaryahu & Kook, 2002; Hammami, 2016; Hammer & Schulz, 2003; Mason, 2007; Peteet, 2007; Saad, 2019; Salih, Zambelli, & Welchman, 2020; Suleiman, 2016; Turan, 2010), these scholars explore Palestinian identity mainly through the lenses provided by social studies, anthropology, political geography or other spatial disciplines. Although extremely valuable and thorough, providing critical insights into many issues surrounding Palestinian identity, these studies by and large suffer from three main shortcomings. First, they struggle to acknowledge and portray the complex mosaic of identities and cultures that is linked to Palestinian migration and that makes up the contemporary Palestinian understanding of nationhood. Secondly, the preference for a specific disciplinary perspective often fails to deliver a more comprehensive picture of the interconnection between socio-cultural constructs, material features of the living environment, time, politics and economics. Finally, the focus on transnational diaspora and refugeehood largely overlooks other, perhaps less sensational but still conspicuous, relevant and tormenting forms of displacement that have proven to be fundamental to the constitution of contemporary Palestine, even though they are less directly connected with Israeli colonisation.

I propose that such answers to the question of Palestinian identity or identities can be discovered through a more empirical approach to the everyday elements of community life, underscored by an interdisciplinary paradigm that tackles in tandem living spaces, ordinary performances and trajectories of displacement. This chapter tackles the Palestinian urban context of the West Bank through the case of Ramallah, the de facto administrative capital city, focusing on the suburban area of Umm Al-Sharayiet – Al-Amari Camp. Using the significance of "microstories" as a methodological approach (Ginzburg, 1986), this chapter investigates the diverse socio-spatial identities of three contexts within the area. Central to the discussion is the space of 'the everyday' as the socially-constructed context that results in a multitude of socio-spatial relations that can themselves change over time. Insights into identity will be sought specifically through the ways in which diverse displacements and homing trajectories materialise in and through ordinary spaces that characterise today's urban West Bank. Spaces of the everyday are explored, here, with reference to Setha Low's concept of "homing the city" (2016) which extends the notion of home to the everyday environment on the urban scale, while contextually recognising its political and economic entanglement. Thus, it puts the concept of domesticity in relation to the different backgrounds, mindsets and personal dispositions of residents.

The aim of this chapter is to present concrete examples of the ways in which major circumstances and very individual conditions intertwine and together build the complex of meaningful environments. These environments in turn constitute the habitat of people's everyday life as the ground of expression of one's identity, conveyed through the demonstration of rights, responsibilities and expectations (Lemanski, 2020). Beyond providing a fine-grained, case-specific knowledge, the chapter will experiment with an interdisciplinary methodological framework better to substantiate the identity of communities expressed in terms of socio-spatial constructs and relations with time and space. Observations for this chapter were collected throughout a period of ten years in the West Bank, and have been integrated with extensive fieldwork performed between 2016 and 2017. This period of time was spent in cities, villages and camps located throughout the West Bank, and was marked by close experiences with everyday life in more than 60 households distributed across these various contexts. Based on these data, the three microstories that make up this investigation exemplify typical and recurrent situations in the local context. The study relies on an empirical approach that combines full-immersive, co-participated ethnographic methods, and a set of visual techniques that draw from architectural practices and discipline which will be used to analyse and represent a sense of belonging and place-making.[2] The field research combined individual and collective methods, with the engagement of local communities and a group of twenty students from Birzeit University's Faculty of Architecture. In respect for academic ethical standards, the names of participants have been changed in order to ensure anonymity and thereby the protection of identity.

The chapter unfolds in two main parts: the first provides an understanding of the interrelation between macro political and economic events, migratory flows and the transformation of the physical and social landscape of the case study. The second analyses three microstories, focusing on the socio-spatial circumstances that brought specific households into being, and highlighting their particular perspective on 'home' and on the temporariness at play in shaping the built environment.

Outlining the local socio-spatial process

Ramallah/Al-Bireh, the de-facto capital of the West Bank, is an urban agglomerate and the result of the progressive merging of two distinct municipalities – Ramallah and Al-Bireh. The three microstories are located in the south-western suburb of the city, in the area locally known as Umm Al-Sharayiet, an urban sprawl that developed along the road that connects Ramallah/Al-Bireh with Jerusalem through the Israeli checkpoint of Qalandyia.

This section will redraw the most significant passages in the socio-spatial development of the context the object of this study, highlighting the influence of

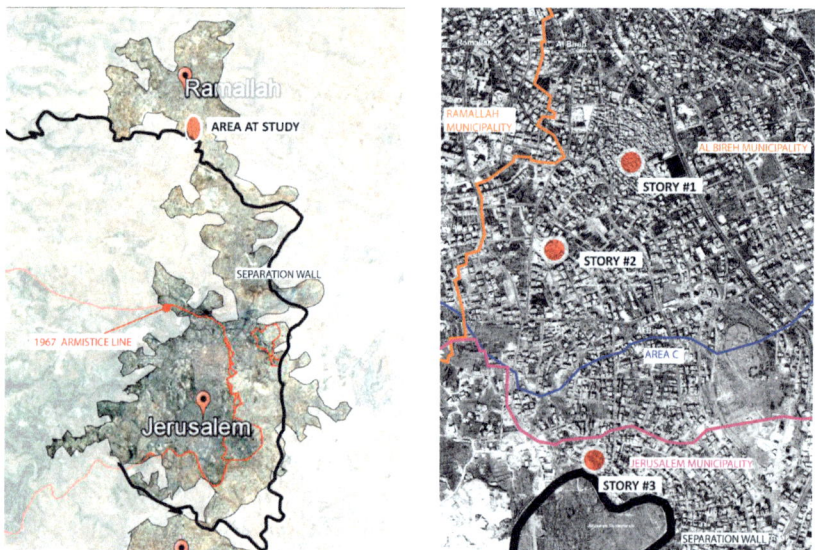

Figure 1. The location of the case study. Source: the author.

major political and economic events on more localised parts of the region. The analysis will focus in particular on the sequence of migratory flows of different natures, and the way these reshuffled spaces, social composition, local cultures and habits until today's configuration. Particular emphasis is given to understanding the early formation of Al-Amari Refugee Camp; this is motivated by the fact that the camp is the core settlement that kick-started the urbanisation of the context under analysis, and its presence influenced the development of the surrounding neighbourhoods.

1948-1967: From agricultural fields to refugee hub

The urbanisation of the area started with Al-Amari Refugee Camp. Located in close proximity to the centre of Ramallah/Al-Bireh, the camp was initially set out informally on rural plots in 1948, as families from several cities and over forty rural villages across the central coastal plain started settling on the site, while escaping from the ethnic cleansing enacted by Israeli armed corps. As emerged through interviews with inhabitants of the camp, the first families found accommodation by negotiating personally with the owners of the agricultural fields.

The current socio-spatial structure in Al-Amari formed in the early years of the camp (1948-55), as refugees with very diverse backgrounds and origins started clustering on the basis of their home town in a "pragmatic, almost organic way [...] appropriating existing infrastructures [...]" (SIAAL – Stuttgart University & UNRWA, 2005, pp. 73–74). The substantial lack of regulation during the first five years brought refugees to arrange spaces by reproducing the pre-existing socio-spatial habitus, "comparable to the spatial order of a typical city centre within the Islamic cultural context" (ibid., p.74) and articulated on the model of urban *haras* and *houshes*.[3] Here, "pre-1948 socio-economic differences were translated into space allocation" (ibid., p. 74), with clans coming from cities gaining more spacious and favourable locations in the camp thanks to better economic power and personal connections. This socio-spatial order of family clusters and quarters is still deeply inscribed into the collective consciousness of the camp, although its role in everyday life has transformed throughout the time. The spontaneous clustering of inhabitants on the basis of the town of origin is motivated by the relevance accorded in the local culture to the extended family and clan as source of protection, stability and support. This is particularly the case in times of exception, that is, in a situation of conflict, exile and expropriation of assets and rights. This social pattern has materialised in the arrangements of quarters inside the camps, each of which features specific everyday practices and cultures, with significant differences between families with rural and urban origins. Such differences were made to coexist side by side in a limited and deprived space, exacerbating the traditional distance between the two communities. Although attenuated, this division is still present today and strongly influences the everyday life of the camp.

In 1952 Al-Amari was formally acknowledged by the United Nations as a refugee camp. This action laid the foundations of the camp as a site of socio-spatial exception: the formal definition of borders fenced the camp and its inhabitants out from the rest of the "regular" context, while causing a significant shift in the legal status of the physical site and that of its inhabitants.[4] Alongside this action came the primary formal urbanisation, with UNRWA trying to arrange the site as a rationalised grid of plots and unpaved roads. However, the reorganisation of the camp succeeded only partially, as the aggregation based on place of birth and extended family kept constantly reaffirming and consolidating itself. For housing, each family – which typically counted 6 to 8 persons – was allocated a 12 m^2 one-room concrete shelter on a plot of 80 to 100 m^2, in replacement for fabric tents (Rueff & Viaro, 2009, p. 344).

With the Six Days War in 1967, the advancement of Israeli forces and the withdrawal of the Jordanian Mandate from the West Bank, a consistent number of Palestinians were induced to flee, with some of them resettling in Jordan. At the camp level, shelters that were left vacant by households that moved away offered residents the opportunity to gain some space for their own growing households.

1970s-1980s: Liberal economies and migration policies reshuffling the socio-spatial structure

In the 1970s, the aftermaths of the Six Days War and Camp David treaties, the swift rise of oil economies in the Gulf and in Libya and the replacement of Arab Socialisms with liberalism (Owen, 1981) brought with them a new wave of "mixed [...] displacement driven by the intertwining of political instability and economic needs migration" (Thiollet, 2011; Valenta & Jakobsen, 2018, p. 22). The Palestinian workforce was simultaneously mobilised by new Israeli policies that sought to incorporate workers from the territories into the secondary labour market (Rosenhek, 2003, pp. 238–242), and job opportunities and immigration schemes into the Gulf area (Thiollet, 2011). The massive wave of migration caused a complex – and very much undebated – transformation in the socio-spatial tissue of Palestine, and in that of the context under study in particular. From the social point of view, access to better salaries and the exposure to different lifestyles in the Gulf and in Israel deepened the social gaps between those who migrated and the poor who did not manage to access employment outside Palestine.

Displacement affected more than the mere income level: it diversified standards and expectations towards the everyday, its spaces and its practices, affecting patterns of spatial and goods consumption. The migration to Israel and in the Gulf respectively inspired quite diverging aesthetics and behavioural codes: this involved ideas of what a proper, beautiful house should look like; practices of leisure; food habits; tastes for garments and social behaviours. It also influenced religious views, especially in relation to the public and the family, a point particularly relevant for Muslim communities.[5] It also meant the conspicuous absence of men aged between 20 and 40, and the consequent reshuffling of gender roles back home, with women increasingly taking over family responsibilities and jobs outside the house (Owen, 1981, p. 9). As migrant workers largely invested their earnings in buying land or properties and in improving their houses in the home country (Ibid.), the whole built environment underwent a process of transformation.

In the case study, the improvement and expansion of houses led to the fast saturation of the camp. This was soon followed by the first exodus of wealthier families who could buy plots around the edges of the camp and build new dwellings (SIAAL – Stuttgart University & UNRWA, 2005, p. 71). The exodus locally had three main effects: the rise of land prices, the design of new houses outside the camp as a material statement of social achievement, and the creation of new relations between the camp and the rest of the city. Under these circumstances, the urbanisation of Umm Al-Sharayiet started in a mostly spontaneous way, constrained by few building regulations from the British and

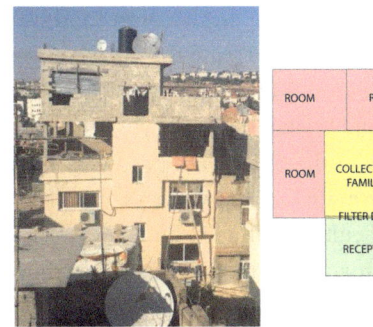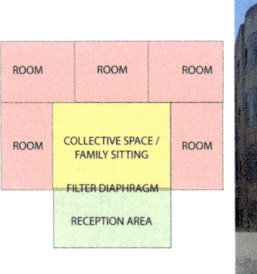

Figure 2. Refugees building homes. A family house built in the camp (left) and outside the camp (right). Although the aesthetics of the respective facades are radically different, their floor plans follow the same scheme developing around a central collective space (in yellow). Areas in red identify the most private parts of the house, accessible exclusively by the resident family (bedrooms, bathrooms, kitchen). Source: the author.

Jordanian mandates, which mainly imposed setbacks from the confining properties and roads (Abu Latifeh, 2013; SIAAL – Stuttgart University & UNRWA, 2005). While the legal framework determined a loose urban tissue of detached buildings, new constructions combined elements from traditional and modern architecture, using elements seen in fashionable bourgeois residences in the city or in the country of migration. New buildings would take the form of one- or two-storey detached cottages each surrounded by a perimetral courtyard. Externally, most designs would adopt modernist-inspired features, with visible investment in the design and materials used for facades. However, the whole architectural concept would still follow traditional schemas. New houses would still be designed with an incremental logic, so as to be enlarged to accommodate sons' families. The floor plan also redraws on the long-established layout of rooms opening on a central collective space (Ghadban, 2008). Nevertheless, interiors' aesthetics were also affected by the a desire to modernise, introducing new materials, finishings and appliances often first seen while working away.

At the end of the 1980s the process of "outpouring" from the camp eventually slowed down due to the outburst of the first Intifada and the rise in land prices following the expansion of Ramallah/Al-Bireh after the Oslo Agreement.

1990s-2000s: The Intifadas and the post-Oslo geography

The years between the 1990s and the 2010s marked another significant turn for the Palestinian context, for its geographic, economic, political and social structure, and for its relations with the Israeli occupier and with the rest of the regional and global context. This period laid down the basis on which the State works today, in an overall trend of loss of ground, tightening of control and surveillance by the Israeli occupation. The Gulf War in 1991 and the forced return of hundreds upon thousands of Palestinians from Kuwait as a consequence of the PLO's support for the Iraqi regime (Valenta & Jakobsen, 2018, p. 36), the rise of the first Intifada against Israel (1987-1993), the Oslo peace process (1993), the Second Intifada (2000-2005) and its aftermath brought about a series of all-encompassing transformations that are difficult to outline in but a few words. Therefore, this section will be limited to an analysis of those elements that most directly drove the socio-spatial process in the case study.

The sequence of crises, armed conflicts and political negotiations that occurred between 1987 and 2015 consistently reshuffled the whole urban hierarchy of Palestine and the West Bank. Major territorial outcomes were the drastic limitations on mobility for Palestinians within and outside the Palestinian territories culminated in the construction of the Separation Wall by Israel, as well as in the enforcement of a new internal geography based on areas with diversified level of autonomy for Palestinians[6] – of which only a mere two per cent came under full Palestinian jurisdiction –, and the establishment of Ramallah/Al-Bireh as the de facto capital of the West Bank.

In the same period, there was also a radical transformation of the political and economic structure of Palestine. The US-sponsored Oslo Agreements were implemented "against the backdrop of the expansion of global capitalism", promoting "new forms of 'peace processes' that are largely based on economic incentives and compromises" (Dana, 2015, p. 457). As the Oslo Agreements had as their primary goal the transition of Palestine from the occupation to being an independent State – under the influence of Israel – such transition was designed according to the logic of neo-liberal state-building and economic development pursued through private entrepreneurship. This was enforced on the ground by Salam Fayyad's administration.[7] The encouragement of trading and private entrepreneurship and the systematic involvement of international agencies in the administrative activities of the Palestinian government, promoted by Fayyad's policies, corresponded to the increasing relocation of offices and businesses in the area of Ramallah/Al-Bireh.

In this framework, Ramallah/Al-Bireh became the destination for heterogeneous migrations, collecting simultaneously political and intellectual exiles returning to Palestine after negotiations with Israel, middle-class families ending their experience in the Gulf and in Western countries, local entrepreneurs relocating firms, and a significant number of people from minor centres in the West Bank searching for job opportunities as clerks and blue-collar workers. Under this pressure, Ramallah/Al-Bireh underwent a fast and once again loosely regulated development, almost entirely driven by private initiatives. Newcomers' spending capacity determined in which area of the city to settle, with lower middle class and under-skilled newcomers finding accommodation in poorer quality urban sprawls mainly located in the southern outskirts of the city.

Umm Al-Sharayiet was among the first to develop under this pressure in the early 1990s. New buildings initially accommodated the offices of ministries and international agencies in adapted apartment buildings, with condominiums housing higher-level white collars with their families. In the early 2000s the decision of Fayyad's administration to relocate public offices in a formal diplomatic headquarter and the construction of the Separation Wall by the Israeli occupation on the southern borders with Umm Al-Sharayiet caused the neighbourhood's downgrading to marginal urban sprawl for lower ranking clerical workers coming from villages across the West Bank. As Umm Al-Sharayiet went on densifying, land prices became mostly inaccessible to the growing population of Al-Amari, which therefore started the vertical development of the camp.

From 2010 and beyond: The socio-spatial reshuffle in progress

During the last decade, Umm Al-Sharayiet continued expanding, overrunning the municipal boundaries and reaching the Separation Wall. The increase in real estate prices and the poorly built environment turned Umm Al-Sharayiet into temporary accommodation, with its inhabitants preferably renting apartments for a few years rather than buying them. The weakening of social cohesion and sense of belonging caused by dwellers' turnover and landlords' speculation caused the progressive deterioration of the local built environment. The socio-spatial pattern is further diversifying, with new migratory flows entering the site: families from East Jerusalem are relocating to the 'Palestinian side' of the Separation Wall due to the growing aggressiveness of Israeli policies and the increase in living costs. The Wall itself caused the depreciation of neighbouring lands, while fencing out an area legally under Jerusalem Municipality jurisdiction, which became actually annexed to Umm-Al-Sharayet and the West Bank. The de facto lawless land so created, however, attracted other, quite specific categories of users, interested in the relatively affordable prices and the lack of authority over spatial development, functions, standards and taxation.

Simultaneously, the almost complete saturation of Al-Amari and the relative improvement of some of its inhabitants' financial conditions have triggered a new wave of out-migration, with numerous households now resettling in the farther afield – and more affordable – outskirts, such as Beitunya and Al-Ramleh. Houses left vacant are offered for rent to an under-skilled workforce migrating to the city from rural villages: these internal migrants represent the poorest and most marginalised layer of displaced people migrating to the city

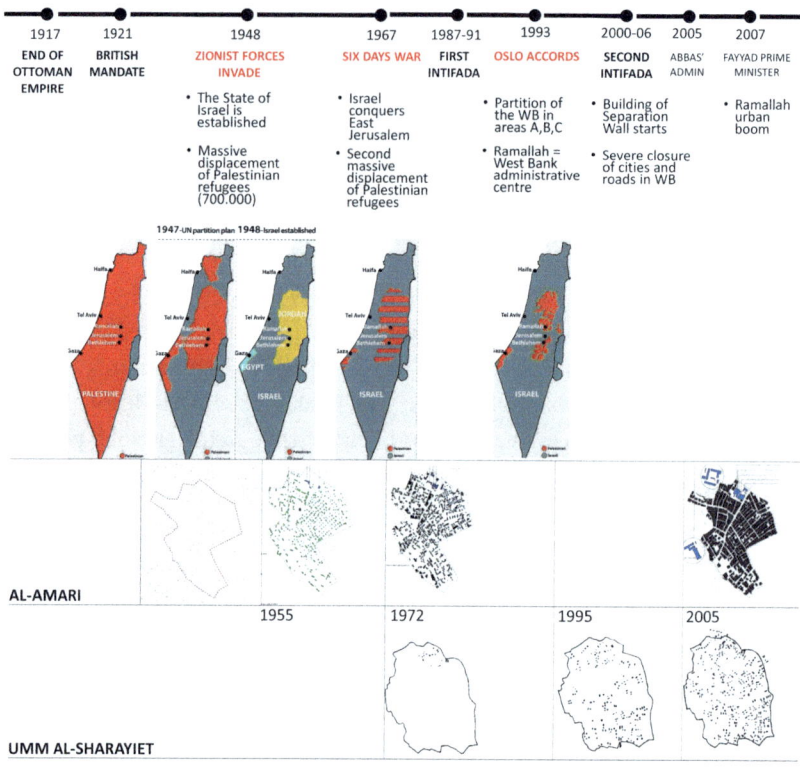

Figure 3. A timeline connecting main historical milestones and the spatial transformation in the region and in the case study. Source: the author.

today, who struggle to integrate into the life of the city and into that of the camp too, with the latter being increasingly divided between villagers and urbanised people, refugees and non-refugees. As per the accords with the UN, Al-Amari enjoys an extraordinary juridical and economic system, which lies outside the administrative and fiscal regulations of the Palestinian government. This translates today into the increasing attraction of the camp for businesses and small manufactures, drawn in by the simplified framework and the access to free supplies of water and electricity.[8]

Homing displacements: Three microstories

This second section narrates the homing processes that are linked to the different experiences of displacement of three households which are respectively to be found in Al-Amari Refugee Camp, the consolidated core of Umm Al-

Sharayiet, and its most southern sprawl flanking the Israeli Wall. The approach proposed here aims to provide an understanding of the internal diversity that characterises the Palestinian nation residing in urban West Bank today. Different identities and (sub)cultures emerge in terms of socio-spatial practices and adaptations pertaining to everyday spaces at the domestic and neighbourhood scale. Microstories contextualise the socio-spatial processes of home-making with different conditions of displacement. Stories eventually bring to the fore the pervasive and often indirect and 'creeping' ways in which the seven-decade-long occupation has affected the temporariness and stability of the home for Palestinian civilians (Rosenhek, 2003, p. 239). At the same time, these cases highlight the (counter-)agency of the Palestinians in fashioning the best possible everyday existence within very variegated sets of constraints and difficulties.

A house in Al-Amari refugee camp

- Fares is a young engineer working for the Municipality of Ramallah. The eldest brother of four and having lost his father, Fares was raised by his mother who made a living out of a manufacturing activity at home and obtained some financial support from other members of the family. This situation is quite common in Al-Amari camp. When we first met, Fares' house was a single-storey building of roughly 80 m² situated along a secondary road in the middle of the camp: replacing the original one-roomed shelter, the house covers the entire surface of the plot, having been delimited on the other three sides by very narrow alleys left by the expansion of the surrounding buildings as a guarantee of the minimum right of passage and ventilation for all the neighbours. The small yard originally in front of the shelter had been progressively covered up to build new rooms and was eventually roofed. The room facing the main street was turned into a mini-market by Fares' father: however, after his death, his widow and the rest of the family decided to close the shop as Fares' mother could not see herself comfortable as a single woman working in a "public" facility such as the neighbourhood's drugstore. Fares' mother is the head of the family; however, she is gradually handing the most practical part of this role over to Fares, as she is growing older and as her eldest son has reached adulthood for a paid job. With a view to providing for his aging mother and younger brother – an occasional construction worker in his early twenties – over time, Fares gradually saved money and built good connections in the neighbourhood and the camp council, so as eventually to be able to start building a second floor. Given the density of their 'hara' and the social etiquette, much of the preparation entailed informing their neighbours in a timely manner of the intention to build in a way that would affect their own environment and daily life: some of these buildings were previously allowed to have windows that looked directly onto Fares' rooftop – used as a terrace for hanging out the washing – and this courtesy was about to be removed; the stairs leading to the second floor could only be built externally, which led to a reduction of one of the alleys' road section, thus affecting the local flow of pedestrians and cars. Moreover, Fares' financial means would not alone suffice to pay for the works, meaning that helping hands and sponsors among friends and acquaintances had to be sought. Finally, being the only graduate in the family and fatherless, it was important for Fares to build a proper house as a demonstration of the family's successful trajectory despite the hardship, and also as a way to honour and compensate for the sacrifices of his mother, who for a long time alone played a role that is typically the prerogative of men according to local customs. Following the initial stages of the works, it became evident that the decision about the design lay mainly in the hands of Fares' mother: this kind of power is locally the indicator as to who holds the 'honorific leadership' of the family, a role that is assigned regardless of who actually pays for the project. Thinking about Fares's future and his steps towards having a family, during the building process Fares' mother insisted on starting the construction of a third floor, even if partial, regardless the limited funding. This was a way to put out a material statement to the neighbourhood announcing the future claim for a further amount of space, light, air and view.

Some important factors underlie the development of a dwelling like that of Fares: the self-design and self-building, the incrementalism, the opportunity that is taken and that it in turn creates for others, and the importance of social relations within the family, with the neighbourhood and with the camp. Self-building and self-designing the family house with limited financial means and without expert guidance leads to a heavy reliance on traditional models, archetypes and knowledge accumulated throughout generations prior to their displacement as refugees. This mechanism equally affects the architectural and the neighbourhood scale. Despite being apparently very different, the refugee camp by and large follows and redraws the long-established socio-spatial processes that formed the kasbahs – fortified citadels – in the Levantine region and in historical Palestine. Hence, contemporary techniques are used for building dwellings that feature the traditional layout of the court house (Awad, 2010; Ghadban, 2008): units grow into family residences accommodating multiple households together sharing a highly collective everyday routine – such as sitting together on a daily basis, cooking and eating collectively, taking care of the children and elderly people

Figure 4. Incremental housing in Al-Amari. Buildings have progressively expanded, saturating the ground floor of the respective plots. Source: the author.

of the family– and are therefore provided with architectural features that accommodate such habits, following socio-spatial criteria that can be found in historical complexes. On a broader scale, buildings aggregate into introverted clusters that foster social and spatial bonds, in a way that, architecturally and functionally, is pretty analogous to that of the typical *housh*. Seen in this way, camps like Al-Amari constitute the last places where historically consolidated ways of producing socio-spatial environments in urban contexts survive in the Middle East and continue their contemporary evolution.

The factors of incrementalism and opportunity together come into play to respond to the conditions of scarcity of space, big families and often modest and sporadic incomes. The combination of these conditions triggers what could be called 'space-grabbing': families may decide to build out of necessity (reasons can include impending changes to family structure, such as new births or sons approaching marital age) and out of opportunity. The latter happens, for example, when a neighbour needs to sell or exchange parts of the house, or when some extra savings are available, and favourable social circumstances occur.

In the crowded social and spatial tissue of the camp, a decision is never made by an individual. Any change to the spatial layout[9] is social – and vice versa; the private house is, in this respect, also a collective endeavour. Beyond the usual negotiation that takes place in any family nucleus when deciding on the interior arrangements of the dwelling unit, the expansion of a building from a single to multiple units belonging to nuclei from the same family is a matter of power geometries based on the factors of age, gender, social status and leadership skills. Seen in the broader picture of the *hara*, someone's expansion corresponds to somebody else's contraction. This concerns not just the physical space, but also less material aspects of everyday life that are equally crucial to people's physical and psychological wellbeing, such as lighting, ventilation, view and, eventually, privacy. Starting from the centre of the plot, where the initial shelter was most frequently located, buildings tend to expand and merge towards the margins of their respective plots. Such edges are the place where spatial and social negotiations between different families happen and materialise. These are also the actual frontiers where social bonds are more likely to be stimulated, whether in terms of solidarity, indifference or conflict. Buildings and their inhabitants have forcibly to talk to each other: the negotiation of rights and needs thus materialises in the pattern of alternating openings, screens, filter spaces and common areas.

The collective dimension of home-making in the camp is also an economic one. As families are numerous and rapidly increasing and incomes tend to be modest, (re)fashioning the house often requires seeking the contribution of family members and acquaintances in the neighbourhood, either for collecting the amount necessary to pay for the works, or to cut back on building costs by recruiting friends and neighbours to work on the site. The ability to aggregate forces around one's project is a matter of social talent, but it is also part of a kind of non-monetised economy based on the exchange of reciprocal favours (Mauss, 2002). The combination of all these factors eventually produces a distinctive environment, with a characteristic aesthetic for the built space, a specific behavioural code and a characteristic pattern of everyday socio-spatial practices and mindsets associated with the various spaces of the camp.

Umm Mahdi and Umm Al-Sharayiet

- Umm Mahdi is a divorced schoolteacher and mother of four. Native of a town in the rural outskirts of Nablus, Umm Mahdi moved to the city after getting married to an employee of the electrical company. She arrived in Umm Al-Sharayiet in the years of transformation caused by Fayyad's policies and the construction of the Separation Wall. For two decades she has lived in a three-roomed apartment in a housing complex formerly allocated to high ranking clerks employed by the ministries. When she moved in, she says, the atmosphere was that of a small elite knowing each other well: the building was well maintained and lively, especially thanks to employees' wives, who would often arrange gatherings and social activities in their apartments or in the complex's common spaces. But, following the creation of the diplomatic quarter and the retirement of some clerks, everything changed: old tenants moved away, renting their houses to new people who are mostly from lower middle-class backgrounds and who do not invest as much affection and effort into the place, as they do not own the property. Meanwhile, Umm Mahdi and her husband divorced. In Umm Mahdi's eyes, Umm Al-Sharayiet is just a facility for staying in Ramallah, a place that means little more than a workplace and lodgings: she cannot wait to return to her village with her children as soon as possible for as long as possible; so as to enjoy her father's country house and to have her daughters and sons play freely in nature; and to enjoy social life with her siblings and old friends while finding some relief from her maternal duties by sharing the task with the rest of her family. The city does not offer her any pleasure: the morphology of the city requires a car or taxi, which as a single mother she cannot afford, just as she cannot afford most of the cafes and restaurants downtown, while the neighbourhood does not have more than a drugstore on each road. The lack of attachment and limited salary push Umm Mahdi to refrain from investing in her house in Umm Al-Sharayiet; her true home is in her native village, whereas the apartment in Umm Al-Sharayiet is so basic and cramped for her and her children such that it constantly appears untidy, ramshackle and overcrowded. However, Umm Mahdi's children do not seem to be of the same opinion as their mother: they are constantly busy with their friends, chatting and playing in the staircases of the building and the surrounding outdoor spaces. This occupation is a matter of concern for Umm Mahdi, so after schooltime she is constantly busy keeping an eye on her sons and daughters, and on whom they hang around with in the neighbourhood. In this, at least, the architecture of the building and the surrounding loose grid of roads and free-standing condos, alternating with empty plots, provides some benefits, offering a panoramic view over what happens around her apartment.

Figure 5. A view of the urban landscape surrounding Umm Mahdi's house. Source: the author.

Umm Mahdi's experience is very common in Umm Al-Sharayiet; the interaction between the built environment and its inhabitants is permeated by the overarching sense of temporariness. The feeling of marginality and exclusion is also characteristic of this context, boosted by the poor living environment which has been produced by profit-driven real estate projects on the repetitive grid of roads and parcelisations laid out by local planning. In a manner similar to what happens in cities that attract migrants in other parts of the Middle East and in South Asia, the majority of people find accommodation in complexes built by private developers. Most of Umm Al-Sharayiet's condos are built by small speculators for an unknown third party, following the logic of maximum profit achieved by savings on materials and by minimising accessory spaces (e.g. living rooms and terraces), and by neglecting the design of outdoor spaces.

The outcome of money-making projects and very basic planning tools and building regulations is an uncohesive patchwork of condos spaced out by undesigned asphalted roads and privately-owned setbacks imposed by the building regulations. The lack of interest in what happens to projects after being sold, the poor design of both the domestic and urban built environment, the highly undesigned and run-down landscape produce a dysfunctional and still expensive habitat, which hardly creates satisfaction in its residents, and thus is hard to appropriate. For this reason, Umm Al-Sharayiet is unlikely to become the lifetime place for its dwellers.

The inconsistency between appropriation and ownership especially shows in the perimetral yards around apartment buildings: being legally jointly owned by residents, who nevertheless fail to form a community, these spaces end up being only lightly and sporadically appropriated, and remain mainly desert and shabby. This outdoor landscape sums up to the empty plots and roads, the only publicly-owned spaces of which people expect the municipality to take full care.

Temporariness, lack of attachment, socio-spatial conditions and morphological features together impede those inhabitants who suffer impaired physical or economic autonomy: toddlers, elderly people, persons affected by handicaps, women and one-income families, from participating in and enjoying urban life.

In spite of this, however, people apply their agency in the determination to create an everyday out of local circumstances. The indefiniteness of Umm Al-Sharayiet offers the opportunity to invent tactics of spatial appropriation: where a plot actually belongs to no-one, anyone can take it over at any time, although informally and temporarily. The vibrant life of places like Umm Al-Sharayiet has to be sought in the ephemeral performances of the everyday, with the youngest generations playing a very active role. While the intimate, collective spaces like that of the *housh* are lacking, the desire to meet is still there and adapts to the corners and recesses of the setbacks. The urban grid takes the place of the structure of the *hara*, which traditionally defined socio-spatial micro-systems, and nevertheless the social distinction into *haras* still survives in people's practices and specific jargon, especially among teenagers, being spatially anchored to gathering points and micro-morphological landmarks (e.g. the drugstore in the street, a parking area, a street curve, a drop in the topography). Urban voids are the terrain for playing, for setting up clashes or holding block-parties, for continuing rural activities in the city; in a word, they are the place for the expression of wills and needs.

A villa with view on the Israeli Separation Wall

- The southern outskirts of Umm Al-Sharayiet are an uncohesive agglomerate of buildings of various kinds: shacks and warehouses next to ten-storey condos and fancy villas, rising on empty lands scattered with wild vegetation, rubbish and broken cars, loosely connected by asphalted tracks. The place is almost impenetrable: although living for more than a year a few hundred metres north of this neighbourhood, I could never achieve a real interaction with this part of the city and its inhabitants. The same could be said for the rest of the team participating in the field research. Finding people to talk with in the streets or asking questions in shops was very difficult, and so was visiting apartment buildings or entering staircases. No-one opened their doors to us, and taking pictures, even in public roads, was seen as inappropriate; indeed, the widespread presence of cameras, fences and gates signalled the inhabitants' concern for privacy and private property with the urge towards surveillance. The overall impression was that of an entrenched and hyper-defensive context, with the built environment reflecting a fragmented, individual-based social landscape. This atmosphere condenses upon moving closer to the Wall, culminating in the very proximity of the concrete fence, where several luxury villas are located. These monumental houses barely show any sign of life from behind their elaborate perimetral fences. During site visits no one was ever seen; windows' shutters or curtains would never move, and no laundry was hung out. At best, an expensive car would be parked in the garden, always carrying an Israeli plate, never a Palestinian one. The fancy features of mansions stand out more dramatically against the background of the military architecture of the Israeli Wall and the surrounding shabby landscape. Instinctively one would wonder who, obviously being so wealthy, would ever invest money in building an extravagant residence in such a context, rubbing shoulders with Israeli guards, choosing the Wall as part of the landscape to enjoy from the living room or the master bedroom, surrounded by a desert where almost no one is able to apply any rule or control. On this very point, how did these people even obtain permits to build so close to the military fence? Do these houses have permits at all? And if so, from whom, and how? After a year of networking, I eventually met Umm Mohammad, a lady in her fifties, one of the very first to settle in the southern part of Umm Al-Sharayiet in the late '80s, when the place was still rural and unurbanised. As a longstanding local, socially skilled and member of the local mosque committee, Umm Mohammad had a grasp of who was living, moving, building in the place, and how the socio-spatial landscape had transformed in the last forty years. Although even this way I could not have access to the villas, thanks to her I could reconstruct the stories behind these architectures. Their similarity in typology and design features corresponded to analogous personal circumstances. Legally speaking, Umm Al-Sharayiet lands bordering the Wall fall within the Jerusalem Municipality's jurisdiction, and thus in that of Israel; however, in practice, being on the other side of the Wall, they are part of the Palestinian socio-economic system, where the cost of living is almost five times cheaper than that of Israel. On the top of that, the juridical ambiguity of this micro-area, its lack of planning and authority, the presence of the Separation Wall, these factors engender a poor socio-spatial context, but also provide opportunities in terms of relatively cheaper land prices – especially when compared with Jerusalem – and almost tax-free and paper-free building procedures. Some middle-class Palestinians residing in Jerusalem are willing to take this chance with its risks and choose a lifestyle as commuters between two states in conflict. In the end, this in-betweenness offers a great compromise that affords status-symbol homes while maintaining Israeli IDs, and the related privileges of jobs and everyday social relations in Jerusalem.

Figure 6. A view of one of the eclectic villas built in the proximity of the Separation Wall. Security cameras and high perimetral fences made proper photographing of the mansions very difficult. Google Streets was used as an integration to images collected on site by the author. Just like in the microstory, the car in this casual picture has an Israeli plate (recognisable by the yellow colour, while Palestinian plates have a white background). Source: Google Streets, 2019.

The physical in-between, where the eclectic mansions rise, reflects the social in-betweenness of Jerusalemite Palestinians, who have now for decades dealt with unpredictable economic and political perspectives and ambiguous juridical situations, the outcome of the increasing pressure of Israeli policies to relocate them outside the city. The riskiness of building in between edges and the daring architectural design reflect an ambiguous type of displacement, which is both internal and trans-national at the same time. Contextually, they also state the agency exercised by this category of displaced persons, who decide to seize the moment and take full advantage of the in-betweenness rather than being trapped by it. Migrating to this paradoxical, lawless place makes anything (good or bad) possible: this is the perfect site for new identities to emerge, with owners being free to talk through their houses with basically no constraints.

The fancy villas bordering the Separation Wall are perhaps the most outstanding expressions of the endemic transformation happening in contemporary Palestinian society, which is rapidly reorienting towards consumerist and individualistic models through massive exposure to social media and international broadcasts, in line with the dominant trend in the globalised world. The villas seem to speak to a neo-liberal idea of home: that is, introverted, individualist and antisocial; very much focussed on one's private life, while being much less interested in relations with the broader community. Spatially, this finds expression in the evident preoccupation with private property and the redundant demarcation of borders: while great investment is made into the landscaping of the outdoor spaces and fencing walls, what is outside the property and how it looks is quite irrelevant, as long as this does not threaten the life within the walls. In this logic, perimetral fences become crucial physical devices that defend, separate and conceal the inner while intimidating, impressing and surveying the outer. Security based on social relations encountered in the camp and, in lesser measure, in the consolidated part of Umm Al-Sharayiet is thereby replaced by cameras. The extroverted side of these homes is their being 'flaunty': although this social function is quite typical of residences, in this case the show-off perhaps does not address neighbours, with whom there is barely any connection, but is more likely to be staged through means like Instagram, Facebook and TikTok. The home as a status symbol is characterised by its large size, the over-abundance of spaces and the tendency towards the spectacular and the scenographic. Although disparate in terms of architectural layout, they all share the same the emphasis on the monumental hall and the use of an eclectic style. Main facades are central to this function, embedded as they are with a myriad of references to external imaginaries of beauty and wealth. They mix features from Gulf mansions seen in popular television series or Californian-style residences, and revise and adapt elements from classical architecture, with the display of expensive marbles, elaborate stonework, frescos, mosaics, decorative lighting systems and complex ironwork.

A final reflection

This chapter has presented only three of the numerous socio-spatial microcosms linked to processes of displacement present in urban Palestine today. Far from being exhaustive, microstories concretely outline the features of some urban communities in Ramallah/Al-Bireh. Their distinctive identity emerges in terms of living habits, everyday practices, social structures, built forms, dwelling culture and citizenship, with the last intended as the expression of expectations, rights and relations with the local context and its actors, unrelated to formal legal status (Lemanski, 2020, p. 591).

Long-term conflicts and colonialism, indeed, are ever-present elements driving the socio-spatial transformation of the context under study, and they act in a way that is much deeper and all-encompassing than one would immediately realise. The microstories highlight how political agendas locally succeed in stirring the Palestinian socio-spatial landscape using the more discrete language of economics, accords and regulations, with effects equally disruptive and often more long-lasting than those of warfare. Seventy years of occupation are no longer a 'time of exception' but have rather become the usual framework with which Palestinians are forced to cope on a daily basis, trying to achieve the best possible life.

'Modernised' urban sprawls, like that of Umm Al-Sharayiet, prove here to be no less significant in providing the dimension of the effects of a long-standing occupation. As in other colonial cities in the past, such as Kabilyia in Algeria (Heynen & Loeckx, 1998), in Umm Al-Sharayiet too the colonial regime manifests itself through economic levers and political relations that influence the local administrative apparatus, macro- and micro-economic structures, socio-spatial transformations, consumption habits, in an all-encompassing effort of normalisation that is aimed at the eventual neutralisation of self-determination. Beyond that, such stories also reveal the role of neo-liberal paradigms and globalisation in the whole process. These tune with the aims of the colonial project, introducing a " capitalist production of space" that responds to "a wider programme of spatial control in which lives are measured and ruled by the dictates of the market" (Awan et al., 2011, p. 30). All these pushes together move people around, more or less willingly, more or less permanently. Against this backdrop, Ramallah/Al-Bireh emerges as the main receptor for a variety of migrations, affirming its identity as an 'enclave micropolis' (Taraki, 2008): a globalised urban agglomerate the social and spatial landscape of which well represents the fragmentation of a nation.

A final reflection comes from looking at the three cases contextualised in the hidden geography defined by the Oslo Accords on the area at study. The invisible lines superimposed by the agreements divide the site into area A and C, partially overlapping with the Jerusalem Municipality. On the ground, this determines very different conditions in terms of legal guarantees, security and autonomy, consistent with the neo-liberal state-building criteria at the foundation of the Oslo Agreements (Dana, 2015). This micro geo-political pattern affects the very local scale, driving spatial patterns and demographics. Better security and administrative sovereignty are likely better to guarantee the stability and legal status not only of dwellers, but also of businesses and properties, with effects on land tenure and prices. At the same time, more stability means more control and regulations over private individuals and their activities. Put simply, what is more secure and stable (areas A) costs more: a better perspective of security, legality and stability becomes a commoditised asset, an investment that requires financial means and longer time horizons. In the context of a fully liberalised real estate market, where no measures have been taken to balance the social mix, diverse profiles of migrants end up sorted to specific locations by the force of their spending capacity and time perspectives.

COHESION AND TURNOVER

- collective society
based on clan/family structures
practice of sharing spaces and goods
- slow turnover, stable community of residents

- individualist society
based of single households
- fast turnover of residents
(average 7 years)

Figure 7. Mapping social structure and population turnover on the built tissue, in relation to the local micro-geography of administrative borders. The degree of temporariness and social disaggregation seems progressively to increase in relation to the precariousness and ambiguity of the administrative status defined by each border. Source: the author.

Acknowledgement

I gratefully acknowledge Eng. Mahmoud Al-Farra, students from the course "Local Architecture" from the Faculty of Architecture at Birzeit University for the academic year 2015/16, and families from Al-Amari Refugee Camp for the crucial contribution to the empirical research for this study.

Notes

1. As per the Cambridge Dictionary, 'nation' in this chapter refers to "a large group of people of the same race who share the same language, traditions, and history, but who might not all live in one area".
2. The ethnographic observation was collected by integrating a variety of tools, including social mapping, formal and informal interviews, carried out both in collective and one-to-one mode, drawing interviews, and full-immersive periods participating in the daily routine and activities in the local communities.
3. Hakim defines the *hosh* (or *housh*) as the Arabic word that designates a cul-de-sac-like cluster of buildings aggregated around a semi-private common court, separated from streets of more public access by a narrow alley working as a filter space. Hara, instead, is the Arabic term traditionally indicating the socio-spatial entity of the block or the neighbourhood (Hakim, 2008).
4. Refugee camps in the West Bank come under the jurisdiction of the UN, which manages the civil administration and security. Refugees residing in officially recognised camps were listed at the UN and provided with refugee cards. On one hand, this would grant them access to UN facilities and support programmes such as food and medical aid, UNRWA primary schools and clinics. On the other hand, it gave them the right to claim for restitution of or compensation for the assets confiscated by the Israeli government and its army in the event of negotiations for peace. Until recent times, the refugee card would be strictly connected to the actual residence in the camp: hence, a refugee willing to settle outside the camp's official borders would be stripped of the card and all related guarantees and protections. See Holzer (2013).
5. Religious life was radically different in 1970s' Israel and the Gulf countries. In Israel, Palestinians would experience a largely secular society, Jewish for the large majority. Gulf countries, which were predominantly Muslim, were characterised instead by a much more prescriptive religious approach that was and remains very different from the approach traditionally observed in Palestine and by Palestinians, and which continues to be strictly regulatory towards social structures and gender relations.

6. The Oslo Agreement segments the Palestinian territories into three areas: 'A' (civil administration and security both under the Palestinian Authority), 'B' (civil administration under the Palestinian Authority, security under the Israeli Army) and 'C' (civil administration and security both under the Israeli Army). Additionally, other special zones are established, like Israeli military zones and refugee camps, with the latter under UN jurisdiction.
7. Salam Fayyad was the Palestinian Minister of Economics within the PLO in the years 2002-2005 and 2007-2012. His policy promoted a highly pragmatic approach with a neo-liberal imprint (Dana, 2015), aimed at demonstrating the reliability of the Palestinian administrative and economic system as a fully-functioning country, able to keep control and manage its territories, citizens and, therefore, its security.
8. Camps in the West Bank are typically provided with water and electricity by Palestinian companies. However, being outside the direct jurisdiction of the Palestinian administration, it is often very difficult for companies to claim back bills and debts.
9. This involves not only the act of building, but also that of demolishing, annexing or ceding spaces to a counterpart, reviewing the internal design of dwellings or making changes to the external façades.

References

Abu Latifeh, R. (2013). *Umm Elsharayiet Neighborhood Analysis*. Birzeit University, Birzeit, Palestine.

Abu-Saad, I. (2006). State-Controlled Education and Identity Formation Among the Palestinian Arab Minority in Israel. *American Behavioral Scientist*, 49(8), 1085–1100. https://doi.org/10.1177/0002764205284720

Awad, S. Q. (2010). *The Peasant House: Contemporary Meanings, Syntactic Qualities and Rehabilitation Challenges*. Graz University of Technology, Graz.

Awan, N., Schneider, T., & Till, J. (2011). *Spatial agency: Other ways of doing architecture*. London: Routledge.

Azaryahu, M., & Kook, R. (2002). Mapping the nation: Street names and Arab-Palestinian identity: three case studies. *Nations and Nationalism*, 8(2), 195–213.

Bhabha, H. (2013). In Between Cultures. *New Perspectives Quarterly*, 30(4), 107–109.

Bjawi-Levine, L. (2009). Childrens' Rights Discourse and Identity Ambivalence in Palestinian Refugee Camps. *Jerusalem Quarterly*, (37), 75–85.

Bshara, K. (2012). *Space and Memory: The Poetics and Politics of Home in the Palestinian Diaspora* (Doctoral dissertation). University of California, Irvine.

Dana, T. (2015). The symbiosis between Palestinian 'Fayyadism' and Israeli 'economic peace': The political economy of capitalist peace in the context of colonisation. *Conflict, Security & Development*, 15(5), 455–477.

Fincham, K. (2012). Learning the nation in exile: Constructing youth identities, belonging and 'citizenship' in Palestinian refugee camps in south Lebanon. *Comparative Education*, 48(1), 119–133.

Ghadban, S. S. (2008). Architecture in Palestine. In *Encyclopaedia of the History of Science, Technology, and Medicine in Non-Western Cultures* (pp. 225–38). Netherlands: Springer.

Ginzburg, C. (1986). *The cheese and the worms: The cosmos of a sixteenth-century miller*. Harmondsworth: Penguin Books.

Hakim, B. S. (2008). Mediterranean urban and building codes: Origins, content, impact, and lessons. *URBAN DESIGN International*, 13(1), 21–40.

Halabi, Z. (2004). Exclusion and identity in Lebanon's Palestinian refugee camps: A story of sustained conflict. *Environment&Urbanization*, 16(2), 39–48.

Hammami, F. (2016). Issues of mutuality and sharing in the transnational spaces of heritage – contesting diaspora and homeland experiences in Palestine. *International Journal of Heritage Studies*, 22(6), 446–465.

Hammer, J., & Schulz, H. (2003). *The Palestinian diaspora: Formation of identities and politics of homeland*. Abingdon: Routldege. Retrieved from https://books.google.ps/books?id=9N4sk-EMEKUC&printsec=frontcover&source=gbs_ge_summary_r&cad=0#v=onepage&q&f=false

Heynen, H., & Loeckx, A. (1998). Scenes of Ambivalence: Concluding Remarks on Architectural Patterns of Displacement. *Journal of Architectural Education*, 52(2), 100–108.

Holzer, E. (2013). What Happens to Law in a Refugee Camp? *Law & Society Review*, 47(4), 837–872.

Johansson, A., & Vinthagen, S. (2015). Dimensions of everyday resistance: The Palestinian "Sumūd." *Journal of Political Power*, 8(1), 109–139.

Khalidi, R. (1997). *Palestinian Identity: The Construction of Modern National Consciousness*. New York: Columbia University Press.

Lemanski, C. (2020). Infrastructural citizenship: The everyday citizenships of adapting and/or destroying public infrastructure in Cape Town, South Africa. *Transactions of the Institute of British Geographers*, 45(3), 589–605.

Low, S. (2016). Homing the City: An afterthought. *Home Cultures*, 13(2), 215–220.

Mason, V. (2007). Children of the "Idea of Palestine"1: Negotiating Identity, Belonging and Home in the Palestinian Diaspora. *Journal of Intercultural Studies*, 28(3), 271–285.

Mauss, M. (2002). *The gift: The form and reason for exchange in archaic societies*. London: Routledge.

Owen, R. (1981). The Arab Economies in the 1970s. *MERIP Reports*, (100/101), 3.

Peteet, J. (2007). Problematizing a Palestinian Diaspora. *International Journal of Middle East Studies*, 39(4), 627–646.

Rosenhek, Z. (2003). The Political Dynamics of a Segmented Labour Market: Palestinian Citizens, Palestinians from the Occupied Territories and Migrant Workers in Israel. *Acta Sociologica*, 46(3), 231–249.

Rosenthal, G. (Ed.). (2016). *Established and outsiders at the same time: Self-images and we-images of Palestinians in the West Bank and in Israel*. Göttingen: Universitätsverlag Göttingen.

Rueff, H., & Viaro, A. (2009). Palestinian Refugee Camps: From Shelter to Habitat. *Refugee Survey Quarterly*, 28(2–3), 339–359.

Saad, D. (2019). Materializing Palestinian Memory: Objects of Home and the Everyday Eternities of Exile. *Jerusalem Quarterly File*, (80), 57–71.

Salih, R., Zambelli, E., & Welchman, L. (2020). "From Standing Rock to Palestine we are United": Diaspora politics, decolonization and the intersectionality of struggles. *Ethnic and Racial Studies*, 1–19.

Sayigh, R. (1977). The Palestinian Identity among Camp Residents. *Journal of Palestine Studies*, 6(3), 3–22.

SIAAL – Stuttgart University, & UNRWA. (2005). *Camp Profiling: Amari, Deheisheh, Fawwar*. Stuttgart: UNRWA.

Suleiman, Y. (Ed.). (2016). *Being Palestinian: Personal Reflections on Palestinian Identity in the Diaspora*. Edinburgh: Edinburgh University Press.

Taraki, L. (2008). Enclave Micropolis: The Paradoxical Case of Ramallah/al-Bireh. *Journal of Palestine Studies*, 37(4), 6–20.

Thiollet, H. (2011). Migration as Diplomacy: Labor Migrants, Refugees, and Arab Regional Politics in the Oil-Rich Countries. *International Labor and Working-Class History*, 79(1), 103–121.

Turan, Z. (2010). Material Objects as Facilitating Environments: The Palestinian Diaspora. *Home Cultures*, 7(1), 43–56.

Valenta, M., & Jakobsen, J. (2018). Nexus of armed conflicts and migrations to the Gulf: Migrations to the GCC from war-torn source countries in Asia, Africa and the Arab neighbourhood. *Middle Eastern Studies*, 54(1), 22–47.

CHAPTER 11

Mediating between Formality and Informality

Refugee Housing as City-Making Activity in Refugee Crisis Athens

Aikaterini Antonopoulou
University of Liverpool, U.K.

Re-thinking urban informality

A place of just over 130,000 inhabitants at the end of the 19th Century (Biris, 1966, p. 246), Athens expanded in size and took the form of a modern European city in the interwar period and was densely built after World War II (WWII). It is very often described as a "modern" city due to the apparent formal similarities of its typical buildings to the modern architecture of the early 20th Century: reinforced concrete frames, white façades, horizontal openings and flat roofs. Yet, this building activity of the first half of the 20th Century carries within it a wide variety of informal actions such that the city could equally be described as an "un-planned" city. None of the masterplans composed since the constitution of the Greek state and the transfer of the Greek capital to Athens in 1834 was fully implemented, and it appears that the citizens have intervened to a great extent in all stages of planning by supporting, resisting or ignoring state decisions (Bastea, 2000, p. 5). In the introduction to the Greek translation of his book *Modern Architecture: A Critical History*, Kenneth Frampton (2009) describes Athens as a modern city "par excellence", focusing on the extent to which the language of modernism was appropriated in the city both formally and programmatically in the 20th Century and manifested itself through the city's urban growth. This manifestation of the modern, argues Frampton, owes itself to the endless repetition and wide spread of the – individually – uninteresting typical multiple-dwelling building, the *polykatoikia* (p. 14). Continuing a very long tradition of "architecture without architects" (ibid., p. 15) in pre-modern Greece,[1] the city has taken its shape not from the vision of a single architect, but instead from the spontaneous and almost autonomous expression of a popular culture.[2]

Ioanna Theocharopoulou (2017) situates urban informality in Athens within the wider social, cultural and economic context of 19th Century Greece. She understands informal activity as an expression of Greek culture that has prompted the modernisation and the urbanisation of Athens, and has enabled small-scale developers and builders, but also non-professionals (such as "housewives"), to take agency in them. Informality is traced in the longstanding divide between the "East and the West" that characterised Greek society in the years after independence – though it may be argued that features of this can still be identified today. The East was reflected in the popular culture that linked to the local Mediterranean traditions and the region's Ottoman past, whereas the West referred to an "educated elite" that made its appearance in the newly constructed state and promoted a rational, ordered and central management of the city and the country in a more general sense. These fundamental class distinctions were, as elsewhere in Europe, supported and extended by access to higher education. This produced "European style professionals", architects and planners (who would then populate the ruling institutions and the private sector), on the one hand, and a large body of on-site, self-taught builders who would "continue to rely on orally transmitted, craft-based trade education" (Theocharopoulou, 2017, p. 60), on the other, very often in direct conflict with each other. Planning was also imported from the West, hence the endless problems in the implementation of any master plan ever composed (Bastea, 2000, p. 44). As Greece progressed into the 20th Century, the discrepancies between the popular and the elite, the private and the public, the formal and the informal never ceased to exist and played out in the rapid urbanisation of Athens post-war (Fig. 1.).

Figure 1. Athens, Gyzi, photo by Yiorgis Yerolympos.

The concept of *urban informality* is traditionally understood as a "state of exception from the formal order of urbanisation" (Roy, 2005, p. 147) and therefore linked to the urbanisation of the developing world, the spread of slums and squatter settlements in the global south (Davis, 2006), the enforced transfer of underprivileged urban residents to peri-urban areas and to conditions of extreme poverty and precarity. However, the dichotomy between the formal and the informal has increasingly been contested in recent times. Urban informality is regarded as a form of urbanisation by itself and as a system of norms that drive urban transformation and connect different forms of economies and spaces to one another (Roy, 2005, p. 148). Then the formal and the informal are both at play in the theorisation of the contemporary city; in effect, it is the intersection of the two that creates tensions between capital and identity (Gaffkin et al., 2011, p. 309). This intersection also allows for more forms of agency to arise: when small-scale developers and builders, permanent and temporary residents take part in shaping their environment, new visions about the city can emerge. If formality and informality are both considered as forms of practice in a complex, multiple, contingent and ever-changing interrelationship (McFarlane, 2012, p. 103), they can also challenge the established classifications, leading to new understandings and alternative productions of urban space.

This chapter mediates between the formal and informal practices that have shaped contemporary Athens. It juxtaposes two very different approaches to housing for refugees – one pre-1945 and a recent one – and examines the relationship between architecture and the city that each one represents. Built between 1934 and 1935, the *Alexandras Avenue refugee building complex (prosfygika)* is a housing project designed to respond to the massive population exchange between Greece and Turkey in and after 1922. The complex proposed a model of housing for refugees that materialised the objectives of the Modern Movement. It was built to set a precedent for the future development of social housing during the rapid urbanisation of Athens and other urban areas in Greece in the coming decades, and to respond to the imminent commercialisation of housing (Stavrides, 2007). The example was never widely followed, however, and eventually the complex itself fell into a state of disrepair. *City Plaza*, conversely, was a squatted former hotel in Athens' city centre which housed an average of 350 refugees per day during the 39 months of its operation from April 2016 to June 2019 in response to the European refugee crisis. The occupied building operated as a cooperative and stood against the formal refugee camps system that has been set up in Greece, and that continues to run at the time of writing, under appalling conditions (Human Rights Watch, 2019; Donaldio, 2019; Kitsantonis, 2019). Between the top-down practice of the *prosfygika* that reflects the social system Greece once sought to develop (but never fully accomplished) and the bottom-up structure of City Plaza, which demonstrates the potential of Athens' much-contested urban informality, this chapter looks at the architecture of the displaced as a city-making activity, which not only makes space for emergency situations but also tests alternative forms of living and working together even in challenging contexts and at the intersections of crises. It focuses on key representations of both housing projects (photographic representation of the prosfygika and online and photographic representation of City Plaza) which, combined with archival research, become drivers to unpack two contradictory visions of Athens.

Prosfygika

In 1922 a failed Greek Army expedition into Asia Minor that aimed at liberating the Greek-origin population living in Turkey led to what in Greece is commonly referred to as the "Asia Minor Disaster", that is, the destruction of Smyrna and the massacre of its Greek and Armenian residents. Following this, a treaty was signed (Lausanne, July 1923) which set out a compulsory, large-scale population exchange and resulted in the relocation of 1,200,000 Turkish nationals of Greek origin (and of the Greek Orthodox religion) from Turkey's Aegean coast to Greece,[3] except for those living in Istanbul, as well as 355,000 Greek nationals (of Muslim religion) from Greece to Turkey (Motta, 2013, p. 365), except for those living in Thrace.

Although the incoming people were of Greek Christian origin and they were granted Greek citizenship upon their arrival (and vice versa), it is important to highlight that this was by no means a repatriation for either group. Asia Minor has hosted Hellenic settlements since antiquity. For the Orthodox Christians, therefore, the exchange was received as a "harsh exile" (Hirschon, 2008, p. 8) and a displacement. For many decades these people were regarded and referred to as refugees and as "mikrasiates" (meaning coming from Asia Minor), which emphasised their cultural differences. Native Greeks depicted them as "Orientals" and attached several stereotypes to them (Gatrell, 2013, p. 67). This was evident in the terminology used by both official agencies (Refugee Relief Fund, Refugee Settlement Commission), local politicians, and less formal references, such as newspaper articles (Gatrell, 2013, p. 64), as well as in the popular place names, many of which are still in use today. The very name of the housing project examined here, *prosfygika* (adjective), means "of refugees" in Greek.

The Greek State's intentions were to keep about half of the refugees around the cities so as to integrate them into the local economy (Stavrides, 2007).[4] Greece was in the middle of a significant financial crisis and in a disorganised state (Biris, 1966, p. 247), lacking both order and social policy. Therefore, the influx

Figure 2. 'Temporary accommodation of refugees from Asia Minor in the Municipal Theatre of Athens, Athens, 1923,' source: Joseph Hepp archive, Hellenic Literary and Historical Archive – Cultural Foundation of the National Bank of Greece Photographic Archive.

of refugees into the country was seen as an opportunity: as low-paid workers in abundance, they would contribute to the development of Greek industry, which was still in its early stages. With most of the industrial production concentrated around the main urban areas of the country, 643,025 people (53 per cent of the total influx) were distributed throughout those city centres and this prompted their further urbanisation (Vlachos et al., 1978, p. 117). Athens, in particular, as the main commercial centre and the place where state decisions were made, offered fertile ground for an extensive manufacturing and industrial zone. Its adjacent Piraeus (the harbour) also offered a prime location for industrial growth. In this context, Athens, a place of 300,000 inhabitants, received 129,380 refugees (a population increase of 40 per cent) and Piraeus received another 101,185 refugees, which increased its population by 74 per cent (Polyzos, 1973, p. 80).

These 129,380 refugees arrived in Athens distressed and deprived of most of their belongings. Without much infrastructure to receive them, the refugees were initially accommodated in every possible public building such as schools, churches and railway stations, and eventually they built informal settlements in the periphery of the city using salvaged insubstantial materials. Architectural historian Kostas Biris describes the Athens of 1925 as a filthy, disordered and crowded space to such an extent that the municipality itself built market stalls all around the central market square to accommodate the refugees' commercial activities (1966, pp. 291-2). A photo from September 1923 (Fig. 2.) becomes emblematic of that period: it shows the municipal theatre of Athens, a neoclassic building designed by Ernst Ziller (completed in 1888) and housing 150 refugee families on its balconies. The temporary residents have raised impromptu curtains to create privacy, while trunks – presumably carrying their few belongings – can be seen piled up everywhere.

Although in 1923 Greece received funds from England and the US to set up the Committee for the Rehabilitation of the Refugees and significant additional support from the League of Nations, it was not until ten years later that these funds were used to clear out the informal settlements and to develop social housing in order to re-house the refugees. Between 1923 and 1930 the efforts and funds of a number of public agencies and committees that were established to deal with the pressing conditions concentrated their immediate reaction to the crisis initially on providing tents and temporary shelters, and later on funding the construction of residential buildings, yet in an equally unplanned manner, which focused on quickly providing shelter rather than a thought-through and designed response. Vlachos et al. (1978) argue that there was no research or any careful consideration of the building process, which resulted in Athens' uncontrolled and undesigned expansion and its monstrous appearance (p. 118).

From 1930 onwards, however, the government of Eleftherios Venizelos began to develop a political agenda with a particular focus on social care, in which the accommodation of the refugees and the clearing of the city from the informal temporary shelters played a central role (Vlachos et al., 1978, p. 118). The *prosfygika* was built in Alexandras Avenue in this context between 1934 and 1935 to provide an alternative model of housing against the incubating commercialisation of residential development in Greece at the time (Stavrides, 2007). Indeed, the privately-funded medium-scale multi-storey residential buildings that Frampton wrote about had already begun to emerge and would predominate in the city after WWII. The complex was designed by architects Kimon Laskaris (1905-1978) and Dimitrios Kyriakos (1881-1971), appointed by the Technical Department of the Ministry of Welfare, which had been founded in pursuit of a more organised response to the refugee housing crisis. Kyriakos had significant experience in designing public and infrastructural projects in Greece, while Laskaris had just returned to Greece from Paris, where he had worked in Le Corbusier's office. In a rational layout, the housing developed in eight blocks consisting of a total of 228 apartments of two types and reflected the objectives of the Modern Movement as expressed at the 4th International Congress of Modern Architecture (CIAM), which had arrived in Athens in August 1933: set at a distance from each other to ensure adequate exposure to sunlight, the blocks were uniform and featured no decoration or any other formal or stylis-

Figure 3. Prosfygika, aerial view; image sourced from Google Earth and adapted by author.

tic concessions in an attempt to impose order on an otherwise unorderly and chaotic city (Fig. 3). The refugee housing prompted research on mass housing and the development of the minimal dwelling that would accommodate the low-income urban resident in a more general sense (Herscher, 2017, p. 64). Testing the minimum essential housing standards, the apartments were of 30.2 or 34.8 square metres and consisted of two rooms, a kitchen and a toilet (Stavrides, 2007). A stairwell would service two apartments per floor. The apartments ran the width of the building and featured a balcony offering outdoor space. Built at the time at the edge of the city centre, the complex marked the city's potential extensions and expressions. Pristine and unpretentious, modern and efficient, it was designed as an example to follow and as an opportunity to impose order and to control the impending urbanisation of Athens (Fig. 4.).

Although a number of such complexes were constructed in Athens to respond to the Asia Minor crisis (Vlachos et al., 1978, pp. 120-124), such housing prototypes were never assimilated into the life or the morphology of the city. For alongside these housing schemes, in the 1920s and 1930s, privately funded multi-storey residential buildings made their appearance, also referring to the Western European modernist examples of the time and accommodating the wealthy urban classes. In its smaller scale and following the street block patterns (as opposed to the prosfygika, which implemented a totally different urban figure), the *polykatoikia* was endlessly imitated and reproduced after WWII to give Athens its very unique appearance. The *polykatoikias* attracted the higher classes by presenting them with yet an extra level of technological comforts (such as central heating

Figure 4. Prosfygika: 'view of the residential building complex constructed for the housing of refugees in Alexandras Avenue,' 1936, Archive of E.R.T., A. E, Petros Poulidis collection.

and elevators) and, most generally, a modern lifestyle. The modest and economical *prosfygika*, conversely, represented the poor and pitiful living conditions of refugees, who continued to be regarded as "others" in the city (Theocharopoulou, 2017, p. 71; Stavrides 2007). Mass housing – and perhaps the fact that its design had not taken into account the refugees' former lifestyle and their abrupt transition to urban contexts[5] – brought with it memories of a sad past and came to symbolise the crisis itself, whereas *polykatoikias* promised a bright future.

Post-war, the privately-funded *polykatoikia* transformed into a scheme that would accommodate the middle and even the lower classes, and eventually they composed a dense and increasingly chaotic environment around the *prosfygika*. New forms of legislation also played an important role in this development. Since 1929, the Law of Horizontal Ownership has allowed the ownership by individuals of a floor (in full or in part) of a multi-storey building and therefore partial ownership of the underlying plot. To this, a "part-exchange" (*anti-paroche*) system was established, which allowed a small plot-owner to turn their land over to a developer in exchange for a few new modern apartments in the final built volume. The two schemes together boosted construction and gave the opportunity, on the one hand, to small and medium scale developers to avoid (partly or entirely) the involvement of banks and other funding institutions and, on the other, to owners of old and badly-maintained properties to renew their housing

Figure 5. *Prosfygika*, current condition; photo taken by author.

Figure 6. Effacing the *prosfygika*, July 2004, source unknown.

and profit from it. Theocharopoulou (2017, p. 142) and Vaiou (2002, pp. 219-220) argue that this informal financing structure facilitated greater class mobility as well as assisting the shift from the rural to the urban and the movement of the population to the city centre. This system, in its scale and operation, has not changed significantly to this day, making the construction industry a key factor in activating (or slowing down in times of crisis) the Greek economy.

In December 1944 the *prosfygika* actively participated in the city's recent history, with its residents forming a solidarity network around the adjacent prisons during the German occupation and the buildings being attacked during the so-called "Battle of Athens", which was a predecessor to the Greek civil war (Stavrides, 2007); however, the project was never seen as an example to be followed. Since the 1960s, the complex has become the site of a long dispute between successive governments and local activists, with the former proposing its demolition and its transformation into a public park and the latter, joined by the local community, protesting for its protection. Eventually it fell into decay (Fig. 5.), providing accommodation – apart from a small number of activists who fought for their preservation – to several marginal subjectivities such as drug addicts and immigrants without papers. In an attempt to efface both the buildings and their occupiers from the image of the city, during the Athens 2004 Olympics, and at a time when Athens had to present an image of glory and cleanliness throughout, the front block was entirely covered by a screen featuring an image of the Acropolis (Fig. 6.). In another attempt to clear out its "otherness" from Alexandras Avenue by means of political privatisation, in the context of the recent financial crisis, the complex was included in the Hellenic Republic Asset Development Fund. In 2003, the two front buildings were declared listed by the Greek Ministry of Culture as representative examples of social housing (Greek Government, 2003), and, in 2009, the entire complex was declared listed. In its latter decision the Ministry recognised the complex's social and historical significance in the integration of the refugees from Asia Minor in the productive and social life of the city as well its key role in the urban history of Athens as one of the few examples of modernist social housing in the interwar period (Greek Government, 2009). Although today the Municipality of Athens has plans to restore the buildings and use them for contemporary social housing, no budget ever became available, and so they stand today taken over by time and roughly repaired by makeshift constructions and salvaged materials.

City Plaza

At the extension of Alexandras Avenue, a couple of kilometres to the west, in Victoria Square *City Plaza* takes the form of a typical *polykatoikia* built in the 1970s (Fig. 7.). City Plaza was a hotel that ceased operation in 2010 due to the financial recession, and had remained empty since then, alongside other retail, residential and hospitality-related buildings in the city centre. In April 2016, shortly after the agreement between the EU and Turkey that trapped thousands of refugees between Turkey and Greece (March 2016), *Solidarity Initiative for Economic and Political Refugees*, a leftist activist group, occupied the hotel's empty building, reconnected the utilities and set up community-based refugee accommodation as a response to the European refugee crisis, which had begun in early 2015 (Fig. 8.). Similar movements that actively opposed Europe's formal migration politics and the power relations connected to them had emerged in many European cities at the time; among others, in Brussels, Rome and Berlin squats offered communal living to refugees as an alternative to the official camps system. In its local context, City Plaza also participated in a network of occupied spaces in Athens (*Coordination of Refugee Squats*) which aimed to accommodate the increasing number of asylum seekers who arrived in Athens from the Greek islands.

In the 39 months of its operation, from April 2016 to July 2019, City Plaza gave space to more than 2,500 refugees from 13 different countries (City Plaza, 2019) until their documentation was complete and they were allowed to continue on their way further into Europe. The building operated in the form of a cooperative, with refugees and solidarity activists living together and participating in both the decision-making and its basic maintenance.[6] About 100 of the 126 rooms of the hotel hosted an average of 350 refugees at any time

Figure 7. City Plaza aerial view; image sourced from Google Earth and adapted by author.

Figure 8. City Plaza, 26 August 2018; photo taken by City Plaza.

(among them an average of 120 children), while the remaining 26 functioned as communal or other support spaces, as storage, and to accommodate volunteers who visited the site (City Plaza, 2019). Volunteers also contributed to the medical and administration needs of the squat and organised Greek, English and German classes. City Plaza did not use any state or Non-Governmental Organisations (NGO) funding, but ran only on individuals' donations – with fundraising campaigns active in Greece and in Germany – and on items and products donated either by local merchants or people residing in the wider area. Its operation critiqued the inhumane and appalling living conditions in the formally organised refugee camps in Greece, as well as their seclusion from the urban centres. City Plaza, conversely, aimed to integrate the refugees into the city centre of Athens and promote their living within the larger community. For as long as their families stayed in the hotel, the children were enrolled in the

Figure 9. City Plaza, "the fight continues," July 2019; photo taken by author.

local schools and were further integrated into the local community. In response to increased pressure from the newly elected conservative government via the Greek police towards the vacation of a number of squats in Athens, in July 2019 the collective decided to hand the building to the hotel's former employees, to whom all the mobile equipment of the building belonged according to a court order that had followed from the hotel's bankruptcy (Fig. 9.).

Throughout its operation, City Plaza maintained an active, albeit with very low means, online presence which communicated and complemented its physical action in the city. It maintained a simply made webpage, entitled "the best hotel in Europe",[7] which advertised its fundraisers in English and in German, and a blog which publicised its needs and actions. Facebook and Twitter kept it connected to its supporters as well as to its networks in the context of which it organised events and protests. Currently, the blog and Facebook page both document City Plaza's daily life and its broader scope until the closure, in the form of an uncurated archive. The webpage hosts the collective's report on the 39 months of its operation and its political position. In its statement, it describes its twofold objective: to provide migrants with appropriate housing in the city centre of Athens and in collaboration with the locals, and to create a political hub of struggle for migrants and locals together (City Plaza, 2019).

The intersection with the city and the integration of refugees in its everyday structure was crucial in this operation, yet this integration did not come without further challenges. As mentioned, the empty hotel was not the first occupied building in Athens that was put to the service of the refugee crisis at the time; however, it is one of very few that were located outside Exarcheia, a highly political neighbourhood known for its anti-authoritarian character and its strong sense of community, whose residents always stood in solidarity to those in need and particularly to minorities, migrants and refugees. Although only a few blocks to the West, Victoria Square, where City Plaza is located, and its neighbouring districts present a more complex background. This part of the city once constituted a middle-class residential district densely and chaotically built in *polykatoikias* in the 1950s via the part-exchange system described above and as Athens expanded to the north. In the decades to come, many of these residents moved towards the suburbs and they were progressively replaced by immigrant populations who arrived in Athens during the 1990s, mainly from the Balkans. After 2000, the growth of the immigrant population (of increasingly diversified backgrounds, due to the recent refugee crises in the Middle East and Africa) and its presence in the city's public spaces, in combination with the declining social conditions of the remaining older residents in the context of the economic recession, have led to the development of aggressive, xenophobic and nationalist behaviours. This has provided fertile ground for the growing popularity of Golden Dawn, a neo-Nazi political party which comes after a long tradition of fascist organisations in post-war Greece and which has re-emerged both in the politics and in the streets of Athens and other urban areas in the country (Dalakoglou, 2012 & 2013, Doxiadis & Matsaganis, 2012, Kandylis & Kavoulakos, 2011, Psarras, 2012). Between 2012 and 2019, the party also enjoyed significant parliamentary representation.[8] During this period Golden Dawn kept an active and visible presence in the streets of the city centre, often claiming territorial control over space in specific neighbourhoods (Kandylis, 2013, p. 274). It developed a social programme to support only the ethnic Greek population (organising food banks and soup kitchens) and even offered them protection (Doxiadis & Matsaganis, 2012, p. 34), often acting as if it could replace the authorities[9] by checking the papers of immigrants and claiming to clear urban areas of immigrant crime.[10]

In this context, migrants, among other vulnerable groups, became increasingly absent from the public spaces of the city during the crisis (Vaiou & Kalandides, 2016, p. 460). Then, the refugees' mere existence in the City Plaza and at the city centre did not automatically provide access to the public sphere, especially due to their close proximity to hubs of xenophobia and racism. The hotel's presence in both physical and digital terms – as a building block in the city and through its updates on social media – suggested instead a play between visibility and invisibility. It was the visibility of its action that kept attracting popularity, volunteers and funds, especially when it was under constant threat of eviction by the hotel's owner. The videos regularly posted on City Plaza's Facebook page give us positive glimpses of the residents' lives both inside and outside the building, from the private rooms to the communal areas and to the clinic, to the street, the park and the square, in an attempt to prompt public dialogue and a sense of solidarity. One of them, aiming at celebrating the hotel's two years of occupation, tells the story of the space by following a little girl who lives there in and out of the rooms until she picks up her backpack and departs for school.[11] On another one, the children of City Plaza describe how a crowdfunding campaign was set up to buy bicycles for them, how they organised a bicycle workshop, and how they used to go cycling in the Pedion Areos Park nearby.[12] This very visibility, however, could also put the refugees in peril as it engendered exposure in the highly contested neighbourhood they were situated in; therefore, City Plaza operated at constant vigilance, with residents taking shifts in looking after the security of the place and making sure that the residents were not exposed to any form of danger.[13] By creating a safe, protected environment for its inhabitants, it was then able to open up to the public and to invite the city to take part in its happenings, from street parties and communal meals[14] to taking to the streets and protesting against the politics of the refugee crisis and against the unliveable conditions of the refugee camps in Greece and elsewhere.[15] Through the highly defended visibility of their actions and everyday activity they established a network of reclaimed and public sites that opposed xenophobic and racist behaviours and instigated new readings of the contemporary city. The adjacent alley, where the street parties were held, the Areos Park, where the kids rode their bicycles, the streets where the protests against the migrational politics took place, as well as the hotel's communal kitchen, the restaurant that had been turned into a communal living room and the room that had been transformed into a classroom together bring a "geography of publicity" (Staeheli et al., 2009, p. 647) in which people claim their right to take part in the public realm. By occupying a pocket of space at the intersection of many conflicting situations, City Plaza became a tool to reveal exclusion, discrimination and inequality; to re-think established concepts and practices; and to expose the diverse realities and unexplored worlds that underpin them.

Making space within informality

The integration of refugees in the communities that receive them may have been a consideration when the *prosfygika* was constructed, but this is certainly not a priority in the way the refugee crisis has officially been handled in recent times. In his book *Displacements: Architecture and Refugee*, Andrew Herscher (2017) argues that the refugee as a political subject and a political community has hardly ever been registered in architectural history and, by extension, in the social reproduction of architecture (p. 3). Following the current of global politics, argues Herscher, architectural history has always treated refugees as human surplus and as people out of place upon whom the exclusions of the nation state apply. When the state foresees the refugees as part of its labour force, then the architecture for refugees focuses on cities and their integration in them; when the state aims to incorporate the refugees in its citizenry, architecture focuses on housing programmes; whereas when the state cannot envisage refugees either as workers or as citizens, then architecture takes the form of the camp, set away from the city and without any interaction with it (Herscher, 2017, p. 8).

Indeed, the first two cases outline the rationale behind the development of the *prosfygika*: although the refugees that it was made for were not integrated in the social and economic life of Athens for many decades, they were envisaged as an opportunity for the development of Greek industry. Then, indirectly, coming from a Greek Christian background, they were also part of a project of homogenisation of the population and therefore they contributed to the formation of the Greek nation-state as a new political community (Gatrell, 2013, p. 80). Conversely, it seems that today the architecture of displacement has been shaped by those who cannot fit into the scheme of nationalities (Gatrell, 2013, p. 53), conceived both as political entities and as systems of representation (Hall, 1992, p. 292). This shift away from the city and from housing solutions to the camp in recent years (Herscher's third case) has accompanied the full political and spatial exclusion of refugees and their constitution as the "rightless" (Arendt, 1958, p. 281). This has led to the construction of the refugee crisis and even the process of asylum – fundamentally a political issue – as a humanitarian problem and, therefore, as a condition that is temporary and can be resolved by temporary solutions, epitomised by the state-instituted refugee camps. Against this never ending temporality and isolation, City Plaza has attempted an active engagement of the refugees with the city and its infrastructures despite the difficulties this entailed within Athens in crisis.

The two approaches to housing for refugees, as outlined by the *prosfygika* complex and the City Plaza, reflect the positions the buildings hold within their respective urban contexts. Built at what was at the time the edge of the city, the *prosfygika* aimed at framing and shaping the city's future extensions. Like the intention to unmix the Greek and Turkish populations via the population exchange, the complex represented a top-down effort at urban purity and order. They were to formulate a new, precise, formal system to organise the built and the unbuilt in the city, as well as urban living itself. However, Athens has expanded through the *polykatoikias* which, despite their formal and material similarities to the modern movement, do not share its political and aesthetic considerations; as such, they have not been able to manifest this radical break from Greece's past and traditions. Biris (1966) argues that the Bauhaus was largely misinterpreted and reduced to a style in Athens (p. 310), while Bastea (2017) writes that "it lacked innovation and precision and shunned any effort towards standardisation […] [i]nstead, it relied on a quasi-craft process of construction" (p. 121). Continuing pre-war traditions and conceptions, the *polykatoikia* was easily assimilated in the Athenian lifestyle and culture, yet it failed to become an object of innovation. It is in this anarchic building culture that "modern" Athens was constructed, and *polykatoikias* tightly surrounded any ambitious attempt at social housing and through that any vision towards an organised urban environment.

Then the city was built from the micro to the macro (i.e. the micro-developer, the micro-owner, the self-funded) and it became a place where decisions at the larger scale were never fully implemented, to take the form of the chaotic and overbuilt environment we encounter today. City Plaza nested within this very same disorderly environment. It occupied an empty building in Athens that was made available by the financial crisis. It stood for long in separation and vigilance, surrounded by centres of xenophobia and racism. Yet through this "crack" its residents promoted new conditions of belonging to the city and they contributed to shaping a political life beyond nation-state citizenship and national identity (Fig. 10.). They set up a communal life in progress, and by that they tested the boundaries of the city and how people can live and work together. But it is perhaps this culture of the "micro", often identified as counter-productive and responsible for the informal development of the city, which allows such gaps within the urban fabric to exist and to give space to other forms of habitation. Indeed, the innumerable ground-level humanitarian initiatives that took place in Athens during both the financial and the refugee crises, from food banks and social health clinics to emergency shelters and the provision of legal support to those in need, support this proposition. Athens' much-contested urban informality seems to bring more agents (and more spaces) into the process of city-making – and perhaps also disagreement and conflict – but along with that a greater degree of adaptability and resilience, and tests unexpected cohabitations such as the one brought about by City Plaza in Victoria Square. As cities today strive to become inclusive, to absorb immigration, to protect health as a shared value, to become sustainable, City Plaza, as a temporal urban experiment, represents a city shaped by its occupants and in an incessant process of transformation.

Figure 10. Street party outside City Plaza, 8 April 2018; photo taken by City Plaza.

Notes

1. See also examples of pre-modern Greek vernacular architecture included in Bernard Rudofsky's (1987) MoMA exhibition "Architecture without Architects".
2. Dimitris Philippidis argues that the 'modern' was adopted in a superficial manner (in relation to the buildings' external appearance as well as to the choice of modern interior equipment) in 20th century Greece and was not supported by a respective advancement of building technologies of the time as elsewhere in Europe. Therefore, it was reduced to a fashionable style, and as such it was re-appropriated by local designers and builders (Philippidis, 1978, p. 106).
3. The Greek Census records indicate a population of 5,021,790 in 1920 (Hellenic Ministry of Finance, Hellenic Statistical Authority, 1920, p. 31) and of 6,204,684 in 1928 (Hellenic Ministry of Finance, Hellenic Statistical Authority, 1920, p. 41).
4. Besides, a considerable number of them were of urban origin (Vaiou, 2002, p. 214).
5. In Vlachos et al. (1978), Yannitsaris & Hadjikostas argue that not all of them were prepared for such a form of "urban living", which meant living in close proximity to each other and with limited space for social interaction; therefore, they began to occupy the open spaces between the blocks for various communal activities (pp. 119-120).
6. Based on their individual capacities and interests, the residents prepared the meals, they cleaned the premises, they worked in shifts for the security of the building on a 24/7 basis, they were responsible for the childcare, and they ran creative and educational activities.
7. City Plaza: The best hotel in Europe; retrieved: https://best-hotel-in-europe.eu/.
8. 21 seats with 6.97 per cent of the total votes in the national elections of May 2012 (Greek Ministry of Interior Affairs, 2012), 8 seats and 6.99 per cent in the national elections of September 2015 (Greek Ministry of Interior Affairs, 2015) and no seats and 2.93 per cent in the national elections of July 2019 (Greek Ministry of Interior Affairs, 2019).
9. Indeed, there have been instances where the Golden Dawn have been supported by the police as the much higher than average percentage of votes by policemen in the national elections indicates (Elafros, 2015).
10. The district of Aghios Panteleimon, located only a few blocks away from Victoria Square, was central in Golden Dawn's operations. In January 2009, a so-called 'residents' committee' decreed that a playground in the neighbourhood's central square should close so that migrant children – and consequently every child in the area – would be unable to use it. The large blue slogan on the pavement of the square that was painted at that time read "foreigners leave Greece" and this led to the space becoming a centre of conflict between anti-fascist groups, who often broke in to make the playground accessible, and Golden Dawn supporters, who re-made the playground's fencing even stronger. Actions such as this, together with many other op-

pressions that were less visible, have shaped the life of the public spaces surrounding City Plaza in recent years (Antonopoulou, 2018; Kandylis & Kavoulakos, 2011).
11. Refugee Accommodation and Solidarity Space City Plaza (2018), 28 April. 2 chronia #CityPlaza! *Facebook*: https://www.facebook.com/watch/?v=1854568548168813.
12. City Plaza Refugee Accommodation (14 June 2018). Bicycle Project. *Facebook*. https://www.facebook.com/1568287556796915/videos/1787014828257519/.
13. Refugee Accommodation and Solidarity Space City Plaza (28 April 2018). 2 chronia #CityPlaza! [2 years #CityPlaza!] *Facebook*. https://www.facebook.com/watch/?v=1854568548168813, 2:50.
14. Refugee Accommodation and Solidarity Space City Plaza (8 April 2018). Kales Giortes! [Happy Holidays!] *Facebook*. https://www.facebook.com/sol2refugeesen/videos/1789790127982486/.
15. Refugee Accommodation and Solidarity Space City Plaza (1 May 2017). *Facebook*. https://www.facebook.com/1568287556796915/videos/1712459915713011/.

References

Antonopoulou, A. (2018). The Online Presence of Golden Dawn and the Athenian Subjectivities it Brings Forward. *European Journal of Creative Practices in Cities and Landscapes, 1*(1), 73-92.

Arendt, H. (1958). *The Origins of Totalitarianism*. New York: Meridian.

Bastea, E. (2000). *The Creation of Modern Athens: Planning the Myth*. Cambridge: Cambridge University Press.

Biris, K. H. (1966). *Ai Athinai: apo tou 19ou eis ton 20on aiona* [Athens: from the 19th to the 20th Century]. Athens: Melissa. [Greek]

City Plaza (2019). 39 mines City Plaza: oloklirosi enos kyklou, arhi enos neou [39 months City Plaza: the completion of a cycle, the beginning of a new one]. Solidarity to Refugees. Retrieved from: https://best-hotel-in-europe.eu/.

Dalakoglou, D. (2012). Beyond Spontaneity: Crisis, Violence and Collective Action in Athens. *City: analysis of urban trends, culture, theory, policy, action, 16*(5), 535-545.

Dalakoglou, D. (2013). From the Bottom of the Aegean Sea to Golden Dawn: Security, Xenophobia, and the Politics of Hate in Greece. *Studies in Ethnicity and Nationalism, Vol. 13*, No. 3, 514-522.

Davis, M. (2006). *Planet of Slums*. London: Verso.

Donaldio, R. (2019, November 15). Welcome to Europe. Now Go Home. *The Atlantic*. Retrieved from https://www.theatlantic.com/international/archive/2019/11/greeces-moria-refugee-camp-a-european-failure/601132.

Doxiadis, A. & Matsaganis, M. (2012). *National Populism and Xenophobia in Greece*. London: Counterpoint.

Elafros, Y. (2015, January 27). Megala Pososta tis Chrysis Avgis se astynomikous [High Percentage (of votes) for Golden Dawn by Policemen]. Ekathimerini, retrieved from https://www.kathimerini.gr/. [Greek]

Frampton, K. (2009). Forward for the Greek Edition. In K. Frampton, *Modern Architecture: A Critical History*. Athens: Themelio, 14-16. [Greek]

Gaffikin, F., Perry, D. C., & Kundu, R. (2011). The City and Its Politics: Informal and Contested. In D. R Judd & D. Simpson (eds.). *The City, Revisited: Urban Theory from Chicago, Los Angeles, and New York* (pp. 305-331). Minneapolis: University of Minnesota Press.

Gatrell, P. (2013). *The Making of the Modern Refugee*. Oxford: Oxford University Press.

Greek Ministry of Interior Affairs (2012, 9 October). National Elections 2012, National Results, http://ekloges-prev.singularlogic.eu/v2012a/public/index.html#{"cls":"main", "params":{}}. [Greek]

Greek Ministry of Interior Affairs (2015, 17 December). National Elections 2015, National Results, http://ekloges-prev.singularlogic.eu/v2015b/v/public/index.html#{"cls":"main","params":{}}. [Greek]

Greek Ministry of Interior Affairs (2019, July). National Elections 2019, National Results, https://ekloges.ypes.gr/current/v/home/. [Greek]

Greek Government (2003, 26 November). *Greek Government Gazette*. Issue number 1747, Vol.2, http://www.et.gr/idocs-nph/pdfimageSummaryviewer.html?args=sppFfdN7IQP5_cc--m0e1_I_A1rdk6dWVOuKoNt-i0W8rzSZFxgk-VP3k-U-ba0QkAYi3ORfmaruPpX-8ezBSEu48JvGR5TH975h8iB-tM3_vKMSuwFT8g8jMbcMCublFfxlNP8qam0Z2NA7o-3J9mzynsRl5LlSqV9gMbsYlqMHvjIM2HaHVZ-g. [Greek]

Greek Government (2009, 13 February). *Greek Government Gazette*. Issue number 62, http://www.et.gr/idocs-nph/pdfimageSummaryviewer.html?args=sppFfdN7IQP5_cc--m0e13UYg1ETLDG-0OmyBFPen068rzSZFxgk-YECNqvEa2PUkAY-i3ORfmarpLtZ11xa1tXkxcPQvNBMtY9T3IvMHxXor4OLuBPgbVM77k1-A9Eyz-7vqZ2xJ5_DbrHsGMnw3mleZRIfaokf59Zx8LQ6t2EFR1pfWwgVfILg. [Greek]

Hall, S. (1992). The question of cultural identity. In S. Hall, D. Held & A. G. McGrew (eds.), *Modernity and its Futures* (pp. 274-325). Cambridge: Polity Press.

Hellenic Ministry of Finance, Hellenic Statistical Authority (1928). *National Census Records of 15-6 May 1928*.

Hellenic Ministry of Finance, Hellenic Statistical Authority. (1920). *National Census Records of 19 December 1920*.

Herscher, A. (2017). *Displacements: Architecture and Refugee*. Berlin: Stenberg Press.

Hirschon, R. (2008). *Crossing the Aegean: An Appraisal of the 1923 Compulsory Population Exchange between Greece and Turkey*. New York: Berghahn Books.

Human Rights Watch (2019). *World Report 2019: events of 2018*, 229-231. Retrieved from: https://www.hrw.org/sites/default/files/world_report_download/hrw_world_report_2019.pdf

Kandylis, G. (2013). The Space and Time of Migrants' Rejection in the Centre of Athens. In T. Maloutas, G. Kandylis, M. Petrou & N. Souliotis (Eds.). *The Centre of Athens as a Political Stake* (pp. 257-279). Athens: National Centre of Social Research. [Greek]

Kandylis, G. & Kavoulakos, I. (2011). Framing Urban Inequalities. *The Greek Review of Social Research*, 136, 157–176.

Kitsantonis, N. (2019, October 31). Greek Refugee Camps Are Near Catastrophe, Rights Chief Warns. *The New York Times*. Retrieved from https://www.nytimes.com/2019/10/31/world/europe/migrants-greece-aegean-islands.html.

McFarlane, C. (2012). Rethinking Informality: Politics, Crisis, and the City. *Planning Theory & Practice*, 13(1), 89-108.

Motta, G. (2013). *Less than Nations: Central-Eastern European Minorities after WWI, Volume 1*. Cambridge Scholars Publisher.

Philippidis, D. (1978). Apartment houses and life in modern Greece. *Architektonika Themata* (1978/12), 103-107. [Greek]

Polyzos, I. (1973). I poleodomiki diamorfosi me tin prosfygiki plimmyrida – apospasma apo anekdoti kai euryteri meleti [Urban development through the refugee influx – excerpt from unpublished and wider research]. *Oikonomikos Taxydromos*, 992 (26 April 1973), 80-82. [Greek]

Psarras, D. (2012). *Η Μαύρη Βίβλος Της Χρυσής Αυγής* [the Black Bible of Golden Dawn]. Athens: Polis [Greek].

Roy, A. (2005). Urban Informality: Toward an Epistemology of Planning. *Journal of the American Planning Association*, 71(2), 147-158.

Rudofsky, B. (1987). *Architecture without Architects: A Short Introduction to Non-Pedigreed Architecture*. New York: Museum of Modern Art.

Staeheli, L., Mitchell, D., & Nagel, C. (2009). Making Publics: Immigrants, Regimes of Publicity, and Entry to 'the Public'. *Environment and Planning D: Society and Space 27*, 633–648.

Stavrides, S. (2007). Heterotopias and the experience of porous urban space. In K. Franck & Q. Stevens (eds.). *Loose Space – Possibility and diversity in urban life* (pp. 174-192). London: Routledge.

Theocharopoulou, I. (2017). *Builders, Housewifes, and the Construction of Modern Athens*. London: Black Dog.

Vaiou, D. (2002). Milestones in the urban history of Athens. *Treballs de la Societat Catalana de Geografia*, 53-54, 209-226.

Vaiou, D. & Kalandides, A. (2016). Practices of collective action and solidarity: reconfigurations of the public space in crisis-ridden Athens, Greece. *Journal of Housing and the Built Environment*, Vol. 31, 457–470.

Vlachos, G., Yannitsaris, G. & Hadjikostas, E. (1978). Housing the Asia Minor refugees in Athens and Piraeus between 1920 and 1940. *Architektonika Themata* (1978/12), 117-124. [Greek]

CHAPTER 12

Making Home in Borgo Mezzanone

Dignity and Mafias in South Italy

Anna Di Giusto
University of Florence, Italy

Introduction

Since the end of the 20th Century, significant demographic studies have highlighted the critical role of European cities in the management of the increased flow of immigration from Eastern Europe, Africa and the Middle East (Cohen & Layton-Henry, 1993; Skelcher, Sullivan, & Jeffares, 2013). The forecast of these studies primarily concerned urban centres that are part of conurbations or international areas of development, such as cities which are otherwise on the road to economic decline, like Foggia. These cities would not have been able to absorb the additional workforce or sustain the costs, thereby making their role one of future transit to other, richer areas rather than one of settlement (Sassen, 1994; Caponio, Scholten, & Zapata-Barrero, 2019). In recent years the application of the Dublin III Agreement and the restriction of immigration policy in Italy have forced many migrants to enter an underworld of illegality and live on the edge of the city, thus foregoing opportunities for integration. In most cases these forced migrants do not have their own funds to use to sustain themselves or facilitate their own means of integration (Ammirati, 2015).

Furthermore, in the last twenty years the Italian government has consistently failed to establish a multi-year plan for migrants' integration into the urban fabric, in contrast to other European countries (Balbo & Manconi, 1990; Macioti & Pugliese, 1996). Consequently, only individuals waiting for their requests for asylum to be decided are allowed access to and to reside in a CARA, but Italian legislation forbids them to have any sort of occupation. Non-asylum seekers are forced to find a place to stay and any kind of job, even an illegal one. *Caporalato* and mafia can prosper in this situation because migrants, who have nothing but their "bare lives" (Agamben, 1995), which is to say no rights to legal or political representation, are easily sequestered in under-paid work in local farms and often end up being detained by employers (Rizzuti, 2019). This situation of exploitation impacts on the local labour market too, as landlords prefer a migrant workforce that is cheap and easily exploitable. It is a vicious circle which provokes tensions with the local Italian community who feel cheated of regular and safe employment. The numerous ghettos that accumulate around urban centres with an agricultural vocation, as in the case of Foggia, increase the degradation of the site and provoke racist and violent reactions against those migrants (Bellizzi, 2019).

This chapter endeavours to explain the 'homing' experience of the Borgo Mezzanone shantytown through interviews with twelve temporary inhabitants about their living conditions and their effort to transform a precarious and illegal housing location into an environment that somehow resembles home. Considering the danger and risks at play for an Italian person, especially a woman, in travelling to this location, it was possible to have only a series of unstructured interviews with a handful of young people, twelve in total, who were associated at the time with a friend of the interviewer, a young boy from the Ivory Coast. He is an asylum seeker first encountered during research in Riace, a small Italian town that has since become famous because of its integration politics. The demographic of the interviewees consisted of men between the ages of 19 and 31, who come predominantly from the Ivory Coast (10), but also from Burkina Faso (2).

Context

Southern Italy has never managed to bridge the economic and social gap between the rich and poor compared to the regions of Central and Northern Italy. Indeed, from the time of National Unification (1861) to the present, this gap has only widened (Novacco, 1992). The disparity was fuelled both by poor political choices, such as the failure to invest in infrastructure, and by the post-Fordist revolution that rewarded investments in the third sector and crushed the more fragile economies, such as those still predominantly agricultural but not sufficiently mechanised (Sassen, 1999). For these reasons, the region has become a laboratory of weaving relationships among indigenous criminal systems, imported mafias, exploitation of human beings, the economy and politics. In the area of Foggia, the capital of a province of 627,000 inhabitants, the practices of *caporalato* (i.e. a form of illegal intermediation and exploitation of migrant workers in the agricultural sector) and prostitution are widespread and well-known by the national and local media (Leogrande, 2016). This situation of degradation gave rise to ghettos similar to those in Libya, which typically have a brothel and a central square suitable for drug dealing (Sagnet & Palmisano, 2015).

Borgo Mezzanone is only 15km away from Foggia, although it is part of the municipality of Manfredonia which is 45km away. The village was founded in 1934 by the fascist regime which reclaimed the area to reduce the flow of emigrants predominantly from Africa and the Middle East to Northern Europe and the Americas (D'Alessandro, 2002). Being located in one of the few plains in the Italian peninsula, Foggia has from the beginning been an agricultural site. For this reason, even today the area is renowned for its agricultural production, especially tomatoes. Half of the Italian tomatoes produced come from this area (Daniele & Malanima, 2011). The production process can be conducted legally, through temporary employment agencies or internet sites, or clandestinely, which benefits from the *caporali* recruiting labour on behalf of landowners. This latter approach produces about 15 per cent of the workforce, who originate from other countries and may or may not have a regular residence permit (Barbaro, 2018). Recent Italian legislation has tried to challenge this phenomenon, recognising it as a crime punishable by severe prison sentences (Di Marzio, 2017). It should be noted nonetheless that in Southern Italy the mafia's reach and control are powerful and have been intertwined for almost two centuries with the economic and political spheres of life, rendering the exercise of law onerous (Ciconte, 2008). Since many migrants cannot be hired on the basis of regular employment contracts, the local mafias present themselves as their only source of employment. This vicious circle fuels illegality and prevents the real integration of asylum seekers and refugees into the Italian social fabric (Liberti & Ciconte, 2016).

Before entering Borgo Mezzanone, it is important to understand what is meant by *caporalato*. The *caporalato* is an Italian word which indicates an informal system of organisation of temporary agricultural work, consisting of labourers inserted into groups of 'work' teams of variable size. The *caporale* is a man who can distinguish himself by the ability to find the cheapest labour for landowners and agricultural companies. He is an illegal labour force broker and the workforce manager of the local farmers (Omizzo, 2018). The *caporale* is the middleman who engages the farmhands on behalf of the owner and sets their remuneration, part of which he keeps for himself. Wages paid to workers or 'days' are considerably lower than those in the regulatory tariff and often do not include social security contributions (Arena, 2012). The contractual hourly pay for casual agricultural workers in Italy was set by law at €6.50 to €9.65, but in the area of Borgo Mezzanone the hourly pay is typically around €3.50 (INPS, 2017).

The Italian legal framework has responded to this phenomenon only in the last few years with the progressive ban on *caporalato* as a criminal practice in the exploitation of labour. In 2011 Italian law nr.148 introduced into the penal code the new crime of *caporalato* as the illicit brokering and exploitation of labour. The penalties provided for the *caporali* are imprisonment from between five and eight years as well as a fine of between €1,000 and €2,000 for each worker involved (Di Marzio, 2017). The government has since announced the use of regulatory measures to punish companies that employ labour through the system of *caporalato* which can result in the confiscation of their assets (Porcelluzzi, 2012). Despite this, in Borgo Mezzanone the reality of *caporalato* is a common one due to the presence of numerous young people, also Italians, but especially those who come from sub-Saharan Africa and who have left a reception centre and have subsequently not found the means lawfully to enter the Italian workforce. Some of them are without residence permits by reason of problems related to Italian legislation (Giuliani, 2015). According to the data collected by the CGIL, one of the most relevant Italian Unions, the business of *agromafie* – mafias working in the agricultural field – has been shown to involve at least 100,000 workers and to make a profit of €48 billion a year (Agromafie, 2018). However, recent decrees, such as that of October 2018 which bans residence permits for humanitarian reasons, have resulted in a large increase in the number of unpermitted residents (Facchini, 2018) and prevented migrants from accessing structures that, although themselves not very efficient, today represent the only form of reception (InfoMigrants, 2018).

Italian and foreign mafias in Borgo Mezzanone

Borgo Mezzanone is considered one of the most complicated situations of migration, illegality, agriculture and government complicity to be found in Italy. On the outskirts of Foggia, the northernmost city of Puglia, a situation of widespread illegality has been created. This is due to the strong demand for labour, employed in the lush surrounding countryside and which benefits from the workers' vulnerability. It is estimated that there are circa 6,000 residents in the area, although an official count is not available (Fig. 1.). The place was built around a pre-existing CARA, guarded day and night by police (Sabetti, 2019). This reception centre, however, has some breaches in its fence on the north and west sides of the perimeter. Via these gaps the residents of the village enter and leave as they please. Therefore, the area under military control – the CARA – has no control of the informal settlement which holds most of the irregular workers of Borgo Mezzanone (Fig. 2.). The people interviewed, coming from the Ivory Coast and Burkina Faso, hint that the breaches, which are large and well known to the military, are used to allow people from the CARA to bring in drugs and prostitutes.

Figure 1. The location of Borgo Mezzanone and the local CARA; image extracted from Google Earth by author.

Figure 2. Bird's-eye view of the CARA and the informal settlement of casual workers that surrounds it; image extracted from Google Earth by author.

In 2016, the Italian journalist, Alfonso Gatti (2016), was introduced into the CARA as a fake refugee. In this way he had the chance to analyse the centre's management. During his week-long stay, he did not see any military leave the square where the guards stay, either to visit or control movements within the barracks where 6,000 migrants are housed. He denounced the inadequate standards of living, the hygiene and food conditions of the refugees, and the mafia connivance of the cooperatives which fail to provide for minimum needs, despite the fact that they receive a contribution of €22 per day for each refugee hosted. This amount, multiplied by the number of guests and the days on which they are required to wait for the Commission's response, reaches the figure of €14,000 per day and €15 million over three years.

Here the Gargano mafia brings in drugs (mainly, Albanian marijuana, cocaine, Turkish heroin and methamphetamine) by car, thanks to a dense network of pushers of different nationalities. The drugs reach the English-speaking part of the ghetto, dominated by the largest Central African criminal brotherhood, called the Black Axe, which works with the 'ndrangheta and the Mexican Sinaloa cartel (Palmisano, 2018). The fact that what happens within the settlement, however criminal, has never been reported by the news media can begin to indicate the ability of these criminal groups to cooperate with each other.

In the shantytown

My personal experience of the Borgo Mezzanone started by my being forbidden to enter the CARA. Instead, the military directed us towards a passage to the north of the centre, where a very damaged road passes through the fields. This path follows a track that endangers the safe passage of cars by huge potholes. Before reaching the shantytown, one sees piles of rubbish, mostly glass, on the edge of the path. However, in all this chaos there is a particular order because garbage is divided according to the recycling criteria and not widespread. This provides evidence that the residents of the shantytown care about the cleanliness of their living quarters, as well as demonstrating how much of the waste produced nearby is reused rather than discarded. Most Africans arrive here on foot or by bicycle (Mangano, 2018). There are a number of cars, all of which are without wheels and have been used as sources for recycled materials; car seats have become sofas, the tyres are used to fix precarious house roofs, while other smaller elements are used to fix walls, curtains or other materials used in the construction of houses (Fig. 3.).

The shantytown is located on the disused runway of a military airport. As can be seen from the satellite picture, the buildings are constructed primarily along the main street, the old runway. The former airport buildings have become the mosque and the church, whereas the other masonry buildings are a

Figure 3. Close-up of streets in the informal settlement; image extracted from Google Earth by author.

Figure 4. Façade of the bar made entirely of recycled materials, located in the informal settlement; photo by author.

mystery; none of the interviewees wanted to give information about their use. Constructions are everywhere and are numerous. The squares are frequented by multi-ethnic groups, but an informal law limits the interaction of people from different countries. In this way, genotypical, linguistic and dialectical differences create invisible walls between various people who have been forced to live in and share the multicultural space.

Figure 5. The interior of one of the two restaurants; photo taken by author.

Figure 6. The interior of the nightclub, frequented by irregular workers; photo taken by author.

Since 2016 the shantytown has expanded due to the arrival of the Nigerian mafia which came via Naples and now occupies half of the track (Zancan, 2017). It has opened a bar (Fig. 4.), two restaurants (Fig. 5.), not to mention a nightclub, which often makes sleeping at night difficult (Fig. 6.). The other half of the track is run by Afghans arriving from
Bari, who have set up a shop for various goods as well as a mosque. The area for Nigerians is forbidden to Francophone Africans, so much so that those who dare to approach it risk their lives.

A normal day

All the interviewees were French speakers, and they were interviewed using the interviewer's Ivorian friend as a translator. He is a boy who can speak about ten African languages and dialects, so the interviewees were able to express themselves freely in their native language. For the researcher, however, it was not easy to make sense of what the translator reported because he was only in his second year in Italy. It is possible that many nuances were lost in translation, but the whole group confirmed the general sense. Some of them refused to answer some questions about the organisation of their work and salary. One of them explained that when he decided to leave his city in the Ivory Coast, he certainly did not think he would end up in a place like Borgo Mezzanone. Usually, the friends closest to the Ivorian boy who acted as translator allowed me to ask more detailed and direct questions; in other cases, it was not possible to collect enough material. It should always be remembered that the conditions of the interview involved a situation of general discomfort, both for the interviewees, caught in a dimension of extreme fragility and discomfort, and for the interviewer, a white woman in an illegal camp inhabited by 6,000 Africans.

All the interviewees live in the shantytown, and not inside the CARA itself. All of them work in agriculture, except the boy, who works in a small restaurant inside the camp. He is in charge of preparing lunch for the few men who are not called on by the corporals in the morning, while in the evening many people are served in his small place. The prices are very cheap (a plate of white rice and stew costs two euros), but the quality of the food is very low, it is almost inedible; the interviewer almost choked on a piece of meat made mostly of cartilage. The restaurateur, however, specified that the meat is purchased from a supplier in Naples to make sure that it is good halal food.

All the others reported on the condition of work under the *caporali* system; in the morning the machines and vans of the *caporali* arrive from the west. Before then, at four in the morning, the labourers line up to fill their water bottles, because the Italian employers no longer provide water. Refugees leave through the four gates, and Nigerian *caporali* vans and ramshackle cars are waiting for them on the runway. The Nigerians take €5 per person by way of commission. Then the labourers are left along the edge of the road that leads to Foggia, where they are loaded into the Italian *caporali*. If one wants to avoid the cost of passage from the Nigerians, one must leave on foot or by bicycle. In the shantytown, one of the interviewees claims to keep his bicycle beside his bed for fear that it will be stolen. Anyone who loses their bicycle is then forced to pay €35 a week to the Nigerian *caporali*, which is in effect the cost of two days' work. The labourers who live inside the CARA are paid less than those who live in the slums because the *caporali* deduct the cost of food and housing which is covered by the prefecture. Because of this, they receive a total of €15 a day, while people who live in the shantytown receive €25 per day (Gatti, 2016).

Many of them return only by ten in the evening, queue for a shower, wash a few dirty clothes, eat something and, by midnight, they sleep regardless of the noise from the nightclub which is run by Nigerian pimps and through which they can prostitute women. After three hours' sleep they get up and leave for a new day, climbing over the CARA wall. In other European countries, especially in the North, during the same reception period refugees are required to follow language courses; otherwise, they are rejected. Inside the CARA, no one has engaged with an Italian course (Palmisano, 2017). So, after months of exploitation, when they are transferred to other regions of Italy, it is as though they have not already been in the country for some time.

Housing and dignity

The situation both inside and outside the CARA is precarious, and people live without a waste collection, water and sewerage system. The lighting system is illegal because it is stolen from the road network. There was a parliamentary inquiry to ascertain faults and failings in the management of the centre, but nothing has led to any concrete results (Senato della Repubblica, 2016). Despite all this, those who live there have tried to recreate an environment that can somehow be described as a home. The reuse of car interiors, the creation of some restaurants, the opening of a church and a mosque, and the development of a recreational area can all be seen as signs of the need for migrants to feel somehow 'at home' (Sennett, 2018). If the weather is dry, it is possible to note that among the dwellings there are clay paths, though these are destined to disintegrate during the rainy season. The search for aesthetic details, such as the reuse of Christmas decorations or any object for the beautification of the premises, testifies to the need to rebuild their dignity as human beings (Carrier, 2018). The interviewees permitted some questions and answers, especially concerning religious practices; many have confirmed that working under the control of the corporals makes it difficult to obtain the opportunity to pray five times a day, as required by the Islamic faith. Since there is a mosque in the camp (all those interviewed are Muslim), many of them catch up on their lost prayers in the evening by praying several times in a row. This practice is widespread in the camp.

The interiors of the houses visited have some functional elements adapted to everyday life, such as car seats or advertising tarpaulins that can become external or internal walls of the houses. However, there are also many objects recovered from waste that become furniture to beautify the interior. Some are Christmas or Easter decorations, but in many cases it is a resignification of the object itself that, in this context, becomes an embellishment. This practice testifies to the desire to make the makeshift house feel more like a home, to produce a sense of ownership and belonging, at least temporarily. Despite their openness to talk about something as intimate as religious practice, they did not allow the interviewer to photograph the interiors or exteriors of their homes. The same prohibition of photography applies to the rest of the camp. A possible explanation of this behaviour could be concern about the use of such pictures by the media and other sources of authority in Italy; it is certainly conceivable that the residents felt a need to protect something which provided emergency relief, and therefore a temporary respite in precarious circumstances, lest the Italian police should seek to tear it down.

Another explanation may be related to the fact that residents perceive the shantytown as a stage on a long journey. From their hometowns they planned to reach relatives or friends in Northern Europe. Borgo Mezzanone would therefore represent an intermediate stage that, for some of them however, risks becoming the ultimate destination. The refusal to permit the photographing of the spaces built with recycled materials could therefore conceal a sort of self-deception regarding their present, which they consider to be a brief passage, not to be remembered and for which they do not want to be remembered.

One angle of migration theory is working on the conceptualisation of a new kind of 'transit mobilities' operating in the Mediterranean region. In academia, the formulation of 'secondary migration' is a step on the path to the migrants' final goal – that is, usually not a country in Southern Europe but in the North (Brekke & Brochmann, 2014). This concept is not adequate to describe the phenomenon of housing in Borgo Mezzanone. This place is full of neighbourhood waste, and on a symbolic level for Italian residents it is full of human 'garbage'. Western civilisation is characterised by excess, redundancy, waste and garbage disposal, so much so that today this last point is one of the most critical challenges for the permanence of a sustainable world. At the same time, the wealthiest part of the planet does not want to share its lifestyle, but needs the exploitation of migrants to maintain it (Bauman, 2004). In the meantime, countries cut off from the benefits of globalisation are dominated by other dynamics, such as the free pursuit of profit and total indifference to the environment (Sassen, 2014). So, one of the macro-economic consequences in those areas is the expulsion of migrants. When they arrive in South Europe, their rights are cancelled by their incorporation into the borders of cities in decline, as in the case of Foggia.

Waste and humanity

In the collective imagination waste is the disturbing counterpart of civilisation. It is the dark side that is disposed of far from sight, incinerated or hidden in ditches that are usually built or dug near degraded suburbs, dormitories for the lower classes (Bauman, 2005). In psychoanalysis, waste would be the removal of consciousness which, consciously, avoids questioning the fate of the production waste that serves to maintain the consumerist machine, even more, voracious in the age of globalisation (Baudrillard, 1976).

Instead, if one thinks of the shantytown of Borgo Mezzanone, the waste that pervades its streets and makes up much of its infrastructure is the predominant element, almost omnipresent. On a symbolic level, it appears that the construction of the shantytown concerns precisely those subjects that have been rejected by the city as human waste (Jamal, 2004). Take, by comparison, the Kibera Slum of Nairobi, which is one of the largest shantytowns in the world: here, the rooms are made of precarious materials and are built close to masonry buildings such that the eye can see a continuity of single-storey building roofs. The waste is located on the edge, where there are waterways or where there is some distance between two dwellings. Kibera acts as a miniature city (with 700,000 inhabitants) which is not allowed to get rid of its waste (140 tons per day) because there is no space for the disposal or burning of refuse (Bodewes, 2005). Garbage is everywhere; the social scale has reached the end of its path of class exclusion.

There are differences, however, with Borgo Mezzanone. Although less crowded than the famous and overpopulated slums of the great modern metropolises, shantytowns like Borgo Mezzanone do not function as the overflow and improvised outskirts of some cities, but rather they welcome those immigrants who have not been granted documents to legalise their presence in the country. In this respect, the French version of Borgo Mezzanone is famously Calais, not by chance stigmatised as a jungle – as if civilisation had stopped at its gates to make a wild and dangerous nature triumph (Agier, 2019). However, why has the Jungle of Calais become famous in the media and in academic studies, while only a little research has focussed on Borgo Mezzanone? It is not easy to try to answer this, but certainly in Puglia there are phenomena that not only differentiate between the two realities but make significant the fact that the Italian one is mostly ignored. In Borgo Mezzanone, in fact, the mafias operate in synergy with the phenomenon of the *caporalato*. The mafias are not merely criminal associations, which can also be found in the illegal smuggling of migrants from Calais to the United Kingdom. The Italian mafias always operate in close contact with the political level, locally but also nationally. At this point, it is clear that the media and journalists, even when they deal with realities such as those of Borgo Mezzanone, impart a moment of brief visibility, but then everything goes opaquely out of the spotlight.

The lack of attention paid to this place then becomes a sort of legitimation of the illegality; what is not reported daily and firmly can be handled in another way, far from legality and the control of the police which, it should be remembered, exists a few metres from this shantytown. Borgo Mezzanone has thus become a garbage dump that nobody cares about, not the Italian inhabitants of the area, nor the general public, nor the national media. There is an evident association between a lack of social acceptance and the world of the landfill: centrifugal force drives out all marginality towards the urban periphery, where the city's drains and marginalised humanity are found. This provides evidence for Michel Foucault's analysis of social marginalisation as a crucial moment or the effects of normalisation (Foucault, 1961).

Like Calais, Borgo Mezzanone is "a prototype city in the making" (Wainwright, 2016). It demonstrates the refusal to survive the physical and ideological assault they suffered in the recent times of political and economical crisis. None of the interviewees considers this place the final goal of their journey, but even if only in passing each of them intends to survive this critical situation by implementing innovative housing strategies. In this way, they are trying to answer the sense of loss of identity because they are driven from their lands and rejected by their host country (Bohmer & Shuman, 2008).

They are forced to live the condition of the so-called "double absence": the lack of original identity due to the elapsed space-time distance, and the difficulty of accessing a new condition of citizenship (Sayad, 2002). The reuse of Italian waste testifies to the resilience and the obstinacy of those migrants. Despite the absence of the rule of law and the presence of different mafias, they are looking for habitual normality that can give them back a sense of dignity. This recreated town can appear only as a 'fake' image of the city they come from or the one they would like to create. The result is an effort to rebuild the spacing and timing of a normal life, in spite of everything.

References

Agier, M. (2019). The Jungle: Calais's Camps and Migrants. Cambridge: Polity Press.
Agromafie. (2018). Rapporto 04. Agromafie e caporalato. Roma: Biblioteka Edizione.
Alò, P. (2010). Il caporalato nella tarda modernità. La trasformazione del lavoro da diritto sociale a merce. Bari: WIP Edizioni.
Ammirati, A. (2015, December 27). Che cos'è il Regolamento di Dublino. Openmigration. Retrieved: https://openmigration.org/analisi/che-cose-il-regolamento-di-dublino-sui-rifugiati/.
Amnesty International. (2017, November 6-December 6). Submission to the United Nations Committee against Torture. Retrieved: https://www.amnesty.org/en/documents/eur30/7241/2017/en/.
Arena, M. (2012). I reati sul lavoro: sicurezza e igiene del lavoro, nuovo reato di caporalato tutela e libertà del lavoratore, risercimenti. Milano: Giuffré.
Avallone, G. (2019). Il sistema di accoglienza in Italia. Esperienze, resistenze, segregazione. Nocera Inferiore: Orthotes.

Balbo, L., & Manconi, L. (1990). I razzismi possibili. Milano: Feltrinelli.

Barbaro, E. (2018, June 4). Il quarto potere nel ghetto di Borgo Mezzanone. Terre di Frontiera. Retrieved: https://www.terredifrontiera.info/quarto-potere-ghetto-di-borgo-mezzanone/

Baudrillard, J. (1976). La società dei consumi. Bologna: Il Mulino.

Bauman, Z. (2004). Wasted Lifes. Modernity and its Outcasts. Cambridge: Polity Press.

Bauman, Z. (2005). Work, consumerism and the new poor. Maidenhead, NY: Open University Press.

Bellizzi, T. (2019, July 16). Foggia, sassaiola contro gli immigrati che andavano al lavoro: due feriti. Repubblica. Retrieved: https://bari.repubblica.it/cronaca/2019/07/16/news/foggia_gruppo_di_migranti_colpito_da_lancio_di_sassi_due_feriti-231303017/

Biffi, P. (2017, August 3). Borgo Mezzanone. Il gioco del mondo. Il dialogo di Monza. Retrieved: http://www.ildialogodimonza.it/borgo-mezzanone-il-gioco-del-mondo/

Bodewes, C. (2005). Parish Transformation in Urban Slum. Voices of Kibera, Kenya. Nairobi: Paulines Publications Africa.

Bohmer, C., & Shuman, A. (2008). Rejecting Refugees. Political asylum in the 21st century. New York: Routledge.

Borgna, P. (2011) Clandestinità (e altri errori di destra e sinistra). Roma: Laterza.

Brekke, J-P, & Brochmann, G. (2014). Stuck in transit: Secondary migration of asylum seekers in Europe, national differences, and the Dublin regolation. Journal of Refugees Studies, 28(2), 145-162.

Camilli, A. (2018, September 24). Cosa prevede il decreto Salvini su immigrazione e sicurezza. Internazionale. Retrived: https://www.internazionale.it/bloc-notes/annalisa-camilli/2018/09/24/decreto-salvini-immigrazione-e-sicurezza

Caponio, T., Scholten, P., & Zapata-Barrero, R. (2019). The Routledge Handbook of the Governance of Migration and Diversity in Cities. New York: Routledge.

Carrier, F. (2018, June 7) Inside the slum that houses southern Italy's migrant workforce. The Local. Retrieved: https://www.thelocal.it/20180607/inside-san-ferdinando-slum-calabria-italy

Chiari, A. (2010). Clandestinità e diritto penale. Il reato e l'aggravante di immigrazione illegale. Parma: Università degli Studi di Parma.

Ciconte, E. (2008). Storia criminale. La resistibile ascesa di mafia, 'ndrangheta e camorra dall'Ottocento ai giorni nostri. Soveria Mannelli: Rubbettino.

Cohen, R., Layton-Henry, Z. (1993). The politics of migration. Northampton: Edward Elgar.

Colombo, F. (2018). Clandestino. La caccia è aperta. Milano: La Nave di Teseo.

Curci, S. (2008) Nero invisibile normale. Lavoro migrante e caporalato in Capitanata. Foggia: Edizioni del Rosone.

D'Alessandro, A. (2002). Borgo La Serpe. Foggia: Di Palma & Romano.

Daniele, V., & Malanima, P. (2011). Il divario Nord-Sud in Italia 1861-2011. Soveria Mannelli: Rubbettino.

Di Benedetto, G. (2017, February 23). Caporalato. Bracciante morta di fatica nei campi di Andria. Repubblica. Retrieved: https://bari.repubblica.it/cronaca/2017/02/23/news/caporalato_6_arresti_per_morte_palola_clemente-158977625/

Di Marzio, F. (2017). Agricoltura senza caporalato. Roma: Donzelli.

Facchini, D. (2017). Diritto d'asilo: il 70% dei migranti "vinceva" in appello. Ma il Governo l'ha cancellato. AltraEconomia. Retrieved: https://altreconomia.it/diritto-asilo-appello/

Facchini, D. (2019, October 2). "Decreto sicurezza", un anno dopo: cosa è accaduto ai diritti. Repubblica. Retrieved: https://www.repubblica.it/solidarieta/immigrazione/2019/10/02/news/_decreto_sicurezza_un_anno_dopo_che_cosa_e_accaduto_ai_diritti-237527428/

Foucault, M. (1961). Storia della follia nell'età classica. Milano: Rizzoli.

Gatti, F. (2016, September 12). Sette giorni all'inferno: diario di un finto rifugiato nel ghetto di Stato. L'Espresso. Retrieved: http://espresso.repubblica.it/inchieste/2016/09/12/news/sette-giorni-all-inferno-diario-di-un-finto-rifugiato-nel-ghetto-di-stato-1.282517

Gatti, F. (2016, September 13). Cara di Foggia, quell'inferno ci costa 11 milioni di euro all'anno. L'Espresso. Retrieved: http://espresso.repubblica.it/inchieste/2016/09/13/news/cara-di-foggia-il-ghetto-di-stato-costa-allo-stato-11-milioni-di-euro-all-anno-alfano-dispone-una-inchiesta-1.282713

Giuliani, A. (2015). I reati in materia di caporalato, intermediazione illecita e sfruttamento del lavoro. Padova: Padova University Press.

InfoMigrants. (2018, October 18). Extreme exploitation of migrants is taking place in Italy, the UN Special Report says. Retrieved: https://www.infomigrants.net/en/post/12752/extreme-exploitation-of-migrants-is-taking-place-in-italy-the-un-special-rapporteur-says

INPS. (2017). Disciplina del lavoro occasionale ex art. 54-bis del decreto legge 24 aprile 2017, n. 50. Regime per l'agricoltura e calcolo della forza aziendale. Retrieved from https://www.inps.it/bussola/VisualizzaDoc.aspx?sVirtualURL=%2fMessaggi%2fMessaggio%20numero%202887%20del%2012-07-2017.html

Jamal, S. (2004). Environmental Perception of Slum Dwellers. New Dehli: Mittal Publication.

Leogrande, A. (2016). Uomini e caporali. Milano: Feltrinelli.

Liberti, S., & Ciconte, F. (2016) Spolpati. La crisi dell'industria del pomodoro trasfruttamento e insostenibilità. #Filiera Sporca. Retrieved: http://www.filierasporca.org/wp-content/uploads/2016/11/Terzo-Rapporto-Filierasporca_WEB1.pdf

Macioti, M.I., & Pugliese, E. (1996). Gli immigrati in Italia. Bari: Laterza.

Mangano, A. (2018, January 22). Noi migranti nel ghetto, prigionieri in Italia. L'Espresso. Retrieved: http://espresso.repubblica.it/inchieste/2018/01/22/news/il-ghetto-degli-ingabbiati-noi-migranti-prigionieri-in-italia-1.317392

Massari, M. (1998). Sacra Corona Unita: Potere e Mistero. Roma-Bari: Laterza.

Novacco, N. (1992). Il ritardo del Sud: aree forti ed aree deboli in Europa e in Italia. Milano: Franco Angeli.

Omizzo, M. (2018, June 07). Le Agromafie, il caporalato e il silenzio del governo italiano. Tempi Moderni. Retrieved: http://www.tempi-moderni.net/2018/06/07/le-agromafie-il-caporalato-e-il-silenzio-del-governo-italiano/

Palmisano, L. (2017). Mafia caporale. Racconti di egemonia criminale sui lavoratori in Italia. Roma: Fandango.

Palmisano, L. (2018, April 25). Foggia, il ghetto di Borgo Mezzanone dove mafia e stranieri sono alleati. Corriere del Mezzogiorno. Retrieved: https://corrieredelmezzogiorno.corriere.it/bari/cronaca/18_aprile_25/foggia-ghetto-borgo-mezzanone-dove-mafie-stranieri-sono-alleati-10642972-485e-11e8-be35-75f4207074dc.shtml

Pighi, G. (2008). Le migrazioni negate. Clandestinità, rimpatrio, espulsione, trattenimento. Milano: Franco Angeli.

Porcelluzzi, A. (2012). Tra schiavitù e caporalato: il lavoro degli immigrati. Modena: Fondazione Marco Biagi.

Quarta, E. (2006). Un'istituzione totale dei giorni nostri: i centri di accoglienza e di permanenza temporanea. Un'indagine sul campo. Milano: Guerini Scientifica.

Sabetti, L. (2019, February 20). Il borgo di Mezzo Mezzanone. La grande vergogna a pochi passi da noi. Foggia Reporter. Retrieved from https://www.foggiareporter.it/il-ghetto-di-borgo-mezzanone-la-grande-vergogna-a-pochi-passi-da-noi.html

Rizzuti, S. (2019, November 4). Il decreto sicurezza di Salvini è un fallimento: più irregolari e più illegalità. Fanpage. Retrieved: https://www.fanpage.it/politica/migranti-gli-effetti-del-decreto-sicurezza-piu-irregolari-e-piu-illegalita-e-sfruttamento/

Sagnet, Y., & Palmisano, L. (2015). Ghetto Italia. I braccianti stranieri tra caporalato e sfruttamento. Roma: Fandango.

Sassen, S. (1994). Cities in a World Economy. Thousand Oaks: Pine Forge Press.

Sassen, S. (1999). Globalization and its Discontents: Essay on the New Mobility of People and Money. New York: The New Press.

Sassen, S. (2014). Expulsion: Brutality and Complexity in the Global Economy. Cambridge: Harvard University Press.

Sayad, A. (2002). La doppia assenza: dalle illusioni dell'emigrato alle sofferenze dell'immigrato (S. Palidda, Trans). Milano: Cortina.

Senato della Repubblica. (2016, September 27). Commissione parlamentare di inchiesta sul fenomeno degli infortuni sul lavoro. Retrieved: https://www.senato.it/application/xmanager/projects/leg17/file/repository/commissioni/infortuni17/stenografici/27_settembre_2016.pdf

Sennett, R. (2018). Building and Dwelling. Ethics for the City. New York: Farrar Straus & Girox.

Skelcher, C., Sullivan, H., & Jettares, S. (2013). Hybrid Governance in European Cities: Neighbourhood, Migration and Democracy. Basingstoke: Palgrave Macmillan.

Wainwright, O. (2016, June 8). We built this city: how the refugees of Calais became the camp's architects. The Guardian. Retrieved: https://www.theguardian.com/artanddesign/2016/jun/08/refugees-calais-jungle-camp-architecture-festival-barbican

Zancan, N. (2017, September 28). Foggia, rivolta contro il ghetto. "Ostaggi della mafia nigeriana". La Stampa. Retrieved: https://www.lastampa.it/cronaca/2017/09/28/news/foggia-rivolta-contro-il-ghetto-ostaggi-della-mafia-nigeriana-1.34427486

PART 4
HOUSE

CHAPTER 13

News from the Living Room

Historiography and Immigrant Agency in Urban Housing in Berlin

Esra Akcan
Cornell University, U.S.A.

Who were these men, who
built these kinds of streets? These houses,
these walls that come out of each other,
these roofs fallen over the top of another,
these sleepy windows under the roofs
that face the pumps on street edges?
…
If they knew these were for us
surely they would have done differently:

Who would you say are those who live here?
…

Aren't they those who asked for their rights
against the state who claimed
rights over them, risking their lives
for the foundations of today's democracy?

Aren't you living in these houses now
who will take on, carry on the days of struggle
In the rotten courtyards at the back?

Aras Ören, *Berlin Üçlemesi* (1980), pp. 82-83, 214 (translated by author)

Two images empower Aras Ören's "Berlin Trilogy" – poems written in Turkish but first published in German between 1973 and 1979 (Ören, 1973, Ören, 1980): the destitute conditions of Berlin-Kreuzberg's apartments in the 1970s and the struggles for the right to the city. The poems' lines render a typical architectural scene: the 19th Century rental buildings creating networks of courtyards behind the streets, the façades with windows stripped of their ornaments, and the cramped Hof-spaces where Ören hopes the revolutionary right-to-the-city movement will begin. The citizen and migrant characters parade before our eyes one after another, carrying not only their personal baggage but also their apartments and streets. They include: Niyazi, an immigrant from Turkey, who witnesses his neighbours' daily lives in Kreuzberg with constant flashbacks of Istanbul; his downstairs neighbour, the 67-year-old widow, Frau Kutzer, who longs for the days when she could enjoy Cafe Bauer and other prestigious socialite spaces of Berlin; Atıfet, an activist for workers' rights, who now lives in a corner at Oranienplatz after escaping domestic abuse in Turkey and surviving her only son's death following a police beating; Halime's naughty children, who spend the entire day in the Hof and throw snowballs at Frau Kutzer's window after their mother goes to work in Telefunken to support them and her imprisoned husband; Kazım Akkaya, the skillful, apolitical carpenter who moved to Berlin due to the declining employment in his small town in Turkey and who now works eleven hours a day to make as much money as possible; Sabri Şen, a worker who dreams of opening a shop but soon finds himself at a bar talking about class consciousness; and Dieter, the exhausted construction worker, who tries to keep things clean and decent in an extremely rough and filthy Kreuzberg and who has a bad dream about being evicted due to urban renewal, which will destroy his old building in order to replace it with a new one the rents for which will be 25 per cent higher.

Ören's poems paint Kreuzberg's main dilemma during the late 1970s: it was a worn-out immigrant neighbourhood in need of urban renewal but threatened by the contemporary renewal policy itself, which would have destroyed the buildings and displaced the residents. The poems end with images of characters struggling for their social rights: Niyazi and Emine write separate letters to the Berlin Senate, the former requesting a two-roomed apartment and the latter asking for her own passport so that she can claim her identity as a resident of Berlin. When I started research on Berlin-Kreuzberg's urban renewal throughout the 1980s for what would become my book, *Open Architecture,* I found out during my interviews that similar memories are still fresh in the minds of the residents who participated in the renovation or moved into the new buildings here.

Concepts

This article draws from *Open Architecture* (Akcan, 2018), in which oral histories with former guest workers and refugees in Berlin reveal both the discrimination against immigrants and their agency in the making of architectural and urban spaces during and after Kreuzberg's urban renewal. What get displaced and replaced here are not only the individuals—migrant workers and refugees—but also the notions of conventional architecture and architectural history. By paying attention to immigrant appropriations of domestic and urban spaces we can register architectural design as something that constantly evolves in time and acquires new forms and meanings with resident architects. By honouring the residents' stories equally with those of the architects, we can admit that architectural history does not end when a building leaves the hand of the professional architect. I ask, in this book, what would have happened if architecture had been shaped by a new ethic of hospitality towards the non-citizen, and I call this 'open architecture'. Looking at the past through the lens of this possibility also reveals prospects for the future, and thereby points to the proactive role of architectural history.

In one of the most significant events of the 1980s, known as IBA-1984/87 (International Building Exhibition), world-famous and up-and-coming architects from Europe and North America were invited to build public housing in an immigrant neighbourhood in the context of the discriminatory housing laws and regulations instituted by the Berlin Senate, the IBA team's employer (Fig. 1.) (Fiebig, Hoffmann-Axthelm & Knödler-Bunte, 1984; IBA, 1984; IBA, 1987; Kleihues, 1981-93; Lampugnani, 1984).[1] I have analysed this project with the overarching theme of migration and citizenship, which allows for a joint discussion of the history of 20th Century public housing, the participatory, postmodernist and post-structuralist architectural debates, and the contradictory relationship between international immigration laws and housing. Exploring the implications of the concept of 'open' as a common metaphor in the era of global connections, and as a foundational modern value, albeit prone to contradictions, I define 'open architecture' as the translation of a new ethics of hospitality into design process. While the book gives equal emphasis to the history of architects' (including urbanists and policy makers), and immigrants' (including social workers) contributions to design both before and after occupancy, this article summarises some of the methodological themes of writing an architectural history that integrates the immigrant voice.

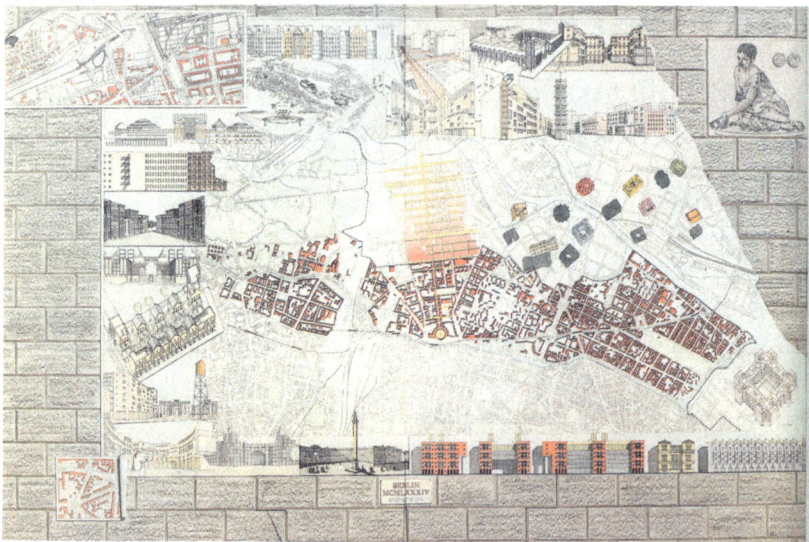

Figure 1. IBA-1984/87 (Internationale Bauausstellung Berlin). Directors: Josef Paul Kleihues, Hardt-Waltherr Hämer. Site plan and drawings of buildings on the plate presented at the 17th Triennial of Milan. Drawing by Giovannella Bianchi, Ebe Gianotti, Werner Oeschlin, Luca Ortelli; courtesy: Werner Oeschlin, Luca Ortelli.

INTERTWINED HISTORY/HISTORY'S ACCOUNTABILITY: Building transnational solidarities or sharpening critical tools against imperial imagination requires, first and foremost, rewriting the past by giving due acknowledgment to its multiple makers. This requires a commitment to a globally inclusive account of the past. There is enough evidence to write the history of modern world architectures in a radically intertwined way, rather than as derivatives of Europe and North America, or as essentially different artifacts as if they were produced in isolated regions (Akcan, 2012).[2] In this conception, global history does not necessarily mean circumnavigating the entire planet, but understanding the connectedness of the world at its every compartment.[3] *Open Architecture* is a global history, even though it concentrates on one single borough in Berlin. It is a global history not only because a large number of established and up-and-coming international architects were invited to build public housing there – making it a microcosm of architectural discourse between the 1960s and 1990s – but also because it exposed the character of Europe as an immigrant continent. Throughout the book, the reader takes strolls in the neighbourhood and stops at seven locations to trace both the local and the global forces acting on design. An additional methodological conclusion is to be drawn from this experience: we need not only to write intertwined histories, but also to admit the accountability of history-writing in producing ignorance that brings conflicts in a world of immigrants. For an inclusive history I invite historians to step slowly out of their areas of expertise and stop perpetuating knowledge about the same places.

ARCHITECTURE'S COMPLICIT OR SUBVERSIVE ROLE: The urban renewal initiative in Berlin's immigrant neighbourhood of Kreuzberg in the 1980s took place in the context of discriminatory housing laws and regulations imposed by the Senate, such as the ban on entry and settlement and the moving quota. Justified as the "integration" of Middle Eastern immigrants, these Senate laws prohibited the movement of additional migrant families to certain boroughs, and mandated that only 10 per cent of residential units be rented to non-citizens in West Berlin. Mid-way, during the realisation of the IBA, the rule in the Senate shifted to the Christian Democrats, who additionally imposed anti-immigration policies. These laws were transposed into the functional programme of new buildings during Kreuzberg's urban renewal in the form of the low percentage of big flats which would have been fitting for extended migrant families. In particular, this programme would either reduce non-citizen families' chances to move into new public housing or welcome them only after they had changed their lives to fit the German family size standards.

In this context, architects found themselves participating in designs from above, policies against equal rights for immigrants, and hindrance of immigrant public housing. But it was important for me also to find out about practices that moved towards a collaborative and cosmopolitan understanding despite the regulatory regimes. *Open Architecture* discloses how policy-makers used architecture as a mechanism of social control and displacement, but at the same time also discusses how architects responded with varying degrees of complicity, irony or subversion to these discriminatory housing regulations. For instance, I argue that a group of architects in IBA-Altbau mobilised tenant organisations, squatter demonstrations, refugee and guest worker participation to carry out a radically democratic process, in a sense similar to the one in which this concept was suggested at the time by intellectuals, such as Ernesto Laclau and Chantal Mouffe. According to the latter, it was necessary for the democratic Left to put a stop to the privileging of a certain class or group as the locus of revolutionary transformation, and to acknowledge that the defence of equality in an irreducibly plural world would involve formerly unimaginable struggles (Laclau & Mouffe, 1985). This should have included the struggle for non-citizen rights whose hints I excavate in the practice of a group of architects in Berlin, albeit not without unresolved contradictions.[4] In this process, the IBA-Altbau's team of architects prepared countless handouts to explain the renewal process and organised *Hausversamlungen* for each and every building to record and negotiate neighbours' conflicting and complementary requirements; the tenant advisors went door-to-door to each and every apartment to discuss the residents' needs and available budgets; translators found on streets or in universities were employed for mediation; the architects removed or added walls, combined or divided units, added stairs and service spaces to optimise the neighbouring tenants' differing needs and financial capabilities; the developers agreed to some low-profit deals for the prestige; the residents agreed to move temporarily to another apartment or to put up with the construction in the house during the renewal process; and the authorities agreed to secure the social housing status of these apartments for approximately twenty-five years, so that no single non-citizen family was unwillingly displaced from its apartment, keeping the original percentage of non-citizens in the area intact (Akcan, 2018; Arın, 1979; Hämer, 1987; Moldenhauer, 1984). This percentage was well above the Senate-imposed 10 per cent. It would have been easy for the Berlin Senate to dismiss this team, but through the amalgamation of participatory architecture and social movements, the Senate's discriminatory laws were subverted by a group of professionals employed by the Senate itself.

RIGHT TO HAVE RIGHTS TO THE CITY: Another important theme, while discussing the role of immigration in urban and architectural history, is human rights. The current Human Rights regime impairs immigrants' right to have rights, and turns them into what Giorgio Agamben calls "bare life" (*homo sacer*) (Agamben, 1998). Namely, states have the power to deprive citizens of their political rights and push them outside the realm that should be protected by citizenship rights. Ever since the first declarations of human rights, natural and civil rights, birth and nationhood have been collapsed into each other, making citizenship the necessary condition for having human rights, and denying many rights to the stateless. The Berlin Senate could pass discriminatory housing laws, such as the ban on entry and settlement and the quota of migrants that could occupy a building, because the migrants were not protected by citizenship rights. The migrants' rights to the city, such as their right to move freely, to choose their neighbourhood, to have equal opportunities in renting an apartment or to move into a building where they could find the support of social and cultural networks were thereby taken away from them with the assumption that their non-citizen status justified this violation. Needless to say, migration is one of the biggest global challenges of our century, but current international laws evict migrants from protection. The refugee or the stateless continues to be prolific, but nothing exposes the unresolved contradictions of the current human rights regime as effectively as the concept of the refugee, because human rights are defined according to the precondition that one is a citizen of a state in the first place.[5]

These contradictions hardly disappear with the transformation from statelessness to citizenry. Former non-citizens continue to be denied social citizenship and social welfare rights (T. H. Marshall, 1965; Bellamy, 2008; Mouffe, 1992; Turner, 1992), as the exclusion of guest workers and refugees from citizenship in the past is projected onto the present in the form of class difference and white supremacy.[6] Étienne Balibar also theorises on the relationship between *internal* and *external exclusions* from citizenship in order to understand the mechanism that denies legal citizens the right to have rights. "An 'external' border is mirrored by an 'internal' border," Balibar writes (Balibar, 2015, pp. 69-70); the myth of a "common belonging" is manufactured to such an extent that citizenship becomes a "club" where one is admitted or refused regardless of one's legal rights (Balibar, 2015, p. 76).

ARCHITECTURAL HISTORY AND FUTURITY: In *Open Architecture* I ask what would have happened if the profession of architecture was more attentive to international migration, and call this 'open architecture'. The chapters define formal, programmatic or procedural strategies towards open architecture, such as latent open architecture as collectivity, as radical democracy and as multiplicity. 'Open architecture' would have been the welcoming of the immigrant into these design strategies. My use of the past subjunctive tense here is not accidental. Historiography in general and architectural historiography in particular concern themselves with the history of actuality. In other words, they seek to explain events as they have actually happened. Unbuilt projects have not changed this rule, despite their ubiquity in history books, since they have usually been discussed for the sake of their actual presence rather than the absence that they create after being designed. *Open Architecture* discusses both built and unbuilt projects, as histories not only of actuality but also of possibility. It defines terms of speech to understand them not as projects per se, but as unfulfilled capacities or as unfinished open histories. Would it matter if we suspended our justifiable curiosity about what happened, and instead tried to look at what did not happen? And would doing so tell us something we did not know about what actually happened? This history of possibility is written in the past subjunctive tense, and simultaneously defines a proactive role for the architectural historian. By both defining and identifying forms of latent open architecture in history, and by exposing their limits, the book makes a call for the future open architecture that builds a new ethics of hospitality towards the immigrant, as opposed to the dominant, Kantian notions of hospitality.

VOICES OF ARCHITECTURAL/URBAN HISTORY: In the context of the immigrant's rightlessness, a related historiographical theme is multiplying the voices that speak for the built environment. In addition to under-represented architects from around the world, this also means including (immigrant) inhabitants' voices in historical narratives. For instance, after ringing every bell in Berlin-Kreuzberg between 2009 and 2017, I tried to configure immigrant voices in *Open Architecture* through a genre inspired by oral history and storytelling, rather than ethnography or sociology. An oral historian refrains from representing an entire ethnicity or group, and adds the name of the under-represented individual into history; and a storyteller acknowledges that the fabric of everyday life unfolding in an individual's experience is also part of a building's history. In this approach, architectural history does not end when the building leaves the hand of the architect. Opening the definition of architecture to resident appropriation is also a feminist gesture to write more women into architectural history. By honouring the stories of resident architects as much as those of the architects, it is possible to stop seeing architecture as an occupation historically practised by men.[7]

Figure 2. View of an apartment in Block 76, renovated by IBA Altbau (team-architect: Heide Moldenhauer); photographed by Esra Akcan, Berlin, 2012.

Indeed, residents appropriated many apartments designed by high-end architects: bridges were repurposed as bedrooms; voids were mechanised as kitchens; unfunctional winter-gardens were turned into playrooms; additional rooms were integrated into apartments from next-door buildings that were on higher levels (Fig. 2.). These oral histories and architectural analyses reveal the spatial agency of immigrants who rightly take credit for the success of the urban renewal and Krezuberg's special place in global imagination. I started with a list of fictional characters in their interaction with Kreuzberg, and let me now continue with a list of real characters in their stories of inhabiting domestic and urban spaces.[1]

Cases

- N.Y., a Kurdish refugee who came to Berlin following an anguished escape from Mardin, lived in asylum sites that separated families and eventually moved into the building designed by the office of Bohigas, Mackay, and Martorell located in Barcelona. What N.Y. appreciates most about her apartment is the open view from her building of the Topography of Terror, another important IBA-1984/87 competition site that used to be the Nazi headquarters. It is not that she, a refugee escaping from Turkish state violence, had deliberately chosen to live in an apartment that overlooks a site that reminds her of the Jews tortured by the Nazi German state, that is in a building block designed by a Catalan architectural firm whose members criticise Spanish fascism and that is located in a neighbourhood in which German discrimination against immigrants from Turkey is a frequent topic of conversation. But she is certainly apt to notice urban signs of state brutality and racism that intertwine the histories of multiple places and peoples throughout the 20th Century.
- Hatice Uzun, a first-generation guest worker, fixed, built parts of and painted her apartments when she lived in three different units located in the building complex whose urban design belonged to Rob Krier's office in Vienna, but which was the result of a collaboration between twenty different architectural firms. Following his own essentialist views about the correlation between nation and form, Krier had incorporated references to traditional "Turkish houses" in the unit plans. This did not need to be recognisable to residents, but it was nonetheless appreciated during my interviews by a family that happened to live in one of these units.
- Günsel Çetiner, N.Y.'s neighbour across the street, is a guest worker's spouse who came to Berlin under the Family Unification Law of 1973 and soon moved into the building designed by the Italian architect, Aldo Rossi,

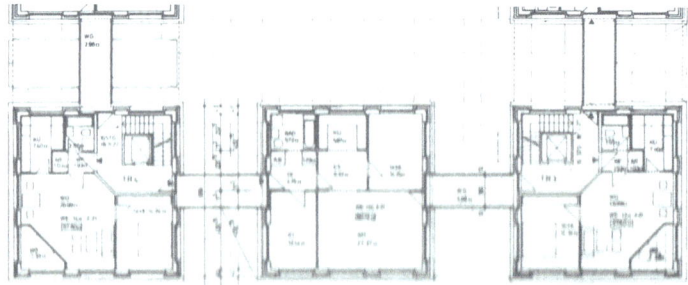

Figure 3. Views of Barış's appropriation of entrance bridges as arrival space (left) and daughter's bedroom (right) in Oswald Mathias Ungers's building in Block 1; photographed by Esra Akcan, Berlin, 2011.

which she could never leave since her husband was suddenly paralysed and became housebound. This building not only embodies the idea of open architecture as collectivity, but also exposes the limits of this openness (Akcan, 2018, pp. 96-148). Rossi expected that a unified architecture would emerge from the collective memory and the collective will of a city, as if a society has no alterity and as if the class-based, ethnic or geopolitical hierarchies had not prioritised one memory and will over others. The role of the immigrant, the newcomer, was largely neglected in Rossi's book, *Architecture of the City* (Rossi, 1982).

- Semanur S. lived with her six children in the building designed by the German architect, Oswald Mathias Ungers. As I visited the building to interview her neighbour, I found a temporary memorial in her name, commemorating the traumatic event that had taken place the night before when her husband had cut off her head and breast and thrown them into the Hof. The nine-square plan of the building, designed by Ungers, creates a square courtyard at the centre of a square building composed of eight square towers, served by four square stairwells, all placed in a city block divided into

Figure 4. View of a balcony in Zaha Hadid's building in Block 2; photographed by Esra Akcan, Berlin, 2012.

a square grid; with all four façades composed of square windows, and the eight free-standing square towers are bridged on the fourth floor, above the square surface with nine-square perforations on three floors. Fatma Barış, who arrived in Germany from Urfa with her family, now lives with her four children in an apartment of this building, where the architect's obsession with geometric order and uncompromising symmetry resulted in the two entrance bridges as big as her home. Barış turned one of these into a bedroom and the winter garden into another bedroom. Understandably so. Living in public housing where every inch counts, she prioritised a room of her daughter's own over the symbol of cosmic order. Her son painted the walls of his siblings' and his own rooms with images appropriate for their ages and preferences (Fig. 3.).

- Sakine Albayrak became the director of a kindergarten following the Montessori system as a result of her own experience with the discriminatory German education system. She has turned the narrow balcony in the British-Iraqi architect Zaha Hadid's building for handicapped residents into a linear garden and a green buffer zone between the interior and the Hof (Fig. 4.).

Figure 5. Heide Moldenhauer, Kita (day care centre) in Block 78, Kreuzberg, Berlin, when built in 1984, and in 2012; photographed by Heide Moldenhauer and Esra Akcan.

- Mr. Tuğrul still remembers the hardships of growing up as a Turkish migrant in Kreuzberg in the 1970s, when his father told him not to tell anyone that his hometown was Dersim —the location of the Zaza uprising against the Turkish government. He cannot forget his neighbour's eldest daughter killing herself by jumping out of a window into their Hof. He now lives in one of the buildings renovated under German architect Heide Moldenhauer's responsibility during IBA-1984/87, and does not want to move out. Practising their Alevi customs occasionally, he and his family can now freely go to the Cem House around the corner, while daycare and a women's support network are provided in the Kita and Family Garden, also designed and retrofitted under Moldenhauer during the urban renewal (Fig. 5.).
- Cihan Çelik, who arrived in Berlin as a child from Erzincan, lives in a building that was renovated by the Altbau team of IBA-1984/87. She vaguely remembers a woman who visited their home to discuss the modernisation process for their building and apartment with her parents. This must have been Heide Moldenhauer from the IBA-Altbau team, who regularly directed tenant meetings for each building in this block, and went door to door to each and every apartment with her translator Necla – a young Turkish migrant that she met in the neighbourhood, spent many hours and prepared an exhibition with. Moldenhauer convinced the German-Turkish artist, Hanefi Yeter, to design murals on the façade of the corner building in Block 76. She was influential in turning the Heile House, occupied by squatters, into a self-help project that supported public service. Today Heile House still functions as a place where a passer-by can use a public toilet; lunch is prepared by immigrants and served in the common dining room almost every day (Fig. 6.).

Figure 6. Views of the Heile House in Block 76, renovated by IBA Altbau (team-architect: Heide Moldenhauer); photographed by Esra Akcan, Berlin, 2016.

Figure 7. Views of an apartment in Block 81 renovated by IBA Altbau (team-architect: Cihan Arın); photographed by Esra Akcan, Berlin, 2016.

- Suzan Nişancı is one of the immigrants who rightly takes credit for making Berlin's Kreuzberg one of the most exciting places in the world to live in. Her apartment is situated in the urban block that was renovated under the responsibility of Cihan Arin – the German-Turkish architect who was also in charge of non-citizen participation in the Altbau section. During the urban renewal, a room from the next door building on a higher level was integrated into her apartment at her request to accommodate the large family, which is why there are now stairs negotiating the level difference inside the living room. She still participates in the protests against the rising rents and complains about her neighbours' reluctance to speak up for their rights and the tenant consulting agencies' disinterest in gentrification, which betrays the ideals on which these agencies were founded in the 1980s (Fig. 7.).
- Yüksel Karaçizmeli, a first-wave guest worker from Adana, vividly remembers her first arrival on the dark train, and the details of the medical exam when German doctors scrutinized her entire body at the border. She was handed how-to-behave pamphlets and official toilet decrees for foreigners, which gave instructions in utmost detail for the proper use of the toilet seat and the toilet paper. She now lives in the building designed by Álvaro Siza's office in Porto. Finding the open kitchen inappropriate for Turkish food due to the strong smells that infiltrated the house, she made herself a two-part kitchen using the unclassified space for flexible use: an open section

Figure 8. Views of the closed and open kitchen in Karaçizmeli's apartment in Álvaro Siza's Bonjour Tristesse in Block 121; photographed by Esra Akcan, Berlin, 2012.

for washing, preparing, storing, and dining; and another divided by a glass partition for cooking. This void space is one of Siza's architectural contributions in the name of participation, since it prescribed a zone for residents' voices to be heard at the very stage of architectural design (Fig. 8.).

Figure 9. View of the semi-annual grill in Álvaro Siza's senior's club in Block 121; photographed by Esra Akcan, Berlin, 2016.

- The seniors' club in the same complex designed by Álvaro Siza's office is a popular meeting place especially for retired workers. It is managed by immigrant volunteers such as Ms. Rukiye, who has been working here for the past twenty years and organising large get-togethers, such as semi-annual grills on Sunday afternoons. The seniors' club has become a major attraction for graffiti enthusiasts, with no white surfaces remaining untouched today. Every time the city repaints the walls white, it takes no more than a couple of weeks for graffiti artists to reclaim them. Unlike the architectural critics who adore the serenity and silence of Siza's buildings, the city's inhabitants have evidently interpreted his modernist white façades as blank surfaces on which to write their own stories. But, no need to take a lofty tone; this is to be expected. When there is no effective public sphere in which immigrants can represent themselves, building walls will host the unauthorised voices (Fig. 9.).
- The residents of Frei Otto's Öko-Haus built their apartments on a tree-like set of platforms, which ended in an agglomeration of multiple dream worlds in no hurry to interfere with each other (Fig. 10.). During the construction process, tenants and architects applied to build their own houses, as a version of a self-help initiative. The twenty-four houses on multilevel platforms have been designed in an ad hoc manner, with a different form and programme for each resident, out of an uncountable number of diverse materials, including different types and colours of wood, metal, brick, stone and glass. No house, window, door, balcony, greenhouse, doorknob or ornament seems to be like any other; many are quite idiosyncratic. This

Figure 10. Frei Otto (with Torsten Birlem, Jürgen Rohrbach, Manfred Ruprecht, and Ute Schulte-Lehnert, et al.), Öko Haus Complex in Block 192; photographed by Esra Akcan, Berlin, 2016.

  open architecture glorifies individual expression to an excessive degree, with no motivation for harmonisation.
- Frau Fokken, a retiree who worked in IBA-1984/87, now lives in the building designed by Rem Koolhaas and Elia Zenghelis's office in Rotterdam. The building was introduced in a professional magazine as follows: "OMA imagined that a section through the building would represent a section through West Berlin: [American] Allies at the base, followed at the middle levels by larger units to be taken up by Turkish guest workers and their families, with Germans living in small units at the top" (Pepchinski, 1990, p. 17). Making non-citizens visible on an urban façade took a critical stance against the anti-immigration policies of the time, but only by having to stamp their apartments as territories of the stateless. This is yet another example where identity markers may function as emancipators of a disenfranchised group, but at the same time freeze and reduce their ever-changing and multiplicitous existence into a boxed category of identity.
- Yeliz Erçakmak, the daughter of two Turkish migrant teachers who grew up in Dortmund, embraces the idiosyncratic and unfamiliar spaces in the American architect John Hejduk's design as an evolving, performative stage, and herself as a meaning-construing participant. A space of curios-

ity is the set of small square balconies. Imagining that the man and the woman of the house would each sit on one of the balconies, her husband joked about constructing a bridge by placing a wooden platform in the air between the two balustrades. Another idiosyncratic feature is the set of transparent bridges one needs to cross to reach the small towers, where a kitchen, a bathroom, a laundry and a reading room are located. Erçakmak particularly appreciates how she can cross the bridge to the reading room, and how that act of crossing creates the feeling of leaving the house, and how that detachment allows her to feel outside if she chooses to close the door, or how an open door instead allows her to stay informed about the inside while still being able to read her book, and how that ability to choose to be inside or outside empowers her. Hejduk himself did not comment on the immigrants' rights to the city, but his idiosyncratic design approach with non-conventional expressions opened up a space for immigrant voices indirectly.

These and many more examples testify to how immigrants make spaces their own against all odds, and how hybrid spaces increasingly define cities. Whether the forces of history will erase essentialist identity categories or sharpen them during this process is yet to be seen.

Actionables

In conclusion, architecture is by definition open: once inhabited, users appropriate it whether the architect anticipated it like Siza and Otto or wanted to prohibit it like Ungers, but this is not what defines open architecture. The author of "open work", Umberto Eco, also emphasised this distinction: it is not interpretability that distinguishes an open work from a closed one, but its intentionally unfinished nature that awaits the performer's or audience's completion (Eco, 1989). In the case of architecture, appropriatability, or the fact that a building is almost always appropriated by the inhabitants, does not make it open architecture. Rather, open architecture is the condition when an architect embraces or anticipates the quality of openness during the stage of design.

In this respect, let me say a few words carrying this discussion on migration, citizenship and urbanism through to our day in the wake of the world's biggest refugee crisis since the Second World War due to the War in Syria or the violation of academic freedom around the globe that pushed countless academics and journalists into exile, or still, the travel ban, DACA termination and family separation in the USA. Due to these recent global developments, I was often confronted with the fact that the forces that had shaped the experiences recorded in the book continue today with little or no improvement; these include rightlessness of the stateless, crises of citizenship categories, state brutality, lack of decent housing, quandaries of public housing, and hostility towards immigrants.

And yet, my book is also a chronicle of hope. It reports inspiring stories against all the odds of immigrants who rightly take the credit for Kreuzberg's place in the global imagination. When there was a lack of hospitality in architecture, it records examples where individual residents triumphed over these non-open spaces, as was the case for Barış' appropriation of Ungers' plan. The book also brings out solidarities between ex-migrants and citizens, despite the overwhelming discrimination, as was the case for Uzun's repairs, Karaçizmeli's kitchen and IBA-Altbau architects' willingness to renovate Nişancı's, Çelik's and others' apartments in relation to their specific needs. Additionally, it records one of the most important chapters of public housing in world history, a programme that has since then almost disappeared from the purview of architectural publications. Paying attention to immigrant appropriations of domestic and urban spaces thereby calls on us to change our conventional ways of designing buildings and writing architectural histories.

Discrimination and migration are longstanding and connected phenomena that reproduce each other. They need our attention also because the future is vulnerable to their multiple effects. The 21st Century will be the century of migrations as a result of the serious global challenges of our time, including climate change, political unrest, social and economic inequality, and food insecurity. However, the current international laws and global ethics fall well short of facing up to this challenge. Rather than rethinking the border systems that block migrations, the world authorities are reacting to this challenge with anti-immigrant and nationalist policies. My book instead calls for a theory of open architecture as an appropriate response to the impacts of international immigration on architecture and urbanism.

Notes

1. Throughout its execution, the IBA published numerous extensive catalogues of the buildings designed, constructed and renovated for the building exhibition. Only the most significant ones are added in this bibliography.
2. For more discussion see also *Architecture in Translation* (Akcan, 2012) which offered an alternative model for global history by developing a vocabulary based on translation theories. I defined translation as the migration of not only people,

but also ideas, images, objects, technologies and information from one place to another, and their transformations in the new locations. Far from a depoliticised description of these migrations however, translation theory allows us to record the geopolitical tensions, psychological anxieties and uneven power dynamics during the history of colonisation and nationalisation.

3. For more see Esra Akcan, "Writing a Global History through Translation: An Afterword on Pedagogical Perspectives," *Modes of Architectural Translation: Objects and Acts,* Karen Koehler and Jeffrey Saletnik (eds.) Special Issue of *Art in Translation* 10:1 (2018): 136-142.
4. Despite the steps towards democratisation against the professional discourse at the time that viewed participation as mediocracy, there were limits to hearing the non-citizens in public spaces, shared areas, public buildings and particularly religious structures. These limits drew the border where open architecture was closed (Akcan, 2018).
5. This includes those expected to be displaced due to climate change, but the existing refugee convention does not even have a provision for climate refugees.
6. Much has been said about T.H. Marshall's (Marshall, 1965) tripartite definition of citizenship as civil, political and social citizenship, challenging him on numerous fronts, especially for his account of the concept's historical evolution and assumption of a unitary process tied to the British context. Nonetheless, his insight into three types of rights has continued to have explanatory power. According to this framework, social citizenship rights are those tied to economic welfare and security, such as insurance against unemployment, rights to healthcare, education and pension.
7. Remembering Linda Nochlin's ground-breaking essay "Why Have There Been No Great Women Artists?" (Nochlin, 1971) I think that historians have filled architectural history books almost exclusively with male characters partly because they defined architecture as an occupation historically practised by men. Yet, if we were to define architecture as design open to residents' appropriation, there would be at least as many women architects as men in history, even though, of course, there is no biological reason why women should be the makers of a house's interior. By relating the history of residents as specific individuals who are as influential as specific architects in designing spaces, I try to contribute to the writing of this feminist history.

References

Agamben, G. (1998). *Homo Sacer: Sovereign Power and Bare Life* (D. Heller-Roazen, Trans.). Stanford, CA: Stanford University Press.

Akcan, E. (2012). *Architecture in Translation: Germany, Turkey and the Modern House.* Durham: Duke University Press.

Akcan, E. (2018). Writing a Global History through Translation: An Afterword on Pedagogical Perspectives. In K. Koehler & J. Saletnik (eds.) *Modes of Architectural Translation: Objects and Acts,* Special Issue of *Art in Translation 10*(1), 136-142.

Akcan, E. (2018). *Open Architecture: Migration, Citizenship and the Urban Renewal of Berlin-Kreuzberg by IBA-1984/87.* Berlin-Zurich: Birkhäuser-De Gruyter.

Arın, C. (1979). Analyse der Wohnverhältnisse ausländischer Arbeiter in der Bundesrepublik Deutschland—mit einer Fallstudie über türkische Arbeiterhaushalte in Berlin-Kreuzberg. PhD diss., Berlin Technical University.

Balibar, E. (2015). *Citizenship.* T. Scott-Railton (tr.). Cambridge: Polity Press.

Bellamy, R. (2008). *Citizenship.* Oxford: Oxford University Press.

Eco, U. (1989). *Open Work.* A. Cancogni (tr.). Cambridge: Harvard University Press. [Translated from *Opera Aperta,* 1962]

Fiebig, K. H., Hoffmann-Axthelm, D., & Knödler-Bunte, E. (Eds.). (1984). *Kreuzberger Mischung: Die innerstädtische Verflechtung von Architektur, Kultur und Gewerbe.* Berlin: IBA, Verlag Ästhetik und Kommunikation.

Hämer, W. H. (1987). Twelve Principles of Careful Urban Renewal. *Domus 685,* 70-71.

IBA (1984). *Idee Prozeß Ergebnis: Die Reparatur und Rekonstruktion der Stadt.* Berlin: IBA.

IBA (1987). *Internationale Bauausstellung Berlin 1987: Projektübersicht.* Berlin: IBA.

Kleihues, J. P. (1981-93). *Internationale Bauausstellung Berlin 1984/87: Die Neubaugebiete – Dokumente, Projekte,* 7 vols. Stuttgart, Germany: Verlag Gerd Hatje.

Laclau, E. & Mouffe, C. (1985). *Hegemony and Socialist Strategy: Towards a Radical Democratic Politics.* London: Verso.

Lampugnani, V. M. (ed.). (1984). *Modelle für eine Stadt.* Berlin: IBA.

Marshall, T. H. (1965). *Social Policy in the Twentieth Century.* London: Hutchinson.

Moldenhauer, H. (1984). Planungsalltag am Kottbusser Tor. In *Idee Prozeß Ergebnis: Die Reparatur und Rekonstruktion der Stadt* (pp.135-137). Berlin: IBA.

Mouffe, C. (1992). Democratic Citizenship and the Political Community. In C. Mouffe (ed.), *Dimensions of Radical Democracy: Pluralism, Citizenship, Community* (pp. 225–239). London: Verso.

Nochlin, L. (1971). Why Have There Been No Great Women Artists? *Artnews* (January), 22. Retrieved: https://www.artnews.com/art-news/retrospective/why-have-there-been-no-great-women-artists-4201/

Ören, A. (1973). *Was will Niyazi in der Naunynstrasse.* A. Schmiede and J. Schenk (trs.). Berlin: Rotbuch Verlag.

Ören, A. (1980). *Die Fremde ist auch ein Haus*. G. Kraft (tr.). Berlin: Robbuch Verlag.

Pepchinski, M. (1990). OMA's Berlin Housing Confronted by Change. *Progressive Architecture* (71/13), December, 17.

Rossi, A. (1982). *Architecture of the City*. D. Ghirardo & J. Ockman (trs.). Cambridge, MA: MIT Press.

Turner, B. (1992). Outline of a Theory of Citizenship. In C. Mouffe (ed.), *Dimensions of Radical Democracy: Pluralism, Citizenship, Community* (pp. 33-62). London: Verso.

CHAPTER 14

The Nubian House

Displacement, Dispossession, and Resilience

Menna Agha
University of Antwerp, Belgium

The house: Making sense of displacement

At some point in the early 2010s I sat in front of a scientific committee of a prominent university in Cairo with the ambition to defend a funding proposal for a research project that would revolve around Nubian architecture. At one point, one member of the scientific committee took it upon themselves to comment: "What architecture? There are only a few small houses in Nubia." Within this statement I found, then and now, a plethora of problematic understandings about the value of housing, the definition of architecture and what exactly deserves our scholarly attention. What the statement exhibited, above all else, was a viewpoint – one that remains unfortunately prominent – that fails to see the meaning of the Nubian house beyond its utility and place of origin.

In what follows, then, I intend to present an alternative lens and perspective, and ultimately an alternative theorisation, of the Nubian house from within the scope of Egyptian Nubian displacement villages. This shift of narrative will therefore follow the story of the Nubian house as it has developed through the 20th Century, placing particular emphasis on the 1963 displacement of Nubian communities for the state-built housing project, then dubbed 'New Nubia' (Fernea & Gerster, 1973). Nubians themselves refer to this project much more unfavourably as *Al Tahgeer*, or 'place of displacement'. In this chapter I will analyse the Nubian house from 'inside the house', which is to say that I will critically approach these spaces through the memories and the stories told about them and as they have been embedded within the Nubian collective consciousness.[2]

The Nubian people or Nubians are an African population who have been displaced and resettled within Egypt (and Sudan) as a result of a nationwide Development-Induced Displacement and Resettlement (DIDR) scheme. Before their displacement in 1963, Nubians occupied the area between the Nile's first and fifth cataracts (Adams, 1978), the area which now lies between Egypt and Sudan. Historically, DIDR schemes are associated with development projects, such as the construction of dams for hydroelectric power, which tend to result in the displacement of large communities and are therefore often associated with the loss of livelihoods and with impoverishment (Cernea, 1996; Drydyk, 2007; Mathur, 2016). Narratives of loss, both during and after their involuntary resettlement, were certainly dominant during my upbringing, as stories of human suffering defined the process of resettlement. And it is safe to say that the process of resettlement into new land and houses does not typically flow smoothly – an undisputed fact both in Nubian stories and in state and academic literature (cf. Allen, 2014; Fernea & Kennedy, 1966; Ghabbour, 1991; Hopkins & Mehanna, 2011; Mahgoub, 1990; Scudder, 2016a; Serageldin, 1982; Tadros, 1979; Tibe, 2015).

For one to be able to to tell a meaningful story of the Nubian house, and to offer a definition of what it is, it must be situated in Nubian histories. The geographic site on which this study focuses is the site of the 1963 Nubian resettlement in Kom Ombo Valley in Egypt, and specifically the village of Qustul, the displacement settlement in which I was raised. While the old village of Qustul in Old Nubia had a built environment that developed organically along the banks of the Nile, the new settlements have a rectangular pattern with housing in rows and minimal design, which was based on modernist methods of urban planning as per the intentions of the engineers and planners of the central government in Cairo. In the settlement one can find a health centre, schools, an administrative building and a central complex of 'public' spaces that consists of a community centre, a coffee house, shops and a mosque.

My aim here is to offer the reader a visual and narrated layout of the different tactics that have affected the Nubian house over a certain period of time. Through this, on a personal level, I want to make sense of *my* world as a Nubian woman, and of my own sense of displacement, in relation to the childhood house. This personal venture has broader ramifications as I endeavour to understand displacement as a spatial issue and in terms of spatial practices. Nevertheless, I will always be reminded of the futility of impartiality, as this more academic endeavour will always be in conflict with the voices of the Nubian women who raised me, given that my familial and social ties to them deny me the 'proper' distance of scientific neutrality. Indeed, the role gender plays is of interest here not only because of its traditionalised role as an apparatus of space making, distribution and signification, but also because Nubians have a history of matriarchy (Fluehr-Lobban, 1998), and an ongoing tradition of (informalised) *matrilineality* that can be detected in and around the space of the house. With this in mind, it should be noted that following their displacement in 1963 until 1964 the role of Nubian women significantly diminished in the resettlement villages.

As I take on the task of reviving a gendered lens of displacement, home and spatial practices, through my own position as a Nubian woman and as a scholar of architecture, I further assert my partiality to this lens with the conviction that research is always biased. Finefter-Rosenbluh (2017) offers me, in this regard, a reflexive toolkit for a rigorous positioning. While not always explicit, this endeavour comprises: (a) the activation of the situated mental process of perspective-taking; (b) the anchoring of my own perspective with the goal of dissecting the perspectives of others; and (c) the establishment of an equilibrium. Therefore, I recognise that the lens through which I look at the Nubian house is a feminist one, even though it might be affected by nostalgia (for I spent my childhood in this particular house) and the tropes of scholarship. Thereby, I seek to anchor myself in pan-African and feminist literature, while taking a critical stance towards and establishing critical distance from institutional narratives. By finding an equilibrium between various perspectives, including my own, I seek critically to negotiate my allegiance and the allegiances of others to a Nubian identity.

A short history of the Nubian house

Nubians are rarely, if ever, the authors of their own stories within academic literature and scholarship, with the exception of a few cases, such as Hassan Dafalla's *The Nubian Exodus* (1975). So, when I started engaging with the literature related to Nubia and to Nubians, I found myself reading about me, my places of residence and my people through another's perspective and lens. Thus, in the majority of cases my engagement with the literature was experienced as its subject – which struck me at first as somewhat 'eerie' and was soon to became infuriating. The story tends to begin with the 1899 dismantlement of Nubian land. At the time, British colonisers had drawn a political border to divide Egypt and Sudan into two different countries. Nubian blogger and storyteller, Mostafa Shorbagy, traces the story back to the day when a community of Nubians of the village of Adendan was surprised by the arrival of the military, surveyors and government clerks on their land. The intention behind these exceptional movements was the marking of the lines drawn between Egypt and Sudan. These lines were further established by the raising of the Egyptian and Sudanese flags above the houses of two brothers which were opposite each other. The Nubian house, in this case, represents the first witness to the break-up of Nubian land, as two housing units which belonged to one family could mark the point in time that forced Nubians, like myself, to embody one side of a story and heritage; in my case, the Egyptian side.

Old Nubia (Fig. 1.) was laid out along the banks of the Nile at high Level so as to avoid floods during rainy seasons (Hopkins & Mehanna, 2011). Altogether there were forty *Nahias*, or districts, of which seventeen were Kenuzi-speaking, five were Arabic-speaking, and eighteen were Fadija-speaking (ibid., p. 10). These districts consisted of dozens of *nagas* – the smaller units of residence, which were the actual units of co-residence, while the district was more of an administrative unit. The Egyptian Ministry of Social Affairs recognised 536 *nagas* between the dam site and the Sudanese border in 1962 (Scudder, 1966, p. 104). The 1960 census records 560 settlements divided between forty districts (Hopkins & Mehanna, 2011).

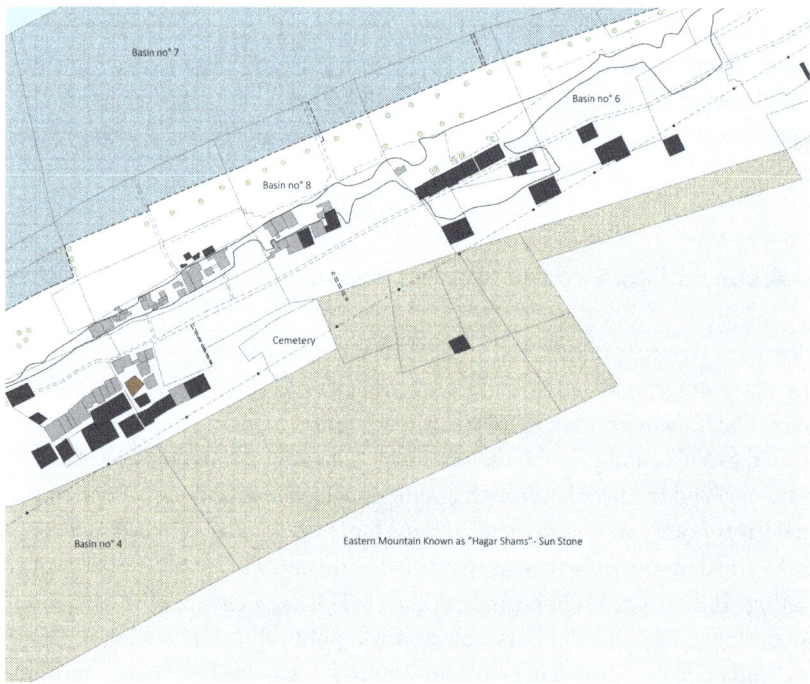

Figure 1. Part of Qustul in Old Nubia by the Nile; image produced by author.

Over the 20th Century, Nubians and the Nubian houses that stood on the Egyptian side of the dividing line faced several hydropower developments that induced a series of displacements, starting with the building of the Aswan Low Dam. The dam was constructed on the first cataract in 1902, and was subsequently heightened twice, once in 1912 and then again in 1933 (Waterbury,

1979). Because of this, Nubians lost a vast area of arable land over the course of the Low Dam development. The Nubian household, as a result, lost a major part of resources as the rise of water levels in 1902 and 1912 flooded arable land, reducing wealth and power produced within the house; this economic dispossession led to the migration of Nubian men to urban centres for waged labour, leaving the Nubian house under the at times exclusive care of women.

In 1933, the heightening of the dam was more severe, as it flooded a number of villages which led to the loss of more land and the increase in labour migration. Nubian houses were then faced with an environmental catastrophe caused by irresponsible state developments. In response, the state offered 75,000 L.E. in order to replace 35,00 of the houses. But in the economic standard of the time this was a shockingly small amount to cover the huge loss of Nubian property and livelihoods. Nubians rallied together, notwithstanding, in order to rebuild their villages in what Hassan Fathy in his historical introduction of El Hakim's book on Nubian architecture dubbed "a miracle in architecture" (El Hakim, 1990, p. iv). The spatial idea and ideal of the Nubian house in this regard was resilient, such that 35,000 houses were rebuilt in twelve months, and as Fathy describes it, "[n]o two houses were the same, each was more beautiful than the other: each village created its own character" (ibid.). Such resilience was the result of a community-based approach to rebuilding, and of an emotionally driven building regime.

The house: Disposition and dispositions

The High Dam was conceived and eventually built in the 1960s in order to fulfil a dream of industrialism and, in turn, nation-making. But, while the rest of Egypt celebrated the dam, Nubians were expected to start living in their newly built environment. The 35,000 Nubian houses that were rebuilt in 1933 were submerged again under the High Dam reservoir, along with all the Nubian houses south of the dam within the Egyptian border. The destruction reached as far as Nubian Halfa valley in Sudan, a fact which resulted in their resettlement in a similar DIDR scheme.

The state produced the plan under the supervision of the Joint Committee for Nubian Resettlement, established in April 1961 (Serageldin, 1982). The planning and design process was hastily finalised and claimed to be "a replica of the original housing schemes with a socialist tinge" (Ghabbour, 1991), which, especially to Nubians like myself, is a lofty claim that barely reflects reality. Most notably, the housing plans were not actually derived from any substantial sociological or anthropological studies as they were finalised before the ethnographic survey of Nubia had even been commissioned (Hopkins & Mehanna, 2011). Moreover, the ethnographic survey, which was first conceived in 1960 (Fernea, 1963), was not tasked to investigate the spatial organisation or dynamics of Nubian houses.

Investments in machines and irrigation systems were the priority of government in the earlier years of resettlement (Ministry of Social Affairs, 1964), with the assumption that the financial support of men and of agricultural practice would trickle down to support women and the household. This, of course, did not always go to plan. As a 67-year-old Nubian woman explained to me: "We didn't have running water at home, and we were not allowed to use public taps to water our [home] garden", for state agents recognised the problem of water scarcity. The ability to have indoor water and electricity, indeed the primary reason that Egypt built the High Dam, was not achieved in the resettlement villages following the first decade of displacement, and effective sewage network systems are yet to reach Nubians in these resettlement villages.

Immediately after resettlement, dwelling units were distributed to families according to their size and according to the Egyptian state's definition of a 'nuclear' family, thus rupturing indigenous systems of spatial organisation and social contracts. Displaced Nubians often recall that their first encounter with the settlements and with their new houses was filled with disappointment: the modern paradise that they were promised was just an incomplete housing project in the desert. Even those who were lucky enough to receive dwelling units received them incomplete, roofless and doorless. Nubian people were therefore required to invest time and resources into building their own new houses.

Nubians have exhibited their dissatisfaction with their newly built environment both verbally, as can be seen by my interviews with them, and in the renovations that they implemented to make the state-built dwelling units liveable in. Since moving into the settlements, they have reappropriated the state-built dwellings; housing units and their facilities which were not complete at the time of the move have since been refurbished. As Saida, a 78-year-old woman in Qustul, said: "When we first arrived here, there was a house for a family and no house for [the] five others, and if one received a house, it would have no roof and windows. We had scorpions and snakes coming in and out." With state investments directed towards retraining men, Nubian women had to spend their savings on repairing and finishing their new units.

Two American anthropologists, Fernea and Kennedy (1966), were responsible for the ethnographic survey in Nubia during and directly after the displacement. They noted the vast construction efforts that took place in Nubian displacement villages during this time:

There is scarcely a neighbourhood in New Nubia in which some houses have not been radically altered through the mounting of china plates above the doors, as in Old Nubia, and by plastering the exterior with mud to create a facade upon which traditional Nubian designs may be painted. (Fernea & Kennedy, 1966, p. 351).

The creation of the house in the 'Nubian way' was crucial to Nubian communities that had resettled; therefore, if they could, they often paid for expensive remodelling of the new settlement (Fig. 2.). "Some house-owners have spent as much as 300 EGP in their efforts to bring the new homes into conformity with traditional Nubian standards" (Fernea & Kennedy, 1966, p. 351). This is an astounding amount of money, especially with the knowledge that in 1960 the Egyptian annual income per capita was 52.4 EGP, and the compensation issued by the government for their displacement equated to 10 EGP per household. Pointing to the dwelling unit in which she and her family lives today, my great aunt mentions how they 'had to sell our gold in Kom Ombo to make this [into] a proper house'. Cash compensation, as Fernea (1967) points out, was given to men and quickly spent on gambling, which meant that the majority of the burden of redevelopment fell on Nubian women who had to sell their coveted gold items to afford the costs.

Figure 2. Nubian dwelling units before and after undergoing transformations; image produced by author.

The changes that were made to the dwelling units are often framed as positive indicators of integration and settlement, and as a reflection of the way in which people coped with the newly built environment (e.g. Mahgoub, 1990; Fahmi, 2014). They are even framed as a sign of the Egyptian state's tolerance of and commitment to ease (presumably, unjustified) Nubian discontent (Fahim, 1983). But, if we look at personal experience and take into account the frustrations and struggles of Nubians who lived through displacement and resettlement, this framing could comprise a kind of epistemic violence. In a situation of displacement, where people endeavour to find adequate solutions to spatial disruptions and dispossession, to give credit to the government and the state which initially displaced people replicates hegemonic narratives about modernisation and progress. Moreover, it explicitly omits to deal with the impact of displacement on the Nubian people and on their relationship to the idea of the Nubian house. It frames the dynamic instead as a story of a 'generous' landlord (i.e. the state) who gave an 'ungrateful' group of people land, without taking into consideration the overall injustice of the situation which prompted that need for state land.

The injustice of displacement without adequate compensation or housing provision forced Nubians to spend two decades rebuilding their livelihoods, which was marked in part by the building and fitting out of Nubian houses. Especially because many of the Nubians in the resettlement had to build their houses from scratch, there was a resurgence of the Nubian style of housing developed in contrast to the dwelling units primarily offered by the state. The resurgence appears as the typology called "Al Ahaly" (Fig. 3.), which roughly translates to 'community-built' housing units, that can be described as self-built houses that follow Nubian traditional typologies, even as they manifest the economic and environmental constraints posed by their new-built environment.

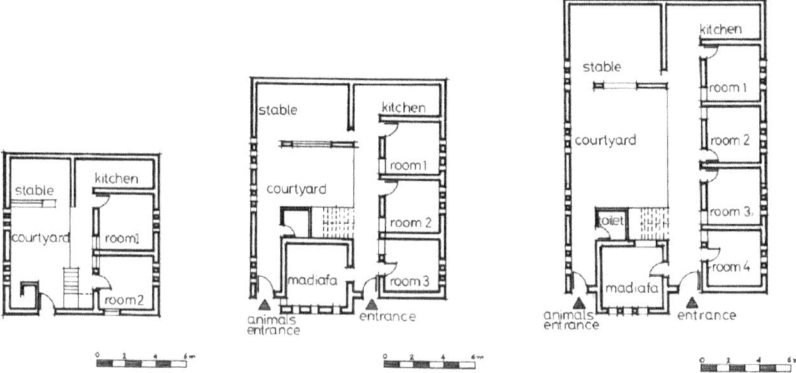

Plans of the three designs offered by the Egyptian state to settle Nubians

Figure 3. Dwelling units offered by the state; floor plans produced by author.

When I asked for the reason why people elected to spend so much on their housing when facing the challenges of poverty, a 57 year-old Nubian man responded that "we had to retrieve our dignity". Dignity and housing are commonly associated with housing cultures. However, for Nubians, dignity is connected to housing, for the organisation of a house attends to a specific political agenda. The Nubian household, not unlike the African household in general, is conceived of as more than a place of residence, but a point of origin for our sense of personhood. The value of the Nubian house is therefore not equivalent to the number of rooms it has, or indeed its price on the housing market, but to the social impact that its organisation has on the larger community, especially with regard to the prominence of the house matriarch. Therefore, post-displacement, building activities aimed at retaining the traditional house and the world that it had produced for the people of a community. Scudder (2016) notes that "Nubians attempted to cling to the familiar during the first year following removal" (p. 5). And it was predominantly women who took the initiative to remodel their housing in order 'to change the government house to a Nubian home' (quoted in Fahim, 1983, p. 79).

Hegemony in design and planning

We can come to see and understand what the Nubian house in Old Nubia looked like only through storytelling. My grandmother's stories often deal with the house as the site of everyday life; and she usually expects me automatically to set the events of her story into the typology of a house, unless told otherwise. Historically, the everyday lives of Nubian women were integrated within the social sphere, as was the house. The house is a place where people meet, eat, sort their crops and divide their shares. Moreover, the house, as per my grandmother's stories, has the ability to transform into a courthouse, a warehouse and a large-scale kitchen, which explains in part the large surface areas of traditional Nubian houses in relation to the number of their occupants, a design element that is distinct from the dwelling units of the Egyptian state in the resettlement village. The Nubian house was in this respect never merely residential or a space of mere subsistence.

The average surface area of Nubian houses, before resettlement, ranged from 500 to 2,000 square metres (Elhakim, 1999), and it is common to find a 1,600 square metre unit that is registered as the residence of four or five people. The state dwelling units, in contrast, offered much smaller surface areas, moving all social encounters, such as weddings and conflict councils, to formally designated 'public' spaces. Dwelling units in the current settlement comprise less than 10 per cent of the average Nubian house, as the state offered units that varied from 100 to 220 square metres (Fig. 4. and Fig. 5.) (Serageldin, 1982), and which resulted in the creation of two separate spheres – one public and the other private – where there used to be no obvious distinction between the two phenomena.

The settlement design offered a modern plan in which 'public' spaces with state-sponsored services and activities were at the centre of the settlement's housing and agricultural uses (Fig. 6). The buildings assigned to that centre are the mosque, a sports centre, a school and community centre. The mosque in the new settlement was different from that of the old one; there was less space

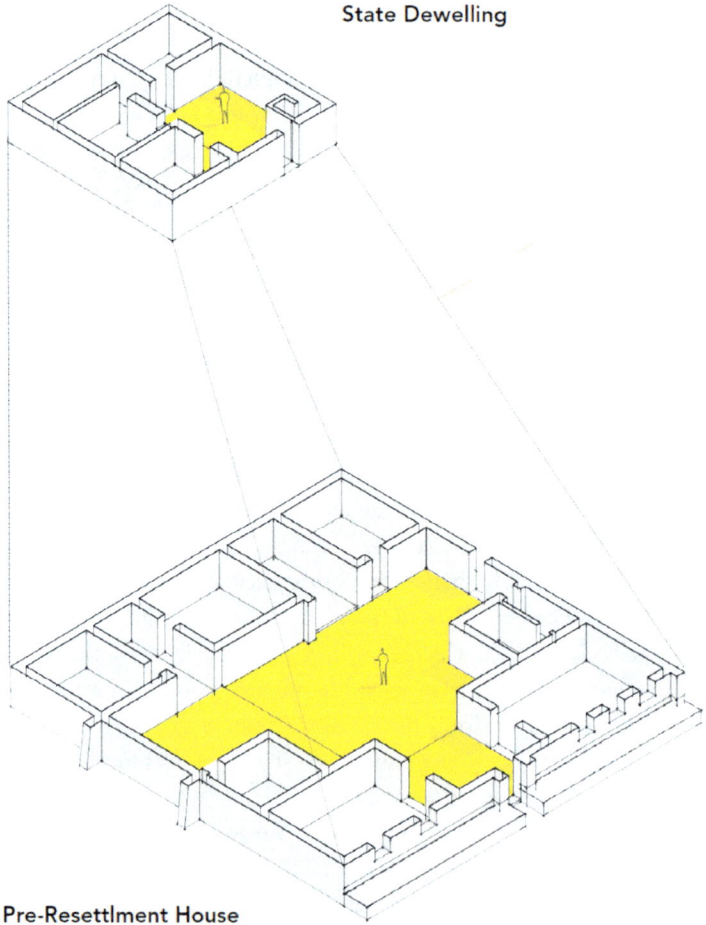

Figure 4. The difference between a Nubian house (Al Ahaly) and a state dwelling unit; image produced by author.

Figure 5. Centre of Qustul in *Tahgeer*; image produced by author.

Figure 6. Illustration of Mastaba in Qustul; image produced by author.

provided for any juxtapositions between Nubian culture and the religious practice of Islam due to the strict governance over religious rituals from "Al Azhar", a state-operated institution with theological authority.

The sports centre was designed for sports recognised by the state; it had a football field and a small administrative building. However, Nubian girls and women did not participate in sports due to the exclusionary narratives around football that depict and allow only men the space to play. And yet, the community centre was and still is operating under the Ministry of Social Affairs whose board consists of ten members, one of whom is a woman. After millennia of socially determinant powers, the role of Nubian women has diminished in the formally-instituted cultural organisations.

The state-built dwellings are modernist in design, and offer the minimum requirements of living space; they contain the minimum surface area required for cooking, cleaning and sleeping. The units were built around a courtyard, as the state architects claimed to draw inspiration from traditional Nubian houses (Serageldin, 1982). And yet, the courtyard was too small in scale to fulfil its environmental role in cooling and ventilating the house or its more social role in fostering political activity and life (Bayoumi, 2018). Because dwelling units were of less than 10 per cent of the average Nubian house, this meant that the reduction in living space resulted in the migration of political activities from the domestic sphere to the state-designated community buildings (Agha & De Vos, 2017). Along with the loss of available surface area in the household, women lost their central position in the creation of and attending to the social and political sphere. Instead, the utilitarian design of the house confined homemaking to the mere act of biological upkeep and, thus, Nubian women lost their place of power in community life. In this way, the architecture of the dwellings limited the social, economic and political functions of the Nubian house, excluding women in the process from what could be and has been articulated as the public sphere. The state-designated dwelling unit thereby destroys the Nubian house as a cultural institution and its constitutive powers. In this case, the existence of new forms of public space became an infringement on the indigenous spatial order in which the house and the women of it were socially and politically involved.

Displacement from the Nubian house was a great threat to the social and political resources that women had previously possessed in Old Nubia. Indeed, Nubian women, who were the most opposed to the idea of resettlement, were once considered the experts on genealogical networks and kinship ties, and they were thus responsible for distributing inheritance and harvest, as they were the most aware of complex family ties and of the ways in which these activities had taken place in the old Nubian house. Nubian women were also in control of zoning their surroundings through different complex processes. They often controlled the spatial organisation of their village by controlling where their descendants lived, with the intention of keeping close ties with people who would ensure that their directions would be followed with regard to working on the land or constructing new facilities. These skills and power were taken away from these women once they were taken over by the formalised legal systems and the judicial power of state agents (Fernea & Kennedy, 1966).

Spaces of resistance and resilience

Even though there was a clear loss of power and influence, Nubian women were not passive victims of the modernising structures that sought to undermine them. As an architectural scholar, I am both expected and inclined to see the multitude of spatial structures and practices that impose a particular social order via a built environment – one, in this case, deigned as suitable and regulated by the Egyptian government. As a Nubian woman, however, I know first-hand as well as through the accounts of my family and community members that we do not sit idly by while we are dispossessed of our social powers, but rather we endeavour actively to resist the systemic changes imposed on us by the built environment.

The dwelling units have undergone – and are still undergoing – many changes. The most common and prominent change is the *mastaba*; a masonry bench that is attached to the house as they were in their old villages. Anthropologists who

Figure 7. Left: images of the Nubians' new system of opening the door from the outside. Right: an illustration of an old lock made by Farag Allah Omeir before displacement; images by author.

witnessed the early years of resettlement note that Nubian women spearheaded the efforts to build these simple benches which were in almost every dwelling unit by the third year of resettlement (Fernea and Kennedy, 1966). A *mastaba* is a place to perform everyday life, indeed a place that does not recognise the hegemonic separation between the inside of the house and the outside as that between the private and the public, and therefore it is a place that may provide a platform for counter-hegemonic practices (Agha & De Vos, 2017).

Another common intervention within dwelling units is the compromised lock. The purpose of a door lock in Nubian architecture is to close the house if it is empty, and not for the purpose of internal security; the lock is therefore situated on the outer side of the door, facing the street, and it is relatively large and visibly decorated with ornaments (Fig. 7.). Nubian houses have retained the tradition of unlocked doors, even in the state-built dwellings; in order to do so, they have each drilled a hole in their door, and extended a string that connects the inside of the door to the outside in a way that allows one to open it from the outside. This ensures accessibility to the house from outside. Growing up, I remember that our door would be opened by visitors from the outside only after three polite knocks to make us aware of their presence. The accessibility of the house and people's desire to access it were matters of family pride. As my grandmother used to say, "Our house is always full".

A complete resummoning and manifestation of the Nubian house has also appeared in the typology of the *madyafa*, or guesthouse (Fig. 8.). The *madyafa*, in the context of Nubian displacement villages, is a replica of a house; it is a feature that Nubians imported from Upper Egypt and was initially the part of the household which hosts visitors. But, large Sa'idi (i.e. Upper Egyptians who inhabit the area to the north of the Old Nubian lands) families have adapted it to be a part of the household (Abdel-Gawad, 2012, p. 26). The *madyafa* is also found in other Arabic-speaking contexts, such as Iraq (Salim, 1962, p. 72–80). Alternatively, Nubians kept the Arabic name but assigned to the *madyafa* a different function and even identity. The *madyafa*, in this context, became part of the community-shared housing and replicates features of the traditional Nubian house without the sleeping component; it has often stood in for the Nubian house for those who were deprived of such spaces by the state's design. They appeared in all villages following the period of displacement, and moreover they served as a new reference for a kind of spatial organisation beyond the state plan of the village, marking the new division of the village for local governance.

Figure 8. Western madyafa in Qustul; image by author.

Qustul, for example, has three *madyafa* buildings, and each serves the area surrounding it and is governed by the association responsible for managing funds and preparing the space for its social functions. Elderly women in Qustul took it upon themselves to reorganise their village and thereby determine the virtual borders of three zones. No map was generated, and the state was not informed of such organisation. And yet, Nubian women collected funds from the village inhabitants to build large houses for events for the respective zones. These buildings were designed to look like old Nubian houses, but they were constructed to accommodate the passing of life events (e.g. the celebration of a birth or a marriage, or providing space for a funeral, etc.), resolve conflicts and function as venues for other sorts of gatherings. When walking by a *madyafa* in Qustul, it is easy to perceive it as yet another *Ahaly* house, and it was this aesthetic veiling of a major community organisation that made it seem unthreatening to the authorities.

The key to open the western *madyafa* in Qustul used to be in the hands of my paternal grandmother, Fato Sakina. She was the initiator and the manager of Quest's western *madyafa*, which was built right opposite our house. To me, the *madyafa* was such a peculiar building: it was closed, typically dead all year long, except when a life event took place; it was never used as a daily space. Nubian women instead extended their houses into the streets using mastabas (Agha & De Vos, 2017) and other transgressive spatial methods, such as the taking over of the street for living and sleeping, to create daily spaces. The *madyafa* was a proxy for a house that was lost, which is to say that it functions as a reincarnation of the house that was typically lent to a family or household during the passing of life events.

The Nubian house, in this case, is actively trying to assert its position as a point where life should happen. This is best embodied in the events of March 2018, when my father passed away. At the time, I travelled to offer my condolences to my great aunt, Zolikha Sakina, who took the place of my father's direct matriarch following the death of his mother. This made it my duty, as his child, to pay my respects to her for the grave loss. I arrived in the afternoon only to find her outraged about the way the village had organisation his funeral: it was to be held in the central area around the mosque, and excluded a visit to her house. Historically, such courtesy was offered to the matriarch of the deceased in her house, and it acknowledged her position and the role her family's house had played in the life of the deceased. In the new settlement houses, however, the available space cannot accommodate such a ceremony. Therefore, people have compromised by conducting the ceremony in the central 'public' space and only then moving to the matriarch's house to offer personal condolences. Nowadays, even this compromise has been lost and respect for the matriarch's house is foregone. Through Zolicka Sakina's outrage, as I see it, the house could still declare a manner of resistance in the face of declining traditions and the dismissal of old cultural practices.

Conclusion: Making sense of the Nubian house

Making sense of the Nubian house in an academic framework comes with some problems which lie largely in the issue of framing Nubian meanings within existing theories of gender and housing; especially at stake is the issue of gender and womanhood, which has been recalibrated, challenged and confronted in the works of afro-womanist scholars on space and place. Even though I view the multitude of feminist analysis as of great value, I struggle to position the Nubian woman and her house under their broad umbrella. Woman is not a gender category in African epistemes (Oyěwùmí, 1997), and this is no sense of Judith Butler's notion of performativity (1990) or Hélène Cixous' linguistic investigation of the place of a woman (1976). The other issue with the existing theory is the lack of African voices in spatial studies that have taken such distances from Western categories and resituated themselves in indigenous episteme. Categories which are significant to Western social, economic, cultural and political thought, such as the distinction between the public and the private, appear ontologically inapplicable; identifying the *madyafa* as a public or private space is therefore not really apposite to explaining the Nubian house (it is, however, a mark of my own epistemic displacement since previous publications). What I endeavour to do now, instead, is to decolonise and to maintain my own stance on seeing the world without being bound to Western categories, such as private/public, even as Western feminists endeavour to unpick them.

There is a strong relationship between Nubian women and their houses, a relationship that does not warrant their exclusion from other spaces, nor does it warrant the marking of this house as a private space. This relationship nevertheless stems from the perception of the house and women as the points of origin, as is the proposition of Afro-feminists like Oyèrónké Oyěwùmí (1997) who suggest that in the (Western) social sciences, a bio-determinism has assumed that the biological differences between men and women 'naturally' result in their being assigned different roles and spaces. However, Oyěwùmí finds evidence to show that the household, as a point of origin, becomes the principal determinant; a household, in this context, can therefore refer to the space of a family and, in doing so, it does not constitute a predetermined relation to biological genders (Ndlovu-Gatsheni, 2018).

In the same vein, it should be stressed that a Nubian house is not severed from its surroundings. It remains accessible and interwoven, such that the Nubian 'inside' (or interior) was never severed or separated from its 'outside' (or exterior); nor is it the case that an open Nubian house constitutes the opening of a private space. Rather, I see the Nubian house as the original space for making the 'social' and the 'political', while technologies such as the *madyafa* are to be considered as a means to give the power back to the house. Thus, in the meantime, what the *madyafa* does is stand idle, waiting for another house to grant it a proxy, and, by doing so, it can perform one of the incarnations of an onto-spatial structure that does not recognise separate spheres.

Understanding the Nubian house post-1963 requires recognising the spatial confrontations between the state imaginary and the Nubian one, and thereby realising that the Nubian house is an active contributor to such confrontations. The state imaginary is built on a utilitarian ethics brought about by its quest for modernism that brings with it in turn modern categories such as the public-private distinction; these categories were not necessarily a part of Nubian's understanding of space but have since been adapted to accommodate old and new ways of living.

Virginia Held offers a criticism of the division and its gendered implications: as long as 'man' has been associated with what is human, 'woman' has been associated with the natural world. Prominent among distinctions reinforcing this view has been that between the public and the private, because of the way they have been interpreted (Held 1990). The private, the woman's house, is a space of biological function, as is the case with the design of the dwelling unit. Such dualities and in particular dynamics of bio-determinism and the assignment of properties based on sex are not applicable in African value systems (Oyěwùmí, 2016), rendering this design decision by state architects and planners a devastating factor to existing gender contracts in a matrilineal society, rendering women increasingly vulnerable to spatial and economic challenges. It is worth mentioning in this respect that Nubian women continue to lose their houses, their status within communities, and their role as matriarchs, a struggle which they arguably share with many other African women across Egypt and even the continent (Ibanga, 2018).

It can be shown how the design of the dwelling units is responsible for imposing such categories that affect Nubian spaces on two levels. First, there is the ontological level, as it devalues and dismisses the activities of Nubian women and the role of the house, over which they preside, to what is natural or biological. In this sense, the Nubian house is associated with reproduction and reproductive activities that have no lasting effects or affects, and so not with the productive activities and with the constitution of histories. The design of the dwelling units enforces a novel ontology of space through a private-public hegemony that discounts more indigenous categorisations of space. Second, there is the political level, whereby government services and activities have continually alienated women from newly-established 'public' spaces because the state predominantly considers men to be heads of the household. The minimal design of the dwelling unit facilitated the movement of social and political spaces to built spaces outside the household, thereby anticipating the movement of power away from spaces typically associated with women, and so limiting their access to power.

In and among all these changes and challenges, however, the Nubian house did not stand idle or passive in the background. It sought to reject its relegation to a 'private' area and hence blur the line between what constitutes an inside and an outside through the use of *mastaba*. It could also extend itself onto the street and expand the spaces used by women. The house sought in this way to reject the barrier imposed by the door and its lock; the house breaks its own lock to assert its accessibility and connection with the community. The Nubian house asserts itself as a space that is neither private nor wholly public, and so cannot be reduced to such simple dualisms. However, the Nubian house remains in confrontation with and resistant to these dualisms for over half a century after displacement. Therefore, to make sense of its contemporary form, I must consider the world in which it emerges and the world that has continued to impose itself on it.

I see evidence in the examples and in my encounters in Qustul of a house that is actively trying to heal itself by reclaiming its power through appropriation and adaptation. The *madyafa*, for example, which appears as a proxy for the Nubian house, stands as a community institution and as a tool of self-governance, or even counter-governance; it acts as a spatial reference for a spatial organisation removed and hidden from the one offered and even tacitly enforced by the state. Moreover, there is significant meaning in the fact that Nubians rebuilt the space of the *madyafa* to replicate the design of a house. With its notably public role, the *madyafa* is a space of community and social constitution. Even though it replicates functions that the state provides through its own form of public spaces, the *madyafa* relocates these functions back into the space of the house, thereby affirming what many Nubian women and men perceive to be the ontological inapplicability of state paradigms and spaces.

What we can learn from these encounters is that the Nubian house resides in Nubian consciousness, as does the Nubian landscape (Agha, 2019), prior to its materialisation. It is therefore an image and an ideal that makes possible and engenders the reclaiming of Nubian social spaces. The activation of the Nubian house is inevitable as it is a location of Nubian power – especially that of Nubian women who have been dispossessed due to state programmes of displacement and resettlement. The Nubian house is as such an ontological paradigm and a carrier of multiple meanings that have been displaced and continue to be displaced by contemporary social, economic and political changes.

Notes

1. More comprehensive stories of these summaries can be found in *Open Architecture*.
2. While I refer to the Nubian land before 1963 as Old Nubia, I will use 'resettlement villages', 'settlements' and *Tahgeer* to refer to the current sites of resettlement which are located near Aswan.

References

Abdel-Gawad, A. (2012a). *Veiling Architecture: Decoration of Domestic Buildings in Upper Egypt 1672-1950*. American University in Cairo Press.

Abdel-Gawad, A. (2012b). *Veiling Architecture: Decoration of Domestic Buildings in Upper Egypt 1672-1950*. American University in Cairo Press.

Adams, W. Y. (1977). *Nubia: Corridor to Africa*. Princeton, NJ: Princeton University Press.

Agha, M., & De Vos, E. (2017). Liminal Publics, Marginal Resistance. *IDEA JOURNAL*, 88-101.

Agha, M. (2019). Nubia Still Exists: On the Utility of the Nostalgic Space. *Humanities, 8*(1), 24.

Allen, S. (2014). *Nubians and development: 1960-2014*. PhD Thesis. Middle East Studies Center. Cairo: American University in Cairo.

Bayoumi, O. A. M. (2018). Nubian Vernacular architecture & contemporary Aswan buildings' enhancement. *Alexandria Engineering Journal, 57*(2), 875–883.

Butler, J. (1990). *Gender Trouble: Feminism and the Subversion of Identity*. London and New York: Routledge.

Cernea, M. M. (1996). Public Policy Responses to Development-Induced Population Displacements. *Economic and Political Weekly, 31*(24), 1515–1523.

Cixous, H., Cohen, K., & Cohen, P. (1976). The Laugh of the Medusa. *Signs, 1*(4), 875-893.

Dafalla, H. (1975). *The Nubian Exodus*. Nordiska Afrikainstitutet: C. Hurst & Co.

Drydyk, J. (2007). Unequal Benefits: The Ethics of Development–Induced Displacement. *Georgetown Journal of International Affairs, 8*(1), 105–113.

El-Hakim, O. (1993). *Nubian architecture: The Egyptian Vernacular Experience*. Zamalek, Cairo: Palm Press.

Fahim, H. M. (1983). *Egyptian Nubians: Resettlement and Years of Coping*. Salt Lake City, UT: University of Utah Press.

Fahmi, W. S. (2014). *The Adaptation Process of a Resettled Community to the Newly-Built Environment A Study of the Nubian Experience in Egypt: A Study of the Nubian Experience in Egypt*. Universal-Publishers.

Fernandez, B. (2018). Dispossession and the depletion of social reproduction. *Antipode, 50*(1), 142–163.

Fernea, R. A., & Kennedy, J. G. (1966a). Initial Adaptations to Resettlement: A New Life for Egyptian Nubians. *Current Anthropology, 7*(3), 349–354.

Fernea, R. A., & Kennedy, J. G. (1966b). Initial Adaptations to Resettlement: A New Life for Egyptian Nubians. *Current Anthropology, 7*(3), 349–354.

Fernea, R. A., & Gerster, G. (1973). *Nubians in Egypt: Peaceful people*. Smithmark Pub.

Finefter-Rosenbluh, I. (2017). Incorporating Perspective Taking in Reflexivity: A Method to Enhance Insider Qualitative Research Processes. *International Journal of Qualitative Methods, 16*(1).

Fluehr-Lobban, C. (1998). Nubian Queens in the Nile Valley and Afro-Asiatic Cultural History. *Ninth International Conference for Nubian Studies August*, 20–26.

Ghabbour, S. I. (1991). Involuntary Resettlement in Development Projects: Policy Guidelines in World Bank-financed Projects. *Environmental Conservation, 18*(1), 91–92.

Held, V. (1990). Feminist Transformations of Moral Theory. *Philosophy and Phenomenological Research, 50*, 321-344.

Hopkins, N. S., & Mehanna, S. R. (2011). *Nubian Encounters: The Story of the Nubian Ethnological Survey 1961 to 1964*. Cairo: American University in Cairo Press.

Ibanga, D.-A. (2018). Concept, Principles and Research Methods of African Environmental Ethics. *Africology: The Journal of Pan African Studies 11*(7), 123-141.

Mahgoub, Y. O. M. (1990). *The Nubian experience: A study of the social and cultural meanings of architecture*. Ann Arbor, MI: University of Michigan Press.

Mathur, H. M. (2016). Resettlement Planning: Reversing Displacement Impacts of Development Projects. In H. M. Mathur (Ed.), *Assessing the Social Impact of Development Projects* (pp. 211–231). Springer International Publishing.

Ndlovu-Gatsheni, S. (2018). *Epistemic Freedom in Africa: Deprovincialization and Decolonization*. New York and London: Routledge.

Oyěwùmí, O. (1997). *The Invention of Women: Making an African Sense of Western Gender Discourse*. Minneapolis, MN: University of Minnesota Press.

Oyěwùmí, O. (2016). Matripotency: Ìyá, in Philosophical Concepts and Sociopolitical Institutions. In Oyèrónké Oyěwùmí (ed.), *What Gender Is Motherhood? Changing Yorùbá Ideals of Power, Procreation, and Identity in the Age of Modernity* (pp. 57–92). Gender and Cultural Studies in Africa and the Diaspora. New York, NY: Palgrave Macmillan.

Rabe, M. (2008). Can the "African household" be presented meaningfully in large-scale surveys? *African Sociological Review / Revue Africaine de Sociologie, 12*(2): 167–181.

Salim, S. M. (1962). *Marsh dwellers of the Euphrates delta* (Vol. 23). London, Athlone P.

Scudder, T. (2016). Aswan High Dam Resettlement of Egyptian Nubians. In *Aswan High Dam Resettlement of Egyptian Nubians* (pp. 1–52). Springer.

Serageldin, M. (1982). Planning for new nubia 1960-1980. In *The changing rural habitat. Volume i: Case studies* (pp. 59–82). The Aga Khan Awards.

Tadros, H. (1979). The human aspects of rural resettlement schemes in Egypt. In B. Berdichewsky, ed., *Anthropology and Social Change in Rural Areas* (p. 122). The Hague and New York: Mountain Publishers.

Waterbury, J. (1979). *Hydropolitics of the Nile Valley*. Syracuse, NY: Syracuse University Press.

CHAPTER 15

Trans-national Homes

From Nairobi to Cape Town

Huda Tayob
University of Cape Town, South Africa

Introduction

Garissa Lodge in the area of Eastleigh, Nairobi, is known as the first "Somali mall". The history of its establishment and growth is recounted through what is often described as the "universal story" of its emergence (Carrier & Lochery, 2013; Carrier, 2017). This often repeated story posits that from the late 1980s, following an increase in the number of refugees arriving in Kenya from neighbouring Somalia, the "two-storey residential block began to be used for trade, through the sale of counterfeit goods and clothing purchased in Dubai. At night, the products were stored under beds, while during the day, the bedrooms became shops" (Carrier & Lochery, 2013, p. 336). Garissa Lodge therefore offered a kind of home and refuge for displaced Somalis. During fieldwork in Cape Town from 2014 to 2016 and in Nairobi in December 2018, I was frequently told various versions of this story describing the semi-formal and multi-use nature of this "Somali mall". More often than not, I was told that the building was indeed always a lodge, the only one in the area when it opened, and one which specifically catered to "Africans", referring to populations from north-eastern Kenya, many of whom are ethnic Somalis or Kenyan Somalis.[1] Mama Layla[2] explained that in the 1980s "the Somalis started to come with their families and they used to sell their things on the bed in the day and sleep there at night. And then they grew and grew, so they expanded the building up to a second floor".[3]

The frequently repeated narrations of the origins of Garissa Lodge as the first Somali mall demarcate it as a "universal story" for Somali malls more generally. Although there are some variations in the different narrations with regard to exactly when it opened, whether it was initially for short or medium-term stays and whether it contained a restaurant or not, certain details remain common: Garissa Lodge was owned by a blind Somali woman named Asha, and it was a space used for residential accommodation and trade (Carrier & Lochery, 2013, p. 337).[4] It is described as the first of its kind formed in the wake of increasing instability in neighbouring Somalia. It was also predominantly ethnically Somali and therefore its origins relate to the particular racial and ethnic identity of Eastleigh as historically demarcated a "Somali" and "Asian" site, defined in the 1948 Masterplan for Nairobi (1948).[5]

In the narrations which recount the establishment of Garissa Lodge a central repeated motif is that it has been a kind of home, hosting regular familial and domestic practices for a forcibly displaced population. Garissa Lodge is widely understood as a point of origin for the typology of the "Somali mall" as a space of both trade and home-making formed in the wake of displacement. This chapter draws on the work of Michel de Certeau (1984) to argue that the narratives and circulation of stories about Garissa Lodge and other similar establishments act as a form of spatial knowledge. De Certeau (1984) asserts that narrations do not just remain in the realm of language as a supplemental discourse to the event itself, but instead are active in "producing geographies of action" (p. 116). Drawing on narrations and stories about Somali malls, this chapter focuses on home-making and unmaking through the central case of Som City, a Somali mall in Cape Town, South Africa. It points to Som City as connected to a wider network of temporary transnational homes, including Garissa Lodge described above. This chapter argues that Somali malls and their associated lodges should be understood as an ambivalent spatial typology as they create a feeling of "being at home", in the context of protracted forced displacement.

I was first told about Garissa Lodge and Somali malls in Cape Town, South Africa. Following De Certeau, I argue that stories such as the founding of Garissa Lodge construct, reinforce and engender particular kinds of spaces associated with Somali refugees, along with a particular kind of home. For Homi Bhabha (1994), the potential of a story is performative and can be understood as a transgressive tactic for those without formal power. Bhabha describes the importance of these stories and their circulation through Ranajit Guha's analysis of a peasant insurgency in India with the "chapati story" in relation to the 1857 uprising. In the chapati story, rumours of a planned uprising against the British were supposedly spread along with the distribution of chapatis, or Indian flatbreads, that were hand-delivered to villages. As Bhabha explains, it is not known whether details of the uprising were actually spread with the chapatis or not, yet this is not relevant, as the circulation of the story was very real and had a wide reach. He points out that the circulation of the story or rumour established a sense of solidarity among the colonised and created widespread unease amongst British colonisers. For this reason Bhabha (1994) argues that the story itself holds a kind of performative power as it circulates in time and space with very real material effects (p. 289). Although a very different context, this chapter argues that the narratives of "home" as constructed and circulated around and within Somali malls are more than invisible stories, and instead both perform and suggest a particular kind of spatiality and a sense of "being at home". In this context, the performativity of the narrations is dependent on the circulation of similar stories among the Somali diaspora.

Figure 1. Advertisement seen in Bellville, Cape Town, "Ideal for Somali Mall", photo taken by author.

This is a form of home with its origin in mass displacement and the civil war in Somalia. Yet, it nevertheless provides an imaginary of provisional domesticity, producing a spatial intimacy across geographies and within contested realms. These are spaces which offer networks of support and possibility beyond the limitations of refugee camp spaces, while remaining ambivalent. Narratives around transnational homes and Somali malls are explored in this chapter using vignettes, with a focus on a lodge in Som City, a Somali mall in Cape Town, South Africa. In drawing out stories about these lodges, the vignettes point to the performative potential of narratives for refugee groups.

Figure 2. Somali Malls in Bellville
1. Bellville Station Mall (1991, 1998, 2009)
2. Oriental Plaza (1995, 2001, 2005)
3. Som City (2004)
4. Anabora Shopping Center 1 (2008 – 2013)
5. Eastern Plaza (2008)
6. Anabora Shopping Centre 2 (2009)
7. Bellstat Junction – Waarshikh Shopping Centre (2009)
8. Welcome Plaza (2010)
9. Western Plaza (2010)
10. Wonderful Plaza (formerly Rodie Rose) (2011)
11. 786 Plaza (2012)
12. United Market (date unknown)
13. FNB building (2014)
14. New Mall (2015)

Home-making and unmaking in Somali Malls

As mentioned, I was first introduced to Somali malls and associated lodges in Cape Town, South Africa. The dismantling of Apartheid and the institution of a non-racial democracy in the early 1990s led to an increasing number of immigrants, migrants, asylum seekers and refugees coming into South Africa from other African countries.[6] While South Africa has become an important site of refuge for many, there have also been growing challenges for new entrants, particularly due to xenophobic violence. In 2008, urban areas across South Africa saw widespread xenophobic attacks that particularly targeted African migrants, asylum seekers and refugees. The violence began in Alexandra township in Johannesburg on 11 May 2008, and within two weeks spread throughout the country. Around sixty-two people were killed and 150,000 people displaced, many permanently (Amit, 2012; Landau & Segatti, 2011). Many of these new entrants are from East Africa and, in particular, Somalia. In Cape Town, their spaces of habitation, established from the mid-1990s have, as in Nairobi, largely been in informal shopping arcades known as "Somali Malls".

These mixed-use markets have been created from old multi-storey office blocks or large individual commercial spaces, which have been subdivided into numerous small spaces to host trading stalls, along with various social, religious and educational services. These malls are central spaces for new entrants, more typically understood as a form of "arrival infrastructure" (Meeus et al., 2019). Yet, I argue that, beyond being important sites of first entry, they are importantly central spaces for gathering, socialising, eating particular foods and meeting for refugee groups. Furthermore, their connection to similar establishments across the continent suggests that these are much more than sites of "migrant[s] as entrepreneurs". Significantly, among their many other functions, these Somali malls also have residential accommodation or lodges which serve a longer-term role as home, short-term accommodation and space of refuge in a time of crisis. These lodges within Somali malls are the focus of this chapter.

By focusing on the home-making and home-unmaking practices evident in these spaces, I have already argued elsewhere that these shopping arcades as a whole and the small shops within are central to constituting an alternative sense of home in the context of large-scale forced migration (Tayob, 2017). Although I was first introduced to the idea of a "Somali Mall" and associated lodge in Cape Town, through my research it became increasingly evident that this is a typology found in other parts of the continent and world, including Johannesburg within South Africa (Jinnah, 2010; Ripero-Muniz & Fayad, 2016; Sadouni, 2009; Tayob, 2019). Through interviews, it became clear that these spaces in Cape Town were in many ways made in the image of places elsewhere. I suggest that these lodges in some ways provide a spatial extension of the camp space as they offer a kind of home that exists at the ambivalent border between processes of home-making and -unmaking. As with camps, they are intended to be temporary and are characterised by transience. They are sites where displaced populations are able to make a home, having been displaced as a result of the deliberate destruction of homes in the past. The temporary nature of these sites and the rudimentary accommodation they offer, however, point to the further imminent unmaking of these sites as homes in the near or distant future. Yet, despite the limitations, in their occupation within broader networks of urban refuge across geographical distances, as narrated to me, they extend beyond the limitations of camp space and have the potential for social and physical mobility, and the imaginary of an alternative future.

In her paper, 'The Idea of a Home', Mary Douglas (1991) argues for a reassessment of what counts as home. In contrast to normative literature at the time, which largely focused on fixed physical domestic space, Douglas (1991) posits that the home is a "kind of space" that is primarily characterised by the regularity of practices, people and things within a fundamentally non-profit-making space. Douglas' reassessment led to the definition of home being expanded beyond the physically defined space of the nuclear family. These re-readings recognise that home is not always ideal: it might be a secure space offering a refuge from persecution, but could also be a space of fear and danger. Yet, this literature largely remains dedicated to domestic spaces behind closed doors (Blunt, 2005; Blunt & Dowling, 2006a; Buchli & Lucas, 2001; Cieraad, 1999; Miller, 2001). In a distinct approach, bell hooks suggests that home is a multiplicity of things and spaces for different groups of people, regardless of material scarcities, asserting the need to question what the home is and to whom. In the context of the segregated south of the USA, home is also importantly a safe space for hooks, free from racism (hooks, 1990a). In a somewhat related critique of Douglas' concept of home, Richard Baxter and Katherine Brickell question the emphasis placed on home-making. They recognise the importance of Douglas' article in noting that homes are created through processes, yet also criticise the idea that home-making is the goal of all homes, where home-making is understood as overwhelmingly positive. Instead, they argue for a recognition of the varied and multiple nature of homes, their different meanings for their inhabitants, and how the processes of home-making always coincide with those of *unmaking*.

Baxter and Brickell (2014) point to a gap in discussions of home-unmaking and suggest that we should view home-unmaking not only as the deliberate destruction of homes (Porteous & Smith, 2001) or as domicide, but also as a part of a broader set of processes. This is particularly salient when one considers protracted refugee situations which often involve multiple and serial displacement. This has been taken up in more recent literature which asks what it means to make home on the move for migrant groups (Boccagni, 2017), sometimes in multiple locations through remittance houses (Lopez, 2010), and how this might redefine our understanding of home and how we study it (Dossa & Golubovic, 2019). This newer literature positions home as located in physical space and determined through temporal processes. This chapter builds on these understandings of home to look into the relationship between home-making and -unmaking vis-à-vis Somali mall lodges and their networks, which extend between a range of urban sites of refuge.

Adopting a view of home-making in relation to home-unmaking, as described through narratives of home, enables a broader understanding of refugee homes beyond their localised specificities. The narratives that circulate about transnational homes suggest a more nuanced reading of refugee homes and the category of the 'refugee'. Following Elena Fiddian-Qasmiyeh (2020), it points to displaced persons as "actively responding" to displacement rather than only being passive recipients, drawing out the importance of refugee-refugee networks of support (p. 3). Garissa Lodge, described at the outset of this chapter, was started up by Mama Asha, where her role as care provider despite a disability was emphasised as she opened the lodge to those who had limited places to stay elsewhere in the city. Most of the lodges described in this chapter are run by refugees themselves, hosting other refugees. Focusing on home-making and the narratives that circulate about it enables a recognition of these marginal and provisional sites of refuge.

Som City

From the 1990s the northern Cape Town suburb of Bellville has emerged as a central area for "Somali malls", and for African migrants, refugees and asylum seekers in general. This is a change that has been seen by the city as problematic with regard to zoning. In an interview with Willem Arendse, the urban manager for the Voortrekker Road City Improvement District (VRCID) at the time, he noted that the general problem in the area was the use of buildings for purposes other than their initial intention. Of particular concern to him was that office buildings were being used for residential purposes. Willem described these buildings as overcrowded spaces where "immigrants" paid minimal rents to wealthy and distant slumlords. Willem expressed his outrage over this practice and this formed part of his reasoning for the need to "clean the area up". Yet, while these spaces were clearly exploitative in Willem's eyes, a different story emerged from the inhabitants themselves. Instead, they pointed to the importance of these lodges to access residential space in a formal area, and

Figure 3. Photograph of a 1st-floor shop in Som City, photo by author.

one particularly understood as 'safe' for new entrants. They further described the value of the short-term leases and the ability to rent spaces on a daily basis. In Bellville, the first of these lodges was started on the upper floors of Som City.

Som City is a Somali mall. The first floor houses a large restaurant, internet café and laundry among a series of shops run by women selling what are described as "Somali goods". The second and third floors above are part of the lodge within the wider mall. Som City was started by Ahmed in 2004, a Somali refugee. Ahmed said that the idea of the Somali Mall with a lodge came to him from Eastleigh in Nairobi, which he passed through on the way to Cape Town. When this particular building in Bellville became available for rent in 2004, he got together with two friends and decided to make an offer to rent it. They converted the ground and the first floors into businesses, and the upper three floors were turned into a lodge. In describing the process of starting the lodge, Ahmed notes the importance of this site as the first of its kind in the area. He said, "You see people come in for buying, for the weekend, for Home Affairs [passports]. They were not having a place to sleep at that time."[7] He therefore explains that starting the lodge in Som City was a response to a need in the area. The reasons given by migrants for staying in Bellville included stocking up for their spaza shops in the various informal settlements, meeting friends for the weekend, and going to Home Affairs to renew refugee permits. Spaza shops are informal grocery stores located in townships – a key source of income for migrants who do not have access to formal employment. Yet, beyond the functional narration of the space, in his initial description, he also described this lodge in direct relation to his personal experience of moving to Cape Town.

When Ahmed first arrived in the city in 2000, he worked as a street trader at Bellville station for four years. He specified that he borrowed 1,000 Rand

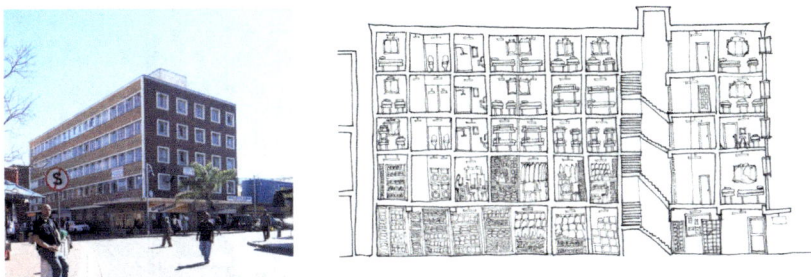

Figure 4. Photograph and drawing of Som City exterior (left) and drawing of first floor (right) (Drawing and Photograph by author).

(about €60 at the time) from his extended family, bought a few items and began hawking on the street, slowly expanding the scale of his trade. When the Som City building became available in 2004, rentals were particularly low, and so, with two friends, he decided to try and start a full Somali Mall. They were helped to pay the initial deposit with assistance from larger and more established Somali refugee-led businesses in the area. Ahmed noted the risk they took in starting the place as it drew on all their savings and put them in serious debt. At the time of speaking to him, however, the shops were all rented and the lodge was completely full three to four days a week.

Unlike the female spaces of the shops, the lodges are primarily male spaces. Som City was a former office block, and so is characterised by a series of small modular spaces. On a tour through the lodge I was shown into the various rooms: most were occupied by two to three beds; the individual rooms housed between two and six people. On each floor, one of the existing bathroom blocks was kept intact, while the second had been turned into a shower room. The bedrooms were all fairly simple and unadorned spaces. Clothing and personal items were stored either on or under the beds. Fig. 5. comprises a plan drawing of Som City, based on sketches done while I was taken on a tour through the site. The drawings emphasise the importance of the physical spaces of accommodation, alongside the narratives that circulate about these lodges.

In asking the manager about the operation of the lodge, I was curious whether rooms could be rented out individually. He responded that this was not a requirement. His response was once again personal, when he said, "Because you see our people they can't afford it, they don't want to pay, everybody is saving. As I told you, you see where I start from." He referred once again to his work as a street trader and noted that he used to live in the lodge himself for the first two years of running it, remarking several times during our interview that he lived there himself, in room 208.

Figure 5. Plan drawings of Som City: First floor trading spaces (left) and second floor lodge (right) (Drawing by author).

Although Som City was the first Somali mall to open a lodge, it soon became a precedent for various other lodges in the area, hosting a combination of transient and longer-term inhabitants, all of whom are refugees. As with the markets themselves, these lodges and guest houses are all ostensibly for profit. As such, following Douglas, they cannot be understood as home spaces for two key reasons: first, according to Douglas, the home is essentially a non-profit-making establishment which means, second, that privacy can be bought (Douglas, 1991, p.298). Yet, these lodges are not like hotels, in that while they are intended for profit, the majority of tenants have limited alternative options. Unlike rented houses which might be used for longer-term stays and therefore allow for one to establish a sense of privacy, in the lodge all that is rented is a bed. There are no formal contracts, and the bed is paid for on a daily basis. However, despite the short-term nature of the accommodation provided, the narratives point to these lodges as stable spaces. Some of the inhabitants stay in these lodges on a long-term basis, while others come into the area for one to three days a week. For the remainder of the week the inhabitants usually stay in their spaza shops in townships.

The occupation of space and beds reflects the migrant trading practices around Cape Town, the high levels of urban violence experienced more generally in South African cities, and the regulation of being an asylum seeker or refugee in the city. Beyond the xenophobic violence of 2008, there have been sporadic yet frequent attacks that targeted African migrants in particular (Amit, 2012). These lodges therefore operate in a liminal zone between a temporary space of accommodation and a safe and stable refuge from ongoing violence. As Dossa and Golubovic (2019) point out, "These interstitial locations should not be excluded from analyses of home-making simply because they are temporary" (p. 173). In a different context, Dominique Malaquais (2004) similarly notes that for many African migrants "the plan to move on, however, is often several years old" (p. 9). In the case of Somali refugees, multiple and forced displacement characterises the protracted refugee situation across generations.

Although home is always subject to a process of unmaking, through moving out or moving homes, forcibly displaced persons face an immeasurable loss. For Dossa and Golubovic (2019), through circumstances of forced displacement the significant labour of home-making becomes visible (p. 172). They describe the labour involved as both a "desire to reimagine a new home after displacement" and a "simultaneous aspiration to maintain a connection to what has been lost" (ibid., p. 173). I suggest that through these lodges not only does the labour of home-making, but also the quotidian process of unmaking homes faced by refugees, become visible. Beyond moments of crisis, the lodges point to the continued and everyday precarity of home. In the stories told of renting small spaces, to save for remittances or future prospects, the narratives that circulate about these spaces emphasise their ambivalence as spaces of refuge and home in the wake of displacement, and hope for another kind of home beyond them.

Figs. 7. and 8. are two photographs of a lodge within Anabora, another Somali mall in the area of Bellville. The photographs point to the bare nature of the space consisting of beds and blankets, and makeshift curtains to provide relief from the sun. These photographs were shared with me by the Problem Building Unit, located in the City of Cape Town municipality. They were taken during an inspection of the building which later led to the eviction of all residents. This is one of the few photographs I have of these lodge spaces, as the fear around possible evictions or immigration raids meant that photographs of these spaces are not particularly welcome. I have argued elsewhere that the evictions are linked to a racialised understanding of the area as a site of urban decay, which is linked to wider patterns of xenophobic violence that particularly targets Africans from other parts of the continent (Tayob, 2017).

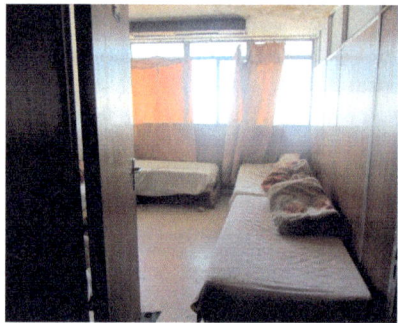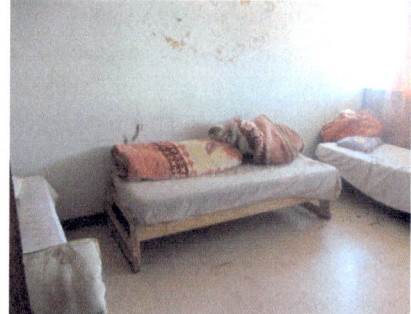

Figures 7. & 8. Photographs of a lodge within Anabora Somali mall in Bellville, Cape Town. Inhabitants were evicted from this space in November 2018.

While the lodge is currently a profitable business for Ahmed, it is also linked to his personal trajectory in the country. This is a significant detail, and common in this type of lodge where, in contrast to Douglas' assertion, there is no clear opposition between profit and home. In the case of Som City, as with numerous other lodges in the area, they transitioned from personal homes to public homes. This reveals a more intimate relationship with the space and the inhabitants and a sense of solidarity with the group which lodges there. Douglas (1991) has argued that home is a kind of embryonic community which is based on the establishment of solidarity, and I would suggest that in the case of these lodges the personal histories of the owners with the spaces result in a kind of solidarity and are one of the ways in which the lodge is defined as a kind of home despite the intention for profit. Spaces of care and refuge, like violent events, remain present in the "form of memory", and, following Golubovic and Dossa (2019), the narrations of them should be recognised for the work they perform (p. 174).

Ilana Feldman (2006) similarly points to the political importance of home as a refrain for Palestinian refugees, where repeated narrations of homeland serve to create a sense of community in the context of displacement. For Feldman (2006), the refrain of home "does not simply give voice to material connections or memories of previous connections but helps to structure people's experience" (p. 17). Although the narrations surrounding the lodge do not refer to some kind of homeland, as in Feldman's Palestinian example, the repetition of certain narratives, starting with Garissa Lodge and with the repeated personal investment in the lodge space, points to the importance of these ambivalent homes for many who have access to little else. The details of personal connections and aspirations for social mobility are located in the narrations of these Somali malls and lodges, along with the ongoing precariousity of the wider situation. As De Certeau (1984) notes, oral narrations act to articulate, verify, collate and compose spaces (p. 123). These stories of the lodges, which move between personal history, entrepreneurial success and spaces of support and care, point to the importance of the narration, narrative and of the physical lodge itself.

This understanding of the lodges as spaces of care is further enunciated by the events of 2008. During the xenophobic violence of May 2008, many migrants from around the city and suburbs of Cape Town fled to Bellville. This reasserts the centrality of these lodges as spaces of refuge connected to the city in a property market that is otherwise exclusively priced and unwelcoming to non-citizens, even to those who can afford to pay. Nationwide xenophobic violence in 2008 led to an increase in demand for space in lodges and a change to the interiors. For instance, the bunk bed is a response to high demand following 2008. At the time, Som City, along with neighbouring lodges, became important as the site of emergency housing, and the Somali malls, in general, were seen as 'safe havens'. Som City and a neighbouring lodge, Oriental Plaza, were turned into what was described as 'a kind of relief centre' providing meals and free accommodation, supported by businesses in the Somali malls (Nicholson, 2011; Meyer, 2010a; Meyer, 2010b).[8] At the time, Ahmed opened Som City to those who were left homeless as a result of the violence. He noted that most people stayed for two to three weeks, but many stayed for up to four months. He articulated that he felt the need to provide free accommodation as many had lost everything in the attacks. While those with money did pay him, around three-quarters of the inhabitants at the time stayed for free. He added, "I could not tell the people just to go out and sleep outside. Especially that time, it was winter time, it was May, it was very cold outside. Everybody must come in, if they had money, they paid, if they did not, I said just stay. Some people lost everything."[9] Ahmed described the severity of the situation and the need to provide free housing for those who could not afford it. In his description he did not see the profit-making intention of the business as something which opposed the idea of the site as a form of emergency housing. He noted that those who could afford to pay were still required to do so. Yet, those who could not and had no alternative means were provided with free accommodation.

Abdoumaliq Simone (2018) suggests that in response to systemic structural violence a kind of urban "politics of peripheral care" emerges by and for marginalised populations with limited provisions (p. 25). These lodges seem to act in a similar manner, to enable the violence to be endured as part of a longer serial form of similar displacements elsewhere through the provision of an emergency home. This role of the lodges as sites of emergency housing in 2008 is significant, as it is one of the reasons given for the rise in the number of lodges in Bellville and the growth of the area as a whole. The response in the area of Bellville has been to accommodate many of these traders in transient and inexpensive housing, and to continue to and consistently subdivide large spaces into small, multiple sleeping areas.

Transnational homes

On the one hand, lodges and the spatial practices that occur within them are closely tied to their particular sites and large political and social forces. On the other hand, perhaps more than responding to the specificities of life in Cape Town, these Somali lodges respond to populations in flux across the continent, along with particular established practices. Ahmed's idea to start a lodge originates from his brief stop in Nairobi and his stay in Eastleigh, an area known for its large Somali population along with Somali malls, hotels and guest houses (Carrier & Lochery, 2013). As discussed at the outset of this chapter, the emergence of mixed-use shopping and residential accommodation characterises the area of Eastleigh and has been described in response to a growing refugee population from the late 1980s, often told through the "universal story" of Garissa Lodge, frequently described as the first Somali Mall.

There are significant similarities in the stories told of these lodges and the proprietors who started them. In the case of both Asha, the founder of Garissa Lodge, and Ahmed, the originator of Som City, the lodge is narrated as located ambivalently between personal profit, the precarious present and a potentially profitable and prosperous future. As Bhabha (1994) reminds us, in relation to the 'the chapati' story it does not necessarily matter whether the narrative is factual. Instead he suggests that we pay attention to the performative nature of the story's narration. Ahmed's description of Som City clearly positions it in relation to Eastleigh and Garissa Lodge. He therefore narrates his own experience as part of a "universal story", situating Som City within a lineage of informal malls and lodges across the continent, all of which have been formed in the context of a civil war in Somali and a large forcedly mobile population. These universals and their repetition are as much about the particular sites they refer to, which are very real, and the narratives of hope for physical and social mobility they suggest in their circulation. As such, the narrations offer us a subaltern form of spatial knowledge about a series of trans-national homes.

Yet this is not to suggest that these spaces are necessarily ideal. As described above, the accommodation provided in Som City is rudimentary. In a retelling of these spaces, Ben Rawlence (2016), for example, relates his interlocutor's experience as follows: "The walls were entirely bare, grubby with the routine of men and work. It was a vessel for sleeping, nothing more. Everything spoke of transience [...] in that sense, it was just like a camp" (p. 260). He emphasises the "bare life" of these spaces, where the material deprivation is foregrounded and choices are limited, where these lodges in Eastleigh mirror those of Dadaab refugee camp. However, a more complex view emerges when one sees these sites as part of a trajectory of spaces that connect Somalia with the border refugee camps such as Dadaab in Kenya and with various urban centres in South Africa. On this journey a further site that emerged as significant is Lusaka in Zambia. In recounting his experience of attempting to travel to South Africa, Mahmoud, a Somali refugee, described a motel of sorts in Lusaka, Zambia, run by a woman known as "Mama Asha". He said of her, "This lady would allow the travelling Somalis and Ethiopians to stay at her home. She also owned a small motel there. If someone could afford to pay her for her hospitality, she would ask for payment. If someone did not have money to pay her, she would allow him or her to stay there free of charge."[10] This description closely echoes what was told to me in Cape Town and Nairobi, where the emergence of lodges as profitable businesses is not at the expense of offering refuge and hospitality without pay. The area where "Mama Asha's Motel" was located was described as similar to Eastleigh, Nairobi. Mama Asha was a Somali refugee herself, and "everybody knew her". Mama Asha's "establishment" was part of a trajectory for Mahmoud that included Dhobley and Liboi refugee camps which are on either side of the Kenya-Somalia border and Dar-es-Salaam in Tanzania. Som City in Cape Town is therefore one point of refuge on a much longer journey. These refugee homes are therefore both specific and located sites, and exceed the framing and boundaries of the nation state in a methodological and physical sense.

Conclusion

The description of a series of similar kinds of lodges in other parts of the continent points to these Somali malls as being part of a wider network of similar spaces that in many cases posit refugee camps as one point on a longer trajectory of multiple sites. In these lodges, guest houses or motels, the transient and mostly refugee populations renting beds daily are not in opposition to a recognition of these spaces as relatively stable sites of refuge and a space for a better future. As Mahmoud has noted, referring primarily to groups of East African refugees, "everybody knows" about these sites. And, as the various vignettes above describe, there are similar kinds of spaces found in cities such as Nairobi, Lusaka, Johannesburg and Cape Town. Central to recognising the importance of these sites is recognising the spatiality of the stories that circulate about

Figure 6. Ahmed's Journey to Cape Town, drawing by author.

them. As De Certeau (1984) asserts, "Every story is a travel story and a spatial practice" (p. 115). De Certeau extends this to argue that narratives are not only descriptive but also produce "geographies of action" (ibid., p.116). He therefore argues that stories are not simply a translation of actions into language, but are instead essential to the organisation of actions. I suggest that it is in these narratives of refugees, and the stories they tell about where they have been and will go, that we find the knowledge of the extended spatialities that are actively reconfiguring regional relationships of home for Somali refugees. Yet, as De Certeau also reminds us, the story privileges "a logic of ambiguity", pointing to the ambivalence of the lodge as home (ibid., p. 128).

Recognising these lodges as home-like might further support understandings of refugees' lives on the continent beyond the limited space of the camp. However, as Dayaratne and Kellet (2008) point out, it is important to recognise that some homes are not necessarily good homes or houses. Indeed, many of these lodges are materially deficient spaces and are formed in the context of forced migration. Their home-making, drawing on familial and faith-based networks, is therefore intimately linked to other forms of home-unmaking, both within and beyond national contexts. These are spaces that offer safety from wider conflicts, but also from violence within the country of refuge. Thus, while it is important to recognise how people find ways of making homes, it is not to valorise these kinds of spaces as they are potentially also spaces of poverty, lack of privacy and possibly exploitation. The lodges are particular spaces, such as Som City, formed in the context of a localised spatial politics and simultaneously as part of a longer and more extensive narration of precarity and possibility.

Taking the narrations and narratives of refugees themselves seriously is a methodological and epistemological positioning to recognise forms of subaltern spatial knowledge and a radically different archive. This chapter therefore builds on the work of authors such as Anooradha Iyer Siddiqi (2020), who argues that taking the refugee's concerns and problematics seriously requires an epistemic shift to understand the refugee as not only and always a passive subject (Fiddian-Qasmiyeh 2020). The lodges discussed in this chapter, from Nairobi to Cape Town, illustrate that the lodge as a kind of home is not simply a symbol or an abstraction. These are very real material spaces tied into histories of colonial planning, refugee policies and the ongoing racialisation of migration. Drawing out the longer histories of these sites through interviews and oral histories means moving beyond the archive of the nation state and NGO or humanitarian network. This chapter points to the ways in which refugee populations negotiate the deep unequal terrains of global capital and global mobility (Nyamnjoh, 2004, p. 44), while remaining active within a precarious politics of care (Simone, 2018). The chapter therefore contributes to a decolonial methodological positioning, in recognising subaltern knowledge formations which point to how displaced populations assemble new spatial and material nodes as a way of overcoming formal exclusion.

Acknowledgement

A part of this chapter has previously been published as part of the essay series Coloniality of Infrastructure (e-flux Architecture, 2021).

Notes

1. Interview with Mohammed, 2018; Interview with Mama Layla, 2018.
2. All the names of interviewees have been changed. This research was conducted in accordance with UCL Ethics guidance projects 5505/001 and 5505/002, and all data were collected and stored in accordance with the UK Data Protection Act of 1998.
3. Mama Layla, 2018.
4. Carrier and Lochery (2013) note the year 1992 as the date on which Garissa Lodge mall officially opened with 92 shops inside (p. 337). Yet in interviews it became apparent that there was a slow transition from more residential to more trade.
5. On the subject of Eastleigh as a site of urban refugee networks see also: Al-Sharmani 2007; Campbell 2006a; Campbell 2006b; Carrier 2017; Omeje & Mwangi 2014; Rinelli & Opondo 2013.
6. The estimates for 2013 are of 565,520 asylum seekers and refugees in the country. Yet, in 2009 alone, there were 220,000 new applicants. South African police force estimates from 2008 suggest that there are 3–6 million undocumented migrants in the country, with other estimates suggesting 8–10 million (Forced Migration Studies Program at Wits, 2009). 6 million would be around 11 per cent of the South African population. The Southern African Migration Project suggests that numbers are closer to 2-3 million.
7. Interview with Ahmed, 2015.
8. Interview with John, 2014; interview with Patel, 2014.
9. Interview with Ahmed, 2015.
10. Interview with Mohmoud 2014.

References

Ahmed. (2015). Interview: Manager of Som City, February 6, 2015.

Al-Sharmani, M. (2007). Contemporary Migration and Transnational Families: The Case of Somali Diaspora(s). Paper presented at the *Migration and Refugee Movements in the Middle East and North Africa, Forced Migration and Refugee Studies Programme*, American University of Cairo, Egypt, October 23–25.

Amit, R. (2012). "Elusive Justice: Somali Traders' Access to Formal and Informal Justice Mechanisms in the Western Cape." Johannesburg: African Centre for Migration and Society Research Report.

Baxter, R., & Brickell, K. (2014). For Home Unmaking. *Home Cultures,* 11(2), 133–43.

Bhabha, H. K. (1994). *The Location of Culture*. London: Routledge.

Blunt, A. (2005). "Cultural Geography: Cultural Geographies of Home." *Progress in Human Geography* 29(4), 505–15.

Blunt, A., & Dowling, R. eds. (2006). *Home: Key Ideas in Geography* Oxon: Routledge.

Boccagni, P. (2017). *Migration and the Search for Home: Mapping Domestic Space in Migrants' Everyday Lives*. New York: Palgrave MacMillan.

Buchli, V., & Lucas, G. (2001). The Archaeology of Alienation: A Late Twentieth-Century British Council House, In *Archaeologies of the Contemporary Past*, (eds. Buchli, V and Lucas, G.) London: Routledge.

Campbell, E. H. (2006a). *Urban Refugees in Nairobi: Problems of Protection, Mechanisms of Survival, and Possibilities for Integration*. Journal of Refugee Studies, 19, 396-413.

Campbell, E. H. (2006b). Economic Globalization From Below: Transitional Refugee Trade Networks in Nairobi. In *Cities in Contemporary Africa*, (Eds. Murray, MJ & Myers, G A), New York: Palgrave MacMillan, 125-147.

Carrier, N., & Lochery, E. (2013). Missing states? Somali trade networks and the Eastleigh transformation. *Journal of East African studies*, 7(2), 334-352.

Carrier, N. (2017). Little Mogadishu: Eastleigh, Nairobi"s Global Somali Hub. Hurst Publishers: London.

Cieraad, I. (ed.) (1999). *At Home: An Anthropology of Domestic Space*. Syracuse: Syracuse University Press.

Dayaratne, R., & Kellet, P. (2008). Housing and Home-Making in Low-Income Urban Settlements: Sri Lanka and Colombia. *House and the Built Environment*, 23, 53– 70.

Dossa, P., & Golubovic, J. (2019). Reimagining Home in the Wake of Displacement. *Studies in Social Justice*, 13(1), 171-186.

De Certeau, M. (1984). *The Practice of Everyday Life*. Berkeley: University of California Press.

Douglas, M. (1991). The Idea of a Home: A Kind of Space. *Social Research* 58 (1), 287–307.

Feldman, I. (2006). Home as Refrain: Remembering and Living Displacement in Gaza. *History and Memory*, 18(2), 10-47.

Fiddian-Qasmiyeh, E. (2020) Introduction. In Elena Fiddian-Qasmiyeh (ed.), *Refuge in a Moving World* (pp. 1-19). London: UCL Press.

hooks, b. (1990a). Homeplace: A Site of Resistance. In b. hooks, *Yearning: Race, Gender, and Cultural Politics* (pp. 41-49). Boston, MA: South End Press.

hooks, b. (1990b). Choosing the Margin as a Space of Radical Openness, In b. hooks, *Yearning: Race, Gender, and Cultural Politics* (pp. 145-153). Boston, MA: South End Press.

Landau, L., and Segatti, A. (2011). *Contemporary Migration to South Africa*. Washington D.C.: International Bank for Reconstruction and Development, World Bank.

Lopez, S. L. (2010). The Remittance House. *Buildings and Landscapes*, 17(2), 33-52.

Malaquais, D. (2004). Douala/ Johannesburg/ New York: Cityscapes Imagined. In S. Parnell, E. Pieterse, A. Simone, & M. van Donk (eds.), *Dark Roast Occasional Paper Series. 20*, Cape Town: Isandla Institute.

Mama Layla. (2018). Interview, December 2018. Nairobi.

Meeus, B., Arnaut, K., & van Heur, B. (eds.) (2019). *Arrival Infrastructures: Migration and Urban Social Mobilities*. Cham: Palgrave MacMillan.

Meyer, W. (2010a). Bellville Hostel Gives Shelter to Fleeing Somalis. *Saturday Argus*, July 17.

Meyer, W. (2010b). Bellville Turns into "Som City" Refuge. *Saturday Star*, July 17.

Mohammed. (2018). Interview, December 2018. Nairobi.

Mohmoud, A. (2014). English Transcription of Oral History Interview with Ahmed.

Mohmoud, July 13, Minneapolis. Minnesota Oral History Project.

Nicholson, Z. (2011b). "Somalis Find a Safe Haven in Bellville." *Cape Times*, May 11, 8.

Nyamnjoh, F. B. (2004). "Globalisation, Boundaries and Livelihoods: Perspectives on Africa." *Identity Culture and Politics*, vol.5, no.1 & 2, 37-59.

Jinnah, Z. (2010). Making Home in a Hostile Land: Understanding Somali Identity, Integration, Livelihood and Risks in Johannesburg. *Journal of Sociology and Social Anthropology 1*(1-2), 91–99.

John. (2014). Interview: building manager for Patel, August 25.

Miller, D. (1987). *Material Culture and Mass Consumption*. Oxford: Basil Blackwell, 1987.

Omeje, K., & Mwangi, J. (2014). Business Travails in the Diaspora: The Challenges and Resilience of Somali Refugee Business Community in Nairobi, Kenya. *Journal of Third World Studies, 31*(1), 185–217.

Patel. (2014). Interview: Landlord Oriental Plaza and Bellville Station mall, August 25.

Rawlence, B. (2016). *City of Thorns*. London: Portobello Books.

Rinelli, L. & Opondo, S. O. (2013). Affective Economies: Eastleigh's metalogistics, urban anxieties and the mapping of diasporic city life. *African and Black Dias*pora, 6, 236-250.

Ripero-Muniz, N. & Fayad, S. (2016). Metropolitan Nomads: A Journey through Jo'burg's "Little Mogadishu". *Anthropology Southern Africa 39*(3), 232– 240.

Sadouni, S. (2009). 'God is Not Unemployed': Journeys of Somali Refugees in Johannesburg. *African Studies 68*(2), 235–49.

Siddiqi. A. (2020). "The University and the Camp." *Ardeth*, 6, 137 – 151.

Simone, A. (2018). *Improvised Lives: Rhythms of Endurance in an Urban South*. Cambridge: Polity Press.

Tayob, H. (2019). Architecture-by-migrants: the porous infrastructures of Bellville. *Anthropology Southern Africa, 42*(1), 46-58.

Tayob, H. (2017). Fatima's Shop: A Kind of Homeplace. In H. Frichot, C. Gabrielsson, & H. Runting (eds.). *Architecture and Feminisms* (pp. 265-270). London: Routledge.

CHAPTER 16

Static Displacement, Adaptive Domesticity

The Three Temporary Geographies of Firing Zone 918, Palestine

Wafa Butmeh
Urban Planner

Introduction: Opening reflections on the new concept of 'Static Displacement'

> It is like time has stopped for the past 71 years. It is with sorrow that I say that Masafer Yatta in the early 1940s was more developed than Masafer Yatta in 2019.
> Com. 1, 2019.

With this testimony the community representative established a direct relationship between oppressive life under Israeli military occupation and the constructed notion of time within the area of Masafer Yatta, also referred to as Firing Zone 918. Masafer Yatta, which could be translated into English as 'the outskirts of Yatta', is a cluster of 18 nomadic communities, scattered to the south of the city of Yatta in the Governorate of Hebron, South Palestine (IPCC, 2013). Control over this area was intended to serve Israeli military purposes, in addition to protecting the illegal settlements' enterprise. Consequently, the authority to govern movement and development within this closed military zone was placed under the jurisdiction of the Israeli military commander, as designated by military laws (Shalev & Cohen-Lifshitz, 2008). For the 1,500 Palestinians living in Masafer Yatta this meant extreme restrictions and the prohibition of any sort of activity within 35,000 dunums of their lands (IPCC, 2013) (Fig. 1. and Fig. 2.). Nevertheless, the community continues to survive and endure the various difficulties, facing the daily threat of forced eviction and uprooting from their homes.

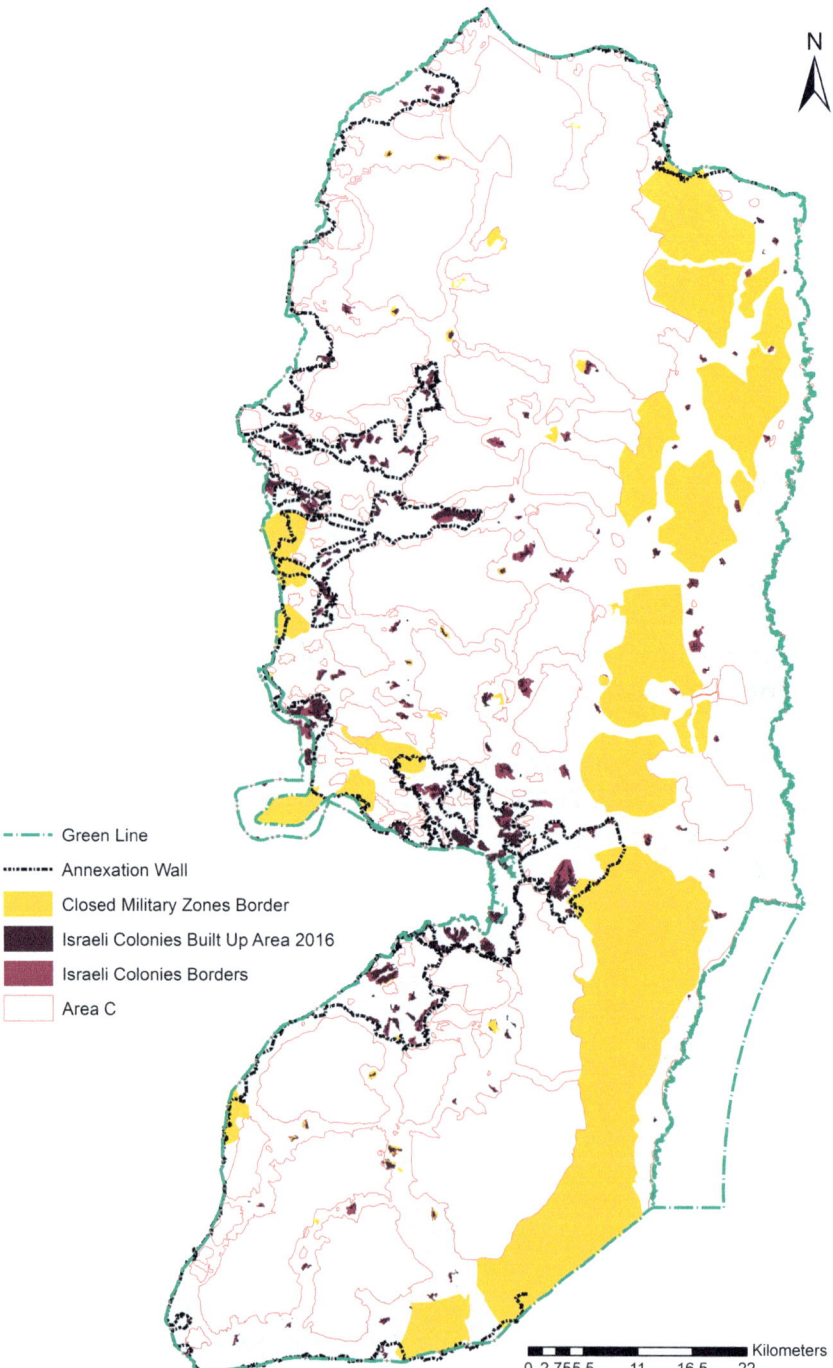

Figure 1. Map of the closed military zones in the West Bank; sourced from MoLG (2018), and produced by a researcher.

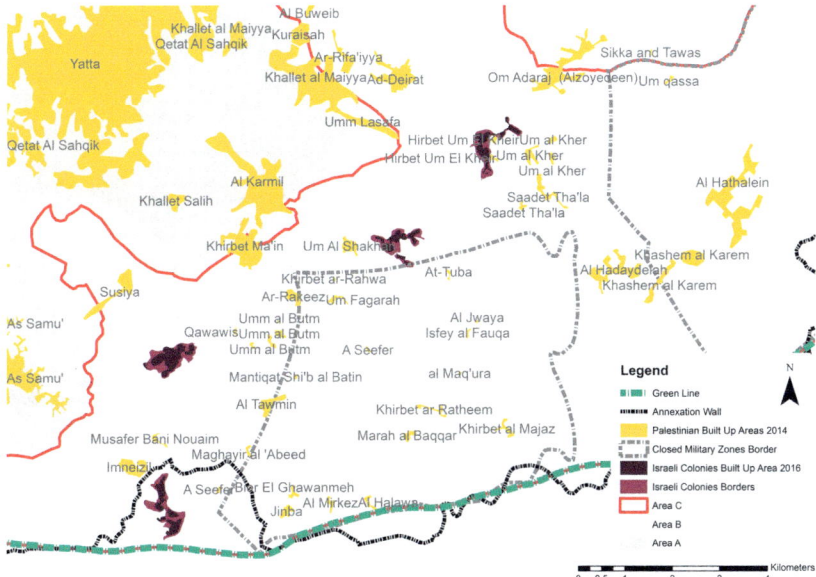

Figure 2. A geopolitical overlay of maps of Masafer Yatta; sourced from MoLG (2018) and produced by the author.

Nowadays Masafer Yatta resembles a unique case within the Palestinian spatial, political, social and economic fabric (Fig. 3.). The restrictions imposed on the community's development can easily be interpreted through the building typologies in Masafar Yatta and the availability of infrastructural networks. Photographer Eduardo Soteras Jalil (2014) described the landscape of Masafer Yatta by saying: "This is the story of Masafer Yatta, a space inside another space, a world that is stranger to everyone […] it's the life of people that live very close to the ground, so close that many of them sleep in its womb, in caves that they, their grandparents, and their great grandparents' dag" (cf. Fig. 4., Fig. 5., and Fig. 6.).

This chapter addresses a form of intersection between making homes and displacement by introducing home-making practices as tools utilised by threatened communities in order to respond to and resist forced displacement. More particularly, this chapter addresses the relationship between the constructed notion of time and the implications of the declaration of Masafer Yatta to be a closed military zone on the spatio-temporal dimensions of livelihood within the communities. In this regard the relationship will be explored by assuming that Firing Zone 918 operates as a unique entity, where the perceived pace of time is regulated by the specific hegemonic and counter-hegemonic practices within the boundaries of the closed military zone. The chapter draws on community testimonies and the oral histories of Masafer Yatta in an attempt to shed light on a rarely explored facet within the broader discourse of displacement.

Figure 3. A hamlet in Masafer Yatta; photo taken in 2014 by the author as part of a UN-Habitat project.

It also introduces the concept of 'Static Displacement' theoretically to unpack 71 years of consciously developing and regulating the communally perceived notions of time and space on different scales inside the entity of this closed military zone, and to employ these constructed notions as tools in the hands of the community to counter the threats of physical displacement imposed by military orders. While the act of displacement is usually attributed to the physical movement of a population, the discussion of the case of static displacement entails rethinking the spatio-temporal aspects that could characterise different geographical realities. This is based on the distinction between the geobody, as a neutral definition of space, and geography, as the construction of socio-cultural practices in time and space (Abrams & Hall, 2006). Thus, static displacement can occur when a certain group of people experiences a shift from one geographical reality to another while remaining physically in place within the same geobody.

The distinction between 'geobody' and 'geography' is particularly relevant within the Palestinian context, where claiming domination over the land represents the core ideology of the Zionist colonial project that has been carrying out a systematic act of ethnic cleansing of the land from its indigenous Palestinian residents by fulfilling the claim of a "land without people" (Khamasisi, 2014). In consequence, Palestinians were put in a position to counter such a hegemonic project by reclaiming their right to the land. On the other hand, the occupation power and the occupied Palestinian communities have been utilising the same Palestinian land for different purposes, supported by different

Figure 4 & 5. Interior shots of a cave in Masafer Yatta; photos taken by Jalil (2014).

socio-cultural, political and ideological claims, where the geobody is rendered differently in the narrative of each party (Khamasisi, 2014). The case of Masafer Yatta illustrates how the two geographical realities of the occupier and the occupied are interpreted and utilised by the dominated community as a tool of prolonged resistance and where the ongoing construction of geography is consciously practised to mitigate the threat of physical displacement.

With the same population remaining within the same geobody, the two changing attributes in a static displacement process are geographical reality and the temporal dimension. Thus, as static displacement takes place, the same geobody operates according to various conceptions of time. Nevertheless, it is important to note that the notion of time has always been socially constructed within certain cultural norms: "[i]n fact, in any culture, we seem to operate comfortably with switchable concepts of time" (Davis, 2012). This understanding of time goes beyond the field of social sciences to reach the arena of natural and cosmic sciences as well. For example, Roville (2017) denies the absolute nature of time, emphasising that what physics describes when measuring time is the local time of an event and it then compares those local times with each other. In this method, time is thought of as a network of local times rather than one linear scale. However, theoretically to conceptualise the temporal dimension of the static displacement process, the concept of 'rhythm', as introduced by Henri Lefebvre, provides a comprehensive framework to study the interrelations of time, space and humans in the scope of everyday life (Maycroft, 2015).

Lefebvre's attempts to think about space and time differently but also together entails the development of the 'rhythm analysis' where he conceptualised rhythm as the unifying concept of space and time. Rhythms simply exist wherever and whenever there is an interaction between time and space, whether in the form of linear or cyclical rhythms. Linear rhythms are associated with the succession of events and are usually characterised by a beginning and an end, while cyclical rhythms last for a while and then restart, and are mostly attributed to cosmic and natural phenomena such as days, nights and seasons

(Lefebvre, 1992). This concept of rhythms provides a theoretical framework for analysing the spatio-temporal dimensions of the geographies of the occupier and the occupied in Masafer Yatta. Arguably, three geographical realities are operative: 1) the geographical reality before the declaration of the military zone, which will be referred to here as the 'domestic geography' of Masafer Yatta; 2) 'the military zone geography', governed by the Israeli commandership and monitored regularly by Israeli soldiers and military technologies such as aerial photography and drones; and 3) an 'adaptive geography', which emerges out of the community's interpretation of the military geography.

Static displacement occurs when the community of Masafer Yatta reidentifies the rhythms generated in each geographical reality to reidentify the spatio-temporal character of the geobody, and thus it could be argued that the geographical reality transfers within the geobody accordingly. In order to demonstrate how the concept of Static Displacement is manifested in the case of Masafer Yatta this chapter explores how the implications of the geopolitical situation on the spatio-temporal patterns in Masafer Yatta as a point of departure then to discuss three temporary geographies of Masafer Yatta, where the concept of home-making is tackled on a larger scale by considering home to be a territorial and temporal entity where a group of people share a sense of communal livelihood and social ties. In this sense, the homemakers are not yet refugees or a forcefully displaced population; they are the indigenous residents of the territory who are anticipating and resisting their displacement.

Figure 6. Exterior shot of a cave in Masafer Yatta; photo taken by Jalil (2014).

The geopolitical situation and the spatio-temporal dimension in Masafer Yatta

Understanding the contemporary spatio-temporal patterns in Masafer Yatta cannot be separated from understanding the geopolitical situation and its implications for the development of certain spatio-temporal patterns in the everyday life of Masafer Yatta's community. In fact, the complex geopolitical situation in Masafer Yatta impacts on every aspect of the life of the community. One way to disentangle the relationship between the geopolitical situation and the community is by investigating how geopolitics frame the spatio-temporal dimension. In the context of this research and concerning the community's perception of the passage of time, which was expressed in the phrase: "[i]t is like time has stopped for 71 years", the metaphor of a 'frozen time bubble' arguably captures the relationship between the geopolitical situation and the spatio-temporal dimension in Masafer Yatta. According to the perception of the community, the geopolitical situation has restricted its ability to accommodate its growing needs, whether the population growth, its ability to expand spatially in terms of building and construction, or having the option to develop in terms of technologies and infrastructure (Com.1, 2018). The declaration of Firing Zone 918 has spatially and temporally segregated Masafer Yatta as a geopolitical entity from the surrounding communities and lands, imposing very restrictive rhythms over the area and thus establishing a frozen time bubble when compared to Yatta, for example, or on another extreme end, when compared to the surrounding illegal Israeli settlements. However, the establishment of the frozen time bubble is not limited to the declaration of the firing zone; rather it is traced back to the War of 1948 when the Negev (the southern extent of Masafer Yatta) fell under Israeli occupation and was then followed by several geopolitical demarcations depriving the community of its right to develop.

As a region Masafer Yatta is cartographically defined by four lines, each delineating a different spatio-legal territory. The first is the demarcation line marked in the 1949 Armistice Agreements, which were signed following the 1948 War between the Israeli army and neighbouring Arab countries, also referred to as the Green Line. Nowadays, this line serves as the de facto border of the State of Israel. Nevertheless, in 1949, it was intended only as a demarcation line and not a permanent border (Sella, 1986). The second line is the Area C territories, a term which refers to the areas within the West Bank that are under full Israeli control, both civic and military, according to the Declaration of Principles on Interim Self-Government Arrangements (Oslo Accords, 1993-1995). The signing of the Oslo Accords, as the foundation for a Palestinian Interim Self-Government in the West Bank and Gaza for a transitional period of five years, was geopolitically translated into the classification of the West Bank into three geopolitical clusters: Area A, which comprises around 18 per cent of the West Bank (mainly including the major urban centres) is under full Palestinian control; Area B, comprising around 22 per cent of the West Bank, is under shared control, where the Israeli Government controls security matters and the Palestinian Government controls civil matters; and the third, Area C, which comprises almost 60 per cent of the West Bank including agricultural and vacant lands and areas inhabited by Bedouin and semi-nomadic communities, in addition to areas established as illegal Israeli settlements prior to Oslo, (Shalev & Cohen-Lifshitz, 2008). The third line is the closed military zone territory, identifying areas that are designated as closed military zones or firing zones, usually utilised as training areas for the Israeli military forces (Etkes, 2015). The fourth line is the planned path of the Segregation and Separation Wall, which serves to define the frontiers of Israel (IPCC, 2013).

The geopolitical demarcations in Masafer Yatta place absolute power in the hands of the Israeli Government, which manipulates the laws and regulations and adopts a very selective, discriminatory formula in implementing such regulations (Shalev & Cohen-Lifshitz, 2008). This manipulation of legal patterns attributed to the geopolitical divisions is a tool of an indirect transfer policy exercised against the Palestinian population, especially in border areas similar to Masafer Yatta, where their lands used to expand to reach the village of "Arad" in the occupied Negev (Aloni, 2016). In the negotiations, which took place in the United Nations, before the 1948 War regarding the division of Historical Palestine between the two states of Palestine and Israel, Negev was allocated as part of the future Palestinian state. Conversely, after the war, Negev was occupied and annexed by the Israeli occupation. Immediately after that, the Israeli Knesset discussed minimising the Arab population in Negev and Israel in general. This was advocated to be done by adopting direct and indirect transfer measures. For example, Moshe Sharett, the second Prime Minister of Israel, had said in the early 1950s that Israel cannot achieve its goal of evicting Arab minorities merely by military forces, adding that measures should be taken to undermine the rights of Arabs living in occupied territories in 1948, yielding to their migration (Masalha, 2002).

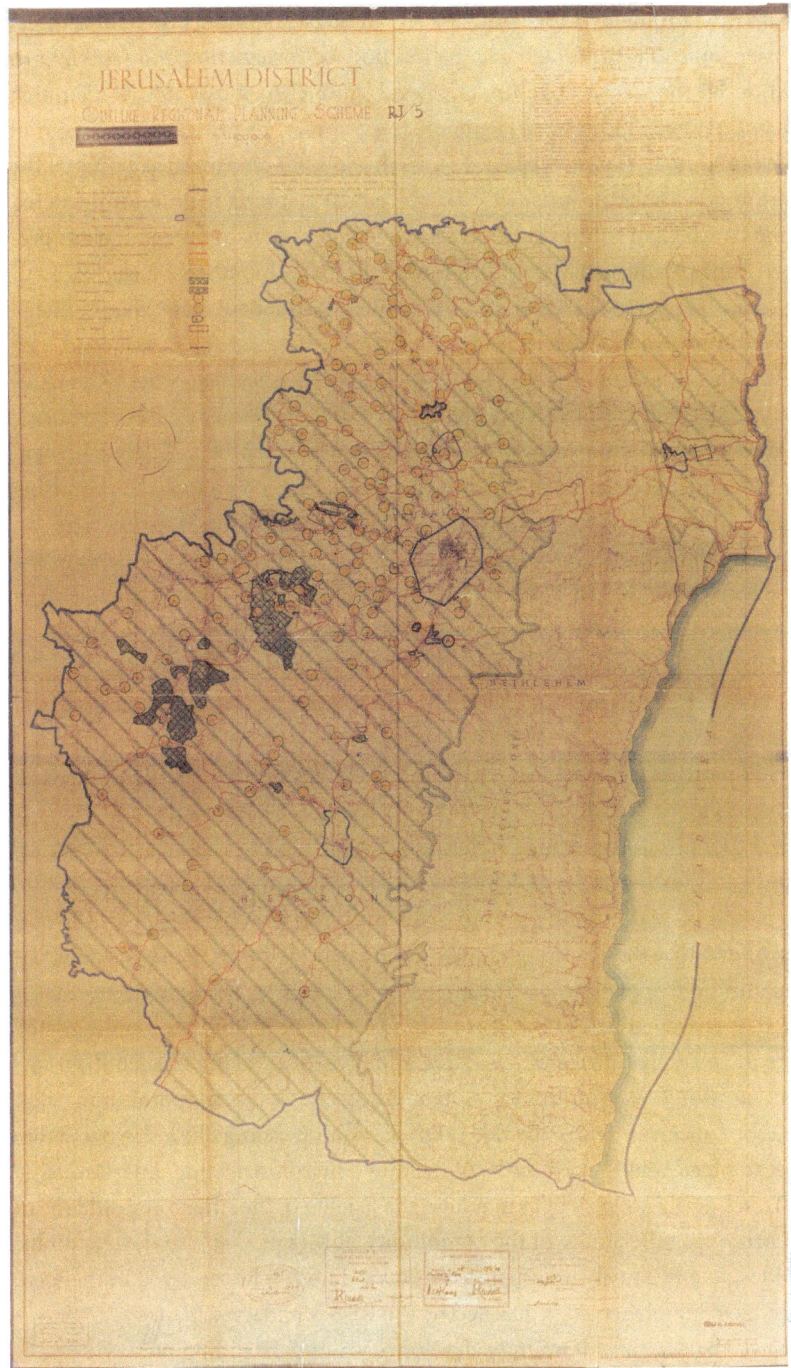

Figure 7. RJ5 Mandatory Plan; sourced from MoLG (2018).

Urban planning and regulations were amongst the most powerful indirect transfer tools that the Israeli occupation utilised for eviction and land appropriation by the Israeli State under a legal guise (Khamaisi, 1997). "Planning practice has been militarized [...] there is a complete prioritization in favour of Israeli interests" (Hague et al., 2015). In the specific case of Masafer Yatta, the entire area is under the jurisdiction of the Israeli planning regime administered by the Israeli Civil Administration (ICA), which harnesses outdated plans prepared under the British Mandate in the late 1930s and 1940s as a basis for "issuing" planning permits (IPCC, 2013). The British Mandate Plans were initiated as diagrammatic maps that illustrate urban centres and the major land uses outside those centres on a district scale across Historical Palestine (Khamaisi, 1997). The Mandate plans had demonstrated Arab-Jewish duality, favouring the development of the Jewish community, an aspect which was very much endorsed by the International Jewish community, which anticipated a promising vision in those plans for the progress of Jewish colonies in Palestine. The two plans covering the West Bank are the S-15 Plan for the Northern parts of the West Bank, approved in 1948, and the RJ-5 Plan (Fig. 7.) for Jerusalem district including Masafer Yatta, approved in 1942 (Crookston, 2017).

Until 1942 the British Mandate RJ-5 Plan was the only approved plan to which the ICA referred and which it interpreted in terms of planning and building activities in the area of Masafer Yatta. According to RJ-5, Masafer Yatta is partly classified as an agricultural and pasture zone, while the rest of the area is marked as desert (IPCC, 2013). The ICA uses these classifications as a legal tool to reject planning applications submitted by the Palestinian community and further to issue demolition orders for any built structures that do not obtain official building permits issued by the ICA (IPCC, 2013). Hence, it is argued that the planning regime dominated by the Israeli military is manipulating the spatio-temporal dimension by pushing for keeping the status quo that prevailed in 1942 as it is or for a worse situation based on outdated plans in a way that disregards the goal and level of detailing of such diagrammatic drawings. Within the Israeli planning system, the temporal dimension could be conceived as an extruded point of time, operating like a sharp line that separates legal and illegal objects of the built environment, and any attempt by the Israeli planning system to maintain the legality of the situation would mean compromising the ability of the community of Masafer Yatta to develop; thus, the local community's constructed notion of time will be rendered in the form of a frozen bubble which is guarded by the RJ-5 Mandatory Plan.

Nevertheless, the community developed an understanding of how demolition orders operate in terms of time; in other words, the Palestinian community was able to conceptualise the temporal dimension of demolition orders, which would normally consist of hiring a lawyer and therefore submitting petitions to the court and awaiting court hearings, a lengthy process which the community would describe as "buying time" (Com.1, 2018). The result was that the number of buildings that were demolished on the ground had always been much smaller in comparison with the total number of buildings that received demolition orders (IPCC, 2013). On 30 April 2019, the use of the mandatory plans as a restrictive wall took an escalated approach, as the Israeli High Court approved Order No.1797, which states that the Israeli military is authorised to demolish any new building in Area C of the West Bank within 96 hours of receiving a demolition order. This drastic change in the Israeli military's approach is designed to be implemented in pilot zones devoid of possible planning, including Firing Zone 918 (Haqel, 2019). This has not just altered the previous conception of the temporal dimension of demolition orders but has affected the overall spatio-temporal aspect of Masafer Yatta, which shall be explained in the following section.

Reflections on methodology and positionality

In November 2013, while I was part of a field surveyors' team conducting a physical and demographic survey in Masafer Yatta, I became curious about the exterior image of the dwellings, mainly one-roomed shacks built of concrete hollow blocks and covered with a piece of fabric. What intrigued me was the piece of fabric, as it did not have any functional or structural value according to my limited technical knowledge as an architect and urban planner. Several hours into the fieldwork, I asked a resident about that piece of fabric, and her initial reaction was to lean towards me and lower the tone of her voice as if she was revealing a secret and say: "we use this fabric so as the buildings will look like tents when photographed by the Israeli military balloon, we want the buildings to look temporary to avoid receiving demolition orders". Her answer drew my attention to the concepts of temporality and permanence and the role of everyday living practices as community tools of resilience in the context of military occupation and forced displacement. This research is a compilation of semi-structured interviews conducted over three periods: spring 2014, summer 2018 and winter 2019. The latter two consisted of the most structured interviews discussing the temporal dimension of everyday living and space in Masafer Yatta.

The fieldwork in 2018 and 2019 included interviews with community members (two men and one woman), in addition to the head of Masafer Yatta Local Council. While the direct quotations in this chapter are from interviews conducted with community members, our research also included interviews with other stakeholders, one being the chief urban planner responsible for the preparation of local outline plans for the hamlets of Masafer Yatta (2018), the head of surveying and the GIS Department (man) and the head of the Planning Department (woman) at the Ministry of Local Government (2018), the official national governmental body following up on the issue of planning and regulation in Masafer Yatta, a humanitarian officer (man) from OHCHR working directly in the field with the local community of Masafer Yatta, and the main lawyers (two women) following up on the legal proceedings with the court.

In addition to the interviews conducted, the research included a review of legal and planning documents with a focus on how time is being tackled in these documents (directly or indirectly), and a reflection on these documents as products in time; included among this are the reviewed plans, planning laws, legal documents, proceedings and decisions of the Israeli High Court. For the purpose of exploring the relationship between the spatio-temporal patterns generated by the Israeli military occupation and the everyday life of the community inside the closed military zone, I will now proceed to compare them to the everyday life of the community prior to the declaration of the military zone, that is, what I have referred to as the 'domestic geography'.

Masafer Yatta: Three geographical realities

The domestic geography of Masafer Yatta, before 1948

Exploring the spatio-temporal characteristics of Masafer Yatta begins with understanding the references to the mobile lifestyle indicated by the word "Masafer", which is derived from the noun "Safar" meaning travel in Arabic (IPCC, 2013). The head of the local council of Masafer Yatta describes the cyclical rhythms of the community and their temporal patterns as follows:

> The name 'Masafer' is derived from the Arabic word *safar*, which means travel. This is due to the mobility of the community. Masafer Yatta's community is neither a Bedouin community nor a settled farmers' one, but rather a hybrid between the two. Its annual calendar consists of three seasonal destinations. One in the summer to Yatta, where people harvest figs and grapes from their fields in the city. The second one begins at the end of summer until the beginning of spring in Masafer Yatta, where families move to graze their sheep and cultivate their lands on the outskirts of the city. Finally,

the third trip happens in spring, where shepherds travel further south, towards the Negev, and temporarily reside in tents in order to graze their flocks during spring. Thus, this demonstrates how the community of Masafer Yatta is mainly dependent on livestock and agriculture. (Com.1, 2018).

Considering the 'rhythm analysis', as introduced by Lefebvre, as a theoretical framework for discussing the three temporary geographies of Masafer Yatta, the transhumance living prior to the year 1948 resembles an overall cyclical rhythm with an interval of one year between each repetitive cycle. In this case, the annual cycle consists of three seasonal cycles that collectively contribute to the overall livelihood of the community. This composition of cyclical rhythms was organically developed through the interaction between the residents of Masafer Yatta and the economic potentials presented within seasons and spaces. Thus, it could be argued that Masafer Yatta as a geographical body was developed as one destination within the broader spatio-temporal patterns economically utilised by the community. In other words, the farming and herding community of Masafer Yatta was able to establish a cyclical rhythm that corresponded to the suitability of the land and seasons to growing crops and grazing livestock as the two major sources of income.

It is evident that natural rhythms are embodied within the cyclical rhythms of the community since the efficiency of the production cycle of agriculture and grazing cannot be sustained separately from natural cycles of resources with little to no interference with the rigid grids that were imposed by modern nation-state ideologies of abstraction and control. Despite the fact that the city of Yatta was its summer destination, the community of Masafer Yatta has managed to figure out a way of living that contrasted with the settled urbanised rhythms established by the modern nation-state in Yatta, at that time the British Mandate. Nevertheless, the two contrasting rhythms coexisted in a beneficial manner, as Masafer Yatta developed to serve as the food basket of the Southern Hebron region. Masafer Yatta used to supply the market of Yatta with wheat, meat and other dairy products (Com.1, 2018).

The closed military zone geography

The closed military zone geography severely alters the spatio-temporal dimensions of the 'domestic geography' of Masafer Yatta. The Israeli occupation, through the militarised legal system, has imposed a linear rhythm that begins with the declaration of the closed military zone and continues to persist as long as this order is in force.

On 25 December 1972, the Israeli Military Commander declared Masafer Yatta a closed military zone, known as Firing Zone 918 (ACRI, 2013). Approximately 36,000 *dunams* of Masafer Yatta were designated as training ground for the Israeli military. This declaration has placed the area under the direct authority of the Israeli military commander, who has the power to determine what spatial practices are allowed within the borders of the closed military zone (Etkes, 2015). This also includes prohibition of the movement of people, livestock and goods across those boundaries. No-one shall enter, leave or remain in a closed military zone without the permission of the Israeli military commander. These procedures are implemented and enforced on the ground by mandates directed to Israeli military officers, who are authorised to expel from the firing zone anyone with no official permit. However, permanent residents who inhabited the land before the closure are exempted by law from being forcefully evicted from those areas. In this context, the definition of permanent residents remains a debatable issue, as the Israeli military uses a very strict formula to identify who is eligible to be considered as a permanent resident (Shalev & Cohen-Lifshitz, 2008).

In the specific case of Masafer Yatta, the declaration of the firing zone has been renewed twice since 1972, once in the early 1990s and again in May 1999 (ACRI, 2013). Nevertheless, the local community of Masafer Yatta was never officially informed by the Israeli government or military forces where the boundaries of the closed military zone lay, even though this could have been done by communicating official maps to the local community or by physically marking the borderlines on the ground. The only marks visible were some concrete blocks indicating that one was entering a firing zone, which were placed on the other side of the Green Line. Thus, families who were living on the occupied side in the 1948 War would see the signs only when crossing the borders to enter Masafer Yatta (Com.1, 2018).

It was not until November 1999, after the second renewal of the declaration of the firing zone, that the community representatives were able to obtain new maps showing the boundaries of Firing Zone 918 clearly. In that same year, the Israeli Military Forces invaded the hamlets following an eviction order issued against the community, and forcibly displaced around 700 residents, uprooting them from their houses along with all of their belongings, and forcing them to leave without any provision of shelter for the nearby village of Al Karmel (ACRI, 2013).

I remember this night as if it had happened yesterday. I was still a bride when we were forced out of our homes with all of our furniture, clothes and others; the caves were emptied and we were living in the streets (Com.2, 2019).

The evicted residents submitted petitions to the Israeli High Court, and in 2000 residents who had been evicted were allowed to return to their caves, fields and flocks in Masafer Yatta (ACRI, 2013). However, this came at a price, in the form of an interim injunction stating that the situation should be preserved and all forms of development activities including construction and cultivation were prohibited (ACRI, 2013). As the community representative describes it:

> Masafer Yatta was a hotel for sleeping and dwelling in only.
> (Com.1, 2018).

Almost twelve years later, in July 2012, the Israeli Ministry of Defence presented its position to the Israeli High Court, stating that Masafer Yatta is vital for the Israeli military, recommending that the need for the firing zone is maintained, and demanding to be allowed to evict the Palestinian residents. In his position, the Israeli Minister of Defence supported his demands by arguing that the residents of Masafer Yatta were not permanent residents who inhabited the closed area all year long even before the declaration of the firing zone (ACRI, 2013).

Nevertheless, it is important here to emphasise that restrictions on movement and alterations to the semi-nomadic lifestyle of the community took the form of indirect transfer measures in the guise of legal processes since 1948, immediately after the occupation of Palestine, and beyond, wherein the declaration of the firing zone added a more extreme layer of control. Such laws and regulations were implemented on the ground by three main actors: the Israeli Military Forces; the Environmental Protection Department; and the Israeli Civil Administration (ICA) (Shalev & Cohen-Lifshitz, 2008). In practical terms, those laws and regulations include, mainly, planning and regulating laws, which prohibit any kind of activity such as the construction of buildings, the erection of tents or fences, and even planting trees without the official approval and permit from the military commander and the ICA (Etkes, 2015). The Ottoman Land Law stipulated that any land found to be uncultivated for three consecutive years was automatically declared to be state property (Shalev & Cohen-Lifshitz, 2008). Finally, the Black Goat Law, which was endorsed by Israel in 1951and which forbids the grazing of black goats in lands outside the registered private property of the shepherd, including an individual dwelling or a private garden, with a special condition that one black goat is allowed to be owned for every 20 *dunums* of registered private land (Nature, 2017).

The execution of the linear rhythm imposed by the Israeli military orders is monitored through different actors and technologies, utilised by the occupation to register unauthorised activities, including sheep grazing, agriculture and construction. This also includes the presence of Israeli soldiers in Masafer Yatta on weekdays and regular aerial photographs of the area captured by a surveillance balloon. The community of Masafer Yatta was able to identify the frequency with which those monitoring activities occurred; for example, the surveillance balloon was observed to appear roaming over the hamlets of Masafer Yatta every three days, while the soldiers were seen almost daily on weekdays. Accordingly, it could be argued that the recurrence of the monitoring activities creates a cyclical rhythm that imposes the linearity of the military zone's spatio-temporal rhythms.

The monitoring of cyclical rhythms enforced by the Israeli military could be considered 'strategies' following De Certeau's definition, for they are hegemonic in nature and are imposed by powerful structures over marginalised communities within spatially defined areas. According to Yilmaz (2012), De Certeau's definition of strategies entails regulations being applied as tools to discipline the population for prolonged periods of time. Thus, strategies are limited by bordered areas over which they have control, while having a limitless temporal nature. Hence, by integrating the concepts of rhythm analysis and strategies, I argue that the military orders have created a spatio-temporal reality that is well-defined in terms of spatial and temporal bordering; the declaration of a firing zone was marked by clear spatial boundaries while, temporally, it resembles a moment that is sought to be preserved by means of the applied regulations for an extended period of time.

The adaptive geography of Masafer Yatta

In the early 1970s the people of Masafer Yatta realised that they had to resist the threat of displacement and protect their land from unlawful confiscation. The community took this decision based on observations and lessons learned from the displacement trajectories of other Palestinian villages and communities after the Wars of 1948 and 1967, as the community representative explains:

> We knew if we were to leave Masafer Yatta, even for the shortest period of time, we would never be back, it would have been 'bye bye London' (Com.1, 2018).

Accordingly, the community of Masafer Yatta had to face the challenge of living under the often vague and certainly discriminatory laws of the Israeli state in general and the Israeli military orders in particular. This act of manipulative existence between the blackness of illegality and the whiteness of legality is what Yiftachel refers to as the 'grey space' (Yiftachel, 2006; see also Kedar, Amara, & Yiftachel, 2018). This research argues that the concept of "grey space" is manifested in the specific context of Masafer Yatta through adaptive geography, where the main objective is to maintain the cyclical rhythms characterising the domestic geography prior to the declaration of the firing zone while creating the least amount of friction with the linear rhythm imposed by the Israeli military orders, which defines the unjust qualities of the military zone geography.

In order to establish this adaptive geography, the community has redefined the spatio-temporal patterns of their activities to keep going the two major sources of livelihood: agriculture (Fig. 8.) and livestock (Fig. 9.). Based on the previous demonstration of the domestic and military zone geographies, it is argued that the adaptive spatio-temporal character reintroduces the domestic cyclical rhythms and attempts to integrate them within the linear military zone's rhythm by ensuring that there is no intersection between the cyclical rhythms of the community and the monitoring cyclical rhythms employed by the Israeli military to enforce the implementation of the military zone's linear rhythm. In other words, the community's cyclical rhythms shall not occur at the same time as the monitoring cyclical rhythms. Hence, it could be shown how the same geobody defined by the military zone borders is operating as different geographies by manipulating the spatio-temporal patterns associated with each geographical setting. This transition of spatio-temporal patterns within the same geobody, as well as from one geographical reality to the other, could be referred to as an act of static displacement.

Figure 8. The agricultural land in Masafer Yatta; photo taken in 2014 by the author as part of a UN-Habitat project.

Figure 9. Livestock grazing in Masafer Yatta; photo taken in 2014 by the author as part of a UN-Habitat project.

The Israeli occupation of Palestine in 1948 and in 1967, and later the declaration of Firing Zone 918 in 1972, have severely affected the annual cyclical rhythm of the community. The people of Masafer Yatta were no longer able to travel to the three seasonal destinations, and so the seasonal activities were spatially modified to take place in and around Masafer Yatta. Moreover, Yatta ceased to be a summer destination, and visits to attend big ceremonies, including wedding celebrations and funerals, were limited. As for the grazing land to the south, where shepherds used to spend springtime, it was confiscated after the War of 1948 and annexed to lands under Israeli sovereignty, an event which has restricted the movement of shepherds and their flocks around the hamlets of Masafer Yatta. Hence, it could be concluded that, on the one hand, the movement of the community of Masafer Yatta was limited partly by the laws and regulations of the Israeli government as a tool of indirect displacement, while on the other hand this confined movement emerged as a technique adopted by the community of Masafer Yatta as a form of resistance against those indirect tools of displacement by creating facts on the ground that contrasted with the ones imposed by the military orders. The community opposed their temporary existence and therefore its vulnerability in being displaced by Israeli military orders.

According to legal experts, the Israeli Minister of Defence does not consider the residents of Masafer Yatta to be permanent residents due to the fact that they had not consistently lived in the area for one complete year before it was declared as a closed military zone. However, using a period of one year as a scale by which to determine the permanence of the community in this case does not take into account the semi-nomadic rhythmic character of the population, where a year is only one cycle that loops. Thus, such an inaccurate scale of measurement simply disregards the social dimension of time, as it could be argued that the annual cycle is a permanently occurring phenomenon that forms the identity of this community. Despite these unjust criteria for defining the temporalities of residents, the community of Masafer Yatta complied with these spatio-temporal conditions and spatially adapted by settling in Masafer Yatta. The main challenge for this community was to identify its geographical extent based on the laws and regulations imposed by the military orders and demarcation lines:

> The demarcation of the Green Line was done through the installation of barrels with metal polls, which were changed from time to time. However, the new barrels were not placed in the same locations as the old ones. Rather they used to be placed within a range of 3 km to 4 km during the years [...] it is 2019 today, and we are still confused where the Green Line is [...] Another point to consider is that no signs were placed to indicate the boundaries or the entrances of the closed military zone since 1977. The only signs that were installed were on the 1948 side of the boundary, facing commuters who were entering the firing zone from the Negev (Com.1, 2018).

After the geographical change in terms of space was identified, the next challenge was to develop a definition based on time and to identify how they unify under the concept of rhythm. The community of Masafer Yatta was able to settle on the rhythm based on observations. By looking into the monitoring rhythms, the community of Masafer Yatta would assume the temporariness of the military zone's geography, refusing to deal with it as one linear rhythm that persists through time. Instead, through looking into closed cyclical monitoring rhythms (taking place at certain times and hours of the day and the week), the community considered the military zone's geography to be of limited duration, beyond which they could resume their domestic activities. Immediately after the declaration of the closed military zone, the presence of its geography was directly attributed to the presence of Israeli soldiers and military vehicles:

> We understood that the military, after all, consists of employees, who operate according to their work calendar. Thus, the community decided that the safest time to graze and cultivate our flocks was after the soldiers' working hours. Hence, the community has converted its activities from daytime to night-time […] the prohibition of construction forced the community to live in caves. From the declaration of the firing zone until the late 1980s, people found refuge underground in the Canaanite caves. During the day, when the military machine was present, people would refrain from leaving the caves until it was night-time; then they would cultivate their fields and graze their sheep (Com.2, 2019).

Thus, the first cyclic monitoring rhythm has followed the cycle of working hours and working days of the Israeli military. The community would carry on performing its domestic rhythms of flock-grazing and cultivation outside those timeframes. Hence, the geobody of the closed military zone would retain its domestic geography at night and during Jewish weekends and holidays.

Later, the Israeli military began to utilise technological advancements in aerial photography to monitor the establishment of the new geography of the firing zone. The regular application of surveillance balloons as tools to capture aerial photographs of Masafer Yatta every three days established another monitoring cycle, which was particularly tied to the time intervals between each balloon trip and the next. Within this paradox of temporality and changing geographies, the onset of aerial photographs introduced another timeframe captured in the photo, which was more permanent than what the community had experienced with the military machine. Accordingly, its domestic activities were considered as both a process that followed a certain rhythm and a product that could be traced on the ground as well as through the aerial photographs.

Adaptive techniques: Farming, livestock grazing and construction

To provide more concrete examples of adaptive geography, this section will address the adaptive techniques employed to redefine the spatio-temporal patterns generated from practising three main activities: farming, livestock grazing and construction. In this regard, concepts of strategies and tactics introduced by De Certeau would appear to be relevant. While his definition of strategies could reflect the status of the closed military zone's geography, the activities carried out by the local community of Masafer Yatta are, arguably, 'tactics', as De Certeau states: "tactics develop as crucial practices that are interferences to strategies or power mechanisms" (cited in Yilmaz, 2012, p. 67). Unlike strategies, tactics evolve in a loose setting, not limited by borders or temporal limits; they are rather temporary arrangements that seize the opportunity to disrupt the hegemonic strategies utilising everyday practices as a form of resistance (Yilmaz, 2012). Hence, to resist the linear rhythm imposed by the military order the local community of Masafer Yatta has restructured its daily practices of farming, livestock grazing and construction as tactics to redefine its cyclical rhythms where time permits without conflicting with the military cyclical monitoring rhythms.

The grazing of its animal flocks was predominantly a daily activity. However, to avoid any kind of confiscation or fines, the community decided to manage this process collectively in shifts in order to protect the flocks. Therefore, instead of families grazing their animals individually, each hamlet would form a group of two shepherds and one watchman who would together graze all the flocks of the families living in the hamlet during the time between dusk and dawn.

The activity of cultivation proved to be more complicated as it includes the process of cultivating the land itself along with ensuring the acceptable appearance of the land in military archives. Although the process is prohibited by Israeli law as it involves the illegal presence of people inside a firing zone, cultivated land is necessary and vital to protect the land itself from being confiscated, which would happen if the land were left uncultivated for three consecutive years, as per the Ottoman Land Law. Thus, the people of Masafer Yatta had to alter their cultivation techniques, cultivating only at night and with a very limited range of crops that required little maintenance and expense, given the fact that they risked being destroyed. This has severely affected the regional position of Masafer Yatta. According to the community, Masafer Yatta used to be the food basket of Yatta, but during the 1970s and 1980s cultivation was no longer practised to produce abundant products, but rather as a tool to create the illusion of cultivated fields for aerial photographs (Com.2, 2019).

Finally, dwelling is the most complicated of all three activities. The community had to adapt to the fact that its construction of shelters would not only be noticed by the military but also captured in the aerial photographs. Therefore, there was an urgent need to create a geography that was suitable for their needs and also justifiable in the eyes of the camera (Fig. 10.). An old lady told the story of the building and constructing of shelters in Masafer Yatta, saying:

We are cave dwellers, but you cannot always live in a cave. Eventually, the families grow in number, and our kids would get married and have their own family at some point, so, we need to grow while surviving at the same time. In the 1970s and 1980s, and even until today, when we build, we make sure that the structure is as small as possible, we build one unit at a time, and we do not have the choice to install a permanent roof […] it is a common knowledge here that when people build with bricks, they would cover the building with fabric create the illusion that it is a temporary structure and could be decomposed […] we have been dealing with the ICA for two decades now, we understand that a demolition order is better than having a stop-work order. Thus, we need to create facts on the ground, establish finished structures, and then fight to prolong them, by submitting petitions to the court. You could say that we buy time. On the other hand, if you receive a stop-work order, that is it, the order is executed on the spot. Therefore, people build at night and on Saturdays, and no construction should take longer than three days to be built […] we notice the surveillance balloon twice or once a week, so we have a chance to create facts on the ground during times where those balloons aren't present, to avoid receiving a stop-work order. (Com.2, 2019).

Figure 10. Dwelling typology in Masafer Yatta; photo taken in 2014 by the author as part of a UN-Habitat project.

Arguably, the accumulation of the different geographies is manifested physically on the scale of an individual dwelling, where two typologies of dwellings are found in Masafer Yatta. The first typology is the cave, which primarily emphasises the spatio-temporal character of the military zone's geography, where all activities, including any type of construction, are forbidden by law.

In this case, the cave resembles the disrupted passage of time imposed by the military order, where a linear rhythm of restriction and dehumanisation prevails, leaving no trace of development in recent decades. At the same time, if we are to rethink the spatio-temporal character of the cave, it could be argued that the cave also represents an adaptive rhythm in which some families live in a manner that belongs to another linear rhythm that ended many decades ago. Thus, dwelling in those caves opposes the linear rhythm of militarisation by living in the remains of a receding rhythm from the past, thereby erecting camouflage by way of the invisible tempos of the past. The second typology of dwellings is the relatively new housing units that are built in brick and covered with fabric to give the illusion of temporariness. In this case, the bricks belong to the domestic geography, while the fabric belongs to the adaptive geography based on the interpretation of the military zone's geography. In this typology as well, the aspirations of the local community to endure a living on their lands are camouflaged under the temporary rhythms of the military zone (Fig. 11.).

Figure 11. Masafer Yatta's hamlets; photo taken in 2014 by the author as part of a UN-Habitat project.

Conclusions: 71 Years of static displacement unpacked

The discussion presented here attempts to demonstrate how the two concepts of home-making and displacement can be intertwined in cases of resistance. It does so by tracing how the threat of displacement affects the built environment and the spatial practices of communities threatened and rendered vulnerable by militarised occupation. Rather than exploring the aftermath of displacement and how it shapes the urban and structural patterns of communities, this research sheds light on the act of resistance as a spatial concept which manifests itself in the daily production of spaces and spatial practices through adjusting the spatio-temporal patterns of geographies by the agency of the vulnerable population.

This chapter has introduced the term 'static displacement' to showcase how the population moves between different time frames and within different geographical realities. The declaration of Masafer Yatta as a closed military zone has drastically changed the domestic geography of the area and has imposed a restrictive time frame on the population, one that was perceived to be paused, statically displacing the community within the same geobody. Nevertheless, the research illustrated that one way to resist such hegemonies is to create smaller segments of time where the community could retain its domestic geography and adapt in a manner that does not place them under the threat of physical displacement and forceful eviction.

The application of static displacement as a concept, integrated with the concepts of rhythms by Lefebvre and tactics by De Certeau, attempts to provide an analytical lens through which hegemonies and systems are studied, by understanding the spatio-temporal patterns embodied within the systems and the counter-spatio-temporal patterns generated as tactics of resistance. The definition of geography through exploring the notions of time as attributed to the different features and practices would contribute to better observation of the invisible aspect of the urban space, and in formulating a social and temporal picture of the static lines and boundaries that are outlined in urban maps. While Masafer Yatta provides a unique case, the concept of static displacement is applicable in cases where different groups holding different power positions use the same geobody to claim their rights to the land. Such cases emphasise the power of collective daily practices in shifting the power scale and creating facts on the ground in favour of the vulnerable and threatened groups.

References

Abrams, J., & Hall, P. (2006). *Else/Where: Mapping New Cartographies of Networks and Territories*. Minneapolis, Minn: University of Minnesota Design Institute.

ACRI. (2013). *Experts Legal Opinion In relation with the Petition filed by Residents of Villages in Firing Zone 918 against the Intention to Transfer them from their Homes*. Jerusalem: Association of Civil Rights in Israel (ACRI).

Aloni, A. (2016). *Expel and Exploit: The Israeli Practice of Taking over Rural Palestinian Land*. Jerusalem: B'Tselem.

Com.1. (2018, June). Mapping the Terrain of Masafer Yatta. (Researcher, Interviewer).

Com.2. (2019, February 10). Adaptive Techniques. (Researcher, Interviewer).

Crookston, M. (2017). Echoes of Empire: British Mandate planning in Palestine and its influence in the West Bank today. *Planning Perspectives 32*(1), 87–98.

Davis, S. B. (2012). History on the Line: Time as Dimension. *Massachusetts Institute of Technology, 28*(4), 4-17.

Etkes, D. (2015). *A Locked Garden, Declaration of Closed Areas in the West Bank*. Jerusalem: Kerem Navot.

Hague, C., Crookston, M., Wegener, M., Platt, C., & Gladki, J. (2015). *An expert international group of planners says a new approach to planning could contribute to peacebuilding*. Ramallah: UN-Habitat Palestine.

Haqel. (2019). *THE HIGH COURT OF JUSTICE APPROVED A DRACONIAN ORDER*. Jerusalem: Haqel, In Defense of Human Rights.

IPCC. (2013). *Masafer Yatta Planning Brief*. Jerusalem: International Peace and Cooperation Centre.

Jalil, E. S. (2014). *Masafer. Life in the Interstice*. Retrieved from Eduardo Soteras Jalil: https://www.eduardosoteras.com/masafer

Kedar, A., Amara, A., & Yiftachel, O. (2018). *Emptied Lands: A Legal Geography of Bedouin Rights in the Negev*. Stanford: Stanford University Press.

Khamaisi, R. (1997). Israeli use of the British Mandate planning legacy as a tool for the control of Palestinians in the West Bank. *Planning Perspectives, 12*(3), 321-340.

Khamasisi, R. (2014). قضايا إسرائيلية. المكان وتهويد الأرض على السيطرة وأدوات سياسات ،أيديولوجية, 13-33.

Lefebvre, H. (1992). *Rhythmanalysis: Space, Time and Everyday Life*. Paris: Éditions Syllepse.

Masalha, N. (2002). التطبيق في الإسرائيلية الترانسفير سياسة :أقل ورب أكثر أرض *1949-1996* (2 ed.). Beruit: Institute for Palestine Studies.

Maycroft, N. (2015). Understanding Henri Lefebvre: Theory and the Possible. *Capital & Class*, 170-174.

MoLG. (2018). *GeoMoLG*. Retrieved from GeoMoLG: https://geomolg.ps/

Nature, T. L. (2017, April 18). *Return of the Black Goat*. Retrieved from Land and Nature: https://www.eretz.com/wordpresshe/?p=2201

Rovelli, C. (2017). *The Order of Time.* New York: Riverhead Books.

Scott, J. C. (1999). *Seeing like a State: How Certain Schemes to Improve the Human Condition Have Failed.* New Haven, Conn.: Yale University Press.

Sella, A. (1986). Custodians and Redeemers: Israeli Leaders' Perceptions of Peace, 1967-79. *Middle Eastern Studies, 22*(2), 236-251.

Shalev, N., & Cohen-Lifshitz, A. (2008). *The Prohibited Zone, Israeli planning policy in the Palestinian villages in Area C.* Jerusalem: Bimkom -Planners for Planning Rights.

Yiftachel, O. (2006). *Ethnocracy: Land and Identity Politics in Israel/Palestine.* Philadelphia: University of Pennsylvania Press.

Yilmaz, G. G. (2012). Tactics in Daily Life Practices and Different Forms of Resistance: The Case of Turks in Germany. *Procedia – Social and Behavioral Sciences, 82*, 66 – 73.

Abrams, J., & Hall, P. (2006). *Else/Where: Mapping New Cartographies of Networks and Territories.* Minneapolis, Minn: University of Minnesota Design Institute.

ACRI. (2013). *Experts Legal Opinion In relation with the Petition filed by Residents of Villages in Firing Zone 918 against the Intention to Transfer them from their Homes.* Jerusalem: Association of Civil Rights in Israel (ACRI).

Aloni, A. (2016). *Expel and Exploit: The Israeli Practice of Taking over Rural Palestinian Land.* Jerusalem: B'Tselem.

Com.1. (2018, June). Mapping the Terrain of Masafer Yatta. (Researcher, Interviewer).

Com.2. (2019, February 10). Adaptive Techniques. (Researcher, Interviewer).

Crookston, M. (2017). Echoes of Empire: British Mandate planning in Palestine and its influence in the West Bank today. *Planning Perspectives 32*(1), 87–98.

Davis, S. B. (2012). History on the Line: Time as Dimension. *Massachusetts Institute of Technology, 28*(4), 4-17.

Etkes, D. (2015). *A Locked Garden, Declaration of Closed Areas in the West Bank.* Jerusalem: Kerem Navot.

Hague, C., Crookston, M., Wegener, M., Platt, C., & Gladki, J. (2015). *An expert international group of planners says a new approach to planning could contribute to peacebuilding.* Ramallah: UN-Habitat Palestine.

Haqel. (2019). *THE HIGH COURT OF JUSTICE APPROVED A DRACONIAN ORDER.* Jerusalem: Haqel, In Defense of Human Rights.

IPCC. (2013). *Masafer Yatta Planning Brief.* Jerusalem: International Peace and Cooperation Centre.

Jalil, E. S. (2014). *Masafer. Life in the Interstice.* Retrieved from Eduardo Soteras Jalil: https://www.eduardosoteras.com/masafer

Kedar, A., Amara, A., & Yiftachel, O. (2018). *Emptied Lands: A Legal Geography of Bedouin Rights in the Negev.* Stanford: Stanford University Press.

Khamaisi, R. (1997). Israeli use of the British Mandate planning legacy as a tool for the control of Palestinians in the West Bank. *Planning Perspectives, 12*(3), 321-340.

Khamasisi, R. (2014). أيديولوجية، سياسات وأدوات السيطرة على الأرض وتهويد المكان. قضايا إسرائيلية, 13-33.

Lefebvre, H. (1992). *Rhythmanalysis: Space, Time and Everyday Life*. Paris: Éditions Syllepse.

Masalha, N. (2002). أرض أكثر وعرب أقل: سياسة الترانسفير الإسرائيلية في التطبيق *1949-1996* (2 ed.). Beruit: Institute for Palestine Studies.

Maycroft, N. (2015). Understanding Henri Lefebvre: Theory and the Possible. *Capital & Class*, 170-174.

MoLG. (2018). *GeoMoLG*. Retrieved from GeoMoLG: https://geomolg.ps/

Nature, T. L. (2017, April 18). *Return of the Black Goat*. Retrieved from Land and Nature: https://www.eretz.com/wordpresshe/?p=2201

Rovelli, C. (2017). *The Order of Time*. New York: Riverhead Books.

Scott, J. C. (1999). *Seeing like a State: How Certain Schemes to Improve the Human Condition Have Failed*. New Haven, Conn.: Yale University Press.

Sella, A. (1986). Custodians and Redeemers: Israeli Leaders' Perceptions of Peace, 1967-79. *Middle Eastern Studies, 22*(2), 236-251.

Shalev, N., & Cohen-Lifshitz, A. (2008). *The Prohibited Zone, Israeli planning policy in the Palestinian villages in Area C*. Jerusalem: Bimkom -Planners for Planning Rights.

Yiftachel, O. (2006). *Ethnocracy: Land and Identity Politics in Israel/Palestine*. Philadelphia: University of Pennsylvania Press.

Yilmaz, G. G. (2012). Tactics in Daily Life Practices and Different Forms of Resistance: The Case of Turks in Germany. *Procedia – Social and Behavioral Sciences, 82*, 66 – 73.

CODA

About the Displacement of Home

Hilde Heynen

This volume brings together a wealth of material that ponders the making and unmaking of homes in displacement as a spatial practice. In this final chapter I am offering a concluding critical overview of the different contributions, which might work as a second bookend, counterbalancing while further complementing the introduction of my fellow editors.

My own interest in dwelling, home and homelessness goes back to my early work on architecture and modernity (Heynen, 1999). The literature I relied upon back then stated that the condition of modernity installs a sense of homelessness in all individuals subjected to it, since the pace of change is so fast that the sense of what is familiar continually withers away (Berman, 1985; Adorno, 1991). Because of that, modernity generates a massive longing for home as the site of belonging; a belonging that is situated either in the past (nostalgia) or in the future (utopia) (Lyotard, 1991; Bloch, 1986). Since that site of belonging is most often perceived as *not* present or in the here and now, this means that home and our experience of it are always already intrinsically displaced.

Taking up this line of thought, authors such as Rose Braidotti have argued for a nomadic way of thinking, one that would recognise this experience of homelessness as a point of departure (Braidotti, 2011). In such intellectual discourse, the figure of the migrant and the condition of exile have long been seen as metaphors, sometimes by authors (such as Adorno and Braidotti) who have themselves experienced exile or migration, but also by intellectuals who have the privilege of writing from the safety of unthreatened personal spaces of belonging. There is, however, a danger in this metaphorisation, as Sara Ahmed (1999) points out: "the act of granting the migrant the status *as* a figure (of speech) erases and conceals the historical determination of experiences of migration" (p. 333). Indeed, the intellectual nomad is most often a privileged one, who has choices and who is allowed legally to cross borders. That privilege is not afforded to everyone on the globe, and Ahmed's warning rightly reminds us that migration as a real-life experience is about lived embodiment as well as storytelling, colonialism, racism, social antagonism, class relations, and about the politics of gender. For Ahmed, these elements have an enormous impact and the experience of migration thus evokes the transformation of the self: "[t]he gap between memory and place in the very dislocation of migration […] becomes reworked as a site of bodily transformation, the potential to remake one's relation to what appears as unfamiliar, to reinhabit spaces and places" (ibid., p. 344).

To reinhabit spaces and places – that is exactly what this volume seeks to examine; the practices of accommodating or appropriating spaces and places that are encountered during a journey in search of a better life, as a result of (forced or voluntary) displacement. Forced displacement, as in the case of refugees, is the focus of most chapters in this book, but some deal with a broader set of displaced people. We should be mindful, however, that there is not necessarily a clear dividing line between the migration of those who seek work and those who seek asylum. Voluntary and forced migration, rather, need to be considered as two poles in a politically constructed bi-polar constellation which does not adequately reflect the experiences and self-descriptions of the people involved (Yuval-Davis, 2011, p. 37). Hence the theorisation that I aim to provide by way of this coda seeks to address a wider spectrum of displacement.

The introduction by Luce Beeckmans, Ashika Singh and Alessandra Gola has already set the scene for this endeavour by unpacking some important themes: the assumed opposition between home and displacement; the importance of spatial agency; the impact of global politics; the merits of interdisciplinary research and of affective (rather than objective) writing. Here, I wish to corroborate and elaborate on the reflections of my fellow editors by pondering and comparing the different chapters from four different points of view. I will start by revisiting the geopolitical conditioning of the meaning of home, framing the longing for home within the politics of the nation-state, colonialism and neoliberal capitalism. A significant dimension in the experience of home-making in displacement is, besides and related to space, that of time. This will be the entry point for the second part of this coda. In the third section I will address the possible role architects and architecture play in situations of displacement. The fourth and last part of this coda will deal with issues of gender and feminism.

Geopolitics of home

The Western bourgeois idea of home, argues Maria Kaika (2004), is a social construction based on the exclusion of undesired elements both in the social realm (exclusion of anomie and social conflict) and in the natural realm (exclusion of cold, dirt, pollution and sewage). The idea of the home as an autonomous, safe and private heaven is thus predicated on the 'othering' of nature: the bourgeois home is where nature is completely domesticated, where clean water and power are supplied through an invisible apparatus of pipes and cables, and dirty water and waste are likewise quasi-invisibly discharged. Whereas Kaika focuses on the historical-geographical processes that dealt with water – namely, the introduction of modern systems of plumbing and sewage – one could apply a similar analysis to socio-economic and political factors. Indeed, the bourgeois ideal of home, as famously formulated by John Ruskin in 1865, can be deconstructed to show how it is imbued with notions of gender, class and nation:

> This is the true nature of home – it is the place of peace: the shelter is not only from all injury, but from all terror, doubt and division. In so far as it is not this, it is not home; so far as the anxieties of outer life penetrate into it, and the inconsistently-minded, unloved, or hostile society of the outer world is allowed by either husband or wife to cross the threshold, it ceases to be a home. (Ruskin, 1901, p. 102).

In Ruskin's depiction of the home a whole lot of things are made invisible: not just women's work in maintaining the home, but also the possibility of domestic violence, as well as the economic basis of the home (earned by the man in the outer world) and the class oppression of industrial and domestic workers that makes it possible. Likewise, the entanglements of this bourgeois home, with its cult of domesticity, and the colonial enterprise are left untouched. Indeed, as Karen Hansen (1992) points out, the etymological nearness of "domesticity" and "to domesticate" is no coincidence: domesticity was often seen in the colonial discourse as part of the civilising mission of the West and the import of domesticity was a crucial factor in the colonial encounter. Hence, the very specific, gendered and class-based bourgeois idea of home was put forward in colonial discourse as universally valid. Anne McClintock (1995, p. 5) comparably argues that the cult of domesticity was a crucial, if concealed, element of the imperial enterprise, while Wendy Webster (1998) unravels the intimate connections, in films from the 1950s and 1960s, between the bourgeois ideal of home and whiteness.

Even though the 19th Century bourgeois cult of domesticity was taken to task by material feminists (Hayden, 1981) and by some Marxist critics (Teige, 2002), it nevertheless had a profound impact on 20th Century housing movements (Heynen, 2005). It is also an important ingredient of the global arrangement of nation-states and institutions that regulate people's lives in displacement. In this global arrangement every corner of the earth is part of a nation-state that gives certificates of belonging (such as passports) out to the people it recognises as 'legitimately' inhabiting its particular corner. With such a certificate of belonging (i.e. the claim to national citizenship) people can travel to other corners of the globe, although this freedom is, generally speaking, restricted to those who have a claim to a passport from the global North and/or can afford the conditions and costs of an entry visa from the country to which they wish to travel. It is this global regime of citizenship that aggravates and prolongs conditions of displacement, because it means that underprivileged people who leave their homes, forced or otherwise, tend to end up in camps or in refugee housing, or in illegal situations in which they are exploited, or in other unsavoury places where no one would wish to raise one's children. Displacement in this sense is the mirror image of the politics of belonging, which symbolically separates the world population into an 'us' and a 'them' (Yuval-Davis, 2011, p. 20), and which motivates political realities such as 'Fortress Europe' (or 'Fortress Australia' or 'Fortress US'). This politics of belonging, I argue, is a further elaboration and extension of the gestures of exclusion that are fundamental to the bourgeois home (see also Brickell, 2012).

As we know, the bourgeois home is completely entangled with the mode of production called capitalism: the 19th Century bourgeoisie was the class of entrepreneurs and businessmen who made their fortunes as property owners and employers of an exploited proletariat, namely, through industries that often thrived thanks to the trade opportunities offered by colonialism (McClintock, 1995; Said, 1994; George, 1999). Colonialism, imperialism and capitalism have collaborated to ensure that in almost all countries across the globe a legal apparatus is in place that assigns ownership of land and buildings to specific individuals, companies or the state. Housing thus became a commodity, often unaffordable for large swathes of a population. In some countries, social welfare policies go a long way to counter the negative effects of this capitalist regime, but in many others social welfare cannot cope with the demand. The welfare state model has, moreover, lost its political appeal in recent decades due to the increasing dominance of neo-liberal ideologies (Cupers, Mattsson, & Gabrielsson, 2020).

All of these factors have been recognised by several authors as constitutive of a series of mainstream political outlooks that tend to conflate 'home' and the 'nation-state' (Duyvendak, 2011; Brickell, 2012; Davies, 2014; Walters, 2004). In a theoretical scheme referred to by many of our contributors, Brun and Fabos (2015) helpfully refer to this constellation as 'HOME'. 'HOME' points to the broader political and historical configuration that embeds this specific notion of 'home' in global institutions and that is often evoked by the perpetrators of nationalist exclusion and violence. Next to 'HOME', Brun and Fabos also distinguish 'Home' as representing values, traditions, memories and feelings of home, and 'home' as the day-to-day practices of home-making. In this volume the three constellations are at stake: the 'spatial practice' of our book's title points at its core to everyday practices of inhabitation, while still, as evidenced by many of the discussions in individual chapters, seeking to account for how 'Home' and 'HOME' shape, complement and/or frustrate such practices.

The political dimensions of 'home', 'Home' and 'HOME' are perhaps nowhere as visible as in the chapters dealing with Palestine. In 1948 the *Nakba* destroyed Palestinian society, resulting in the forced displacement of more than 700,000 Palestinians from their homeland. Since that moment, many of these refugees and their offspring have continued to live in what were originally conceived as temporary camps and they still claim their 'right to return'. This right to return is denied by Israel, hence many Palestinians live in a kind of limbo as de facto stateless persons. Although the Palestinian camps have undergone major transformations, and are now dense urban tissues rather than collections of tents, they are clearly places of ambivalence: for instance, improving the camps and making them more homely and more inhabitable might make a lot of sense from the point of view of 'home', but not from the point of view of 'Home' and 'HOME'. Some Palestinians continue to feel that they should not settle – not make their home – because settling might be seen by others, including the rest of the world, as foregoing the right to return. This political omen is part and parcel of the lived reality of the residents of Nahr Al-Barid in Lebanon and it continues to impact on their every decision regarding their built environment, as explored and pondered by Ashika Singh (Chapter 2).

A similar dynamic played out in Sheikh Radwan in Gaza City, a neighbourhood planned and developed by the Israeli state between 1967 and 1982 in order to broker a 'permanent solution' for the residents of the nearby Shati refugee camp. By accepting a plot in the new neighbourhood these residents in fact gave up their right to return – which was clearly one of the goals of what Fatima Abeek-Zubiedat sees as 'colonial urbanism' (Chapter 4). Another version of Israel's statecraft in unfair dealings with Palestinians is discussed by Wafa Butmeh (Chapter 16). This chapter focuses on Firing Zone 918, an area to the south of Hebron which includes Masafer Yatta, which is home to 18 semi-nomadic Palestinian communities. By declaring this area a military zone Israel imposed severe restrictions on these communities by, for example, forbidding the erection of new permanent structures as well as the inhabitation of existing ones. In the process, Israel made the continued survival of a traditional Palestinian way of living close to impossible.

In these three chapters, as in that of Alessandra Gola (Chapter 10), it becomes very clear that for many Palestinians the consistency between the three constellations of 'home', 'Home' and 'HOME' is non-existent and that this absence, this gap, is integral to their identity as Palestinians. They are forced into a situation where day-to-day home-making practices are necessarily at odds with the values and traditions of the homeland to which they cannot return and where geo-political conditions continue to disqualify them as equal citizens or even as citizens tout court. This is somewhat different in the Syrian refugee camps of Iraqi Kurdistan on which Layla Zibar and her co-authors focus (Chapter 3). Here, the authors describe the experience of their interlocutors as a "falling out of Syrian citizenship into a longed-for sense of 'Kurdishness' (one claimed in time and space)" (p. 81). Indeed, Syrian Kurds could flee from the civil war in Syria to Iraqi Kurdistan, and although the autonomy of this region is not fully secure from a geopolitical point of view, there is a shared language, a shared culture and a shared sense of welcome that foster the rapid transformation of these camps into 'towns in the making'. In this particular case, therefore, 'home' and 'Home' can be practised and lived, even if 'HOME' is not lawfully recognised. In fact, one may even claim that the enactment of 'home' and 'Home' is made possible by the camp community's exploration of the very potential of realising 'HOME' at some point in the future.

This point resonates with the way Iris Katz (Chapter 6), calling upon the work of Hannah Arendt, exposes the inherently *political* nature of any act of home-making in such conditions of displacement. Her argument shows how displaced people, by appropriating and beautifying their surroundings in daily acts of inhabitation, materially claim their right to citizenship by marking their presence and thereby making it visible. For Palestinians, the political aspect of dwelling plays out on different levels: many of them are acutely aware that each and every decision they make regarding the homes they build (or do not build), or regarding the structures they inhabit (or fail to inhabit), is a move in a power play where the state of Israel has the upper hand. Even the simple act of having a home and living an everyday life is experienced as an act of resistance, because it manifests Palestinians' refusal to be over-determined by the conflict with Israel. Nobody thus needs to tell them that the political is in the everyday – they indeed live it every day (Feldman, 2006). Likewise, the active home-making practices studied by Layla Zibar in Iraqi Kurdistan play a political role in that they render visible the claim to citizenship and to a viable Kurdish state.

Huda Tayob's chapter on 'Somali malls' in Cape Town, Nairobi and Lusaka (Chapter 15) outlines an even more hybrid configuration of domestic practices, which show how the lived reality of transnational movements in Africa ignores and combats the geopolitical reality of nation-states and their borders. Abdou-Maliq Simone (2011; 2012) has long argued that transnational movements and exchange are crucial elements of African urbanity, and that the assemblage of discrepant materials, sentiments, forms and efforts of various peoples in hybrid configurations makes up for a messy reality that cannot be adequately grasped by the logics of economy, demography or planning. The Somali malls are such a configuration, made up of transnational trajectories, informal economies, commercial arrangements, domestic practices of hospitality as well as exchange between people from different backgrounds and in different stages of their lives. According to Tayob, these malls, which originated because of the mass displacements enforced by the civil war in Somalia, provide "an imaginary of provisional domesticity, producing a spatial intimacy across geographies and within contested realms'" (p. 378). At the same time, Tayob recognises that they are often spaces of poverty and exploitation. Although they offer an alternative to the camps that are the global geopolitical institutions' answer to crisis and displacement, they still should not be romanticised as adequate solutions for people on the move.

Exploitation is also a key term in Anna Di Giusto's contribution on Borgo Mezzanone in South Italy (Chapter 12). This chapter shows the disastrous consequences of European asylum policies in combination with situations of social isolation, various mafia organisations and labour exploitation. In Borgo Mezzanone, official policies erected a reception centre for asylum seekers, but many more so-called 'illegal' migrants inhabit the informal settlement that sprung up next to it and that lacks basic infrastructure and security. Even in these dire conditions, Di Giusto argues, the inhabitants of Borgo Mezzanone demonstrate survival skills and home-making practices. In so far as these practices remain invisible to the surrounding context, however, they fail to realise the political dimension that Irit Katz recognises in the very act of making oneself visible to the outside world. Nevertheless, according to Di Giusto, through sheer persistence and by accommodating the needs and desires of its residents, this shantytown in some ways manages to recreate an environment that can be called home. Its inhabitants have, for instance, arranged for a mosque, and many of them recover objects from waste in order to beautify their respective shelters or set up cafés. These spatial practices and the material traces that they impart mark their aspiration to a sense of dignity as human beings. These efforts – even if invisible to the rest of the world – should be understood as politically significant as this is how the residents of Borgo Mezzanone enact resistance and resilience against a geopolitical constellation that would crush rather than support them.

Arrows of time

Home, says Mary Douglas (1991), "is located space, but it is not necessarily a fixed space." Home also has regulated cycles of home life: when to rise, when to take meals, when to go to bed; hence, "a home is not only a space, it also has some structure in time; and because it is for people who are living in that time and space, it has aesthetic and moral dimensions" (p. 289). This sense of home becomes more complicated in situations of migrancy and displacement. Migrants leave a home behind because it does not hold enough promise for the future, and they make a new home in a different country, which is – inevitably – discontinuous with the old home. This experience of disruption, states Mirjana Lozanovska, provokes many migrants into repetitive building, in their newly adopted country and in their country of origin, each time aspiring to build a dream house that embodies the idea of belonging. This process, however, can never be completed, because, she argues:

> The objective to build a house is exceeded by a condition of serial house building, and repetitive and serial return travel to the homeland, which interfaces housing with acute displacement and (a lack of) settlement. Building a house becomes an endless ongoing process, a psychic journey that can never be completed because the migrant is unable to reconstruct the belief in the 'wholeness' of housing. (Lozanovska, 2019, p. 205).

In the experience of dwelling, multiple time frames are indeed at stake. There is first of all the linear time frame that speaks of the biography of individuals, and that is always already embedded in a collective imagination depicting the past and dreaming the future (Dossa and Golubovic, 2019). This collective imagination works as well on the scale of the family (e.g. the memory of a childhood home that one shares with one's siblings, the dream of the home-to-be made by newly-formed couples) as it does on the scale of the community (what one's town used to be and what it should become, the past or the future homeland of one's people). A second time frame is that of the cyclical time: the cycle of day and night, the cycle of work days and weekend, the cycle of the seasons and the holidays – all of which are marked by certain routines and rituals. For many individuals these time frames work well together, because they manage to deal with major changes in their life trajectory, marked by new home settings, by quickly building up new routines and new rituals, while not necessarily completely losing the old ones (think, for instance, of adult children returning to the family home for Christmas or Eid celebrations). In conditions of displacement, however, it is this smooth co-existence between linear and cyclical time that breaks down.

What is often mentioned as part of this disruption is the protracted sense of waiting that seems to be characteristic of displaced persons' experience. Prospective migrants have to wait for visas; if they are already in the country where they want to settle, they have to wait in order to attain the right residency status allowing one to work or to have access to social housing; one might have to wait at the border in order to clear administrative hurdles; one might have to wait in order for family members to be able to come over, etc. For those living under the humanitarian regime of camps or refugee shelters, this sense of waiting might seem endless. Elizabeth Cullen Dunn (2017) thus wonders, "How [do] the practices of international actors, the dictates and programs of nation-states, the politics of local government, and the beliefs and practices of IDP's themselves intersect in ways that often trap displaced people in the suspended temporality of camp life […] in prolonged liminality?" (p. 7) For Dunn, this situation boils down to the impossibility of home-making, as indicated by the title of her book: *No Path Home. Humanitarian Camps and the Grief of Displacement.* In refugee centres in Western Europe residents are also seen as people-in-waiting whose material conditions boil down to the bare minimum (such as "bed, bath, bread", as it is called in Belgium and the Netherlands) and whose agency is minimised in that they are not allowed to choose their own room-mates, to cook for themselves, or even to add pieces of furniture or decoration to their rooms (all in the name of efficiency and safety) (Beeckmans & Vanden Houte, 2019).

Alternatively, Cathrin Brun analyses how people involved in these extended periods of waiting for a 'durable solution' cope, usually by somehow making the best of the situation in which they find themselves, still without giving up hope of a possible, future return or resettlement. She considers this attitude one of 'active waiting'. Many of her interviewees reported periods where their thoughts and emotions were totally focused on the past, but many of them also managed to frame their future orientations in terms of hope. As Brun puts it herself:

> Agency-in-waiting requires an understanding of waiting as hope for the future. People use hope to cope with an uncertain future; they take on hopeful waiting in the positive anticipation that it will help them stay afloat. However, hope may also indicate resignation as an active strategy. In this case, it is often experienced as boredom and commonly results in less investment in the present. But it is when people stop waiting – when future time is delinked from everyday time and the past – that agency-in-waiting cannot be realized. (Brun, 2015, p. 33).

Notably, what Brun here calls 'agency-in-waiting' often has to do with day-to-day practices of home-making: cooking, caring for children, cleaning, gardening, decorating a room.

Ilana Feldman (2006) elaborates on another understanding of the cyclical moments of home-making. In a contribution aptly called 'The Refrain of Home', she analyses narratives and practices of Palestinians who had been displaced to Gaza and detects how re-connecting with 'home' takes form in rhythmic moments of repetition. These cyclical moments are found, on the one hand, in the repetition of narratives related to the loss of the former home during the *Nakba* and survival strategies in its immediate aftermath. On the other hand, Feldman makes note of the back-and-forth movements between Gaza and the places people originate from – whether this be to retrieve possessions, to steal from Israeli settlements, or to stage *fida'iyyin* attacks. She observes how in these repetitive tactics a sense of home is reproduced, but also transformed, and how these repetitions, incantations and circulations introduce a kind of security in a world that is otherwise full of disruption, if not chaos.

Several of these threads come together in the contribution of Anooradha Iyer Siddiqi and Somayeh Chitchian (Chapter 1). They stress the importance of time in emergency environments, where, they argue, time shapes space. Time shapes space because inhabiting a camp after displacement involves a "malleability that makes tangible the accompanying liquidity of time, of pasts, presents and futures. [...] It is simultaneously of here and there, of then and now, of that which is yet-to-come" (p. 41). Like Lozanovska, they insist that the experience of (the lack of) home involves recalibrations of past, present and future; like Brun as well as Feldman, they show how the protracted temporality of waiting does not imply a freezing in time, but rather a constant renegotiation of the home yet-to-come, anchored in the past yet projected into the future, and partially realised in the present through the agency of inhabitants of the camp.

The last chapter by Wafa Butmeh (Chapter 16, already mentioned) further develops the idea of rhythmic gestures as constitutive of dwelling. Her case is rather unique in that she deals with what she calls 'static displacement' – the dispossession of a group of semi-nomadic dwellers whose practices of inhabitation are severely hindered by the Israeli military, without them being officially displaced. Butmeh discusses how this community manages to resist the spatial logic imposed by the military (namely, that their area is turned into an uninhabitable firing zone) by cleverly playing upon different temporalities. They 'buy time' against the demolition orders by going to the courts; they figure out at which moments of the day and the week the military conduct visual control of their area; they use the downtime of Israeli soldiers for sheep grazing, agriculture and even construction. They thus create a cyclical rhythm that counters the linear rhythm imposed by Israel's military. Whether such tactics are effective against military strategies in the long run may be doubtful, but they remain lasting proof of the active agency and the resilience of this oppressed group.

Alessandra Gola (Chapter 10) shows how the geopolitics of home intersect with the arrows of time to produce divergent socio-spatial realities in urban Palestine. The West Bank, occupied by Israel but also home to a nascent Palestinian State, consists of a patchwork of areas with different political status – some under the control of the Palestinian Authority; some under the control of Israel; some under the control of UNRWA (United Nations Relief and Works Agency); and some that fall outside these demarcations. This patchwork generates very different conditions on the ground with respect to economic opportunities and building codes. While the Israeli-Palestinian conflict still has no lasting solution after more than 70 years, life went on: refugees had children; farmers went on farming; villagers moved to the city; young men and women decided to move country for work and send money back; some families stagnated while others became wealthier. All of them needed homes and all of them somehow dealt with the exigencies of daily life, even while Israel was building a Wall and the conflict continued. In the process they transformed the landscape, the towns and the villages: Ramallah, for instance, became a big city with sprawling outskirts that in the south touched Israeli-occupied East Jerusalem. Gola describes this complicated inhabited landscape with great sensitivity for the interplay of different temporalities – the political one that plays out over decades; the economic one that differs over years; the biographical ones marked by births and deaths as well as by the home-making routines that make up the everyday.

The role of architecture and architects

The world of architecture and that of displacement do not often encounter each other, except in the stories of displaced architects who supposedly took modernism from Europe to other parts of the world, such as Walter Gropius, Ludwig Mies van der Rohe and Lina Bo Bardi. The standard histories of 20th Century architecture, however, barely mention refugee housing or emergency shelter. It is rare that, for example, Le Corbusier's *Maison Domino*, known to every architectural student, is correctly put in its historical context by being discussed as accommodation for bombed-out refugees in World War I. In the interbellum period there were also other architectural projects explicitly meant for refugees, such as refugee housing built by Ernst May in Silesia in the early 1920s (Herscher, 2017, p. 51–59) or the so-called *prosfygika* or refugee housing-blocks from the early 1930s in Athens, designed by architects Laskaris and Kyriakos. As Andrew Herscher argues:

> After World War II, however, refugee housing disappeared from architectural agendas. [...] In the interwar period, in those situations where refugees were recognized as conationals, the accommodation of refugees was a housing issue; after World War II, when refugees became a humanitarian problem, permanent housing would be replaced by seemingly temporary camps. (Herscher, 2017, p. 70–71).

At the end of World War II (WWII) there were an estimated 11.5 million displaced persons in Europe (Shephard, 2012, p. 59). The allied forces managed to repatriate many millions of them in the following months, but there were still considerable numbers of those who found themselves unable or unwilling to 'go home', because their 'home' no longer existed. These people left no traces in the architectural history books, although they continued to be around in Europe for a very long time – until the end of the 1950s. They were accommodated in barracks and camps, which were transformed or dismantled after their inhabitants were finally absorbed into the general population or left, whether that be for Israel, Latin America, Australia, Canada, the USA or for a country to which they supposedly belonged based on ethnic identity or racialised perceptions (Shephard, 2012; Gatrell, 2019).

There are only a few exceptions to the rule that post-WWII refugee housing is absent from architectural history books. One such exception is the refugee centre in Banja Koviljace designed by Mihajo Mitravic in 1964, the focal point of Aleksandar Stanicic's contribution to this volume (Chapter 7). Commissioned by the United Nations, it was a prestige project meant to highlight the global relevance of Yugoslavia's non-alignment movement and to showcase Yugoslavia's hospitality towards foreigners in need of assistance. The centre is a very elegant building with a welcoming and open atmosphere – especially in the wing with communal spaces. Its use of local materials and its formal references to vernacular traditions render it part of a regionally inspired soft modernism that manages to combine local anchoring with international significance. According to Stanicic, the architect managed to resolve the contradictions inherent in humanitarian architecture – the tension between lofty ideals and down-to-earth necessities, or between the architect's intention to provide a home in the here-and-now and the refugee's awareness of temporality and insecurity.

Yet, it is doubtful whether architects *can* manage that tension. Aikaterini Antonopoulou (Chapter 11) compares the formal, top-down approach to refugee housing exemplified in the already mentioned refugee housing – the *prosfygika,* purpose-built in Athens in the early 1930s with the ad hoc, informal and bottom-up accommodation provided by City Plaza, a former hotel occupied and used during the 2015 European refugee crisis. The *prosfygika* was part of official welfare state policies, and was built according to very low *Existenz-minimum* standards, offering 30m² two-room apartments with kitchen and toilets. It never became popular as a housing type, and in fact fell into decay from the 1960s onwards. Alternatively, City Plaza was not purpose-built to house refugees, but functioned very well as such, operated by a cooperative with refugees and activists living together and participating in decision-making and in its maintenance. Because it was centrally located and because of its community life, the refugees that it (unlawfully) accommodated found a good foothold in the city. Their very presence and visibility, argues Antonopoulou, made the building into a tool exposing exclusion, discrimination and marginalisation. Athens' much-contested urban informality thus offered these migrants more agency and equipped them with more resilience than any 'official' solution might have done.

There is a certain tendency among our contributors to consider the official commissioning of architects by the state as part of the problem rather than the solution. That is certainly how Fatina Abreek-Zubiedat (Chapter 4) interprets the work of architects, urbanists and planners who worked on the Sheikh Radwan neighbourhood in Gaza City between 1967 and 1982. Her understanding is that the Israeli occupier promoted 'normalisation' as an instrument of control. Palestinian refugees were offered the opportunity to acquire a plot for a self-built house in the new neighbourhood, but only on the condition that they demolished their house in the refugee camp. In this very cost-effective way, Israel managed to combine economic development with the cultural-political assimilation of Palestinians, while remaining in sync with architectural strategies and forms promoted by well-known international architects, such as those of Team X. Through this colonial urbanism, the architects and planners actually collaborated with the Israeli oppressors.

Iyer Siddiqi and Chitchian (Chapter 1) seek a way out of this conundrum by turning to the residents of the camps as co-producers of its architecture. They call for "an epistemic shift of both the *site,* the *time,* and the *subject* of knowledge production" (p. 39). Spatial authorship, they argue, is performed not only by professional architects or planners. Many camp residents themselves take up the challenge to arrange, de-arrange and re-arrange the fabric of the spaces they inhabit, and deepen their spatial knowledge in the process. It is their continuous negotiation of these entanglements that defines the space of the camp, and not just the professional interventions of emergency architects or humanitarian officials. By offering this *other* reading of authorship, Iyer Siddiqi and Chitchian in fact contribute to a re-conceptualisation of what architecture is all about: not just the specialised field of knowledge in which only professional architects are initiated, but rather a much larger endeavour in which many different layers of spatial knowledge come together, including the everyday, hands-on spatial knowledge of inhabitants and users.

Such a reconceptualisation of architecture is also at stake in Esra Akcan's chapter on immigrant agency in urban housing in Berlin (Chapter 13), based on her book, *Open Architecture* (Akcan, 2018). Open architecture refers to the idea that architecture does not coincide with the design and construction of a building. Rather, states Akcan, architecture pertains to the lifespan of a building – including its use and its appropriation by inhabitants. Moreover, residents often develop and apply spatial knowledge, and their dealings with interiors are often crucial in order to make these spaces more comfortable and more functional. Architects would therefore do well to anticipate, welcome and accommodate the changes residents might bring to their buildings.

Akcan's discussion of the immigrant inhabitation of the postmodern IBA housing of the 1980s might be compared to a recent article on 'Architectures of Asylum', which focuses on the more recent production of collective accommodation for asylum seekers in Berlin (Steigemann & Misselwitz, 2020). Although they do not use this particular term, Steigemann and Misselwitz point out that the architecture of container housing is not 'open'. This is not due to any intrinsic characteristic of the design of these temporary homes itself: three interconnected containers with kitchen, toilet, bathroom and a small porch in front. Rather, it has to do with the bureaucratic rules imposed by the administration, which forbid, for instance, inhabitants to add or remove furniture, or restrict the cultivation of a garden near the container. These constraints tend to be justified by the administration with reference to fire hazards and security issues, but at the same time they install a regime of disciplining and control. Through their fieldwork and community activities (such as workshops), the authors and their students mitigate the tension between the administration's code of conduct and the residents' tactics of personal appropriation, but their discussions clearly reveal that architects can only do so much, and that the housing regime in which refugees or immigrant find themselves is composed of more than buildings alone.

That is also the point made by Paolo Boccagni (Chapter 5), who recognises that in many temporary housing situations residents develop practices of homemaking that help them to negotiate complex interactions between their past, present and future. The materiality of refugee centres or other forms of refugee housing therefore matters, because some organisational and built forms are more beneficial for these practices than others. Whether or not residents have cooking facilities, whether or not they can host visitors, whether or not they can plan gatherings in semi-public spaces, whether or not they can change the furniture or decorate a room – all of this matters because it allows residents to regain a certain control over their lives. All of this nevertheless matters only 'so much'. Indeed, what is in the long run most important for asylum seekers, refugees and migrants is whether or not they will be allowed to stay in their arrival country. Hence, the architectures of the accommodating buildings are important because they might be part of a longer trajectory towards making-a-new-home, but they alone cannot solve the existential and political questions that are crucially at stake in this trajectory (see also Boccagni, PéRez Murcia & Belloni, 2020).

Home, displacement and gender

In recent decades migration flows have changed in terms of gender. Where men used to make up the bulk of migrant workers until the 1970s, there has since been a huge increase in migrating women. Right now over half of all migrants worldwide are female, and they usually take up jobs as domestic workers or as care-workers in the health sector (Gündüz, 2013; DeParle, 2020). Furthermore, women and girls make up around 50 per cent of refugee populations (UNHCR, n.d.). The UNHCR prides itself on explicitly taking their specific needs into account: by providing reproductive health services; by individually registering them as eligible for food rations and other benefits; and by designing and implementing educational and empowering programmes (Buscher, 2010). Still, the UNHCR acknowledges that refugee women who are unaccompanied, pregnant, heads of households, disabled or elderly are especially vulnerable (UNHCR, n.d.). Refugee women in Europe too are exposed to risks of sexual exploitation and/or gender-based violence (Freedman, 2016). Gender is thus an important factor in the lived experience of displacement.

Jennifer Hyndman and Wenona Giles (2011) argue that refugees in situations of protracted waiting are subject to what they call "a feminization of asylum". They contend that such refugees are positioned as helpless victims, who need humanitarian aid but receive it only on condition that they give up their right to mobility. Thus, they are put in a position of dependency, first of all by the charitable systems that manage them and secondly by the way they are not entitled to any legal status anywhere (although they may receive one in the long term if they behave well and are elected in a relocation programme). This feminisation is thus "a material condition, a representational issue and a political dilemma" (Hyndman & Giles, 2011, p. 369). However, if refugees leave their camps and try to enter countries in the global North as asylum seekers, they are framed and masculinised as security threats. It is thus a gendered dynamic that makes up the global refugee regime as "a matrix of exclusion and containment" (ibid., p. 374).

The bourgeois notion of the home that we encountered earlier is also thoroughly gendered. It comprises the idea of the husband and father as breadwinner and the wife and mother as 'Angel in the House', the one who manages the household and makes sure that it is a heaven for all its (other) occupants. As Susan Fraiman (2019) reminds us, the Angel in the House is still with us – as the housewife representing 'family values' or as the symbolic icon of a domesticity that coincides with tradition and conformity (p. 3). Many sociological phenomena indeed prove her continuous impact: the gendered division of labour, the glass ceiling, the pay gap, etc. (see also Heynen, 2005).

All of this means that gender *matters* when we are discussing practices of home-making in displacement. Thus, one might expect that there are significant differences in the home-making practices of men and women in displacement. This difference is rarely thematised in most of the chapters, perhaps because fieldwork research focusing on material practices is so thin on the ground that it has not yet dealt with this issue. Generally, however, contributors do recognise that an intersectional approach is necessary, because there is a variation in lived experiences of displacement in terms of gender, age, culture, religion, class, caste, etc.

Romola Sanyal (Chapter 9) explicitly develops such an approach, working with upper-caste, middle-class women refugees who, after Partition, settled in self-built colonies in Calcutta's periphery. With fieldwork done in the 2006-2007 period, the women she interviewed were advanced in age and their memories had become somewhat unreliable. Nevertheless, Sanyal was able to piece together significant narratives of women's role in the heroic struggle to construct the colony spaces: they acted as guards to protect the plots against eviction; they carried sacks of soil and other building materials; they formed women's committees to organise the community; they made homes habitable despite enduring poverty and they engaged in waged labour to help support their families. They thus actively participated in the construction not only of a material home, but also of a future where the state acknowledged their right to belong and their right to housing.

Menna Agha (Chapter 14) also explicitly addresses issues of gender in her contribution on the Nubian house. She argues that the displacement enforced upon Nubians in 1963 because of the Egyptian government's construction of the High Dam not only caused economic hardship, but also disrupted a long matriarchal tradition that had materialised in the Nubian vernacular. By imposing 'modern' houses and 'modern' spatial dichotomies between public and private on the community, the Egyptian state transformed the built environment in such a way that it was difficult for families to continue traditional practices of co-habitation and hospitality. For Agha, "the state-designated dwelling unit thereby destroys the Nubian house as a cultural institution and its constitutive powers" (p. 364). She nevertheless observes in the current situation in the displaced villages certain instances of cultural resistance and resilience (such as communal houses) that might contain the promise to give the power back to the Nubian house – and in that gesture empower the women who preside over it.

Several of our authors intentionally position themselves within feminist scholarship. That is the case for Siddiqi and Chitchian (Chapter 1) as well as Akcan (Chapter 11), who advocate an epistemic shift in the conceptualisation of architecture and authorship. Traces of the impact of feminist scholarship are also found in other contributions, which carefully reflect on issues of positionality and situated knowledge. Most explicit in this respect is Maretha Dreyer, who calls her contribution 'a feminist ethnography' (Chapter 8). Drawing on Sara Ahmed's post-colonial theory on representation of 'others', she uses participant observation, self-reflection and architectural analysis as research methods in her study of an institutional accommodation for asylum seekers in Dublin. Acutely aware of the legacy of colonialism, she ponders how the neo-gothic character of this building – that she herself experiences as rather pleasant – might evoke quite different feelings in the refugees it houses. Her fieldwork furthermore reveals how the residents' movements are determined and controlled through rules and surveillance, and how little opportunity they have to modify or personalise their living spaces. Her research thus intensifies and substantiates her awareness of her own privileged position as a white, highly-educated South African woman engaged in research in Ireland, vis-à-vis asylum seekers (possibly from the same continent) who are 'othered' and largely stripped of agency and self-determination.

In conclusion: inhabitation as political praxis

In her book *Extreme Domesticity*, Susan Fraiman (2019) freely acknowledges how she struggles with the Victorian-age 'Angel in the House'. She wishes to sever domesticity from its conformist overtones and to kill the Angel once and for all – not, however, by shunning houses and housekeepers altogether, but rather by valuing feminine domestic practices that also can be lived and cherished outside the heterosexual norm and outside patriarchy (p. 3). Critical geographers and urbanists are likewise rethinking 'radical housing' (Lancione, 2020) and 'practices of inhabitation' (Boano & Astolfo, 2020) in order to strip the idea of 'dwelling' from its Heideggerian conservative overtones, and to open up these concepts in order for them to include liberation from oppression and care for the planet. Indeed, these critical interpretations take their cues from marginalised urban practices, where people *are* inhabiting places that seem uncanny and uninhabitable from a mainstream point of view. Boano and Astolfo (2020) thus propose to expand "the notion of dwelling to include intersecting forms of caring, repairing and imagining the future", substantiating the concept of 'inhabiting' "as a relational practice occurring in marginal and fragile environments, constituted by multiple incremental and transformative acts with the ultimate purpose to hold and resist marginalisation" (p. 555)

Mariana Ortega (2014) also offers an interesting approach through her conceptualisation of 'hometactics'. Recognising that 'home' can become a space of exclusion despite its many possibilities of providing nurture and inclusiveness" (p. 180), she proposes to negotiate home's ambiguities and contradictions through tactical moves in space and time that can be spontaneous and provisional yet offer a sense of familiarity in an environment to which one cannot fully belong. Seeing that, from an intersectional perspective, individuals inevitably have multiplicitous selves and that there often are cracks and paradoxes between these selves, home is to be negotiated again and again in a rhythm that refuses to crystallise into a final and fully accomplished sense of being-at-home. The mobility that characterises the life of migrants and refugees accentuates this condition, and brings into sharp relief the provisionality of any sense of home, as became clear in many chapters of this book. Through their practices of inhabitation, they moreover challenge the ideas of home and belonging that their host countries try to impose on them – which is why habitation can be called a political praxis.

This means that there is – inevitably – a certain uncanniness to the home, even to the most bourgeois of homes as described by Ruskin (Leach, 1998; Kaika, 2004), since home is as much a place of restriction and control as it is a place of nurture and care. Often it is through the *unmaking* of home that individuals emancipate themselves: adolescents leaving their childhood homes; husbands or wives leaving an abusive partner; villagers leaving the countryside to explore life in the city; migrants seeking a better life elsewhere. In all these cases people are unmaking their home of old in order to make room for a new and (ideally) better one. Home is a continuous process of *becoming*, rather than a stable situation of being.

References

Adorno, T. W. (1991). *Minima Moralia – Reflections from Damaged Life*. London: Verso.

Ahmed, S. (1999). 'Home and Away: Narratives of Migration and Estrangement'. *International Journal of Cultural Studies* 2 (3): 329–47.

Akcan, E. (2018). *Open Architecture: Migration, Citizenship, and the Urban Renewal of Berlin-Kreuzberg by IBA-1984/87*. Basel, Switzerland: Birkhauser Verlag GmbH.

Beeckmans, L., & E. Vanden Houte. (2019). 'Asielcentra Herdacht'. *AGORA Magazine* 35 (2): 35–38.

Berman, M. (1985). *All That Is Solid Melts Into Air – The Experience of Modernity*. London: Verso.

Bloch, E. (1986). *The Principle of Hope*. Translated by Neville Plaice. Oxford: Blackwell.

Boano, C., & G. Astolfo. (2020). 'Inhabitation as More-than-Dwelling. Notes for a Renewed Grammar'. *International Journal of Housing Policy* 20 (4): 555–77.

Boccagni, P., PéRez Murcia, L.E. & M. Belloni. (2020). *Thinking Home on the Move: A Conversation across Disciplines*. Emerald Publishing Limited.

Braidotti, R. (2011). *Nomadic Theory: The Portable Rosi Braidotti, Rosi Braidotti*. Gender and Culture. New York: Columbia University Press.

Brickell, K. (2012). 'Geopolitics of Home'. *Geography Compass* 6 (10): 575–88.

Brun, C. (2015). 'Active Waiting and Changing Hopes: Toward a Time Perspective on Protracted Displacement'. *Social Analysis* 59 (1): 19–37.

Brun, C., & A. Fabos. (2015). 'Making Homes in Limbo? A Conceptual Framework'. *Refuge* 31 (1): 5–17.

Buscher, D. (2010). 'Refugee Women: Twenty Years On'. *Refugee Survey Quarterly* 29 (2): 4–20.

Cupers, K., Mattsson, H. & C. Gabrielsson, (eds). (2020). *Neoliberalism on the Ground: Architecture and Transformation from the 1960s to the Present*. Culture, Politics, and the Built Environment. Pittsburgh: University of Pittsburgh Press.

Davies, M. (2014). 'Home and State: Reflections on Metaphor and Practice'. *Griffith Law Review* 23 (2): 153–75.

DeParle, J. (2020). *A Good Provider Is One Who Leaves: One Family and Migration in the 21st Century*. New York, NY: Penguin Books.

Dossa, P., & J. Golubovic. (2019). 'Reimagining Home in the Wake of Displacement'. *Studies in Social Justice* 13 (1): 171–86.

Douglas, M. (1991). 'The Idea of a Home: A Kind of Space'. *Social Research* 58 (1): 287–307.

Dunn, E.C. (2017). *No Path Home: Humanitarian Camps and the Grief of Displacement*. Ithaca: Cornell University Press.

Duyvendak, J.W. (2011). *The Politics of Home: Belonging and Nostalgia in Western Europe and the United States*. Houndmills, Basingstoke, Hampshire; New York: Palgrave Macmillan.

Feldman, I. (2006). 'Home as a Refrain: Remembering and Living Displacement in Gaza'. *History and Memory* 18 (2): 10–47.

Fraiman, Susan. (2019). *Extreme Domesticity: A View from the Margins*. New York: Columbia University Press.

Freedman, J. (2016). 'Sexual and Gender-Based Violence against Refugee Women: A Hidden Aspect of the Refugee "Crisis"'. *Reproductive Health Matters* 24 (47): 18–26.

Gatrell, Peter William. (2019). *The Unsettling of Europe: How Migration Reshaped a Continent*. New York: Basic Books.

George, Rosemary Marangoly. (1999). *The Politics of Home. Postcolonial Relocations and Twentieth-Century Fiction*. Berkeley, CA: University of California Press.

Gündüz, Zuhal Yesilyurt. (2013). 'The Feminization of Migration: Care and the New Emotional Imperialism'. *Monthly Review*, December 2013. Available at http://dx.doi.org.kuleuven.e-bronnen.be/10.14452/MR-065-07-2013-11_3.

Hansen, K. T. (1992). 'Introduction: Domesticity in Africa'. In Karen Tranberg Hansen (ed), *African Encounters with Domesticity* (pp. 1–33). New Brunswick: Rutgers University Press.

Hayden, D. (1981). *The Grand Domestic Revolution: A History of Feminist Designs for American Homes, Neighborhoods, and Cities*. Cambridge, Mass: MIT Press.

Herscher, A. (2017). *Displacements: Architecture and Refugee*. Critical Spatial Practice 9. Berlin: Sternberg Press.

Heynen, H. (1999). *Architecture and Modernity. A Critique*. London: MIT Press.

Heynen, H. (2005). 'Modernity and Domesticity: Tensions and Contradictions'. In Hilde Heynen and Gülsüm Baydar (eds). *Negotiating Domesticity. Spatial Productions of Gender in Modern Architecture* (pp. 1–29). London: Routledge.

Hyndman, J., & W. Giles. (2011). 'Waiting for What? The Feminization of Asylum in Protracted Situations'. *Gender, Place & Culture* 18 (3): 361–79.

Kaika, Maria. (2004). 'Interrogating the Geographies of the Familiar: Domesticating Nature and Constructing the Autonomy of the Modern Home'. *International Journal of Urban and Regional Research* 28 (2): 265–86.

Lancione, Michele. (2020). 'Radical Housing: On the Politics of Dwelling as Difference'. *International Journal of Housing Policy* 20 (2): 273–89.

Leach, N. (1998). 'The Dark Side of the Domus'. *The Journal of Architecture* 3 (1): 31–42.

Lozanovska, Mirjana. (2019). *Migrant Housing: Architecture, Dwelling, Migration*. Routledge Research in Architecture. London; New York: Routledge.

Lyotard, Jean-François. (1991). *The Inhuman: Reflections on Time*. Cambridge: Polity press.

McClintock, A. (1995). *Imperial Leather: Race, Gender, and Sexuality in the Colonial Contest*. New York: Routledge.

Ortega, Mariana. (2014). 'Hometactics: Self-Mapping, Belonging and the Home Question'. In Emily S. Lee (ed), *Living Alterities. Phenomenology, Embodiment and Race* (pp. 173–88). Albany, N.Y: State University of New York Press.

Ruskin, J. (1901). 'Of Queens' Gardens (1870)'. In *Sesame and Lilies, and, The Crown of Wild Olive*. New York: The Century Co.

Said, Edward W. (1994). *Culture and Imperialism*. London: Vintage.

Shephard, B. (2012). *The Long Road Home: The Aftermath of the Second World War*. New York: Anchor.

Simone, AbdouMaliq. (2011). 'The Urbanity of Movement: Dynamic Frontiers in Contemporary Africa'. *Journal of Planning Education and Research* 31 (4): 379–91. https://doi.org/10.1177/0739456X11416366.

Simone, AbdouMaliq. (2012). 'Introduction: Enacting Modernity'. In C. Greig Crysler, Stephen Cairns, and Hilde Heynen (eds), *The Sage Handbook of Architectural Theory* (pp. 213–30). London: Sage.

Steigemann, A.M., & P. Misselwitz. (2020). 'Architectures of Asylum: Making Home in a State of Permanent Temporariness'. *Current Sociology* 68 (5): 628–650.

Teige, K. (2002). *The Minimum Dwelling*. Cambridge, Massachusetts: MIT press.

UNHCR. n.d. 'Women'. UNHCR. Accessed 15 June 2021. Available at https://www.unhcr.org/women.html.

Walters, W. (2004). 'Secure Borders, Safe Haven, Domopolitics'. *Citizenship Studies* 8 (3): 237–60.

Webster, W. (1998). *Imagining Home: Gender, 'Race' and National Identity, 1945-64*. London: The UCL Press.

Yuval-Davis, N. (2011). *The Politics of Belonging: Intersectional Contestations*. London: Sage.

About the Authors

Fatina Abreek-Zubiedat is a co-founder of *Zubiedat Architects* office, an architectural historian and theorist. She completed her Ph.D. from the Technion – IIT (2018) (1st Prize of Arthur Schragenheim Memorial Fund for an outstanding thesis) (Israel). Currently, she is a *post-doctoral fellow* at the Institute for History and Theory (gta), ETH, Zurich. Her research focuses on architecture in conflict, Palestinian cultural historiography, urban transformations in contested cities, (post-)colonial development discourse, refugee camps and urban citizenship. Abreek-Zubiedat is the recipient of several prestigious recognitions, including the *Rothschild Fellowship*, the *Neubauer Fellowship*, *Azrieli scholarship* and the *Council for Higher Education Award*.

Nurhan Abujidi is an Associate Professor at Zuyd University of Applied Sciences (Netherlands) and Head of the Smart Urban Redesign Research Centre. She leads urban renewal projects in multiple neighbourhoods and cities in the Limburg Region. Abujidi holds a Ph.D. in Architecture, Urban Design and Regional Planning from the University of Leuven (Belgium), where she also obtained her M.A. in Architecture and Human Settlements. Abujidi was a teacher in international, postgraduate programmes at a number of Belgian universities, including the University of Leuven and the Vrije Universiteit Brussel (VUB). At VUB, she was also the academic coordinator of the Erasmus Mundus UII-module Urban Studies. As the vice-dean and senior researcher at the School of Architecture of San Jorge University (Zaragoza), Abujidi led multiple research projects on urban development. Her expertise includes urban renewal, public space revitalisation and tactical urbanism. She has published extensively, including the book *Urbicide in Palestine: Spaces of Oppression and Resilience* (2014).

Menna Agha is a Nubian Architect and researcher. Previously, she was a visiting Assistant Professor and a spatial justice fellow at the University of Oregon. Menna holds a Ph.D. in Architecture from the University of Antwerp (Belgium) and an M.A. in Design from the University of Cologne (Germany). She is a third-generation displaced Fadidcha Nubian, and her research interests include the questions of gender, space, territory and displacement.

Esra Akcan is Professor in the Department of Architecture and currently the Director of European Studies in the Einaudi Center for International Studies at Cornell University. She completed her architecture degree at the Middle East Technical University in Turkey, and her Ph.D. and post-doctoral degrees at Columbia University in New York. She has taught at UI-Chicago, Humboldt University in Berlin, Columbia University, New School and Pratt Institute in New York, and METU in Ankara. Akcan has received awards and fellowships from the Radcliffe Institute for Advanced Studies at Harvard University, Graham Foundation (3 times grantee), American Academy in Berlin, UIC, Institute for Advanced Studies in Berlin, Clark Institute, Getty Research Institute, Canadian Center for Architecture (twice a scholar), CAA, Mellon Foundation, DAAD and KRESS/ARIT. She is the author of *Landfill Istanbul: Twelve Scenarios for a Global City* (2004); *Architecture in Translation: Germany, Turkey and the Modern House* (2012); *Turkey: Modern Architectures in History* (with S. Bozdoğan, 2012), and *Open Architecture: Migration, Citizenship and Urban Renewal of Berlin-Kreuzberg by IBA 1984/87* (2018). Currently, she is editing the anthology "Migration and Discrimination" and working on her books "Intertwined Histories of Seven Other Wonders" and "Right-to-Heal: Architecture in Post-Conflict and Post-Disaster Societies".

Aikaterini Antonopoulou is a Lecturer in Architectural Design at the Liverpool School of Architecture (University of Liverpool), where she also coordinates the first year of the Master of Architecture programme. Her research focuses on mediated representations of the urban and on the politics of the image in the contemporary city. Most recently, her work has focused on the interaction of the digital with the phenomena of the financial, urban and refugee crises in Athens, Greece: how the homeless, the unemployed, the immigrant, whose active presence in public is minimal, seek to create new grounds for social interaction and a new sense of belonging; how propaganda videos by Far-Right supporters on YouTube reveal unknown Athenian landscapes; how violence, austerity and poverty become aestheticised on the walls of the city via the Internet and mass-consumed through the social media. She holds a Diploma in Architecture from the National Technical University of Athens, an M.Sc. in Advanced Architectural Design from University of Edinburgh (UK), and a Ph.D. in Architecture from Newcastle University. From 2016-2018, she was the Simpson Postdoctoral Fellow in Architecture at the Edinburgh College of Art.

Luce Beeckmans is Assistant Professor in Architecture and Urbanism related to Migration and Diversity at Ghent University (Department of Architecture and Urban Planning) and a senior post-doctoral research fellow funded by the Flanders Research Foundation (FWO). As FWO-postdoc she is affiliated to Ghent University (Department of Architecture and Urban Planning, head institution), Antwerp University (Urban Studies Institute) and KU Leuven University (Interculturalism, Migration and Minorities Research Centre) in Belgium. In her interdisciplinary research she works on the intersection of migration, city and architecture. She explores the materialities of trans-national migration and the spatial dimensions and implications of urban diversity, with a particular focus on home-making and housing of migrants and refugees in the transnational field between sub-Saharan Africa and Europe. Currently, she is running and participating in several research projects on these topics, including an FWO project ('Housing for Refugee Inclusion'), a HORIZON2020 project ('ReROOT: Arrival infrastructures as sites of integration for recent newcomers') and a BELSPO project ('REFUFAM – From policy gaps to policy innovations. Strengthening the well-being and integration pathways of refugee families'). She has published widely and co-curated exhibitions and co-organised (international) conferences and debates on these topics.

Paolo Boccagni is an Associate Professor of Sociology at the University of Trento, Italy, and leads the ERC-StG research project 'HOMInG' – The Home-Migration Nexus (homing.soc.unitn.it; 2016-2021). His main areas of expertise are international migration, transnationalism, social welfare, care, diversity and the concept of home. His research concerns processes of home-making and home-feeling with a primary focus on migrants and ethnic minorities. This focus is strategic for understanding the everyday negotiation of boundaries between native and foreign-born populations. His publications include *Migration and the Search for Home: Mapping Domestic Space in Migrants' Everyday Lives* (2017), "What's in a (migrant) house? Changing domestic spaces, the negotiation of belonging and home-making in Ecuadorian migration" (2014), and "At home in home care: Contents and boundaries of the 'domestic' among immigrant live-in workers in Italy" *(*2018).

Wafa' Butmeh is an urban planner and a member of the HAYA Joint Programme Team in the UN-Habitat, Palestine Office. Previously, she has worked for the Ministry of Local Government, Palestine, on community-driven local outline plans for marginalised and threatened communities in the West Bank, and with the Beit Sahour Municipality as an urban planner on the development of the Master Plan for Beit Sahour. She completed her M.Sc. in Urban Strategies and Design from the University of Edinburgh Heriot-Watt University (UK) and her B.A. in Architectural Engineering, with emphasis on urban design, at Birzeit University (West Bank, Palestine).

Somayeh Chitchian is an architect, urban researcher and doctoral student at Harvard University's Graduate School of Design. She is also a doctoral fellow at the Max Planck Institute for the Study of Religious and Ethnic Diversity in Germany. Her research focuses on the urban geography of immigration., and lies at the intersection of critical urban theory and migration studies. She explores the reciprocal relationship between processes of urbanisation, changing geographies of urban governance, and spatialities and institutional terrains of migration. Moving beyond the inherent 'city'-centric and ethno-centric focus in migration research, Chitchian's work seeks to reconceptualise the object of the analysis of migration studies in the context of contemporary urban forms of geo-economic and geo-political inter-scalar restructuring, and aims to open up new cartographic and representational tools and techniques for geographic analysis. Her research, "Middle Eastern Immigration Landscape in America", won the Harvard ESRI Development Center Student of the Year Award in 2014. Chitchian is a trained architect from Delft University of Technology in the Netherlands and holds an M.A. degree in Design Studies in Critical Conservation (distinction) from Harvard University's Graduate School of Design.

Bruno De Meulder teaches urbanism at the University of Leuven (Belgium), and is the current Programme Coordinator of MaHS and MaULP as well as the Vice-Chair of the Department of Architecture. With Kelly Shannon and Viviana d'Auria, he formed the OSA Research Group on Architecture and Urbanism. He studied engineering-architecture at the University of Leuven, where he also obtained his Ph.D. He was a guest professor at TU Delft and AHO (Oslo), and held the Chair of Urban Design at Eindhoven University of Technology from 2001 to 2012. He was a partner in WIT Architecten (1994-2005). His doctoral research dealt with the history of Belgian colonial urbanism in Congo (1880-1960) and, since then, has laid the basis for a widening interest in colonial and post-colonial urbanism. His urban design experience intertwines urban analysis and projection and engages with the social and ecological challenges that characterise our times.

Anna Di Giusto is a teacher, journalist, writer and independent researcher, who lives in Florence. She holds graduate degrees in Philosophy and Cultural Anthropology. She obtained two post-degree M.A.s in multicultural diversity management. She participated in the QuaMMELOT Project – Qualification for Minor Migrants Education and Learning Open Access (Erasmus+) at the University of Florence (Italy). She recently enrolled in an M.A. in Contemporary History at the University of Florence. She has published articles with FrancoAngeli, ArcHistoR, ISRPt Editore, the University of Leuven, Istos-Istanbul and Russia Pannonica. She is Art Director for the Graphic Novel Section at the Middle East Now Film Festival and deputy editor of www.gufetto.press. Anna is a member of CRIF-Italian Research Center for Philosophical Inquiry, ISRT-Historical Institute of Resistance Movement in Tuscany, SIS-Italian Society of Women Historians and Libera.

Maretha Dreyer is a registered architect and lecturer in Cape Town, South Africa. Her research takes a multidisciplinary approach, focusing on the intersection of architecture, gender and mobility studies. She completed her studies in architecture at the University of the Free State in Bloemfontein. After several years working in an architectural practice, she joined the Cape Peninsula University of Technology as a lecturer in the Department of Architectural Technology & Interior Design. In 2015 she received an Erasmus Mundus Scholarship and subsequently completed her M.A. in Gender Studies at University College Dublin in Ireland. She has been working as voluntary scientific researcher with Hasselt University in Belgium since 2019 and has recently received a grant to complete a Ph.D. at that university.

Alessandra Gola is an architect and researcher born in Bologna (Italy) in 1983. She co-founded The Yalla Project (Palestine), an interdisciplinary applied research hub that deals with the interrelation of built space and social constructs approached through "learning by doing". Alessandra is concluding her Ph.D. in Architecture at the University of Leuven (Belgium) with a thesis on the production of spatial domains in the contemporary Palestinian context. After obtaining her M.A. in Architecture from the University of Ferrara (Italy), she graduated at the Masters of Human Settlements at the University of Leuven. Her work combines professional practice and academic teaching, with her expertise focusing on grounded research and socio-spatial design, and she has been collaborating since 2006 with universities and international institutions across Europe and the Middle East. Her interests focus on the relationship between society, built environment and rights, with a particular concern for the experience of displacement within contexts of conflict and social unrest.

Hilde Heynen is a professor of architectural theory at the University of Leuven, Belgium. Her research focuses on issues of modernity, modernism and gender in architecture. In *Architecture and Modernity. A Critique* (MIT Press, 1999), she investigated the relationship between architecture, modernity and dwelling. She has also engaged with the intersection between architecture and gender studies, resulting in the volume *Negotiating Domesticity* (co-edited with Gulsum Baydar, Routledge, 2005). She co-edited the 2012 *Sage Handbook of*

Architectural Theory (with Greig Crysler and Stephen Cairns). More recently she published an intellectual biography of Sibyl Moholy-Nagy (Bloomsbury, 2019; Sandstein, 2019).

Anooradha Iyer Siddiqi is an assistant professor at Barnard College, Columbia University. She specializes in histories of architecture and spatial practice centering African and South Asian questions. She is the author of numerous articles and two book manuscripts, *Architecture of Migration: The Dadaab Refugee Camps and Humanitarian Settlement* (Duke University Press, 2023) and *Minnette de Silva and a Modern Architecture of the Past*. She is the editor of the collection *Architecture as a Form of Knowledge* (*Comparative Studies of South Asia, Africa, and the Middle East*) and co-editor of the collections *Feminist Architectural Histories of Migration* (*Architecture Beyond Europe, Canadian Centre for Architecture, Aggregate*) and *Spatial Violence* (*Architectural Theory Review*, Routledge). She directs the Columbia University Center for the Study of Social Difference working group *Insurgent Domesticities*, co-chairs the Columbia University Seminar *Studies in Contemporary Africa*, and convened the web/podcast series *Building Solidarities: Racial Justice in the Built Environment* (Barnard College/Columbia University Institute for Comparative Literature and Society) and *Caregiving as Method* (Society of Architectural Historians).

Irit Katz is a lecturer in Architecture and Urban Studies at the Department of Architecture, University of Cambridge (UK), and has practised as an architect in Tel Aviv and London. Her work focuses on built environments created and shaped in extreme conditions, and is strongly engaged with cultural and political theories. She has published extensively about spaces of displacement and the camp, including the co-edited book *Camps Revisited: Multifaceted Spatialities of a Modern Political Technology* (2018).

Romola Sanyal is an Assistant Professor of Urban Geography at the London School of Economics, having spent time at the Development Planning Unit at University College London. Her main research interests and expertise include the social and political implications of architecture, urban geopolitics, urban theory, housing and citizenship rights. She has written on the politics of space in refugee settlements, looking at processes of 'informalisation' in the global south with particular focus on Lebanon and India. Her current research turns to the urbanisation of specific areas in Lebanon through the infrastructures of humanitarian aid and development, having recently arrived in response to the Syrian refugee crisis. Sanyal obtained her Ph.D. at the University of California, Berkeley. Her journal publications include 'Squatting in Camps: Building and Insurgency in Spaces of Refuge' (2011), "Urbanising Refuge: Interrogating Spaces of Displacement' (2014) and 'Refugees and the City: An Urban Discussion" (2015).

Ashika Singh obtained her doctorate at KU Leuven (Belgium) from the Faculty of Architecture and the Husserl-Archives, Institute of Philosophy. She works conceptually on the intersection of 'home' and 'dwelling' in experiences of forced displacement. Central to her research is a phenomenological approach, advocating in its ability to understand the human condition in relation to one's built environment, spaces of habitation and political expression. She was a visiting scholar at Columbia University's Graduate School of Architecture, Planning & Preservation, New York, and has facilitated workshops and spoken and published on the themes of political phenomenology, feminist and decolonial theory, and the architecture of emergency shelter and refugee camps. She is on the editorial board for the journal on political philosophy, *Krisis*, and is currently a reader in English law.

Aleksandar Staničić is an architect and Assistant Professor at TU Delft Faculty of Architecture and the Built Environment, the Chair for Methods and Analysis. Previously he was a Marie Curie Postdoctoral Fellow at TU Delft, research scholar at the Italian Academy for Advanced Studies, Columbia University, and post-doctoral fellow at the Aga Khan Program for Islamic Architecture at MIT. Aleksandar's work stems from two book projects, *War Diaries: Design after the Destruction of Art and Architecture* (co-editor, University of Virginia Press, 2020) and *Transition urbicide: Post-war reconstruction in post-socialist Belgrade* (sole author, forthcoming). He is the recipient of multiple grants and fellowships from the Graham Foundation, Government of the Lombardy Region, Italy, and Ministry of Education, Republic of Serbia.

Huda Tayob is senior lecturer at the University of Cape Town and a Canadian Centre for Architecture Mellon Fellow on the project Centring Africa. Her research focuses on minor, migrant and subaltern architectures and the potential of literature to respond to archival silences in architectural research. She is co-curator of the open access curriculum Raccspacearchitecture.org with Suzanne Hall and Thandi Loewenson, and co-curator of the digital podcast series and exhibition Archive of Forgetfulness (Archiveofforgetfulness.com).

Layla Zibar is an architect and urban practitioner, and a doctoral researcher for both Brandenburg University of Technology (Germany) and the University of Leuven (Belgium). Her research focuses on spatial transformations of the Kurdistan Region of Iraq (KRI)'s refugee camps, in relation to their specific geopolitical, socio-cultural backgrounds and home/homeland factors. She explores the long history of Kurds' forced migration waves in the region, and the spatial dimension of "sites of displacements", which appear to be (re)shaping the overall urban landscape. Layla obtained her M.A. in Architectural Engineering from Cairo University (Egypt -2016) and B.A. in Architecture from Aleppo university (Syria-2010).

21W63668/ T1/ 9789462702936